T0191004

THE
INTERRUPTED
FOREST

THE
INTERRUPTED
FOREST

A History of Maine's Wildlands

NEIL ROLDE

*Maps by
Rosemary Mosher and Kristen Read Boettcher*

Camden, Maine

Down East Books

An imprint of The Globe Pequot Publishing Group, Inc.
64 South Main Street
Essex, CT 06426
www.globepequot.com

Distributed by NATIONAL BOOK NETWORK

British Library Cataloguing in Publication Information available

The Tilbury House Publishers edition of this book was previously cataloged
by the Library of Congress as follows:

Rolde, Neil, 1931–
    The interrupted forest : a history of Maine's wildlands / Neil Rolde.
        p. cm.
    Includes bibliographical references and index.
    1. Maine—History. 2. Maine—Environmental conditions. 3. Wilderness
    areas—Maine—history. 4. Land settlement—Maine—History. 5. Natural
    history—Maine. I. Title.
    F19. R638 2001
    333.73'09741—dc21   2001036786

ISBN: 9781684751280 (paperback) | ISBN: 9781684752706 (ebook)

∞™ The paper used in this publication meets the minimum requirements of
American National Standard for Information Sciences—Permanence of Paper
for Printed Library Materials, ANSI/NISO Z39.48-1992.

Dedicated to the memory of
the late Honorable Ezra James Briggs of Caribou,
who first made the "North Country" real to me.
Would that Jim were alive today
so that we could all hear him thunder
about the "foolishness" going on.

TABLE OF CONTENTS

MAP LIST

ACKNOWLEDGMENTS

SINCE I NO LONGER plan to run for any office in Maine or else-where, I can safely go ahead and offer thanks to those who helped me in this project—without that politician's lingering fear I might inadvertently have left someone out and thereby risked losing a vote. My gratitude to:

Mary Alyce Higgins, Roger Milliken, Jr., Clinton "Bill" Townsend, Connie Baxter Marlow, Mary Adams, Dean Bennett, Tom Gaffney, Harrison Richardson, Denise Pike, Danny Smith, Rob Gardiner, Joseph Lupsha, Andrea Maker, Jym St. Pierre, Jonathan Carter, Rudy Engholm, Deborah Staber, Doug Stover, Jim Haddow, Peter Kellman, Herb Adams, Mark Lawrence, Staff at the Maine Historical Society Library, Staff at the Maine State Library, Staff, Special Collections at the Fogler Library, Staff at the Bangor Public Library, William Hilton, Jr., Richard and Mary Alden, Denis Thoet, Tim Caverly, Charles "Chuck" Dow, and Calvin Hosmer III

And, of course, Jennifer Elliott, my editor and publisher, and all the gang at Tilbury House.

Neil Rolde
York, Maine

INTRODUCTION

The Personal Connection

O N OCCASION, when bored or restless, I often like to peruse maps. Thus do I satisfy my wanderlust cartographically, browsing through atlases, dreaming of one day setting foot on the exotic, odd-sounding name places inked on each attractively colored page. Thanks to indulgent parents, their eventual bequest to me (an only child), a way of life not tied to regularity, and an equally travel-mad spouse, many of those impossible destinations have been reached—far-off real fantasy lands like Tajikistan or Slovenia or New Caledonia or Niue.

But my clearest memory of sitting and poring over a section of the globe that brought me an unforgettable rush of excitement was one much closer to home. It happened almost fifty years ago and in New York City, downtown Manhattan, West 86th Street, where I shared a post-graduate-school bachelor apartment with two friends. Both of my roommates were at work and, temporarily tired of the writing I was doing, I picked up my trusty college atlas and opened it at random. Of all places, it fell open to Maine!

What an anticlimax! Gosh, my father had been born in Bangor. We'd flown together to go fishing at Grand Lake Stream and on Sysladobsis Lake. I'd spent five camp summers in Casco. From home outside of Boston, my buddies and I would take summer day trips to Ogunquit.

So I turned the page—right? No, wrong, because my eye was caught by a corner of the state's configuration—the northwestern-most boundary, to be exact. A space of dramatic emptiness had arrested my attention. A river ran through it—at least one I noted immediately—the Allagash—then another, the upper St. John, and, hidden along another border, the St. Francis. There were lakes galore in the region, and no markers whatever to designate towns. *Terra incognita.* Smack in my own New England. Now that was exoticism in spades!

The awe with which I inspected that lost section of our country could not have been more genuine had it been the valley of the Amazon or the sands of the Gobi. What I didn't know at the time was the true extent of Maine's "wilderness" in the northern half of the state nor that, within a decade, it would be thrust more directly into my life. How could I possibly have guessed I would later sit as a member of the Maine legislature's Special Select Committee on Public Lands? After all, when I laid my atlas down in Gotham and glanced out our windows, it was pure city, the Big Apple, ceaseless traffic, constant noise, and wall-to-wall buildings, a setting where I thought I would remain, making my fortune, forever.

This enduring flash of memory can be dated to around 1956. Ten years later, I was paying my first visit to Maine's "North Woods" (not counting those fishing trips Down East) and becoming aware of its *issues.* Like Dickey-Lincoln. As a gubernatorial campaign staffer in late October 1966, I attended a luncheon meeting in Fort Kent with my boss Ken Curtis and U.S. Senator Edmund S. Muskie and listened to local business people chide these Democrat leaders because the dam project seemed to be stalled in D.C. Ed Muskie, in his magisterial manner, tried to articulate the realities of how things got done in Congress and only partially soothed them. As one of these locals commented, building a dam in Aroostook, bringing cheap power and manufacturing opportunities, was neither a political issue nor an economic issue in the County. "It's a religious issue!" he bellowed.

And in that era, it seemed as if proponents of what Ken Curtis, when governor, called "non-trend development"—big industrial projects not in the Maine tradition to jump-start growth in the ultra-rural backlands—were in the ascendance. There was a hunger for quick, monumental action: Quoddy, the fabled tidal-harnessing effort linked to Dickey-Lincoln dam; oil refineries and docking facilities for supertankers at Eastport or Machiasport; an aluminum smelter at Trenton; and the upstart sugar beet factory at Easton, which required the polluting of the Prestile Stream. These ghosts of past bitter contentions still haunt the northern landscape—but none has ever seen the light of day. So much for moving in a *non-trend* direction.

So what has been the trend? Fishing, farming, and, above all, forest product use, whether logging for lumber or cutting pulp to turn into paper or, since at least the end of the nineteenth century, felling trees for both.

Within such a stasis of resource exploitation, there have been controversies enough. In my own first term in the Maine legislature, 1972–74, we had not only the "Public Lots" question to contend with, but in my own regular assignment, serving on the Natural Resources Committee, we struggled with forestry practices; spruce budworm spraying (basically who would pay for it); the Land Use Regulation Committee, which brought zoning to the Unorganized Territories; and what to do about saving unique natural areas. The history of Maine is replete with issues that have boiled up out of its woods, even long before the idea of conservation was in anybody's mind.

That the future of the millions of acres comprising this vast land mass seems to revolve about contending uses—a national park, tourist development, industrial forestry—is somewhat of a recent phenomenon.

Nowadays, the headlines come thick and fast. Huge tracts change hands. Isolated Maine can no longer escape the global economy. A way of life, based on paper manufacturing, seems threatened. Will these vast private acres, which have been available as if they were public property, be closed off—sold to upscale buyers intent on their own privacy? This is non-trend development as scary as any oil refinery.

Today's clash over resource utilization may well be the central human drama of our time. Up to now Maine people have had a piquant shorthand for it—"payrolls or pickerel"—that no longer quite fits the bill. Global warming has entered the debate, and so has biodiversity. Ecology—a new word since the 1960s—is tossed around liltingly; hard-nosed, for-profit companies find themselves having to take such matters into account. The voters of Maine have thrice now gone to the polls to decide on an issue incomprehensible to the lumbermen of old: should the state government ban the clear-cutting of timber? The inconclusive results of those referenda indicate that the matter will be back before the electorate again and again.

Likewise, each of us has perhaps a secret sense of loss of place, a well-traveled and well-loved spot now gone forever. My own were the woods in a suburb of Boston where I played as a boy—long since turned into garden apartments by an insurance company. It was ridiculously skimpy in the way of wilderness; in fact, it bordered a golf course, but there were boulders to climb, a pine-shrouded "cliff," several swamps to mud around in, tadpoles to catch, skunk cabbage, uprooted trees after a hurricane, and a personal spatial geography still summonable after more than half a century. The Maine Woods can't be personal on the same scale, but those marvelous expanses capture souls just as surely. Their future means a lot to a great many, both here and "away." Besides, Maine people love a good story—all the better if it's one they've pretty much forged themselves.

THE
INTERRUPTED
FOREST

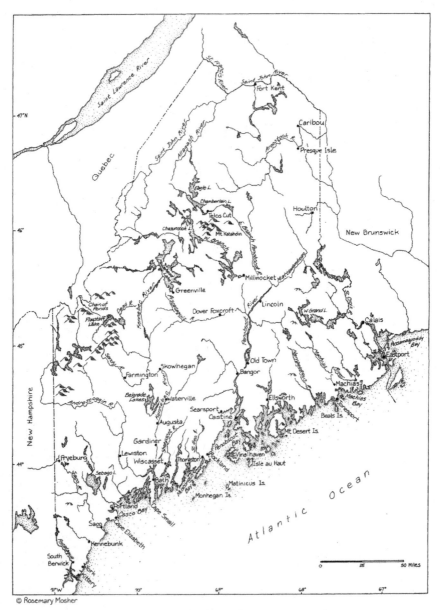

Maine Today

© Rosemary Mosher

ONE

Nowadays

IT'S LIKE BEING IN A WAR. That was my thought, although patently inappropriate to the spectacle before us. But I had somehow been reminded of the movie *Battleground*, where a newspaperman turned infantry grunt (played by John Hodiak) always complained he couldn't tell how his squad fit into the overall strategy of the campaign. In other words, what we were seeing was a tiny corner of a far greater conflict. The machine noises could have been clanking armored vehicle treads in a tank attack. The cutover land was as desolate, if not as shell-pitted, as Verdun. And figures in ranks were toppling, in this case, tall trees—but not so much falling like grenadiers in marching order before a fusillade, as snipped off individually by a monstrous mobile instrument, which we had just learned was called a "feller-buncher." We—a group of seventeen observers—were with the Champion paper company deep in the woods of Hancock County, Maine, watching a "clear-cut."

Deliberately and thoroughly, a patch of wooded Maine was being divested of its trees. None were spared. And a single man, half-hidden in his cab, was doing the work, replacing the platoon of chain-saw-wielders who formerly would have been needed to strip this lot.

A century and a half ago, a veritable army was needed to accomplish the same job. The "choppers" were multitudes of axemen, capable of downing the largest giant of the forest, white pines that might reach more than 200 feet in height. Later, the two-man saw proved its efficiency and the beloved (but dangerous) axe was laid aside. Once toppled, before they could become logs, these pines (or spruce or fir or hardwoods) were delimbed, another labor-intensive process. Then, all this dead weight was moved, primarily by ox teams. So there were "teamsters," especially adept at managing to lug sledloads bearing tons of wood through the wilderness. Roads were required and "swampers" built them, crudely engineered thoroughfares generally passable only in winter when iced over and worn smooth. Their destinations: the banks of waterways from which "river drivers" in the spring would take the mass of logs and float them to sawmills. Completing the vast personnel were "mill workers" and "sailors" aboard vessels transporting Maine's finished lumber and wood products to markets.

Now, in September 1998, here was one employee (of the contractor hired by Champion) doing the bulk of the work, with but one other employee in sight, down the slope, manipulating another futuristic-looking massive gizmo on caterpillar treads that sliced away branches, then cut each denuded trunk into desired lengths and piled the results into neat bunches for trucks to pick up at the roadsides.

No oxen or horses or farms to raise fodder for them, nor food for the huge number of "lumberjacks" crammed into "camps," as they were during the heyday of Maine's logging past. In terms of *productivity*, that magic bullet for capitalism of output per worker, nothing could have been finer than this Hancock County operation of the Champion International Corporation (the company's exact legal title) at the very tail end of the twentieth century.

The productivity concept had a less obvious side, as well. The grove being clear-cut was of one species—beech—and while its wood would be utilized, the space it occupied would soon be put to more profitable use. Replanted in place of these diseased beech trees (victims of a noxious but nonfatal organism called *beech nectria*) will be fast-growing black spruce, one of whose other qualities is that it is resistant to the most dreaded of silvicultural enemies in Maine—the spruce budworm.

The plot of barren ground being created would not, as mostly happened in Maine from its inception in the early 1600s, become farmland, a clearing where a rugged, hand-hewn dwelling could be erected and crops planted. Indeed, 150 years ago Maine had less forest than it does today. Particularly in the more settled parts of the state, those in which the *townships* laid out by surveyors drew enough population to transform themselves into *towns*.

Historic reasons underlie the fact that huge swaths of Maine, once surveyed and laid out in townships, never fulfilled their promise of turning into municipalities. There are still millions of acres of Maine included in a legal entity known as the Unorganized Territories. These are named and unnamed townships where no local government exists, the state of Maine controls all public functions, and the land, to an overwhelming extent, is privately owned.

To observe the clear-cut, we had traveled by bus from Bangor via Aurora on a road universally referred to in Maine as the Airline (otherwise Route 9) and then had plunged into wilderness on a woods road out of a hamlet-sized incorporated town called Great Pond. If you locate Great Pond on a map, you'll see unincorporated squares of land all around it with cryptic designations like T34 MD, T40 MD (a bit north), T3 ND (more northerly still and in Penobscot County, not Hancock), and T5 ND BPP (Washington County).

Such mysterious codework translates as follows:

T34 MD (Township 34 Middle Division)

T40 MD (Township 40 Middle Division)

T3 ND (Township 3 Northern Division)

T5 ND BPP (Township 5, Northern Division, Bingham Penobscot Purchase)

A common designation elsewhere in Maine might be T3 R9 (more famous as Katahdin Township), standing for Township 3, Range 9, with townships running horizontally, like latitude, and Ranges perpendicularly, like longitude.

Also, there is a dizzying array of initials that might be attached, several relating to historic gigantic ownership patterns, like those of U.S. Senator William Bingham or General Samuel Waldo.

It had been explained to us earlier in a preliminary briefing that we were in the Great Pond *Diversity Unit*. The foresters acting as our hosts took special pains to elucidate this concept, which was at the heart of their management plans for Champion's 930,000 acres

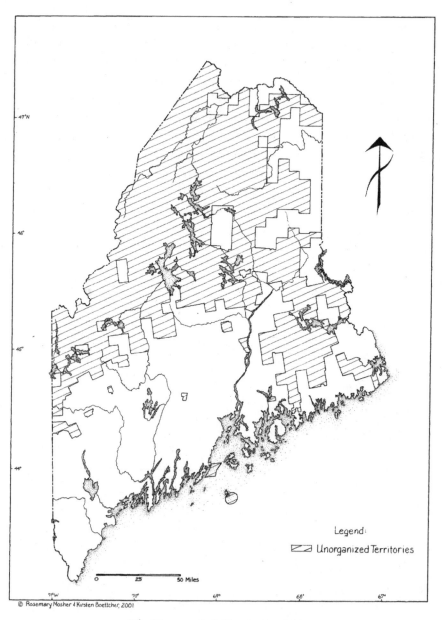

Legend:

▨ Unorganized Territories

The Unorganized Territories, 2001

in Maine. A Diversity Unit is an area of 20,000–40,000 acres and every Diversity Unit is mapped for four different types of land use:

Special Value areas

General Management areas

Protection areas

High Yield areas

The first two categories have excited little or no fuss. Both allow lumbering, with extra care taken where there are *special values*, e.g., wildlife habitats. Under *general management*, a variety of harvesting techniques are used in good timbering locations. No cutting is allowed in *protection* zones and here, the complaint is simply that there aren't enough of them. It is *high yield* policy that causes the biggest public flaps.

For high yield involves clear-cutting and spraying.

The clear-cutting part was what we were observing that day on Champion land. The spraying would come later after the black spruce seedlings had been planted. Those herbicides—harmful only to plants, we were assured—would be dumped on competing growth to allow the desired species to spring up.

The underlying feelings about this trend (combining clear-cutting and spraying), which took some time to imprint itself on Maine's public consciousness, really boiled to the surface in 1995. That summer, a group of environmental activists hosted the Maine Green Party's monthly meeting on Sears Island, where opponents of a proposed container port were waging an ultimately successful attempt to block the project. Jonathan Carter, a faculty member at the University of Maine, Farmington, the party's candidate for governor in 1994, brought up the idea of a statewide referendum campaign to ban clear-cutting. After a certain amount of debate, the notion was accepted.

For a fledgling political organization like the Greens, a formidable task lay ahead. Maine's constitution allows citizens to initiate a referendum if they can gather enough signatures of registered voters to total 10 percent of the votes cast in the previous gubernatorial election. Carter and the Greens and their allies needed 52,000 bonafide signers.

And they got them! What Mainers put their names to was a

legislative document—entitled Initiated Bill to Promote Forest Rehabilitation and Eliminate Clear-cutting—to be entered in the legislative session starting January 1996. The Maine lawmakers had only two options vis-à-vis this measure. They could adopt it as law, or they could reject it; they couldn't amend it; and killing it sent it out automatically to the electorate for a referendum vote.

That vote was eventually scheduled for November 1996. Not enough support existed in the legislature to enact the Greens' proposal. In fact, the opposition there and statewide was fierce. But polls also showed strong public feelings against clear-cutting. As a result of nervousness that the ban might go through, plus the fear of even some strong environmentalists that such action might be too extreme, a strange bedfellowship developed. Led by Governor Angus King, a pro-business Democrat turned Independent, the big paper companies, timberland owners, and other logging interests joined forces with their usual antagonists, the mainline environmental organizations such as the Maine Audubon Society and the Natural Resources Council. They named their bill the "Compact" and it was a grabbag of measures for reforming woods operations which, if adopted the Greens charged, would be worse than doing nothing, while a third player, a mostly rural coalition of property rights advocates, calling itself "Stop the Backroom Deal," claimed it was simply Draconian governmental interference with free enterprise.

The upshot was a trifurcated ballot, dictated in part by a ruling from the state supreme court. Since the initiated referendum was not passed, it *had to* go on the ballot, and the governor's proposal could accompany it as a competing measure. Joining these two choices was a third that offered essentially none of the above.

On the ballot, itself, Question 2 was divided exactly in such fashion: 2A, the Ban on Clear-cutting; 2B, the Compact; 2C, No Change in Forest Practices.

Complicating matters was another ruling from the law court that a plurality would not be sufficient to declare a winner. If no measure achieved 50+ percent, the top vote-getter would have to go on the ballot again in a future election and be voted up or down.

The campaign at first seemed to the political cognoscenti like it would be a one-sided romp for the Compact. Its chief spokesman was the very popular governor—a seasoned television commentator before being elected, Angus King was a highly articulate speaker. His 2B committee would also be the recipient of large infusions of cash from the paper companies (they were eventually to spend $5 million to their opponents' $400,000). The major environmental organizations, although a bit uncomfortable, still exhorted their faithful to vote for the Compact. Albeit polls continued to show strong support for the 2A Ban, previous elections in Maine on populist matters had proved that repeated television and other advertising could turn them around. Mary Adams, the spokesperson for the 2C No forces was not exactly a slouch, herself, when it came to debating referenda questions. Billed as a "housewife" from the tiny town of Garland, she had once led, in the '70s, a successful grassroots effort to help remove a state property tax provision from a school funding law.

This fiercely fought electoral battle ended inconclusively in November 1996. The totals gave 2A, the Ban, 29.3 percent of the vote (171,286); 2B, the Compact, 47.2 percent (276,261); and 2C, No, 23.5 percent (137,350). Since it was a presidential year, that was a big vote—almost 585,000—in an election where Maine had the largest percentage turnout in the nation, 65 percent. But it was obvious that Maine people couldn't quite agree on giving the Compact a majority. The governor's program would have to face the voters the following November.

Because 1997 was an off year, the secretary of state predicted a fairly low turnout. He figured 25 percent or around 240,000; it turned out to be 37 percent, or more than 342,000, and the Compact once more did not inspire enough confidence. It lost 161,839 to 179,050.

The same warring forces from the previous November traded blows, except that now Jonathan Carter and his Green allies did not have to tout the virtues of a ban on clear-cutting. All they essentially had to do was shout NO! At the last minute, they were also able to come up with enough money to run effective and frequent enough ads casting doubt on the Compact. Their primary angel was revealed to be Donald Sussman, a Connecticut investment banker with landholdings and a vacation home in northern Maine. They were on television and could buy newspaper space. For instance, in a full-page ad in the *Portland Press Herald* just prior to election day, "Citizens to Protect Maine's Future" harped on the twin specters they saw haunting the Maine woods:

> Now the corporations who write the Compact are going all out to preserve their current forestry practices, including clear-cutting and aerial toxic spraying.

It also featured a Portland homemaker, Susan Nixon, posed with her daughter, saying: "I realize it [the Compact] won't reduce clear-cutting and it won't reduce dangerous pesticide spraying."

And then an appeal to those who had backed the ban:

"WE CAN DO BETTER."

Despite the fact the Carter-led forces raised $870,000 and Mary Adams and her property rightists a mere $85,000, some losing Compact backers thought her effort had won the day. Said Bill Vail of the Forest Products Council, "I don't think Jonathan Carter had nearly the impact Mary Adams did."

A spokesman for Governor King thought Carter had brought out the No Vote among environmentalists in the bigger cities and suburbs and Adams had done it in the smaller towns. "She provided the margin," said Dennis Bailey, the governor's press secretary.

The two No Vote leaders were hardly allies—even on election night Adams's waspish comment that the Compact was defeated by "people who earn a living in the woods not those who dabble in the environment" was taken as a slap at Carter.

Not quite as waspishly but rather plaintively, he offered an olive branch of sorts: "Rather than continue on the warpath, she should try to work with us in a cooperative way to address the concerns of the small woodlot owners."

There were still eleven bills before the legislature and Jonathan Carter's basic argument had been: if the Compact were defeated, public pressure would force the lawmakers to enact a stronger bill.

But the lesson in Augusta just as easily could have been that Maine people wanted little or nothing done. There were clear signs at the statehouse that the marriage of convenience between the paper companies and mainline environmentalists had come unraveled.

The Interrupted Forest

In the end, in April 1998, a single bill was produced and the *Portland Press Herald* said it brought to a close the debate over clear-cutting—"at least temporarily."

All the legislators could agree upon was a requirement for minimum buffer zones around clear-cuts, requiring justifying plans for clear-cuts greater than 35 acres, for inventories to determine timber supplies, and for annual reports summarizing clear-cutting activities.

Predictably, the ban clear-cutting forces declared these palliative measures hardly went far enough. Speaking for the Forestry Ecology Network, Patricia Lamarche, later the Green Party's candidate for governor, called the bill that her future competitor, incumbent Angus King, had signed and praised, "deeply disappointing."

The issue was not going away.

This capsulized historical review became a flashback in my mind while standing before that newly emerging field in the Hancock County woods. We were told by the Champion foresters it would not remain a field for long. Green growth would start almost immediately, natural replenishment by fast-rising species like quaking aspen ("popple" to Mainers), pin cherry, elderberry, and raspberry bushes. "Great for deer," we were informed. Human planting would take place simultaneously. One-year-old black spruce, spaced seven to eight feet apart, 750–800 to an acre, were to fill the area. Quick-growing, maturing to harvest size in 25–30 years, they could not outrace, however, the popple and other non-desirables, at least not at the beginning.

Thus, once the little black spruces had shut down their growth metabolisms for the year, the plot in question would be visited by a spray helicopter. The herbicide used was generically known as Round-up. The object was solely to "release" the black spruce, the foresters said, to let them have an exclusive on the territory until tall enough not to be blocked or dominated by the popple, etc. With such a "head start," these black spruce can put on two to three feet a year and soon are of sufficient height to continue on their own, without further spraying.

We were shown an example of what they meant. A particular cleared area, leveled ten months earlier, was now alive with sprouted plants. Traces of the trauma still were evident: stumps, brush piles, patches of scraped and bare earth. But the initial greenery of new growth was in full view, higher and greener than the black spruce seedlings previously hand-planted. These latter, looking like miniaturized Christmas trees, their evergreen needles a much darker verdant hue, had to be accompanied by small blue flags; otherwise, they would have been even harder to spot than they were. As our hosts explained it, the spraying they did was a reluctant duty on their part. They applied the glyphisate (to give Round-up its more chemical name) with every scruple possible. They continually studied its effects and, so far, had found it had none on non-target populations. Maine law required that they keep the spray a certain distance from waterways and they did that. Since Champion adhered to the Sustainable Forestry Initiative of the American Forest and Paper Association, SFI's guidelines had to be followed on company lands and among them was "use forest chemicals prudently."

This SFI program, with its elaborate set of goals plus a scoring mechanism, had been entered into voluntarily by Champion. In this, it was joined by practically every other paper company and major landowner in Maine. Each year, a "Third Party Review" is conducted to see how well the participants do in attaining twelve distinct objectives and the companies are ranked. The highest mark is a 5 and the scorers are stingy and tough. In 1998 Champion had an overall rating of 4.07, up from 3.7 in the previous marking period. On "the prudent use of chemicals," it registered 3.4, yet insisting it had instituted the strongest possible set of internal policies on safe use while continuing to look for alternatives to herbicides and fertilizers.

By now, it must be apparent that what was going on here was a "selling job." The seventeen of us had been invited by Champion to partake in one of their forestry tours, a two-day affair which would showcase, as they put it, "a visionary forest management plan that attempts to address and accommodate the various demands on our 900,000 acres of forest land in Maine." The date was mid-September 1998, almost a year after the second referendum defeat for the Compact. Champion, admittedly among the more progressive of the Maine paper companies, was anxious to get its story out—how it was really trying to do right by the woods and still sustain itself as a business. The "concerned citizens" on these tours were hardly chosen at random. My own connection had come through Andrea Maker, director of public affairs for the company in Maine, an old friend, who had perked up when I mentioned the project of this book I was contemplating. Several journalists were with us, several state employees, several academics, and several legislators—or, to be more exact, legislators-to-be; both Republicans and Democrats, they had won their parties' primaries in June and faced no opposition in the general election. It was, if not a wholly feisty group, at least a questioning bunch. We had been told:

> Come see for yourself our carefully developed, balanced, long-term approach to clear-cutting, herbicides, planting and re-growing, selective cuts, hardwood growth, protection areas, and special value areas, including wildlife corridors along waterways.

Champion International Company was then no small operation. (The company has since been bought by International Paper.) Active in the United States, Canada, and Brazil, headquartered in Stamford, Connecticut, this multinational owned 11 million acres worldwide. Its seven paper mills in the U.S. manufactured more than 3.7 million tons of paper a year. They also produced half a million tons of marketable pulp.

Material for construction was another Champion product: plywood, studs, and lumber—close to 1 billion feet a year. The operations in Maine started with a paper mill at Bucksport, where half a million tons of coated paper are made for magazines and catalogs. The employees liked to boast that their customers are such well-known entities as *Time, Newsweek, Reader's Digest, Sports Illustrated,* and the L. L. Bean, J. C. Penney, and Land's End catalogs. On the lumber side Down East were two Champion-owned stud mills, both near the Penobscot River, in Costigan and Passadumkeag (and since closed by IP).

Historically, a merger of Champion, originally an Ohio concern, and the St. Regis Paper Company occasioned its entry into Maine. Company spokespersons liked to portray that event as the arrival of a "white knight" on the scene to rescue a corporation in trouble. That is to say, St. Regis was about to be hostilely gobbled up by an aggressive entrepreneur named Sir James Goldsmith, who already owned the Diamond International Company, a major landowner in Maine, and wanted to add St. Regis's 750,000 acres to his empire. St. Regis, itself, had earlier displaced the Maine Seaboard Paper Company, builders of the Bucksport mill, in 1930.

With the St. Regis tie-in, Champion doubled the amount of its timberland, making it one of the largest private landowners in the U.S. It proudly boasted that in a survey of more than 3,500 chief executive officers from around the world, conducted by Price Waterhouse Coopers for the *Financial Times* of London, it was chosen as "the world's most respected paper and forest products company." Or rather, it was tied for first with a European company.

This global aspect of the pulp and paper and wood products industry can never be overlooked in any discussion of the future of the Maine Woods. Nor can the pressures of markets and stock exchanges—myriad actions far removed from our scene in the Maine wilderness.

Thus, the pronouncements of Champion's CEO Richard E. Olson, as broadcast on the Internet, focused in 1998 on "maximizing shareholder value." Olson was happy to announce that Champion's year 2000 goal of increasing its pre-tax profitability by $400 million would be reached a year ahead of schedule and that another profit-improvement program to boost pre-tax earnings by $285 million would be instituted, including a new gas-fired turbine generator for Bucksport.

How remote these city-slicker concerns might seem from the vantage of the forest primeval in Maine. Yet those twin bugaboos of clear-cutting and spraying that have so agitated Maine public life are directly related to them.

If anyone among our entourage most epitomized the skeptical if not hostile Maine people who had supported the Ban, it was Representative-elect Joanne Twomey of Biddeford. In that quintessential small industrial city in the very southern part of the state, she had carved out a political career as an outspoken environmentalist—no small feat in a community dominated by conservative, economy-minded Franco-Americans, many descended from immigrant

Canadian factory workers. What had started Joanne off was the building of a waste-burning incinerator in the center of the city. She fought it at every step, achieving a name for herself, was elected to the city council, and ultimately, after several tries, won the Democratic nomination for state representative in her district, which assured election since Republicans scarcely ever run in Biddeford. For the Champion foresters with us, led by their chief Joel Swanton, Joanne Twomey was a constant and not-always-so-gentle foil. As we watched the clear-cut operation, saw the tractor-treaded feller-buncher snipping those ill but majestic beeches and lugging the bodies away, one could see this blonde housewife's features tighten. She soon was asking why single-species, even-aged replacements (the black spruces) had been deemed necessary. She refused to believe that any spraying was benign, despite assurances about Round-up. She worried aloud about impacts on wildlife and did not seem mollified by listening to and being shown the extra effort Champion was making to reduce those impacts. When the wildlife specialist employed in this area by Champion, an ex-Maine Department of Inland Fish and Wildlife specialist, spoke of having to bait bears or else their populations could not be thinned enough by hunting, Joanne was outraged and said so. Through her, there was a clear sense of the average Mainer reacting emotionally and with a palpable sense of distrust toward official pronouncements, especially from self-interested corporations.

One tended to feel a bit sorry for Joel Swanton and his crew. Implicit in their dismay was that they were facing an ignorance of the past; no benchmarks to measure progress; none to contrast their caring attitude toward the woods with the atrocities of yore. Not long ago, there was no forestry; trees were butchered, the great white pines brought crashing down until no vestiges of them were left except a few accidentally overlooked. Deeryards were blithely leveled in the good old days—who worried about wildlife when lumbering? Wonderful trout brooks silted up from the runoff caused by skidder ruts taller than a man. Spraying—why the whole forest was sprayed, right to the river's edge, the poison drifting carelessly for miles. We won't speak of men's lives lost or carelessness with fire and whole townships burned flat. Compare today. Compare the planning that went into the Sustainable Forestry Initiative, compare the mapping of the Diversity Units, or that Protection Areas exist, so that every last bit of growing fiber isn't axed or chain-sawed, as it was, and the barren ground left to regenerate itself haphazardly. Behold the poor wildlife expert, aghast that someone might react against bear-baiting, struggling to explain patiently the dogma of his trade—that if you had too many animals of a species in one habitat, all could die from overcrowding, that they had to be culled, and that the 21,000 black bears in the area were far beyond the carrying capacity. Or pity the foresters, some who had advanced degrees, wanting to instill confidence that they had the scientific knowledge to know what they were doing.

How about a little appreciation, if nothing else, for the complexity of the problem, and the added cost, millions to Champion, of going these extra miles to meet public expectations and fears? Also, it should never be forgotten they were still running a business. Common sense, alone, informed the knowledge that mills, whether for paper or building supplies, had to be fed an endless parade of wood. A lot of Maine jobs depended on such continuity. Above all, the most unspoken message was the forester's creed, their basic value judgment: that the highest and best use for a tree is use. To let one grow beyond maturity, reach old age, topple, and rot, never to be made into anything, is a sinful waste, maybe even a crime. The exceptions, of course, granted grudgingly over the years, are trees that grow in areas better protected for other values. Rational planning like the Diversity Units could allow these special places to be saved and offer a range of options for the rest of the forest to achieve maximum production with minimum impact.

In addition to seeing clear-cuts, new and old, we were taken through selectively logged sections and to streamsides where shade was maintained over the water by strips left so that foliage could fall in and provide nutrients for aquatic life. Whoever heard of a logging outfit doing phytoplankton studies? But Champion was conducting them. Different standards of strip size for different waterways had been established, ranging from 100-foot setbacks to ones of 600 feet. We were introduced to the mysteries of basal areas, a way to measure how crowded the clusters of uncut trees should be. A concept referred to as TRIAD was explained; really, another means of saying that if you can intensively manage a portion of your land, you can less intensively manage the rest of it. However, this involves herbicides and other forest chemicals such as fertilizer. The company will continue to look for alternatives, we were told, but presently TRIAD can't exist without their application. In the words of one company employee, "Banning them would flip all our management objectives on their ear." An attention to visual aesthetics was pointed out: a clear-cut done in such a manner that it couldn't be seen from the road. The skyline of silhouetted trees, at least to those at ground level, still denoted a distant wilderness scene.

After a full day of viewing and listening, the tour continued with an overnight stay at Nicatous Lodge and Camps. We were now in Penobscot County, at the north end of Nicatous Lake, and the nearest town was Burlington. We might have been in the middle of nowhere, except the next morning we were witness to a bridge rebuilding done with heavy equipment right next to this year-round, rustic resort. Something of the flavor of the old lumbering camps was presented here, certainly in the gargantuan supper and breakfast meals served to us, and we had that end of the lake to ourselves for the boat and canoe rides we took.

Who doesn't like to recreate in the Maine North Woods? There has always been a special magic to this comparatively comfortable mode of "roughing it." Before heading back to civilization, a visit to one of Champion's own recreational spots brought in another dimension of a great Maine landowner's concern: what to do about people who abuse the privilege of being allowed to use private land. We traveled to deserted Mopang Lake, where a private sporting camp adjoining a magnificent beach had been inherited by Champion from St. Regis. No longer used by Champion for its own employees, it had been closed and gated following a trashing of the beach by interlopers in a four-wheel drive. But as if to bring the problem of trespassing into clear focus, we arrived to find that the lock on the fence had been clipped. Remnants of fires littered the sand. The discovery set the stage for a litany of complaints from our hosts, who were the custodians of this and many other recreational sites. In Maine, alone, Champion has 2,000 miles of road to maintain, roads that provide access for hunters, fishermen, and others using their land. There are 1,200 existing recreational leases. At one time, people were allowed to camp anywhere; now there are six formal camping areas, which temporarily have been leased to the Maine Forest Service. All-terrain vehicles (ATVs) and snowmobiles are allowed and present safety problems. Locals are let in to "tip," i.e., to collect boughs for making wreaths. And all of this permissive good neighborliness by the company helps contribute to a sense many full-time residents of these northern climes have—to wit, that the land is really theirs.

Plus, to quote Chief Forester Swanton: "Public interest in private lands is light-years from twenty-three years ago."

Then, in 1975, the spruce budworm was ravaging the Maine Woods. The paper companies, carrying on pretty much as they had since the turn of the century, still had the state picking up most of the cost of spraying their lands. The public showed little interest in what was happening, except when spray was dropped carelessly and blown onto people's homes in Washington County. Incidentally, Champion was nine years away from buying St. Regis.

Think now of the concerns of this or any multinational corporation. A company statement addressed global climate change. The Kyoto Protocol worried them deeply. That draft document would require developed countries like the United States to reduce total emissions of greenhouse gases to an average of 5.2 percent below their 1990 figures. Developing nations would not have to reduce at all. "Some of these countries also represent the strongest competitors to the U.S. forest products industry because of their low labor and forestry costs combined with new world-class equipment," the Champion document complained. Their cost of complying with already existing environmental regulations, $6 billion to $10 billion, was cited. Then, stating that the Kyoto pact "recognizes the high value of our forests as "sinks"" or places where carbon is stored, and that their "forests and wood products could partially offset our manufacturing emissions," it pointed out that credit would only be given for forests planted after 1990.

Coming full circle was the question of planting forests which, in Champion's scheme of things, comes under *high-intensity forestry*, the touchiest part of their whole operation since it involves clear-cutting and spraying. The company—presumably also with other pulp and paper corporations and major landowners—therefore supported the Reforestation Tax Act of 1999 in Congress, designed to "encourage both individuals and companies to plant and grow trees, as well as to reforest their land after harvest."

So much for these global players. Champion may not be totally representative of all the big-time owners and users of the Maine North Woods in that its reputation was of a company perhaps more scrupulous than the others. With great pride, Champion released the news that its Northeast Region wildlife biologist, Gary Donovan of Bucksport, was a recipient of a 1999 National Wetlands Award for his work in Project SHARE (Salmon Habitat and River Enhancement), an effort to conserve Atlantic salmon in Down East rivers.

In the same year, MEBSR (Maine Businesses for Social Responsibility) gave Champion its Eagle Feather Award in the category of businesses of over fifty employees. MEBSR is well regarded as a membership of businesses run on policies of a "reform capitalist" type, treating their employees and the environment well.

But for a segment of the Maine population, these good practices do not seem good enough to deal with the new problems in the Maine North Woods, or, for that matter, the world at large. Our tour, in their eyes, would have been to a set of "Potemkin villages," mere facades arranged to dazzle and impress, with nothing solid behind them. Project SHARE would have to give way, in their view, to listing the Atlantic salmon in Maine as an endangered species. Clear-cutting and spraying must cease. In other words, coming next is the view from the other side—from those pejoratively labeled "tree-huggers."

TWO

The Tree-Huggers

A CAMPAIGN FOR THE FOREST is the title of a thin book written by Greg Gerritt, described on the back flap as "a longtime Green activist." The work was published in 1997 by Leopold Press, Inc., Raymond, Maine, and Gerritt, it said, lived "until recently" in the rural Franklin County community of Industry, Maine. The campaign in question was the 1996 effort to ban clear-cutting in Maine, in which Gerritt played a prominent proponent's role.

His writing, while polemical, is often candid about the weaknesses of his own side, at least as political neophytes going into battle against some of the strongest forces in the Pine Tree State. Their passion is perhaps best expressed by the harsh language used by Gerritt to characterize their major enemy. There are no shadings here vis-à-vis the paper companies and large landholders. Those Champion foresters who seemed like decent individuals trying to do a difficult balancing act are lumped by Gerritt into a single amorphous mass he calls the FPI (the Forest Products Industry). Nor is this faceless, undifferentiated force indigenous to Maine or to our day and age. After touching briefly on the early history of lumbering in Maine, Gerritt states that the "FPI shifted its investment to the exploitation of forests in the Southeast, the Upper Midwest, and the Pacific Northwest between the end of the Civil War and the early part of the twentieth century."

Now actually globalized, the FPI as such has continued its sprawl across the length and breadth of the planet. Gerritt writes: "Deforestation is now a worldwide problem, with the loss of at least

25 percent of the world's forests having taken place since 1970," a figure he attributes to the World Watch Institute's "State of the World, 1995."

Worries about a too rapidly disappearing forest cover throughout the earth may account, in part, for the adherence of so many voters in conservative Maine to the rather radical positions of the clear-cut Ban promoters. The statistics pouring into public discourse are often even more alarming than those presented by Gerritt. The prestigious National Academy of Sciences printed an article in its Winter 1997–98 *Issues in Science and Technology* magazine that states baldly: "We have lost almost half — 3 billion hectares — of the forests that once blanketed Earth."

The authors maintain: "Just 22 percent of Earth's original forest remains in large, relatively natural ecosystems." What they call *frontier forests* in temperate zones (like the U.S.) are the most endangered. Almost 85 percent of the threat in North America is from logging, and the use of paper products worldwide has risen from 50 metric tons per 1,000 people in 1961 to 170 metric tons in 1994, while global wood consumption in almost the same period went from 100 million cubic meters to nearly 150 million cubic meters. The chilling conclusion that the world will one day relatively soon be without trees if nothing is done gains added poignancy from the debate about global warming. With forests viewed as "carbon sinks," it is possible to wince inwardly at the thought of even a single living tree being slain, never mind millions upon millions.

Thus, the utilitarian view — that a tree is primarily a means to a commercial end: lumber, paper, fuel, jobs — is tilting against a new ethic, or rather an old one that is suddenly finding fresh strength. Trees kept alive have other uses — higher priorities for humankind, as Henry David Thoreau intuited a century and a half ago, suggesting it was no more a tree's highest destiny to be turned into lumber than a man's to end up as manure. Nowadays, when *ecology* has become a household word, supra-utilitarian benefits of the forest are easily delineated with the help of science: not only helping to ward off the heating of the planet but also saving God's creatures from extinction. The idea of *wildlife corridors* is but a practical underpinning for the more mystical notion of "wilderness" as a good unto itself. We are in the realm of religion here, sometimes unabashedly so. Herman Daly, for example, in his book *Beyond Growth*, waxes absolutely theological when he writes:

> To hand back to God the gift of Creation in a degraded state, capable of supporting less life, less abundantly, and for a shorter future, is surely a sin. If it is a sin to kill and to steal, then surely it is a sin to destroy carrying capacity—the capacity of the earth to support life now and in the future.

Daly, however, is not an ordained churchman but a University of Maryland academic, described as "the dean of ecological economics." He, himself, says he is a Christian and wonders if the churches today, because of their slowness to speak out on issues of environmental protection, are in the grip of some world-hating heresy, like Manichaeism and Gnosticism in the Christian past. For God created the world, Daly says, and the Creation was declared good by God and "if we love God we will love God's world," and not ignorantly harm it, "like a curious child playing with a grasshopper."

There are powerfully motivating thoughts in such a line of reasoning. No doubt it has led believers to climb atop great trees and live there until the loggers get tired and go away or to climb into small boats and buzz like mosquitoes at whaling ships and help their quarry to escape. Harmful extremes are always possible, too, like driving spikes into trees and causing injuries, but the case can certainly be made that protection of the planet in its natural form is doing God's work.

It is in this sense of degree that a "new wave," so to speak, of defending the earth has seemingly set itself apart from the conservationists of the old school. Their split in Maine in the battle over clear-cutting is not surprising, perhaps inevitable and, in some respects, a modern play-out of an earlier division. Muir versus Pinchot was a former way of putting it: John Muir, the pioneer of preservation versus Gifford Pinchot, the apostle of careful resource use.

The Champion International Company foresters, with their plot plans and intricate zoning, can be deemed the heirs of Pinchot who was, himself, a forester—indeed, often called "the Father of

U.S. Forestry," and founder of its first school, using his family's money, at Yale. Muir, the Scottish immigrant to the Wisconsin woods, the inspirer of Yosemite and Alaska's Glacier National Park, would have felt right at home in the ban clear-cutting effort.

Another dimension to add to the religious strain is the political. After something went wrong with Marx and Lenin's prediction that capitalism would disappear, the most virulent form of the socialist solution, its Soviet phase, collapsed. One of the major impulses for communism's demise was its atrocities against the environment. Its emphasis on production at any cost led to crimes against the earth on a scale unthinkable in the latter-day capitalist world. So, since capitalism has been left in the saddle, the only show in town, it is the *corporation* that is now the target.

A Sierra Club book, *The Corporate Planet,* by Joshua Karliner, executive director of the Transnational Resource and Action Center in San Francisco, spells out a rationale for the current intensified activism in the environmental movement. He does so through reference to a campaign in the early 1990s by Greenpeace to produce and promote "Greenfreeze" refrigerators that would not use ozone-depleting chemicals. Karliner states as his thesis:

> ...these campaigns hold a great potential to serve as
> building blocks toward a more fundamental change—
> the transformation of political power to an order that
> will make corporations truly accountable to the public
> good.

A suspicion the goal may be more ambitious—to get rid of corporations altogether—is, not surprisingly, an assumption of some of those on the receiving end. During the clear-cutting ban debate, a friend of mine, a quintessential establishment environmentalist whose family had a corporate landholding heritage, exclaimed in exasperation after an encounter with opponents of the Compact: "Those people are communists! They don't believe in private property!"

Be that as it may, echoes of the old Cold War dichotomy have entered this discussion. Norman Mailer, in the blurb he wrote for *The Corporate Planet,* is his usual choleric and somewhat leftist but perceptive self, arguing:

The corporation, by its nature, is as blind as it is powerful. Spiritually blind, morally blind. As a collective
entity, it is worse than any of the individuals who make
it up....

And he finishes his mini-jeremiad by praising the author for
opening "a vision of how dangerous to the future of our globe is
global capitalism, itself."

As we have seen in Seattle, the cry of *global capitalism* usually
phrased as the unfettered rule of corporations, was powerful enough
to draw 50,000 demonstrators to disrupt the World Trade Organization's meeting. Among the top burning issues, possibly the most
attractive to the younger element in the crowds of demonstrators,
was the environment.

The attitude toward the WTO's apparent blind eye to habitat
degradation in its promotion of world trade has been aptly
expressed by a Sierra Club spokesman, Carl Pope, who says: "It
turns out that the WTO's rules are made of, by, and for the transnational corporations and adjudicated by anonymous judges meeting in secret with confidential legal briefs." Then, Pope follows with
an even stronger message: "In the end, the WTO is about coercion,
about making the world safe for companies that don't want to make
decent products in a decent way."

The mainstream environmental organizations engender
equally jaundiced views, and especially taint themselves by taking
corporate contributions. The National Audubon Society gathers
about 2 percent of its income from giants like Chevron, Dow,
Dupont, Motorola, Scott Paper, etc. Worse, individuals with con-
nections to polluting businesses have sat on National Audubon's
board. The National Wildlife Federation, the World Wildlife Fund,
and the Nature Conservancy are likewise impure. Proof, in the eyes
of the greener groups, was evidenced in the clash over NAFTA (the
North American Free Trade Agreement). By "forsaking confronta-
tional tactics in favor of a false harmony approach," as Joshua Karliner put it, the mainstreamers gained a "toothless environmental
commission" and shattered a solid environmental front against free
trade. A similar sort of ill feeling, accompanied by attacks on people's integrity, was engendered among Maine environmentalists dur-

ing the clear-cutting referendum. The depth of the antagonism to corporations has led a state of Washington branch of Earth First! to issue a mock certificate dissolving the corporate charter of the Weyerhaeuser organization. A Maine activist, both as a labor union leader and Green Party member, Peter Kellman of North Berwick, espouses the same tactic. His as yet unpublished manuscript, "The People's Republic of Jay," the story of the 1987 strike in Maine against the International Paper Company, advocates that:

> When we are in fights with corporations that are responsible for the deaths of our people or are trying to destroy our unions, we should organize to get the corporate charter revoked and have the assets of the corporation divided among the workers and communities affected.

So anticorporationism will remain a strong tone as Maine debates the future of its forests. The phenomenon is not exactly new Down East. Governor Percival Baxter, in the 1920s, had his public brawls with the Great Northern Paper Company and the Central Maine Power Company over matters related to the environment. Yet, in the most heated of these contentions, his goal was not to stop the state's largest power company from damming the Kennebec nor, heaven forbid (Percy was a Republican), put it out of business, but simply to get CMP to pay a fair price for the state land it was using on which to build its dam. Jerome Daviau, a muckraker of the 1950s, addressed his concerns to the waterways the corporations had degraded. Especially galling to Daviau, a lawyer from Waterville, was the effect of their operations on the fisheries in the state's rivers. Lack of effective fishways was his number-one *bête noire*, closely followed by the pollution they were dumping. But Daviau was not anticorporation. Just as fervently, he declaimed: "We should not abandon our efforts to obtain new industries."

Then came *The Paper Plantation* in 1974, a report of a Ralph Nader Study Group. Viking Press of New York City published it, obviously with an eye on the burgeoning U.S. interest in the environment. Nader's introduction sets the direction of the discussion:

> Maine is poor. Maine is corporate country—a land of seven giant pulp and paper companies, imposing a one

crop economy with a one crop politics, which exploits the water, air, soil, and people of a beautiful state.

There were then sixteen pulp and paper mills in Maine. They were the state's largest landowners. In 1971 they owned outright 7.5 million acres, or 37 percent of all Maine land, up from 27 percent since 1959. They employed one-quarter of the manufacturing work force of Maine and produced $714 million worth of products.

Each of the seven biggest companies had gross revenues greater than those of the state of Maine, itself. The four largest at the time—International Paper, Great Northern Paper, St. Regis, and Scott—had two to six times Maine's revenues. The report's preface thus extrapolates that:

> The political and economic control of Maine by a hand-
> ful of absentee corporations has turned the state into a
> paper plantation....

Yet, by the standards of our present-day polemics, *The Paper Plantation* seems rather tame in hindsight. Many of its concerns no longer resonate today, like the ending of log-driving in the rivers or the lack of waste treatment for paper company discharges into those same waters. Any mention of clear-cutting is rather skimpy, too, limited by the fact that only one of the companies was doing it—the Scott Paper Company. Or Scott, as it turned out, was the only one admitting the truth. The others would try to cover themselves by leaving a few sticks standing!

In the mid-1970s, the spruce budworm spraying began. It lit a spark that has belatedly left a deep imprint on our current controversies in the Maine North Woods. *Beyond the Beauty Strip* by Mitch Lansky did not appear in print until 1992, but its genesis was an incident of carelessness occurring in June 1976.

Mitch Lansky had moved in 1973 to one of the remotest corners of Maine on the Aroostook County side of its border with Washington County. The official community was the quasi-municipality of Reed Plantation, but where he lived is better known as Wytopitlock, a name symbolic in Maine for the most boondockish settlement we have. When the spray planes flew over that particular stretch of dense forestland in June 1976, they let fly their loads on the farm Mitch Lansky had carved out of the wilderness. He sued, won an out-of-court settlement, and used the money to found a group called PEST—Protect Our Environment from Sprayed Toxins.

More than 3.5 million acres were sprayed in Maine that year. It was a huge operation. Eventually, though, the companies lost their federal and state subsidies, were required to use more and more Bt (a nonchemical biological spray), suffered the pesky attacks of Mitch Lansky's PEST group, and found this mode of budworm control increasingly expensive. So the spray program ended. Opponents all along had claimed that the budworm were cyclical creatures who would eat themselves out of house and home if left alone and that spraying merely prolonged the plague. Once the woods were left unsprayed, this prediction seemed to be borne out—at least there have been no budworm outbreaks since.

However, spraying remained an issue. Another bit of aerial sloppiness in 1979 in connection with a St. Regis (Champion's predecessor) clear-cut in Washington County drew unwanted publicity and a lasting bad image. This occurred when a large number of gardens near Dennysville were contaminated by herbicide drift. Public awareness was further roused when Maine people learned in 1989 that herbicide spraying not only hadn't ceased but had reached a total of 80,000 acres. The next year, the figure had increased to 90,000 acres.

Two years later, Mitch Lansky's book burst upon the scene. He is a tough writer and a meticulous researcher. From the very start, like the talented polemicist he is, he employs the sardonic import of his title to drive home a hard-hitting anticorporate message. An example:

The beauty strip works somewhat like Lewis Carroll's looking glass. To step beyond the beauty strip is to step into a world of distorted priorities, distorted metaphors, and distorted logic. If what you see looks degraded and ugly, the fault (according to corporate spokespeople) lies with your vision rather than industry's management. Once you learn the proper attitude, it should all look acceptable, if not admirable.

Beyond the beauty strip, the priorities for the forest

are industrial priorities. From the industrial perspective, the forest is not a biological community to which we belong and which we must maintain. It is a resource to exploit.

Beyond the beauty strip, forest and society are described with industrial metaphors that help to justify industrial actions. The forest becomes a pulpwood factory, a fiber farm, or just biomass. It is a commodity to be bought or sold. Rivers become an energy source or (along with air) a pollution sink. Human beings are labor (to avoid), consumers (to entice), or stockholders (to please).

Suddenly, Nature was being looked at in a different way. It had value in and of itself, without reference to what its resources might become. The "industrial forest" was a brilliant pejorative term, a great rallying cry for those who were asking Maine people to ban clear-cutting. Even "biomass," which during the OPEC oil crisis had taken on a green tinge as wood—a *renewable* resource—was burned instead of petroleum, was now condemned since it stripped the forest of vegetation that would rot and engender new growth. Plus, whole areas were being ravaged bare in its name. In a sense, it was a conservative creed Mitch Lansky had promulgated. Leave Nature alone. Stop doing things to her.

If their antagonists disagreed, labeling Jonathan Carter and his forces radicals, another force—super-radical in the industrialists' eyes—also entered the picture. These people not only wanted cutting to be dramatically curtailed, or ended altogether, they wanted to turn the woods back to the way they once had been!

RESTORE, they called themselves, making the point right away, before adding The North Woods in upper- and lower-case letters. But their enemies know them by that single stark resonating verb in capitals, as in the bumper stickers seen that proclaim: NO RESTORE FOR ME (using the age-old Down East pun to play on the word forming both the first-person objective pronoun and the abbreviation for Maine).

RESTORE The North Woods has shaken the region as much as the clear-cutting ban by proposing a 3.2 million-acre Maine

Woods National Park and Preserve. It is a project that has the full support of Jonathan Carter and his supporters, now banded in a nonprofit organization called the Forest Ecology Network (FEN). Another ally is the Northern Appalachian Restoration Project, whose publication the *Northern Forest Forum* has Mitch Lansky as its assistant editor and features contributions from Jym St. Pierre, RESTORE's Maine director.

The proposed national park would include Baxter State Park. RESTORE's effort would stretch its forever-wild protection in all directions, encompassing all of Moosehead Lake to the southwest, then north to the Allagash River, and as far west as the Quebec border above Jackman. Some other outstanding physical features of the state that would fall within its borders are: Gulf Hagas, Maine's version of the Grand Canyon; Ripogenus Gorge, with its precipitous 80-feet-in-a-mile-and-a-half drop; Big Reed Pond, site of 5,000 acres of the last remaining old-growth forest in New England; as well as locally famous water bodies such as the Debsconeag Lakes, Lobster Lake, and Umbazooksus Stream and Lake.

While the scope of the project has taken breaths away and brought forth cries of outrage, the notion of a national park here is not new.

As far back as 1913, a Republican congressman from nearby Dover-Foxcroft, Frank Guernsey, tried to interest his D.C. colleagues in approving a Katahdin-area national park, but bills he put in that year and in 1916 died in committee. Around the same period, an effort was underway to create the one national park Maine now does have — Acadia National Park — with the full support of Maine's then-dominant GOP political leadership. While governor Percival Baxter actually lent his name to support a national park on Mount Desert Island, despite his dislike of federal activity in Maine. Then, in 1937, there was an attempt to form a national park Down East that would have subsumed his own Baxter Park. A leader of the move was another Republican congressman, Ralph Owen Brewster, once Baxter's ally, later a bitter enemy. With every ounce of wit and energy, Baxter fought Brewster and his cohort, Myron Avery, chairman of the Appalachian Trail Conference. And he won. Congress lost interest. Talk of a 1 million-acre national park and national for-

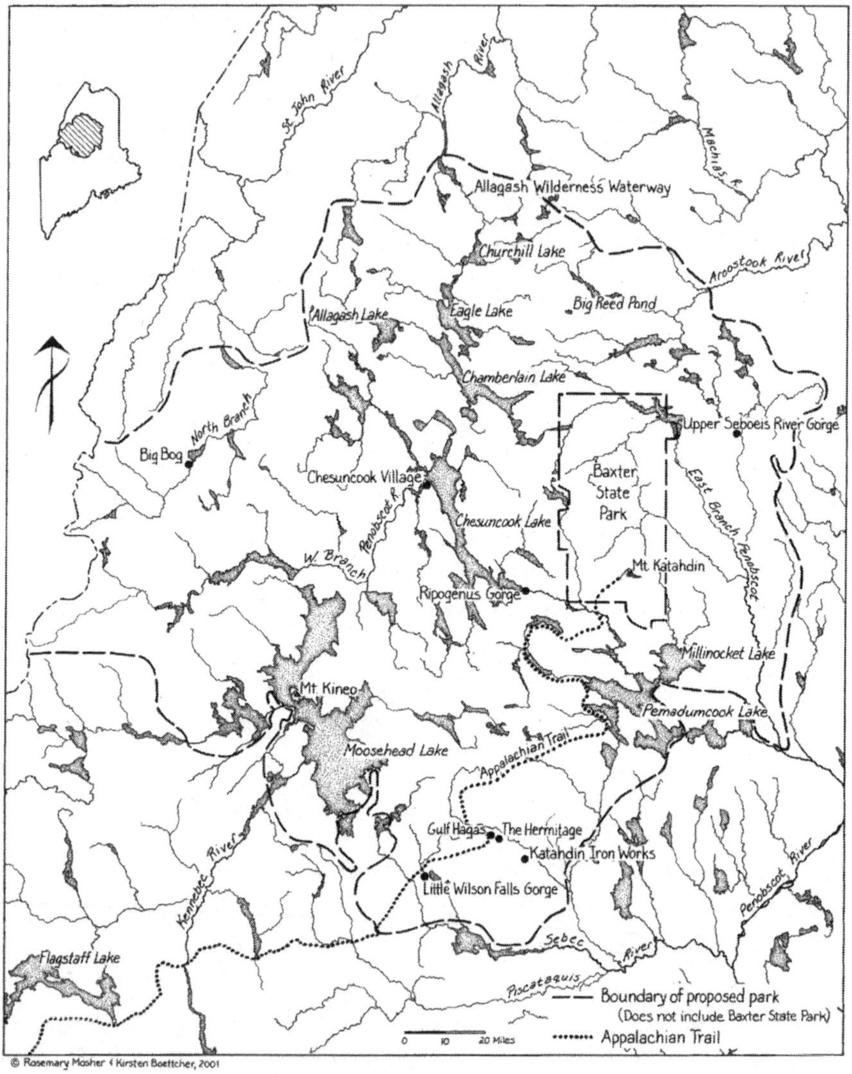
St John River
Allagash River
Machias R.
Allagash Wilderness Waterway
Churchill Lake
Aroostook River
Allagash Lake
Eagle Lake
Big Reed Pond
Chamberlain Lake
Upper Seboeis River Gorge
North Branch
Big Bog
Chesuncook Village
Baxter State Park
East Branch Penobscot
Penobscot R.
Chesuncook Lake
W. Branch
Mt. Katahdin
Ripogenus Gorge
Millinocket Lake
Mt. Kineo
Pemadumcook Lake
Appalachian Trail
Moosehead Lake
Gulf Hagas
The Hermitage
Katahdin Iron Works
Kennebec River
Little Wilson Falls Gorge
Penobscot River
Sebec River
Flagstaff Lake
Piscataquis
Boundary of proposed park
(Does not include Baxter State Park)
0 10 20 Miles
Appalachian Trail
© Rosemary Mosher & Kirsten Boettcher, 2001

RESTORE's Plans for a National Park

est, also spurred by Democratic Governor Louis Brann, faded away completely. Many landowners, even the most conservative, hurt by the Great Depression, had been willing, if not eager, to sell out to the federal government. Eventually, the field was left to Percy Baxter, who spent the next thirty years adding parcels to his *state* park.

Knowledge of Baxter's hostility to the national park idea led in 1999 to an informal meeting between the promoters of the Maine North Woods Park and members of the Baxter family. As a Baxter biographer, I was invited to be present. Some of the attendees came from as far away as Colorado and California. It was explained there would be no change in Baxter Park's status if incorporated into the new national park entity. Governor Baxter's deeds of trust, enshrined in state laws, would still govern, and administration would remain with the Baxter Park Authority. The results of the conclave were somewhat inconclusive: some Baxters for, some against, others undecided.

RESTORE has been touching bases wherever possible to explain its concept. Since one of the arguments is the national park's economic benefit, it sponsored a trip for four residents of the Greenville-Moosehead Lake region to Ely, Minnesota, a one-time iron-mining and logging center that now earns the bulk of its living as a "gateway" into an area of vast parks, including the Boundary Waters Canoe Area, a 1 million-acre federally designated wilderness.

The Ely trip was a follow-up to a well-attended meeting at Greenville High School, organized by the Greenville Economic Development Committee, to discuss a report from RESTORE entitled: "Gateway to a Healthy Economy. The Proposed Maine Woods National Park and Preserve and the Future of the Moosehead Region of Maine." Other groups, including the Sportsman Alliance of Maine (SAM) and representatives of the paper companies, were also invited to present their views.

RESTORE based its arguments on economic factors, beginning with the proposition that "over-reliance on the forest products industry for jobs has weakened the Moosehead Region." The percentage of people thus employed in and around Moosehead was stated as 13.4 percent of all jobs and 19.6 percent in the entire area of the proposed Maine Woods National Park and Preserve, using figures derived from the Maine Department of Labor. A drop in these jobs from 1984 to 1994 was then cited—a loss of 450 for Moosehead and 3,500 in the MWNP region. Predictions of further such job losses in the future were added to the mix.

Emphasizing the need to diversify, RESTORE made the statement that to do so "requires the protection of the special wildland values that distinguish the region." Therefore, "a Maine Woods National Park could protect the special values of the Moosehead Region and sustain a healthy economy."

Another enticement was that if the entire MWNP were acquired, the local governments and the state of Maine would receive a multimillion-dollar payment-in-lieu-of-taxes greater than the property taxes those bodies were already receiving. Still another lure was that in the *Preserve* part of the Park, hunting, fishing, and snowmobiling would be allowed. Tourist revenue, "at even modest levels of visitation," was estimated to be more than $100 million in annual expenditures for goods and services and the provider of more than 5,000 jobs.

That meeting at Greenville High School was in April. In August the flight to Minnesota took place. Two small planes, one piloted by Rudy Engholm, RESTORE's board chair at the time, transported the "three businessmen and one teacher" who went along, plus Jym St. Pierre. Once in Ely, they spent two days meeting with community and business leaders. To quote Jym St. Pierre: "One thing Ely people said: 'Capitalize on the concept of wilderness.'" By doing so, apparently, Ely attracts some 200,000 visitors a year and houses twenty-two professional outfitting and guiding services. The former iron-mining town whose ore played out also boasts a three-year-old International Wolf Center, bringing $3 million a year and 66 new jobs into the local economy, with plans for a $750,000 addition and a North American Bear Center. Jym added that many visitors to Ely do not go into the wilderness Boundary Waters Canoe Area, but its mere presence attracts them.

All of this activity took place in 1996 and, in the ensuing years, it is hard to tell that the Maine Woods National Park idea has made substantial progress. The current push is to convince Congress to fund a feasibility study, but the level of hostility to RESTORE remains so high that this seems a real uphill fight.

Adding to the difficulties are several ancillary issues, vigorously supported by RESTORE, that cause even harder feelings. The top two are the reintroduction of wolves and the listing of Atlantic salmon as an endangered species.

In a region where many people would like to bring back the bounties Maine once paid on large predators, the thought of reintroducing a beast it took years to exterminate strikes some of our citizens as perfectly loopy. They see the deer herd disappearing as a result, the moose population devastated, and their pets and children at peril. They find it bad enough that coyotes have filled in the niche once occupied by *Canis lupus* and now no one can seem to get rid of them. This wolf business, on the other hand, is a problem that may solve itself. Several gray wolves, straying from Canada, have infiltrated and been shot in Maine in recent years.

As for salmon, the uproar has been deafening, led by Governor Angus King, who sees a federal listing as a dire threat to Maine industries in the northeast, particularly the thriving aquaculture operations in Washington County. The attacks on the federal bureaucrats involved, who are seen as engaged in massive overkill, does not make the job easier for those who wish to see a huge federal park in the state.

Still, the leaders soldier on. A flight with Jonathan Carter and Rudy Engholm over the territory scheduled to be in the park showed that neither of them had lost their enthusiasm for the project nor seemed disheartened by the odds they faced. I had been invited to tour with them, along with Rob Gardiner, best known as head of Maine Public Broadcasting but whose interest stemmed from his stint in state government, running the Bureau of Public Lands.

Rudy Engholm, whose plane we were in, has been ferrying people up over the proposed MWNP area on a regular basis. The previous summer, he took Governor King, an open opponent of the park, to see it. Our own trip began in Portland on a very cold January morning, with a stop in Augusta to pick up Jonathan and Rob. The temperature outside the cockpit, according to Rudy, was something like 50 below zero, but it was an extraordinarily clear day. We had no problem seeing Mount Washington in the far-off White Mountains of New Hampshire, a "record distance" for him, Rudy said.

On our way toward the north country, Jonathan couldn't help but remark how good the relatively uncut forests in the "organized territories" looked from the air.

When did we cross into the "unorganized," or what could be considered the North Woods? That is always a subjective question, but when you're at Greenville, flying over Moosehead Lake, you can say for certain you're there. Mount Kineo loomed below, dramatic dark rock jutting above blue water as the tip of an almost unreachable peninsula. Some call it Maine's secondmost dramatic (and famous) mountain, next to Katahdin. Then, we were over another dramatic Maine mountain, Bigelow, and down below, cheek-by-jowl with that rocky upthrust, was Flagstaff Lake, man-made, a village drowned, its houses invisible beneath the icy, dammed-up waters. "Start watching for clear-cuts," Jonathan alerted us as we passed above—and not too high above—Bigelow's ridgeline.

With snow on the ground, they were like big patches of white, studding a brownish ground space. Green wasn't a prevalent color here, although perhaps this might have been due in part to the prevalence of leafless hardwood trees in the area. This westerly section of Maine does tend to grow more deciduous trees than evergreens.

We were to fly all the way up to the Allagash and over such fabled lakes as Chesuncook and Chamberlain and Churchill, the great water system that would anchor the Maine Woods National Park—a feature as telling as the cutover lots was the ubiquity of the roads. Strings of tannish-colored dirt seemed woven through every terrain we traversed.

A paradox, then. Rob and I were told the land we were viewing—and, for that matter, all of Maine's North Woods, was the least inhabited region in the lower forty-eight states. Yet it sure couldn't be called *wilderness*, with all those roads and signs of logging.

One might well facetiously wonder if Donn Fendler, lost in

Baxter Park for twelve days in 1939 and whose book about the ordeal still sells well to Maine youngsters, would be so far immersed in impenetrable woods today. With a cell phone, you might be able to direct a vehicle to you in short order. But, then again, young Fendler was lost in the wilds of Baxter and when, on our flight, we reached the famed state park's borders, we could see the difference. Those 200,000 or so acres have been called "a tiny postage stamp of green stuck on a much larger, much less healthy background." That was the verdict of Charles Fitzgerald, an environmental activist and supporter of more public park land in Maine. But before Percy Baxter's death in 1969, he, himself, voiced aloud the concern that his generous gift might someday be the only patch of green left in Maine.

A good deal of the land he bought had been logged over and in one section of his park, he established a "Scientific Forest Management Area" where the latest in forestry techniques could be practiced. As we flew toward Katahdin's summit over a landscape of dense green, Jonathan was eagerly pointing out we were passing the SFMA, extolling the fact that great forestry was on display there. A high point of the flight occurred shortly afterward. We flew past the peak of Katahdin. Rudy had warned we would experience a bump. The wind-draft (or whatever rocked us) was actually far stronger than he'd predicted. A real bang! Only that wasn't the excitement. There were elements of a thrill ride, to be sure, but it was really the majesty of the mountain at such close range, the massive, extended, bare boulder "knife-edge" that made the moment so emotional. Then, this wink of time and awesome vision was gone, as we flew on.

Another high point, another memorable experience, occurred as we circled above Gero Island. Its good-sized hunk of heavily forested land lies in the northern reaches of Chesuncook Lake. It is designated in Delorme's *Maine Atlas and Gazetteer* as Maine Public Reserve Land and represents one of the choice pieces of North Woods property that came into the state's possession when Rob Gardiner was director of the Bureau of Public Lands. Rudy banked the plane and we soared down around the outline of that wooded isle, a true "postage stamp of green" with its pointed tree crowns now emergent, around and around, with symphonic music from the plane radio punctuating a sense of grandeur and peacefulness. A bit of stagecraft had made its point: Katahdin, along with Bigelow, along with the lakes, along with the vastness of the countryside, roads and cuts notwithstanding—all spoke of how genuinely heroic a concept the Maine North Woods Park was and of how it could capture the enthusiasm and loyalty of the people determined to fight for it.

This latest thrust for a national park in inland Maine had its own history. Originally proposed by the Wilderness Society, whose call was for a 2.5 million-acre Maine Woods Reserve surrounding Baxter Park, the idea caught the interest of another group, the Northern Forest Alliance, a coalition of forty conservation organizations covering Maine, New Hampshire, Vermont, and New York State. Still another catalyst was a federally funded Forest Land Study, authorized by Congress, to look at 26 million acres of forest from the Adirondacks to Maine, for which a major impetus was the breakup of Diamond International's ownership in those four states. Begun in 1988, the study had a deadline of spring 1990. Its work led to the creation of the Northern Forest Lands Council, run by the U.S. Forest Service, which had a beleaguered existence from 1990 until 1994. Its recommendations for restricting land use caused such a backlash that Maine's U.S. senators at the time, George Mitchell and Bill Cohen, usually environmentally minded, backed away from any support. An appropriation of $13 million for planning never materialized and the Council went out of business.

The Northern Forest Alliance, heavily funded by foundations like Rockefeller and Pew, came forth in 1995 with its own proposal for ten wildlands areas to save, five of them in Maine. Some of these coincide with the acreage designated for the MWNP; others are outside, like the upper St. John headwaters or the western Boundary Mountains or the Androscoggin headwaters, plus also a "Greater Baxter Region" encompassing the Debsconeag Lakes, the East and West Branches of the Penobscot, and the Moosehead Lake/Roach River Watershed. Their approach is to push for land acquisition funds at the state (Land for Maine's Future) and federal (Land and Water Conservation Fund) levels.

RESTORE, which later left the Alliance, was started by

Michael Kellett in 1992 and had developed its own, more geographically focused 3.2 million-acre plan by 1994.

Events in the Maine North Woods have since become a continuous news story, almost a frenzy of action and change. The clear-cutting referenda form but a part of it. Beginning in the spring of 1998, a titanic game of North Woods Monopoly, of buying and selling forest land in immense parcels, began to reach a crescendo. The immediate inception was the revelation by SAPPI, Ltd. (South African Pulp and Paper Industries) that it contemplated selling its 911,000 acres of timberland in Maine. SAPPI had acquired all of Scott Paper's facilities here, including the lands gained from Scott's earlier takeover of S. D. Warren, and had emerged as Maine's largest pulp and paper employer. On October 8, 1998, the world learned that SAPPI's entire Maine landholdings, but not its mills in Westbrook and Hinckley, had been sold to Plum Creek Timber Company, Inc. of Seattle.

Already, before the buyer's identity was known, alarm had been spread throughout the state by SAPPI's intended move. Most cogent, perhaps, and most indicative of the feelings of the local people, was a piece in the *Moosehead Messenger* under the byline of Jeff Gibbs. Noting that 50 miles of prime Moosehead Lake waterfront were now on the auction block along with 50 more miles of frontage on nearby tributaries, Gibbs touched directly on the locals' single worst fear: loss of access:

> Just when we all thought that continued public access for recreation was in the bag, we face the prospects of a new owner's potential property access rules. In Maine, we fight for individual property rights — embracing large corporate landowners within the definition of individuals — so long as we continue to have unfettered access.

In that one paragraph, Gibbs summed up a common feeling of many of the residents of the North Woods region: it's our land, even if we don't own it. This attitude has deep historical roots in Maine, and is one of the prime motivating forces behind the fact that Maine today is a separate sovereign state and not still part of Massachusetts. The Maine Woods National Park is often attacked on the basis

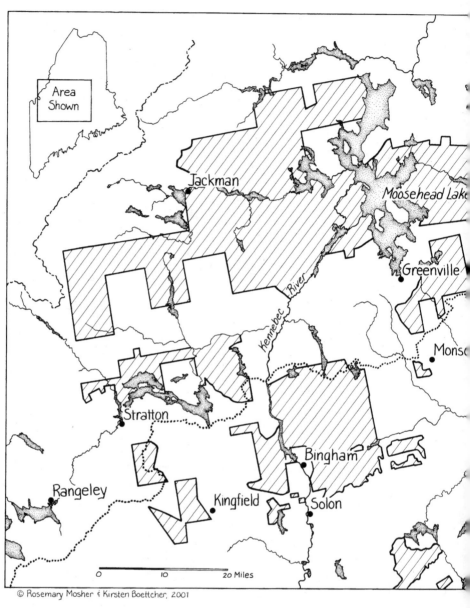

Area
Shown

Jackman

Moosehead Lake

Greenville

Kennebec River

Monso

Stratton

Bingham

Rangeley

Kingfield

Solon

0   10   20 Miles

© Rosemary Mosher & Kirsten Boettcher, 2001

SAPPI Holdings Sold to Plum Creek, 1988

36

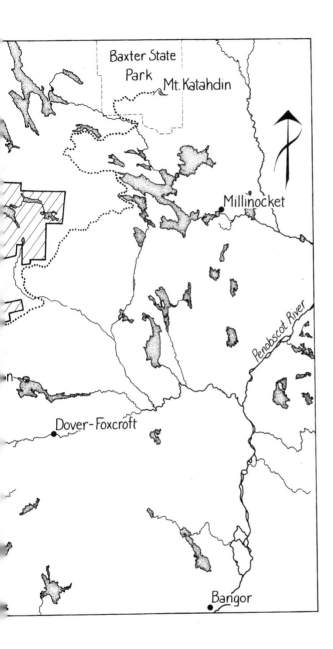

Baxter State Park

Mt. Katahdin

Millinocket

Penobscot River

n

Dover-Foxcroft

Bangor

that it is not needed. A sporting-camp owner in Kokadjo, Fred Can-
deloro, boasted to the *New York Times*: "Right now, with SAPPI, we
have the best land-use deal in the world." And as a Wayne W. Duf-
fett put it in a letter to the Portland newspapers: "We already use the
woods as guests of the paper companies at a nominal fee.... So why
spend millions of dollars to buy something we already have?" (The
same logic was used in the 1920s to shoot down Percival Baxter's
attempts to get the state to buy Katahdin.)

Another part of the worry Fred Gibbs voiced lay in the fact the
Maine Forest Service had confirmed that SAPPI, who'd only owned
its Maine land for four years, had cut it "harder than any other
paper company in the state," and thus:

> It is feared that SAPPI harvesting practices have
> reduced the value of its Maine holdings to the point
> where short-term gain-minded buyers would demand
> that the most valuable of the land—the Moosehead
> and rivers waterfront—be developed into vacation
> home lots.

The sale to Plum Creek can only have intensified this anxiety.
The West Coast company has a mixed image. Some of its lands, like
12,000 acres along the Black River in Montana, have been sold to
the Nature Conservancy but its website does advertise multimillion-
dollar lots for trophy-home development in that state and elsewhere.
A Montana conservationist who pegs Plum Creek's gilt-edged real
estate there at 150,000 acres, adds that most of their merchantable
timber is gone and that's why the company is going east to Maine.
Almost immediately upon their arrival Down East, Plum Creek officials did begin to talk about selling the state shoreline easements
along Moosehead and Flagstaff Lakes.

SAPPI's first announcement in June 1998 spurred the state's
editorial writers to start jumping on Governor Angus King. Said the
Lewiston Sun, a particularly conservative paper, "Gov. King should
seize the opportunity, proving his leadership in environmental concerns once and for all." That opportunity, as they put it, was for the
state to gain control over some spectacular pieces of land and to "do
so before another international giant buys the property, subdivides
paradise, and puts up condos and marinas." The *Portland Press Her-*

ald added: "Maine will not have this opportunity again soon, if ever."

King was taking heat because of his position in the previous legislative session regarding the amount of funding for public land acquisition. The governor had requested a rather paltry $10 million bond issue, which the lawmakers rejected and replaced with a mere $3 million appropriation. Before long, there were fifty requests for it.

The next blow to Maine's nervous system, after learning that Plum Creek was buying *all* of SAPPI's land, came from the state's second largest pulp and paper company, Bowater Great Northern Paper. All of its 2.1 million acres of land in Maine had been put up for sale!

In June 1998 it was still the conventional wisdom in Maine, reinforced by a company statement, that despite interest by some buyers in taking all of Bowater's Maine assets, only the Millinocket mill would be sold. Moreover, $200 million was to be invested to modernize its East Millinocket plant. Imagine the shock, on July 11, for the state to learn that Bowater's president and CEO, Arnold Nemirow, had just told a gathering of New York investors and financial analysts that everything owned by the company in Maine was for sale!

The catalyst appeared to be Bowater's impending purchase of a Canadian paper producer, Avenor, for $2.5 billion, and the load of debt this would entail. Nemirow, speaking at New York City's Waldorf-Astoria Hotel, made no bones about the fact that Maine was now extraneous to the South Carolina-headquartered company's financial picture. "We own all these big, great, efficient newsprints up in Canada now," Nemirow allegedly said in his briefing at the Waldorf-Astoria. "We don't need to own Great Northern in order to serve customers in the Northeast."

Here was a prime example of Maine caught up in globalization. In 1998 Bowater had also bought a South Korean newsprint mill. But in 1998 this originally English company, named for Sir Eric Bowater, which had bought its Maine operations from Georgia-Pacific, was struggling with its image on Wall Street. There had been downgrades of its stock from Morgan Stanley Dean Witter and B. T. Alex Brown. The Waldorf-Astoria announcement was an attempt to reverse the course.

Apparently, it worked. In March 1999 Bowater sold 981,000 acres of Maine land to New Brunswick's J. D. Irving Company and another 650,000 acres the following month to the McDonald Investment Company of Birmingham, Alabama. Both buyers agreed to keep supplying wood to the Millinocket and East Millinocket mills. Arnold Nemirow's "spin" to the financial world in their own somewhat arcane language was that "this transaction [the sale to McDonald] continues the company's redeployment of its rich asset base for greater shareholder value." Chris Lyddan, a writer for the trade organ *Pulp and Paper,* cheered him on: "Bowater is clearly on a trajectory to reposition itself in the global economy. Paper companies are getting lean and mean to respond to Wall Street's criticisms."

Shortly afterward, Bowater's stock was upgraded by B. T. Alex Brown and J. P. Morgan, and the company saw its earnings per share shoot up from 59 cents in 1998 to $1.89 in 1999.

The next big transfer involved the two mills, themselves. They went to a little known corporation out of Quebec called Inexcon, Inc. Until then, an effort had been underway for an ESOP, an employee buyout of the older Millinocket plant. Not only was this attempt derailed, but Inexcon made it clear that it wanted the workers to take a 10 percent pay cut, contribute more to the cost of their health insurance, and agree not to ask for a pay increase for five years. Later, the 10 percent pay cut demand was dropped, but the workers had to extend their present contract.

Environmentalists also were concerned by this sale since there were still 380,000 acres of former Bowater land left in the deal with Inexcon, including the Debsconeag Lakes and Rainbow Lake. Particularly worrisome was the possibility Inexcon would be taking on a good deal of debt to accomplish both its purchase and a planned conversion of the East Millinocket mill from newsprint to specialty papers. The pressure might be on the Canadians to generate cash by selling high-priced Maine lakefront property.

Given these two headline-generating land sales totaling more than two and a half million acres, other such transactions in Maine might be excused for seeming anticlimactic. International Paper went on the market with 185,000 acres around the headwaters of the

St. John River. The Nature Conservancy's Maine chapter convinced its parent organization to loan it $35 million to make the largest purchase in the history of the organization. Georgia-Pacific, through a subsidiary called the Timber Company, sold 440,000 acres that will be managed by Wagner Forest Management Ltd. of Lyme, New Hampshire, which will also be managing some of the former Bowater lands. All in all, when the dust settled, some 3.3 million acres had changed hands in Maine.

As an added fillip, there was the Pingree Project. Billed as "the largest conservation easement project in the world," it involved a Massachusetts group, the New England Forestry Foundation and the Pingree Associates, the descendants of David Pingree, and 754,673 acres of the land in Maine that this Salem, Massachusetts, tycoon had begun amassing in the nineteenth century. To a degree, the arrangement doesn't change much for the Pingrees, except it avoids the temptation to yield to financial pressures that sales for development might relieve, and gives them $30 million for doing so.

In the public buzz over all these goings-on in the Maine Woods, an operative word in the media and other publications was "Opportunity." Here was a golden chance for the state to acquire choice acreage. The miserly percentage of land not in private hands Down East (0.9 percent in federal ownership) was advertised. The *Maine Times* even ran a lead story captioned: "Searching for Percival" and subtitled: "Money Like Baxter's Is There, But Is There The Will?" A not too subtle dig at Governor Angus King, it coupled this piece about the famous Maine philanthropist's gift with both a listing of potential latter-day Midases and a sidebar interview with King, who essentially said one Baxter Park was enough. His meaning was that he didn't think it was necessary to have "a new park like Baxter Park where nothing goes on but recreation." He added he was "more interested in how public values can be preserved without locking up the whole thing."

But interested he was, as figures for a new Land for Maine's Future bond issue began to be tossed about: as much as $100 million was mentioned while the governor at first indicated he could go as high as $30 million. At the previous session no more than $3 million had been eked out, so these were giddy numbers. The environmentalists in the legislature settled on a $75 million proposal, sponsored by the senate majority leader, Chellie Pingree, a coastal Democrat from the island of North Haven. Polling supposedly showed that 70 percent of Maine people supported a bond issue that large, which would have made it, if passed, the largest in the state's history not devoted to transportation. Complicating deliberations in the capital was the fact the governor's own proposed package of bond issues violated the unwritten 90 percent rule of not issuing new bonds in excess of 90 percent of those being retired. When the Appropriations Committee finished its annual wrestling with such conundrums, there was a bond issue for land acquisition of $50 million.

Conservatives in Augusta, led by a Republican named Henry Joy from the minuscule southern Aroostook County town of Crystal, voiced their loud opposition to the price tag and to the very idea of buying more private land and making it public. Another articulate opponent was Jon Reisman, a professor at the University of Maine at Machias, who had been the GOP's unsuccessful Second Congressional District candidate in the previous election. He was identified in an op-ed piece he wrote for the Portland papers as a "spokesman for Keep Maine Free, a coalition that supports the private ownership and stewardship of land." Ordinarily, Reisman is a firebrand on the land issue: "I'll be forced to remind you that Adolf Hitler and the National Socialists were truly committed Greens," he stated in one column; or "What economic system is it when the government owns the land? It ain't capitalism." But as the referendum went out to the people and seemed to gather momentum, he was somewhat muted, noting ruefully that the top Republican leaders in Augusta had caused hard feelings in the party by actually cosponsoring the governor's $50 million bond issue request.

The polls were close to accurate. On November 2, 1999, the Maine voters passed all five bond issues on their ballot and the land bond received a 70 percent approval vote. It carried every Maine county and over 80 percent of Maine towns. No new Percival Baxter had stepped up to the plate but the political climate that had made him dig into his own pockets to save key land had clearly shifted. At least for the time being.

THREE

The Property Rightists and Other Populists

To UNDERSTAND FULLY the role of Mary Adams in Maine's anti-clear-cutting referenda, it is necessary to go back to 1973, the year the legislature passed a new education funding law and financed it with what has been described as a *statewide property tax.* Emerging from obscurity à la Joan of Arc to lead a crusade against the imposition was the "little housewife from Garland," a hamlet-like town in central Penobscot County. Her referendum efforts were successful in repealing the "tax" (to the great surprise of most political pundits), although the law and its formula for distributing school subsidies remained on the books. Governor James Longley, a fellow grassroots fiscal conservative, then placed Mary on the Maine Board of Education, where her ideas and trenchant wit drove the educational establishment wild. Longley's successor, Joseph Brennan, a fairly liberal Democrat, declined to reappoint her for a second term.

Her reentry into public life in the 1996 referendum was based on her previous experience, not on any expertise in forestry (or so she told me in an interview we had in Bangor). She was recruited in a meeting in that same city when a group gathered who were opposed to both Jonathan Carter's ban on clear-cutting and Governor Angus King's *middle-way* Compact. In Mary's words, these were "just people who lived in the woods" and who saw these proposed laws as having an adverse impact on rural Maine. Mary had been sought out because she knew about referendum electioneering.

This is not to say that her heart wasn't with them. She spoke with genuine anger about the Compact. The role played by the large paper companies and landowners not only in endorsing it but in promoting it was a particular sore point. In her eyes, they "split the family" of people who operate in the woods. They also played hardball. "People lost their jobs," Mary said, citing the case of an electrician at a paper plant who was fired for having a VOTE 2C sticker on his truck. "Paper company employees lost their First Amendment rights," she indignantly insisted.

Worse, the fissure caused by the Compact could be felt even within the core of her own support. According to Mary, the Maine Forest Products Council, made up mostly of small- to medium-sized landowners and lumbermen, was polled on the issue and opposed the Compact. Yet because its president, Jim Robbins of the Robbins Lumber Company, was for it, the organization was officially recorded as endorsing Governor King's pet plan. "Why did he [Robbins] do this?" Mary asked rhetorically. Hints of muckraking Populism appeared as she mentioned property Robbins was trying to sell to the state around Nicatous Lake.

A sense of class or social division also appeared in her characterization of the Compact's supporters who could be represented as both big-business executives and wealthy environmentalists. Mary suggested they were analogous to the Brahmins of Boston who don't say they bought their (Beacon Hill) homes but that they "have" them. "These people don't buy their lands. They *have* them," she said, alluding to the Compact promoters. "There is a big difference between them and the people who have to pay for their land and," she added tartly, "satisfy the bank."

It was in this context that she made her widely circulated commentary about the Nature Conservancy's purchase of International Paper Company's 125,000 acres on the upper St. John River, which they intended to continue logging. "Yes," Mary said scornfully. "They'll be practicing wine and cheese logging."

The "enviros," as she called them, received more than scorn. To her, they were a danger. An example of how they affected "her people" was given of a piece of property in Somerset County, owned by Central Maine Power Company, that was cruised for timber and a bid to cut it accepted. However, before the contract was let,

CMP sold the acreage to a land trust and the woods operator was out of a job.

That the opposite of "wine and cheese logging" might be the stripping of an entire acreage posed no problem for Mary Adams. She made a positive virtue out of the enviros' worst nightmare. "Cutover land allows young people to buy land," she argued. "How else are young people going to get a stake? Cutover land is cheap land. Having it available is the only way young people can come in and build a land base."

What was happening now was "not true to the reality of people earning a living in the woods," she went on. The referenda are "not about forestry, but about politics. The neighborhood is changing. More pretty people are owning land."

Trying to put in perspective the sentiments of property rights proponents, Mary began with the phenomenon of globalization. "Everything is being standardized worldwide," she declared in something of a standardized statement, itself. However, her use of "Latvian mittens" to illustrate what might be lost showed a piquant originality. Except that Latvia is full of birch forests, the simile seemed to this interviewer about as far from Maine as one could get. But my incomprehension diminished when she explained that in old Latvia, every village had its own pattern of knitted mittens; no two communal designs were ever the same. It is that individuality, woven into a sense of parochial togetherness, that the local folks in northern Maine felt slipping away, afraid that forces greater than themselves, statewide and planetwide, were conspiring to obliterate their comfy, if tough, insular world. They saw no understanding nor sympathy for their way of life. At the extreme, such worries turned into "black helicopter" types of fears. The fact that GIS satellites observe every inch of the earth bothered them. They wanted to work their land and they were worried that they wouldn't be able to do anything with it. When the Nature Conservancy bought 125,000 acres of northern Maine, that troubled them because they knew that often the Nature Conservancy re-sold its land to the government. In their eyes, Augusta was a place where policies could be passed that would affect them drastically. Thus, some felt they would like to be separated from the state of Maine and run their own show, without having to fret over salmon being listed as an endangered species or about the lynx and wolves being reintroduced or having others' ecosystem ideas foisted upon them.

It is a scary universe in which today's loggers must operate. Working for the big paper companies on contract has never been easy for them. Mary spoke of a "nobleman-serf" relationship and of company vice-presidents with southern accents. Referring to the J. D. Irving Company, the New Brunswick, Canada, giant conglomerate with huge landholdings in Maine, she said, "They either can't or won't pay our loggers enough," and the result is "they can't meet payroll."

"Loggers do the same thing over and over again. They have no niche. They have nothing that anybody needs...and they don't have the luxury to re-create themselves." Mary's plaintive voice drew a truly pathetic picture, to which she added the vignette of a recent gathering of woods workers where grown men cried at the hopelessness of their prospects. "Like fishermen and farmers," Mary said, adding the image of the latter-day lumberman the gallery of industries that once symbolized a flourishing Maine economy, all were but gone now, like the Latvian mittens of yesteryear.

Conspiracy isn't a word that Mary used openly in bemoaning this state of affairs, but the implication always appeared there. She cited a recent book titled *Undue Influence* by Ron Arnold of the Center for Defense of Free Enterprise, who is described as a leader of the "wise use" movement on the West Coast. His book revealed the alleged role of tax-free foundations in promoting a plan to "dry up rural areas"—that is, to put 50 percent of their land into wilderness areas. "That road thing of Clinton's," Mary claimed—meaning the President's attempt to stop building roads in National Forests to facilitate logging—was an inspiration of the Sierra Club, which wrote the executive order. On the Adams Report home page she has titles like: "Batscam, the Latest Enviro Attack on Vermont's Economy: EXCLUSIVE INSIDE REPORT. Green Scheme of Massive Land Control Revealed at Recent Maine River Summit." She is also quoted as stating that the term *Northern Forest* is "a weapon in a subtle war to help people envision the region as one big park."

Yet if Mary was somewhat muted in what opponents would no

doubt leap upon as evidence of paranoia, the tabloid *All Maine Matters* published out of Sullivan, Maine, contained more explicit references, specifically that the problem was the United Nations and its plans to rule the world. Excerpts from the Tom DeWeese report, volume 4, issue 8, of March 1998, later reprinted, spelled out the plan:

> International treaties that ignore American property rights and commerce are the real threat. UN plans for global governance, UN taxation, and a UN standing army threaten America's sovereignty.
>
> These are not pipe dreams or "right-winged conspiracy" theories. The information comes from the UN's own documents.

One particular document cited is the report of the UN Commission on Global Governance, a 400-page "blueprint to achieve global governance by the year 2000." In addition to the UN standing army, UN taxation, and International Court of Justice proposals, there would be a parliamentary body of nonelected private organizations (which brings the matter closer to home) "like the Sierra Club and the Nature Conservancy, called NGOs."

The activities of the nongovernmental organizations are then underscored and include the Biodiversity Treaty, the Convention on Climate Change, the UN Rights of the Child, the Rio Declaration, etc. In another section of the same issue of *All Maine Matters*, the columnist R. O. Voight, who has titled his topic "The Amazing Forests of Maine," relates the UN theme to our North Woods. The goal of the "radical enviros," he says, has been a relentless, unceasing effort "to shut down all wood industry and return the forest to primeval wilderness. It is all covered in the four-inch-thick United Nations protocol to the Biodiversity Treaty."

The sixteen-page newspaper in which these and other property rights sentiments are expressed lists its editor as Robbie McKay of Kingman Plantation and its publisher as Helen D. Gordon of Sullivan. Fishing, as well as forestry, is covered, some farming, too, and a great deal of politics. Just before the November 1998 elections, a full-page ad urged votes for "Maine's Bravehearts"—essentially the Republican slate for Congress and governor and various GOP candidates for the state senate and house in the rural districts—plus pleaded for the defeat of "The Dirty Dozen who attacked rural Maine," i.e., Democratic incumbents in some of those seats. A half-page ad likewise promoted Jon Reisman, challenger to the Second Congressional District Democrat, John Baldacci. Reisman's slogan had a rustic tone: "Join the LEAVE US ALONE COALITION." Letters to the editor, including one by Mary Adams as "Co-chair Common Sense for Maine Forests. Former Chairman of Stop the Backroom Deal, Vote 2C," also supported individual candidates.

In addition, *All Maine Matters* carried numerous commercial advertisements, many predictable, like realty companies, timberland owners, guide services, seafood companies, lobster industry suppliers, etc., and at least one surprise amid so much republicanism, the United Paperworkers International, AFL-CIO, Local No. 396, out of Lincoln. Some 20,000 copies of the paper were distributed from "Eastport to Kittery, North to Lincoln, Millinocket, Island Falls, Crystal, and Houlton, West to Greenville, Dover-Foxcroft, Dexter, and points in between and beyond." A nice homey touch amid the often strident tones of the articles is Robbie McKay's column, "Of Biscuits, Breads, and Berries," offering recipes for such mouthwatering items as Molasses Whoopie Pie, Hawaiian Hamburger, and Squash Gourmet. The name on the masthead may well be a deliberate in-your-face rebuke to a similar tabloid put out by the Maine Chapter of the Appalachian Mountain Club, which the enviros have dubbed "Wilderness Matters." After the election of 1998, in which all three of the major Braveheart candidates and a number of their state-level candidates lost and a majority of the Dirty Dozen were returned to office, a special conclave was held in Lincoln. *All Maine Matters* reported it as "a meeting of historic proportions." More than fifty delegates from Hancock, Penobscot, Aroostook, Piscataquis, Somerset, Franklin, and Washington Counties gathered "to discuss secession from a bloated, socialistic entity known as the State of Maine." They drafted a Declaration of Independence for New Maine and—a special feature—"joined in common cause with a group of loggers who have sparked renewed interest in protecting sovereignty in the north woods with their recent blockade of Canadian labor at the Quebec crossings."

Robbie McKay introduced the loggers' leaders, Hilton Hafford and Stacey King of Allagash, and a spirited exchange followed on the "lack of progress and lip service" those woods workers had received from state and federal bureaucrats, which had caused them to do what they did to gain attention to their low pay and the jobs they were losing to foreigners. Several delegates told the men the bureaucratic inability to act was due to treasonous international trade treaties like GATT and NAFTA, although it was recognized the loggers were not yet ready to join the secession movement.

The relationship of "New Maine," as the breakaway entity would be named, to Canada was a subject of considerable discussion. To quote the report: "The option of forming a separate sovereign nation in conjunction with one or more secessionist elements from Atlantic Canada was discarded as treasonous and likely to result in the absorption of the counties into the Queen's domain." Then one of the Bravehearts who was reelected, Representative Henry Joy of Crystal, declared to them that a secession attempt "to create State 51 was reasonable, feasible, and desirable."

Earlier, in June, during that same election cycle, Joy had been a candidate for the Republican gubernatorial nomination. Although he came in second, his total among GOP voters was a mere 22 percent, nearly 40 points below the candidate chosen to lead his party, former Congressman James Longley, Jr. In the general election, Longley, himself, was similarly trounced by Independent Governor Angus King (the Democratic standard bearer did even worse). Through a legal maneuver, Henry Joy was still able to put himself on the ballot for his old seat during the November 1998 contest. Popular with his conservative rural constituency, he was sent to Augusta for a third term, and two years later for a fourth.

A man now in his mid-sixties, Joy is a former teacher and school administrator with a master's degree in Education from the University of Maine at Orono. A lifelong resident of southern Aroostook County and an Air Force veteran, he shares that jack-of-all-trades syndrome common to many rural Mainers who have to grab whatever opportunities they can in order to make a living. So Henry has added to his CV that he has been a hospital administrator, a logger, a house builder, and the manager of Joy's Texaco Station in the town of Sherman. His organizational memberships are those one might expect: Masons, Lions, Big Valley Sno-Club, Island Falls Fish and Game Club, NRA, American Legion. Politically, he says he is a former "Truman Democrat" and now a "Jefferson Republican."

To Democrats, who claim Thomas Jefferson as the founder of their party, this latter coupling might seem an anomaly and an outrage. But many of the "natives" in rural Maine, knowingly or not, retain the political instincts of their ancestors, who were clearly Jeffersonians, so much so that they separated from Federalist Massachusetts.

Henry Joy touches deep roots Down East.

Nor is he afraid to wear his heart on his sleeve. He is not a cautious legislator.

A steady stream of bills bearing his sponsorship should serve as an unexpressed platform for Joy and his supporters. That some might be patently unconstitutional and that none passed does not seem to stem the flow. For example, seeking to correct the imbalance of population in Maine, he sought to fly in the face of the *one person, one vote* principle and amend Maine's constitution to give each county in Maine, no matter what their population, *two* state senators. Quixotic, yes, but not entirely unfounded, given the makeup of the U.S. Senate. Nevertheless, both bodies in the Maine legislature killed the measure. The same was true for a more constitutionally acceptable but equally bumptious proposal incorporated by Joy in his "Act To Limit Publicly Owned Land." If passed as written, this law would have allowed no more than 7 percent of the land area of Maine to be in public ownership, and in any single county that restriction would be 10 percent. Coming out of committee was a split report with the minority in favor of adopting an amendment — to wit, the 10 percent rule would be waived in Piscataquis County, which already had more than 10 percent of its acreage in public lands. Notwithstanding which, both the house and senate accepted the majority report of Ought-Not-to-Pass and another Henry Joy bill bit the dust.

Sometimes his proposals did not even get this much of a chance. Under Joint Rule 310, the Maine legislature has decreed that any bill coming from committee with a *unanimous* Ought-Not-to-Pass report is automatically dead and cannot be debated. Thus bills of Henry Joy's like "An Act To Require Economic And Taking Impact Analyses To Protect Individual Rights," "An Act To Require That Local Officials Take On-The- Record Stands When They Are Responsible For Laws That Decrease Property Taxes," and "An Act To License Hikers, Canoeists, Kayakers And Off-Road Bicyclists" were dead-on-arrival when they hit the house and senate floors.

The bill to license hikers, etc., was what we would have called a "fun bill" when I was in the legislature; i.e., a bill you could have *fun with* in annoying some group, but weren't serious about getting passed. Henry Joy's intent may simply have been a slap at those who were alien to his way of life and thinking who are now invading his territory in increasing numbers, and also to ask the question: "If fishermen and hunters and snowmobilers have to buy licenses, why not these other consumers of wilderness values?" The bill, as written, actually would have exempted any hiker, etc., who had already purchased a hunting, fishing, or snowmobile license.

This sense of *them and us*, two Maines that will never quite understand each other, emerges in even more subtle ways than an attempt to license nature lovers. The Associated Press news story covering Henry Joy's announcement of his run for governor is a case in point. It starts: "Inveighing against incursions on property rights, Joy declared his intentions at a news conference at De Laite's General Store in Macwahoc," setting a scene in a humorous-sounding deep rural crossroads, actually Joy's birthplace, and then adding gratuitously, "which is closer to Molunkus on the west than it is to Wytopitlock on the east." These are all Maine hamlets whose names are used like Podunk or East Podunk to symbolize hickdom in the state, and no one could blame Henry Joy if he felt resentful that he was being patronized by some "flatlander" writer.

Then, again, Henry's continuous assault sometimes comes close to success. Witness a bill in the second regular session of the 119th Legislature entitled "An Act to Create a Governance System for Unorganized Towns."

This measure, as amended, actually first passed in both bodies. The inspiration behind it had a seemingly irresistible logic. *Let the*

people decide, or *home rule*, for the Unorganized Territories, a sprawling land area close to half of Maine, whose small number of inhabitants (maybe 10,000) have no local government but rely on Augusta
for schooling and, most contentious, their zoning. Since the 1970s,
the latter function has been the responsibility of the Land Use Regulation Commission, LURC, whose rules often have not been
received kindly by those in the region.

Joy's original bill was put in as a "concept draft," a device by
which legislators can present elements of a broad idea without having to detail the specific legal language. Under his plan, a single
"council-type government" would be created for all unorganized
townships. Each populated unorganized community would have a
representative to this council, elected on a one person, one vote
basis. In addition nonresident property owners could select representatives to an advisory board to the council. The unorganized
townships would establish their own school system. After three
years, LURC would be phased out and replaced by a locally constituted "body to oversee land and economic development." No land in
the Unorganized Territories could be removed from the tax rolls; in
other words, there could be no further public ownership of land,
whether by government or land trust or nonprofit organization
unless taxes were paid. It would require Native Americans—
Maine's landowning tribes such as the Penobscots and Passamaquoddies—to establish zoning and land plans for their
properties in the area, but would not affect their sovereignty there.
Finally, it would allow present municipalities to *deorganize* and join
this new government, with the permission of the legislature, a practice available to towns currently and occasionally sought because it
can be cheaper for some existing very small towns to come under the
state rather than continue struggling to support themselves.

Legislative Document 299 was, in time-honored legislative
tradition, eventually turned into a study. Created was "the Committee to Study the Governance of the Unorganized Territories," with
seventeen members, including five legislators, four residents, several
county commissioners, two nonresident public members, and four
landowners. They were to report back on questions concerning: the
effectiveness of the present governance structure; the need for

mechanisms to promote greater citizen participation, particularly on matters of real estate, taxation, education, etc.; and the financial impact of any governance changes. This watered-down, seemingly more reasonable approach did not encounter serious resistance and in early April 2000, sailed through both bodies. But then a funny thing happened. On April 27, without any discussion, the amended bill was indefinitely postponed (killed) in the house and senate.

These were the waning moments of the session when, as all legislators know, any bills with a price tag on them are either accepted or rejected by the Appropriations Committee. Joy's governance bill had a paltry $7,250 as its fiscal note, primarily to pay per diem and travel for the members of the study committee and to print its report.

Sometimes legislators will vote for a measure they don't like, knowing it will die on the Appropriations table. This may account in part for the amended version's easy passage. But not funding a mere $7,250 also shows a decided albeit disguised hostility to the whole notion. Henry Joy, himself, might have been angry his original proposal was so effectively gutted, but amenable to a study—often a foot in the door to further action.

Or perhaps Joy found he had bigger fish to fry. After the deadline for submitting bills, he arrived with one to promote the secession of northern Maine from Maine. In these cases of late bills, the Legislative Council, made up of the ten leaders of the House and Senate, can allow bills in if six of its members consent. Henry Joy did not receive that permission for his secession bill.

No doubt it could be said the main thrust of the property rights movement is to keep land in private hands. The argument is often raised that the only reason the Maine North Woods is as it is — is because it has been in private hands all these years. The owners have been good shepherds, it is claimed. What is certainly true is that, for the most part, the owners have left their land open for the local folks to use as if it were their own.

A corollary to that innate sense of possession arises, too, in the thorny issue of camp leases. These are, in essence, grants of lots to favored individuals, frequently on lake shores, where the recipients are allowed to build vacation dwellings, known universally in Maine

as *camps*. That these are temporary land grants and revocable sometimes on a yearly basis is a potential peril traditionally ignored by
lease holders. As a legislator, I became aware of the problem
through a constituent who had a camp lease from the state of Maine.
After decades at the same place, plus an investment of many thousands of dollars (these "camps" are not "shacks"), he was suddenly
told his lease would not be renewed. The past was catching up with
a small number of people who'd had friends high in state government in the old days, encountering a new administration with different ideas. Without warning, these folks faced having to abandon
personal property of significant dollar and emotional value.

Unconsciously borrowing a page from the book of Maine's
first governor, William King, who tried to help "squatters" in pre-
Maine Massachusetts, I thought a reasonable response would be to
allow these camp owners to buy their leaseholds and have the state
use the money to purchase comparable land for all of the public. I
devised a bill to this effect and teamed up with the late Representative Eddie Dexter of Kingfield, one of those Braveheart Republicans
the property rightists backed, a wily codger who referred to himself
as "just an old ignorant woodsman." Despite the protests of the
bureaucrats that we were rewarding favoritism, our bipartisan effort
got the bill passed and *that* particular hornet's nest eliminated.

However, the issue has since risen to the fore on the *private*
level, now that so much land in northern Maine is being bought and
sold. The good ol' relationships are becoming tenuous and a lot of
leaseholders are worried sick. In an article published on July 25,
1999, the *Maine Sunday Telegram* aired their insecurities.

When Bowater, Great Northern's parent company, sold a
656,000-acre parcel of its land to McDonald Investment Co. of
Birmingham, Alabama, McDonald acquired some 300 leaseholders
who owned camps or businesses on this property. Management was
then subcontracted by McDonald to Wagner Forest Management of
New Hampshire. Changes were immediately effected, most notably,
as reporter Roberta Scruggs wrote, in "new gates, new fees, new
leases, new fears."

Camp leases on private land apparently began in the 1930s. It
was a paper and lumber company policy aimed at attracting new

workers and rewarding old employees; a key stipulation was that leaseholders had to build nice places—no trailers, no tar-paper shacks. As expressed by a present-day leaseholder, an ex-majority leader in the Maine house, Paul Jacques of Waterville: "They said: 'Go ahead. Build a nice place. Enjoy it. Don't worry about it. You'll always have your lease.'" The camp Jacques has had with two friends for eighteen years is now worth over $100,000, but he argues that more than money is at stake. Leaseholders, he says, "have invested their hearts and souls in this property based on an agreement they had with the former owners of this land."

Originally, leaseholders paid nothing to go through company gates to reach their camps. Now, under new rules, they must buy a season pass for $25—no, actually *two* season passes, one for summer and one for the fall—and stop every time at a gate to fill out a "land use and camping permit."

Al Cowperthwaite, representing the landowners' consortium, maintains that the gate check-in deters vandalism, litter, and unsupervised fires, and that leaseholders and visitors, who have to pay $4 a day (Mainers) and $7 a day (nonresidents), will get used to the system. Great Northern, he argues, could afford to provide free services like hauling garbage, grading roads, giving out firewood-cutting permits, etc., because of the profits from their mills, something his group can't do. But if Cowperthwaite believes those affected will be swayed, listen to Paul Jacques, a self-described "fiery Frenchman," regarding the new arrangement. "It was...an insulting lease...it set people off when they read it."

The Maine Leaseholders Association was exercised enough to hire the Portland-Augusta law and lobbying firm of Preti, Flaherty, Beliveau, and Pachios to fight for leaseholder access. The organization has 600 members and estimates there are 6,000 such leases in the Maine Woods. Even more apoplectic were the members of Millinocket's Fin and Feather Club, well known for their feisty efforts to maintain and increase access to both public and private land. In 1996 the club made a deal with Great Northern: in return for Fin and Feather support for federal relicensing of the company's dams, Great Northern would give Maine residents free access to its 1.2 million acres on the Penobscot's West Branch. McDonald has disavowed that agreement. One Fin and Feather member precipitously took action: sixty-seven-year-old Vern Haines got himself arrested by walking through a checkpoint without paying, setting the stage for what the Club maintains will be "the biggest class action lawsuit this state has ever seen." A statewide petition drive has been mentioned. Another jolt came in the winter of 1999 when the Penobscot Nation, owner of 20,000 wildland acres in the western Maine town of Carrabassett Valley, posted its land. Said one local partridge hunter denied access to his quarry: "I feel like I'm under house arrest." The town declared its economic future was imperiled unless it could use this private property.

Thus, the beat goes on in the Maine North Woods, issue after issue, with some spilling out into areas other than strictly land use. A jet-ski ban on many of northern Maine's lakes and ponds was fought by state representative Joe Clark of Millinocket, a Democrat who teamed with Henry Joy to try to repeal legislation to keep the noisy craft off of 245 bodies of water, mostly in the Unorganized Territories—another North-South, Two Maines issue those lawmakers argued, but to no avail. Henry Joy then teamed up with three fellow Republicans to attack the Natural Resources Council, demanding it be investigated for testifying in favor of a bill to withhold state subsidies from polluters. Cries of "intimidation" and "suppression of free speech" followed the GOP effort, which Henry Joy said was "particularly necessary given the NRCM's call before the legislature to treat the business sector with such a heavy hand regarding environmental laws."

Yet subsequently there was the spectacle of Henry Joy on another bill that took a position similar to the NRCM's, this time toward large landowners, corporate and otherwise. At stake in Legislative Document 2486 was the access question raised by the Leaseholders Association and the Fin and Feather Club. Sponsored by a first-term Democrat, Representative Monica McGlocklin of rural Embden, and including as cosponsor Henry Joy, the measure would have removed a state subsidy, the Tree Growth Tax, from owners of 1,000 acres and up in the Unorganized Territories who charged fees or restricted access. This mixture of property rightist and anticorporate welfare sentiment, however, failed to gather enough support.

Lines *can* become fuzzy here. The plight of Maine loggers and their efforts to gain attention have already been mentioned. The property rights people have tried to woo them, yet Mary Adams's eyes narrow and she bridles when she hears the name of one of their number, Jimmy Freeman of Verona Island. To her, he is a dangerous radical, an Earth First! member and rabble-rouser who publicly said the Lincoln Pulp and Paper Company should be shut down.

Hilton Hafford of Allagash, that leader of the loggers who recently blockaded three Canadian border crossings and who attended the secession meeting in Lincoln, was interviewed for the *Northern Forest Forum* in July 1999 and his views were distinctly at odds with those whose frustrations make them seek separation from Maine. Everything they were against, Hafford said, he and his fellow protesters—as authentic a group of woodsmen as one could find—were for:

> We were all in favor of banning clear-cutting. Every logger I ever talked to around this area was in favor of banning clear-cutting. Everyone I talk to now is in favor of turning it into a Park and stopping the cut. Talk to the loggers in our group. They'd support a National Park. If they turned it into a National Park, there would be something left here.

Then, there is Bill Butler of the tiny Washington County town of Aurora, one of the leaders of the first woodsmen's strike in 1975 and co-founder of the now-defunct Maine Woodsmen's Association. The organization, which existed for eight years, had followed on the heels of a woodsmen's boycott in 1970, when wood was withheld from major paper companies, but which ended when a judge declared them in violation of a state price-fixing law. It is Butler's determined opinion that the reason for the Two Maines issue has nothing to do with environmentalists or government regulation. "The diversion of the forest resource and the associated logging jobs to Canada is at the root of why northern Maine is poor."

Bill Butler, who has spent half a century in Maine's woods, has an attitude toward Mary Adams comparable to her attitude toward Jimmy Freeman. In an account Butler wrote for the *Northern Forest Forum*, Butler witheringly stated: "Now comes Mary Adams, a Betty

Boop voice of the property-rights absolutists" (Mary *is* short and wide-eyed and *does* have a high-pitched voice), but adds with some respect, "who can claim sizable credit for defeating the industry Compact." Indeed, he ends a rather satiric description by reminding his readers of Mary's upset of the uniform property tax, "one of the more equitable revenue structures we have seen" and concludes: "If Mary is crazy, it's like a fox—a rabid fox."

So Bill Butler is a Populist whose essential plea is not "leave us alone" but give us a more equitable distribution of the benefits to be derived from the forest resource, good employment, good returns to small growers, maintenance of clean air, water, wildlife, and recreation not in an artificial setting. He quotes an executive of the Canadian-owned Fraser Paper Company as saying Canada views Maine as a third world country. "That we are," Bill Butler agrees sadly. Another of Butler's co-strike leaders in 1975 was Mel Ames of Dover-Foxcroft and this veteran of woodsmen agitation puts a different spin on the future of our great forest area. "The real solution," he says, most likely in jest, is to "cut the state in half at Calais and let northern Maine go with the Canadians."

A Janus-faced throwing up of hands over what to do in the Maine North Woods will undoubtedly not be the final answer. While staying tuned, let us now go back, back in time and see how this astonishing region, unique in our country and the world in its particular political and economic configuration, took shape and came to be as it is today.

FOUR

Geology and Prehistory

O LD BERT, LOUNGING AROUND the dock down at the *hahbah*, knows as much about the Maine coast as any man. But just try asking him if he'd ever heard tell of the "Iapetus Ocean" in these parts and you'll get an wicked cross-looking stare because Old Bert doesn't like to be stumped. For that matter, ask any Mainer, male or female, and except for a few *smaht* geologists, you'll have stumped them, too. What the heck is *Ira Peters'* Ocean, anyway?

Throw in the "continent of Avalonia" and folks Down East will think you are awful peculiar.

But if the geologists are right, these totally unfamiliar geologic features, now no longer in existence, had a good deal to do with the eventual formation of the land mass we now call Maine.

The story goes back a long, long time. The oldest rocks ever found in Maine, the Chain Lakes Massif, are a type of gneiss, 1.6 billion years old, surviving from the core foundation of the North American plate. They're located in the Unorganized Territories, in Chain of Ponds Township northwest of Eustis, close to the Quebec border. These are stony remnants from an era when only the most primitive form of protozoan life (simple algae) occurred on our planet and underscore the volatility of the seemingly stable world we currently inhabit. Great chunks of time allowed huge land masses to move about in ways unimaginable until the "Plate Tectonics" theory of geology was introduced in the 1960s.

It's no wonder Old Bert would have a puzzled look. The *tectonic* story concerning Maine goes like this: About 500 million years ago, coastal Maine wasn't part of North America at all. It was lodged on the western edge of a continent, which scientists have named Avalonia. Modern Europe was included in Avalonia, as well, and between it and North America, which contained the Chain of Ponds rocks, lay the ocean these same scientists call Iapetus, after the mythic father of the mythic Atlas. The Iapetus Ocean was the precursor of the Atlantic.

For more than a billion years, those Chain Lakes Massif rocks had been undisturbed, when Avalonia began to travel west. Within 100 million years, it slammed (in a manner of speaking) right into North America and fused with the latter, displacing the Iapetus Ocean, which disappeared. From all over the globe at this time, continents were converging until they blended into a single super-super continent. *Pangea* is how scientists refer to this configuration.

Local geologist David L. Kendall wasn't kidding when he wrote in his book *Glaciers and Granite*: "It turns out that Maine has been anything but fixed in its present place on the globe...."[1] According to Kendall, 250 million years ago the Pine Tree State was at a latitude of 5 degrees north and longitude of 0 degrees. If you went to that intersection today, you'd be in Africa, in Ghana.

Allegedly, then, Maine was at the equator, in a hot but dry place many thousands of miles from any seawater. How did it get to its current position?

Another 70 million years passed. Pangea commenced to split apart. The northern and southern hemispheres broke from each other and moved away, heading, naturally, north and south. Maine was in the northern portion called Laurasia, which, itself, developed rifts that separated along east and west lines. Into one of these humongous cracks, a new ocean slowly poured, the Atlantic. When the right side of Laurasia, containing most of Europe, went east, a section on its left sheered off and stayed stuck to North America.

As the two opposing pieces of north Pangea drifted away at a steady snail's pace of 2–5 centimeters a year (about as fast as your fingernails grow), the entire New England coast was in the section that formed its Atlantic edge. Yet Maine was still on the move. All of North America rotated—counterclockwise—until Maine reached

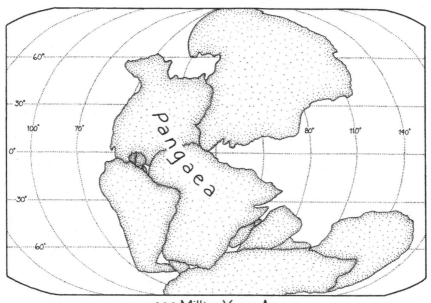

200 Million Years Ago

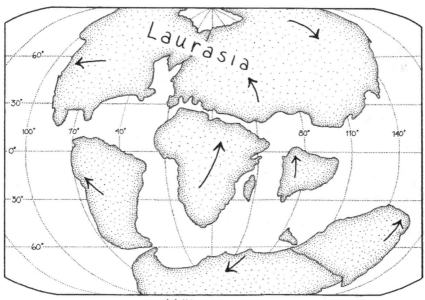

65 Million Years Ago

Maine's Geologic Evolution

its contemporary location, latitude 45 degrees north, longitude 69 degrees west. We're still moving even now, Kendall tells us, and in 50 million years, we'll be where Minneapolis is but presumably still on the shore of the ocean that a vastly expanded Atlantic has filled. Old Bert's umpty-ump descendant may likewise be lolling among the drying lobster pots at the *hahbah* when that day comes and most likely with no more sense of having been shoved around than his distant sire.

About 25 million years ago, Maine finally became rooted and has essentially stayed put down to the present. The biggest events affecting it physically have been the glaciers, somewhere between four and ten of them during the last million years, the Pleistocene Epoch. Their ice covered the land (and out to sea), melted, returned, and this fairly brief geologic bit of time, which we are still in, has earned the title of the "Ice Age." The most recent of these glaciers, the one that has left the most lasting imprint on Maine, reached its maximum extent about 40,000 years ago. Not only did it blanket all of Maine with its mile- or two-thick ice, but also had oozed its great bulk into the Gulf of Maine and beyond to approximately Georges Bank, 180 miles east of Cape Cod.

Anyone who has seen the edge of a glacier where it reaches the sea will never forget the sight. Towering above your puny boat is a wall of blue ice, stained with dirt, craggy and jagged in the parts where pieces, some weighing hundreds of tons, have sheered off. "Calving" is the nickname for these dramatic, fast, sudden quasi-avalanches that occur more and more frequently as the ice sheet "retreats." There is often a roar as the mass of frozen, compacted snow cracks loose and hits the water below with a force that can send out serious waves.

When Maine's last glacier started the process of shrinking 20,000 years ago, no one was yet around to witness these spectacular ice drops. Within 6,000 years, the glacier had come in from its long stretch into the Atlantic to about the position of Maine's present-day rocky seacoast. After 1,000 more years, that shoreline was much farther inland, all the way to Livermore Falls (on the Androscoggin), Medway (on the Penobscot), and Bingham (on the Kennebec). The reason for such flooding: the tremendous weight of the glacier had depressed the land, the melting ice had filled the sea, and not for another 1,000 years did the land rebound.

We are now down to 12,000 years ago and still another millennium was needed before the final icecaps disappeared in northern Maine and from atop mountains like Katahdin where they had existed in alpine cirques.

Since human habitation in Maine is generally dated between 11,000 and 10,000 years ago, there may have been eyewitnesses to these ultimate glacial spasms. However, we have no testimony left to us by those most ancient *Paleo Indians* (*paleo* is the Greek word for *old*). The signs are exclusively physical. They can be read in any roadside cut and from any plane flight over our lake-scarred topography and fringed, island-studded coastal zone. Experts can tell "glacier" everywhere, although since that last one has gone, the pebbly deposits and scraped surface bequeathed as its legacy have been altered beyond recognition by natural regeneration.

At first, what grew in Maine was tundra. Vegetation of the same sort, seen today in places like northern Canada and Alaska, is treeless and bleak, yet not destitute of nutrients. Animals can live off it and humans off the animals.

Maine, bared by the final glacier melt, was still a cold land. Its size was somewhat smaller than now, since even 12,000 years ago ocean waters still flooded some coastal sections. Needless to say, as a vast acreage prepared to receive its first inhabitants, it was not recognizable as either Maine or even New England. South of our state's modern configuration, where Massachusetts is now, dry land currently underwater stretched well out beyond Cape Cod almost to George's Bank. The lonely haunt of wandering herds of caribou, reindeer, musk oxen, and tusked, woolly progenitors of elephants, those barren carpets of Arctic grasses awaited prehistory, nameless, as yet unpeopled, for maybe another 1,000 years.

Certain scientists who call themselves palynologists study pollen, reading it like tea leaves for clues, not to the future, but to the plants of yesteryear, including those of millennia ago. They can tell when trees and shrubs supplemented the tundra. They can tell when there was, as Maine archaeologist David Sanger writes, a "dramatic demise of the tundra."[2] That momentous happening is

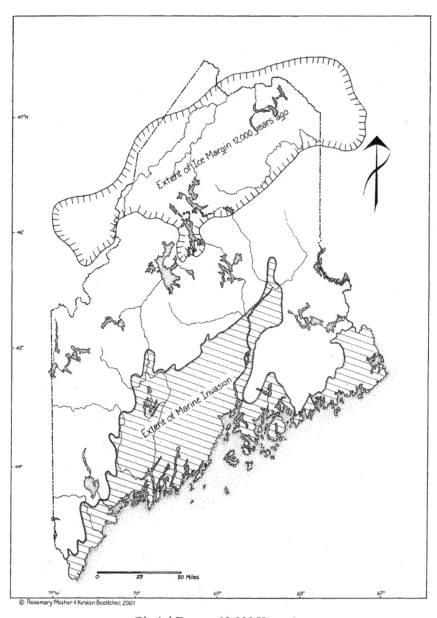

Extent of Ice Margin 12,000 Years ago

Extent of Marine Invasion

47°N

46°

45°

44°

71°W   70°   69°   68°   67°

0   25   50 Miles

© Rosemary Mosher & Kirsten Boettcher, 2001

Glacial Extent, 12,000 Years Ago

pinpointed to have occurred 10,000 years ago. What is less clear is when the first humans arrived in today's Maine; some claim more than 11,000 years ago; others that it was *between* 11,000 and 10,000 years ago. What does seem evident is that the arrival of these earliest occupants of our territory, the Paleo Indians, coincided with the tundra era and its prolific animal life.

How the Paleo Indians reached Maine is also fuzzy. Until recently, the conventional wisdom was that they had originated in Siberia. When the immense North American ice sheet covered the whole north top of our continent from east to west and out to the Aleutian Islands, so much water was sucked from the oceans that dry land existed in locations presently buried fathoms deep. Another unheard of name to bedevil poor old Bert with is *Beringia*, given to the Bering Straits and its surroundings when they formed a 1,200-mile land bridge across which tribes poured into America.

Recently, however, this classic explanation of the Native American peopling of the New World has been beset by new discoveries leading to new theories in the same manner plate tectonics upset the scientific world's geological dogma with notions initially sounding like science fiction.

The battle over who were the "First Americans," where did they originate and when, will likely go on for decades. Nor has the discussion been confined to the quiet but fiercely contentious pages of the professional journals. In its April 26, 1999, issue, *Newsweek* magazine made the subject its cover story. One shocking idea put forth was that some Native Americans, especially those on the U.S. East Coast, may not have arrived via the Siberian land bridge. They could have come to our Atlantic shores, this revolutionary theory maintains, via a northern route through Iceland, Greenland, and Canada. More shocking still, it's claimed they weren't of Asiatic origin, as all Native Americans have been purported to be. And they came to the North American continent much earlier than any scientist has hitherto dared suggest.

This brings us to the "Clovis" argument. The name is taken from Clovis, New Mexico, previously considered the oldest Paleo Indian site in the Americas. So adamant has been the archaeological profession's insistence on the Clovis date of 11,000 years ago that

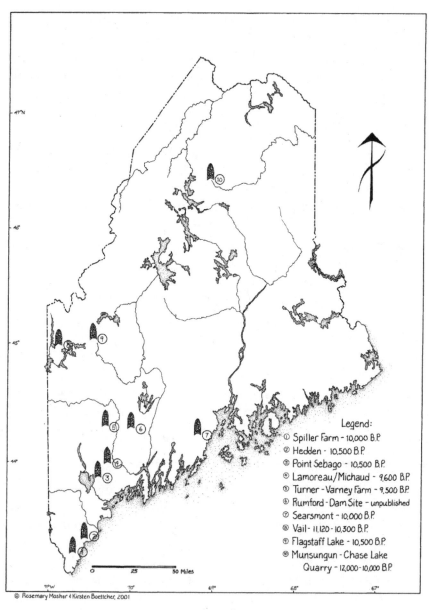

Legend:
① Spiller Farm - 10,000 B.P.
② Hedden - 10,500 B.P.
③ Point Sebago - 10,500 B.P.
④ Lamoreau/Michaud - 9,600 B.P.
⑤ Turner - Varney Farm - 9,500 B.P.
⑥ Rumford - Dam Site - unpublished
⑦ Searsmont - 10,000 B.P.
⑧ Vail - 11,120 - 10,300 B.P.
⑨ Flagstaff Lake - 10,500 B.P.
⑩ Munsungun - Chase Lake
    Quarry - 12,000 - 10,000 B.P.

© Rosemary Mosher & Kirsten Boettcher, 2001

Major Paleo Indian Sites

digging deeper below its strata has not been done. But suddenly, things have changed, starting with a find in Chile, 12,500 years old, at a place called Monte Verde. Tools found near Saltville, West Virginia, were in a layer 14,000 years old. In Virginia, a layer 15,050 years old contained worked stone.

The question thus arises: if there were tool-users in the east of the U.S. this early, could they have traveled across *Beringia* since glaciers existing then would have barred the way? Also, why is there such a striking similarity between Clovis culture and almost identical stone tools found in France? Consequently, the *Newsweek* advances the startling supposition of some paleontologists that they might "have navigated along the ice sheet and seasonal pack ice that spanned the ocean from England to Nova Scotia." Ice Age Europeans on our eastern shores!? Is this more than simply journalistic hyperbole?

As to the tribes in Maine, the Abenaki or "People of the Dawn," there has always been some confusion over their contention that they are the *oldest* of the Native Americans. Had their ancestors come across the Bering Straits and had they been the first, why would they not have stopped in Alaska or on the Pacific Coast? Couldn't they actually have been the *last* to come, traveling the thousands of miles east to their present location, and are thus the *youngest*? Yet what if their people had come via Europe? The claim of *oldest* would make more sense. Plainly, a lot more scholastic tectonic plate shifting is in the offing until a new paradigm is, if ever, accepted.

That leaves the traditional view, often in technical language, of how Maine was populated after the last glacier.

We have, to start with, the Paleo Indians. Three major sites have been found for them in Maine: at Munsungan Lake in northern Piscataquis County; on the shore of Lake Azicohos, Oxford County, a body of water dammed by the Central Maine Power Company, which revealed its secret when the level was lowered; and at the Adkins site nearby, not far from the Androscoggin River. A fourth can also be added in Debert, Nova Scotia, since these earliest "Down Easters" existed in an extended, undifferentiated neighborhood, taking in what today would be all of Maine and the

Maritimes. The "projectile points" (arrow and spear heads) found among these Paleo Indian remains are of the fluted style first unearthed at Clovis. Either the invention of fluting spread rapidly among Paleo Indians already living all over North America or Paleo Indians, themselves, spread rapidly across the continent after inventing fluting, according to Esther and David Braun in *The First Peoples of the Northeast*.[3]

Their favorite material was chert, a hard but easily flaked stone they could groove and attach to weapons needed for hunting. Despite the sparseness of the tundra and the coolness of the climate, there was more than sufficient food for the small bands, probably numbering a few hundred people each, who roamed these subarctic-like plains. Some plants of the grasslands could provide nourishment, but for the most part, they lived off meat. The Vail Site at Lake Azicohos has been described as a "killing ground," into which herds of caribou were lured and slaughtered. At the Munsungan-Chase's Lake Site evidence was uncovered that one band, at least, had established a "chert mine," allowing them to set up a primitive tool and weapons manufactory. With signs the weather was warming—trees like spruce, birch, jack pine, and red pine were taking hold—the migratory herds of caribou, musk oxen, and even mastodons and mammoths began to disappear. The wide-open lands turned into spreading forest enclosures. The Paleo Indians faded away.

They were followed by other prehistory folk. Their DNA, if we had any, might or might not link them to their successors, who emerged out of the mists of time through the clues they left. Thus, these still shadowy ancients have been dated by their surviving artifacts. Listing them in broad categories, like *Archaic* and *Woodland* (or *Ceramic*), the scientists further subdivide these categories into *Early*, *Middle*, and *Late*.

From the end of the Paleo Indians to the present, there are about 10,000 years to cover. The Archaic extends to 3,000 years ago; the Woodland takes us to about 1500 AD David Sanger prefers to use Ceramic "because the major defining features of the Woodland are not characteristic Maine traits, there seems to be little point in using that term."[4]

A layman can easily get lost in the labyrinth of terminology and fine distinctions. What emerges for the scientists through this segmented parade of thousands of years are cultural distinctions they can label, denoting them as Traditions, Phases, Complexes, etc. We still don't yet see our familiar Penobscots, Passamaquoddies, or Maliseets arising out of these geological depths. We are told instead of the Laurentian Tradition, implying influence from the north, or the Susquehanna Tradition, arriving Down East from the south. We see, perhaps, a burial society, surrounding their interments with red ochre, which led an early and eager archaeologist from Massachusetts named Warren K. Moorehead to sensationalize them as a lost tribe of "Red Paint Indians." That brief cultural spasm is now more sedately referred to as the Moorehead Complex. A sense of the life of these by-gone inhabitants of Maine is only tangentially glimpsed. There are swords of swordfishes among the detritus of their Hancock County campsites; *ergo*, we know some of them went to sea. They made certain kinds of pottery in the ages dubbed Ceramic. They used this or that artifact in this or that style. Lost, however, are the intangibles. What did they think about their world—about themselves? How can they speak to us as fellow dwellers in land now ours?

The legends perpetuated by those Native Americans we know today in Maine may offer some clues.

It was an elaborate and complex mythology developed who knows when over who knows how many years. Yet *mythology* may not be a fair attribution for this vast collection of tales, handed down orally, since there is a religiosity here, too, and this view of origins and morals holds as sacred a quality to the northeastern Algonquins as the stories in the Bible do to believers in Christianity and Judaism. Genesis, in this instance, revolves about the dominating divinity figure of Glooskap (there are innumerable spellings and the pronunciation appears to be *Glooskaby*). Charles G. Leland, who plumbed these matters in his 1884 book, *The Algonquin Legends of New England*, describes him as follows:

> Glooskap is the Norse God intensified. He is, however, more of a giant; he grows to a more appalling greatness than Thor or Odin in his battles. When a *Kiawaqui* [a

type of demon] rises to the clouds to oppose him, Glooskap's head touches the stars and scorning to slay so mean a foe like an equal, he kills him contemptuously with a light tap of his bow....[5]

Glooskap created the first humans in Maine and its northern surroundings, according to the Wabanaki. But where did he come from? There is a hint of old religious ideas in the explanation: the battle of Good and Evil, Light and Darkness, Cain and Abel—for Glooskap was originally a twin. He represented the Good Principle and his brother, Malsum the Wolf, the Evil Principle. One reason he is sometimes spoken of as Glooskap the Liar relates to how he handled his bad sibling's attempt to kill him. When asked by Malsum what it would take to overcome his immortality, he replied that a blow on the head by a cat-o-nine-tail would be fatal—a patent falsehood. So, in the middle of the night, when his brother treacherously bashed him with a piece of marsh reed, he awoke and dispatched his villainous twin.

Some legends speak of Glooskap as having been born in the land of the Wabanaki, but it's also said he came over the sea in a great stone canoe, which was actually an island of granite covered with trees.

This second version is interesting, given the new controversy about the "First Americans" possibly arriving from across the Atlantic. One particular legend, as related to Leland, starts:

Glooskap came first of all into this country, into Nova Scotia, Maine, Canada, into the land of the Wabanaki, next to sunrise. There were no Indians here then....[6]

The Indians he created to populate these northern climes were made from the trunks of ash trees. Leland, whose whole work is devoted to his thesis that the Wabanaki tales are infused with Norse and Eskimo influence, emphasizes that in the Icelandic Eddas, man was also made from an ash tree. He expands such points of similarity to all these poem-legends.

They are handled in the same bold and artistic manner as the Norse. There is nothing like them in any other North American Indian records. They are, especially those which are from the Passamaquoddy and Penobscot, inspired with a genial cosmopolite humor....[7]

A Norse connection to the denizens of the Wabanaki realm is no longer mere conjecture. While rumors that Leif Erikson's Vineland was located in New England have been put to rest by excavations at L'Anse aux Meadows in Newfoundland, the discovery of an authentic Norse coin from the eleventh century among material uncovered on the Maine coast has lent reality to some contacts, even if archaeologists were quick to surmise that the rare penny came to these Maine Indians via trade with Indians to the north.

Linkages with folks much farther north might also buttress Leland's other supposition—that Eskimo traits were also implanted in the Wabanaki folklore, particularly the darker side—the monsters, the witches, the cannibals, the would-be doers of evil whom Glooskap must combat. Leland maintains that *Eskimo*, itself, is an Algonquin word, meaning people who eat raw fish or flesh. We now know Eskimos prefer to be called by their own name for themselves, *Inuit*.

Like Adam, Glooskap gives out names, starting with the animals, like *mooin*, bear, or *mi-ko*, squirrel, or *kwah-beet*, beaver. Presumably, he named places, too. For in one of his adventures, when Whin-Pe the sorcerer kidnaps the old woman called Noogumee, grandmother, and a youth nicknamed the Marten, they travel a route from Menogwes to Kee-poog-itk to Oona-maghik to Uktukkamku before he catches up with them. On a modern map, this pursuit would be unfolding around New Brunswick, Nova Scotia, Cape Breton Island, and Newfoundland. The geography of the legends implies a wide geography in the Wabanaki mind, with a range from Uk-tuk-amqw, Newfoundland, south to Samgadihawk, Saco, and west to El-now-e-bit, the White Mountains, and Oonahgemessuk, North Conway.

This territory was not a blank space on the map when the Europeans arrived Down East. The idea *they* had been *discovered* had to have galled the Wabanaki, enough to create a counterlegend:

So they sailed across the sea. This was before the white
people had ever heard of America. The white men did
not discover this country first at all. Glooskap discov-

ered England and told them about it. He got to London. The people had never seen a canoe before. They came flocking down to look at it.[8]

France was the next stop. Not a friendly place. They fired cannon at Glooskap's stone canoe, but ineffectually. In retaliation, he beached all their men-of-war. "They took him prisoner. They put him into a great cannon and fired it off. They looked into the cannon and there he sat smoking his stone pipe, knocking the ashes out."

The historical period had infiltrated the Wabanaki's age-old oral tradition. But how did they account for the historical fact their great hero-god could not defeat the invaders of their land? There is thus another explanation for the title Glooskap the Liar—that is, as Leland writes, "because it is said that when he left Earth, like King Arthur for Fairyland, he promised to return and has never done so."

But such a harsh judgment could not be left to stand alone. How could it be? Of Glooskap, it was said:

He loved mankind and wherever he might be in the wilderness, he was never very far from any of the Indians. He dwelt in a lonely land, but whenever they sought him they found him. He traveled far and wide; there is no place in all the land of the Wabanaki where he left not his name....

It is now more generally acknowledged that Glooskap is hidden in a secret cave on Katahdin, preparing arrowheads for the day to come when the Indians will reclaim their land.

NOTES

1 David Kendall, *Glaciers and Granite*. Unity, ME: North Country Press, 1987.

2 David Sanger, *Discovering Maine's Archaeological Heritage*. Augusta, ME: Maine Historic Preservation Commission, 1979. Page 18.

3 Esther and David Braun, *The First Peoples of the Northeast*. Lincoln, MA: Mocassin Press, 1994. Page 13.

4 Sanger, page 9.

5 Charles G. Leland, *The Algonquin Legends of New England*. Boston: Houghton-Mifflin Co., 1884. Page 2.

6 Ibid., page 15.

7 Ibid., page 13.

8 IIbid., page 128.

FIVE

The Historic Period Arrives

O NE OTHER FEAT credited to Glooskap before his disappearance was the creation of rivers and streams. It all started when the people complained to him there was no water left in the land because every drop had been consumed by Oglebamu, the giant frog. Glooskap took care of that problem with a smash of his stone axe to the amphibian's back, causing its mouth to open and pour out floods everywhere and its much reduced progeny to inherit the look of a slightly deformed spine forever. That gush of liquid resolved itself into the foremost feature of the Wabanaki territory—most particularly, the big rivers and their tributaries, along with the chains of lakes that welded the whole into a single, effective transportation system.

All the way north to the St. Lawrence, all the way south to the Saco, the birchbark canoes of these northern peoples skimmed their way in the most efficient manner possible to navigate this great wilderness. In a few days, a paddler could go from the St. John to the mouth of the Penobscot, and a round trip from the Maine coast to the present site of Quebec City could be done in three weeks. It was the prevalence of white (or paper) birch in their land that had given the Wabanaki this advantage, along with the cultural ingenuity to invent and engineer such a useful craft. Below the Saco, there was nothing indigenous like it; not enough of those lightweight bark producers grew and the natives there had to resort to clumsy dugouts they carved out of entire tree trunks.

The Wabanakis stayed close to their rivers, built their villages

The Interrupted Forest

alongside them, and relied on them for fish and other food. Their identification with some of the major confluences led in time to their being identified *by* them by others; the English, especially, began to refer to the Penobscots, the Androscoggins, the Kennebecs, the Sacos, the St. Johns.

Names become a nightmare as we enter into this history. A Wabanaki geography, had it been printed before the white man appeared, would have been replete with places they knew by the descriptions of what happened at them. The almighty Penobscot River, the heartland of the present-day Maine North Woods, was originally a stretch of water (allegedly around Verona Island and Orland)[1] where, quite literally, "the rocks widen and open out." In the Penobscot language, it would have sounded something like: "bahahwehbzkek" [*P* and *B* are interchangeable; our *Penobscot* can also be pronounced *Benopscot*]. The Androscoggin was "river of rock shelters," the Ossippee, "river alongside," Chesuncook Lake, "location at the big outlet," and Kenduskeag Stream, "stream with water parsnips." All these names, by the way—Androscoggin, Ossippee, Chesuncook, Kenduskeag—which we take to be Indian names, the Penobscots regard as English names. They are mere approximations of the original designations.[2]

This portion of planet Earth released by the last glacier rolled into its present place by tectonics over hundreds of millions of years, grown up to thick forests and laced with watery roadways, was now a known entity—that is, known by the people who inhabited it. That it was unknown across the Atlantic, unknown to the courts of monarchies that would eventually lay claims to it, made no difference. Tribes had formed and staked their own claims, using, admittedly, different criteria from what was to come: communal, not individual, property rights. But even within tribal limits, there were traditional family rights, hunting grounds that from time immemorial had been parceled to specific groups, a kind of unspoken, respected, even inalienable ownership.

Trespass was a known violation; it could send tribes to war against each other and could lead to a clan's taking action against interlopers. In Frank Speck's epochal study of the Maine Penobscots, *Penobscot Man*, he inserts a map showing the boundaries of the

Penobscot tribal territory, from the mouth of their namesake river north to the St. John.³ To the east and west of them were other distinct tribes: seaward, the Passamaquoddies in their niche in today's Washington County, and above them, the mostly New Brunswick Maliseets; while the long-vanished Wawenocks of Knox County, the equally fugitive Norridgewocks and the almost extinct Aroosaguntacooks occupied the inland flanks. The Penobscots' lines ran right through Moosehead Lake and encompassed Katahdin, and Speck has numbered from 1 to 22 the family hunting districts and placed them appropriately throughout the Penobscot tract. Albeit unsurveyed, these "properties" were nevertheless denoted (by the birchbark figurines of animals) and, in following the seasonal rhythms of these peripatetic peoples, occupied, if only for the privilege of harvesting game. The land the tribes lived on was anything but a tabula rasa; it was always somebody's.

The proliferation of tribes and, even more so, of the names for them, is a trial for any historian and his or her readers. Even in as restricted a capsule of territory as the northeast corner, there are numerous variations. We still encounter names from the past that are no longer in currency today: Tarratines, Etchemins, and those in *la langue français*, Souriquois and Armouchiquois. The first named are said to be the contemporary Micmacs, then fierce seagoing raiders. The Passamaquoddies' own name for themselves was *Skið-jim* meaning "men" or "the people," which might have given rise to *Etchemin*. The Penobscots self-styled title was *Alnanbiak*. The French labels quickly passed into disuse, since they were the defeated party in the wars for domination that eventually consumed the historic period.

But well before the Europeans invaded in numbers, a population was in place, scattered throughout Maine, that had developed a distinctive way of life. North of the Saco River, this way of living was similar to but slightly different from that of its fellow Algonquian-speaking neighbors to the south. In the colder climes, there was simply less reliance on agriculture.

There was also a history of which we are but dimly aware. Warfare between tribes was widespread, if intermittent. When one reaches the cusp of the 1600s, facts emerge, as well as the names of

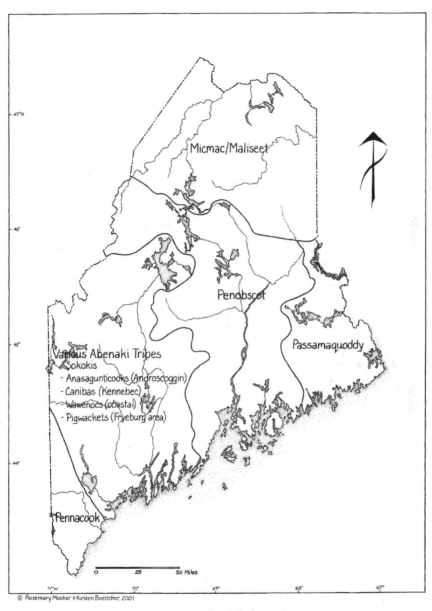

Micmac/Maliseet

Penobscot

Passamaquoddy

Various Abenaki Tribes
Sokokis
  - Anasagunticooks (Androscoggin)
  - Canibas (Kennebec)
  - Wawenocs (coastal)
  - Pigwackets (Fryeburg area)

Pennacook

0   25   50 Miles

47°N
46°
45°
44°

71°W   70°   69°   68°   67°

© Rosemary Mosher & Kirsten Boettcher, 2001

Maine's Early Tribal Groups

warriors. Around 1607 a series of battles erupted that have been recorded. Iouaniscou, a Micmac, led one of the usual Tarratine raids southward and westward, probably upon the Western Abenaki Sacos, and massacred some of his prisoners on Mount Desert Island. Seeking revenge, the Sacos killed a Micmac named Panounias, but did it on the territory of the Penobscots, whose famous chief Bessabes apologized to the equally renowned Micmac sachem Membertou. The latter never believed Bessabes's protestations of innocence and never forgave him. Not only would the Micmacs continue to harass the Sacos but in 1613, in an alliance with the Maliseets, Passamaquoddies, and the far northern Montagnais, they entered upon an all-out war against the Penobscots and slew Bessabes in 1615.

More dreaded even than this intra-Algonquin warfare were the periodic raids by a wholly foreign group from the west, the Mohawks, who belonged to the Six Nations Iroquois Confederation and whose language was utterly different. The enmity between these two peoples was centuries old. It has been speculated that the Algonquins who became Maine Indians were originally driven from a homeland in the vicinity of the Great Lakes by other imperialistic Iroquois.

What would have become of these inhabitants of the Maine North Woods had there never been any immigration from Europe? Would they have found a genius of a leader to unite them, as the Iroquois found in Deganiwadah who fashioned their powerful union of Six Nations? (Bessabes was allegedly headed in this direction when he was slain.) Would they have continued their hunting-fishing-canoeing culture ad infinitum? Would they have consolidated into considerable cities like the Aztecs and Mayas? Would their oral tradition of communication ever have been committed to writing?

As Speck writes: "Theirs was a cultural identity thwarted by the interruptions of an alien civilization—the end of a primitive Utopia."[4] And in further describing the northern Algonquins and their long experience of living in the cold evergreen forests, he states his opinion that:

> They will not reveal themselves as a people planted in
> an inimical environment but as the denizens of a zone

well provided with the means of enjoying that state of well-being and satisfaction which a Father-Creator affords for his children as the Wabanaki claim to be.[5]

Hunting was the keystone of their existence. It was suffused, as was most of their daily life, with religious connotations — a sense of sacredness that applied to all the world, animate and inanimate. Their notion, so seemingly strange to us, was that the animals on whom they lived would offer their lives willingly if approached the right way, and they not only had to be killed in the appropriate ritual manner but their spirits had to be respected and thanked for their sacrifice.

There were different types of hunting, with different designations: "still hunting and stalking," starting in February, taking moose and beaver; "hunting seal" in July and August, by the shore; and "the fall hunt," when moose, deer, and caribou were in the lakes and rivers to escape droves of tormenting flies, and could be approached from canoes. Before muskets were introduced, bows and arrows, lances, and knives had been the means of dispatching their quarry. Stone blades and arrowheads were used in the old days. Moose was king. The Wabanaki became proficient at imitating the calls of the cows during mating season and luring the bulls into target range. They employed birchbark cones made for this purpose, becoming very adept at the practice. The large amount of meat was shared with the rest of the village and the first man to bag a moose (or deer) did not partake of the feast; it would be bad luck. That communal idea was instilled early. A boy celebrating his first kill must never eat any of it himself or he would never be successful again. The Wabanaki hunted bear, too, ate the flesh of beavers they trapped for fur, took caribou, snared birds, rabbits, even deer, and actually had young men so well trained and in such great physical shape they could run down fleeing game on foot and dispatch it. Purification ceremonies in sweat baths were required before undertaking any major hunt. Their legends even reflected memories of hunting elephant-like mammoths and mastodons.

The symbiosis with animals was woven deep into the fabric of their lives. Their hunting bands bore totemic animal names. With territories generally configured by bays or rivers or coastal estuaries (these territories were often referred to as "rivers"), there were among the Penobscots: Bear, Frog, Squirrel, Beaver, Hare, Whale, Lobster, Wolf, and Eel clans or (more commonly) *families*, to cite but a sampling. Names even extended to those of such undramatic creatures as Toads and the fishes Yellow Perch and Sculpin.

Most of their territories were specifically known. For example, the Lobster (and Crab) family was situated on the shores of Penobscot Bay with headquarters at present-day Castine and a clamming site at Stockton Springs. Their current descendants include a branch of the prolific Mitchell family, and another Mitchell branch comes from the Bear clan, whose nearby lands were on the lower western banks of the Penobscot River, and around Belfast. The Eel group—noted for its Neptune members, particularly the famed chief John Neptune—were located inland in the valley of the Kenduskeag and north to Pushaw Stream and Lake. Another illustrious family, today's Atteans, who formed the Squirrel clan, stretched from Caribou and the Ragged Lakes, west of Chesuncook, to Black Brook Pond. A few groups, like the Whale and Beaver, had somewhat indeterminate territories; the former in the Piscataquis River and Millinocket Lake area; the latter east of the Penobscot.

There were social rankings, too, among the bands. The two highest were the Frog and Squirrel, with chiefs being chosen from both of them. The Sturgeon (Sockalexis family) and Bear were also highly ranked. The Eel (Neptunes) had the reputation of being magicians. There were also lower castes, like the Toad, said to be slovenly folks, and the Hare (or Rabbit), reputedly poor hunters, and the lowest of all was the Yellow Perch, who were branded "lazy and shiftless, after the manner of yellow perch." The Whale family may have been so named because its members were "large and dark people."

On a more individual basis, animals also played a defining role in the lives of young Abenaki males who, around puberty, were sent out on a vision quest. The aim was to encounter a manatou, a spirit guardian in the form of a mammal, fish, or bird, and this totem would supply him with a signature for the new name he would adopt. Alone in the wilderness, without food, sleep, and possibly having ingested hallucinogenic herbs such as hellbore, he awaited a sign, a dream image, a gift of insight from the spirit world. It did not always occur and sometimes the ordeal would have to be endured more than once. Armed with a successful experience, the putative warrior had an identity to last a lifetime and a symbol to mark on the bodies of those he killed in battle or, in later years, to append to treaties with the Europeans.

That glimpse into the surreality of the Native American cosmology was often stronger in some individuals than in others. The shaman (the term used by anthropologists) was an important figure among the Wabanakis, as among many if not most of the American tribes. Magic was a vital component of the Wabanaki world view, and those who could practice it in the appropriate spiritual manner commanded great respect and power. They were "medicine men," as they have been called, with an extensive pharmacological knowledge of the plants of the forest and their uses in curing diseases, which were regarded as having been caused by malevolent spirits and evil personal intentions. They also had what we would call regulatory functions, i.e., one of the most effective means the Penobscots had of preventing trespass on the territories of their hunting families was to invoke the magic of a *M'teoulino*, to use the Penobscot word for a shaman. Quite often, great Wabanaki chiefs whose renown has echoed through the ages—Membertou and Bessabes and Madockawando and Passaconaway—were such wizards. Latter-day examples of persons who can work inexplicable wonders have survived in the Penobscots' John Neptune, a late eighteenth-century and early nineteenth-century figure, and the twentieth-century "medicine man" of Indian Island known as "Senabeh."

The powers imputed to these people have never been better illustrated than in a story told by Fannie Hardy Eckstorm in her book *Old John Neptune and Other Maine Indian Shamans.*[6] To her, John Neptune was a man of flesh and blood, who lived down the road from her family home in Brewer and sat by the Franklin stove and warmed himself when visiting her parents and grandparents. As she wrote, her grandparents "were orthodox and fastidiously moral" [Christians] who would have nothing to do with witchcraft or magic or supernatural powers"[7] and remained totally unaware of his powers or those of his common-law wife, old Molly Molasses. Of John, the "wizard of the tribe," Mrs. Eckstorm cataloged a number of incredible traits:

> ...who could make his voice heard a hundred miles away, who could walk in hard ground sinking up to his knees at every step, who could find green corn in winter and tobacco in the forest where there was none, and who had fought and overcome that slimy, devouring monster, the dreadful *Wiwiliamecq.*[8]

This last reference is to a water monster John Neptune fought in Boyden's Lake in Washington County. The Neptune family, you will recall, were under the sign of the eel and the episode reinforces the intense identification of the Wabanaki with their totemic animals. In this case, because of John Neptune's special gifts, he became a giant eel in order to destroy a sea serpent—a snail-like, outsized creature described also as a crocodile, hippopotamus, and big soft lizard. This evil giant, in turn, was the transmogrified version of a Micmac chief who had done an injury to a Passamaquoddy kinsman of Neptune's. The epic combat of these *poohigans* or familiar spirits took place in the lake (which is only four miles from the Pleasant Point Passamaquoddy reservation in Perry) and roiled the waters so badly they were muddy for days. The dead, thirty-foot-long *wiwilimecq* was dragged ashore by Neptune and its bones left to rot.

Or so the story goes, and it is told over and over again. Fannie Hardy Eckstorm believes it is an ancient Passamaquoddy tale borrowed by the Penobscots and attached to their own John Neptune who, as she says, when he "found himself being credited with 'witchpower'...was far too shrewd to deny any marvel told about him: it was greatly to his interest to make the most of his prestige."[9]

More to the point is the fact this sense of a mythic, wondrous other world interchangeable with reality continues to be part of the Wabanaki belief system. By the time Europeans were about to interact with them in the sixteenth century, that cultural pattern of spirituality had had a huge time period in which to develop. Their material culture also had adapted to the physical setting and sustained a way of life for their people. It could adapt to slow change, so it was not fixed forever. But in all innocence of what was to come, it was a satisfactory answer to the question all peoples must answer: how do we survive, even prosper, and assure an enduring future for ourselves?

A sense of what it must have been like for the Wabanaki in their fairly isolated existence (isolated, at least, from the Europeans and their utterly alien influences, albeit not from their Iroquois enemies) can be gleaned from a piece in their own resource book publication *The Wabanakis of Maine and the Maritimes*. This fictional slice of life is titled: "A Micmac Woman Speaks to Her Granddaughter: 1400."

"Granddaughter, the bloodroot dye has turned orange. Bring your quills and we can begin to dye them." Thus does the story commence of the two Wabanaki females sitting outside their wigwam during an era when Europe, itself, was still turned inward and mostly believed the world was flat and unexplorable. The Micmac ladies are about to embark on decorative work, embroidery on moosehide with porcupine quills, which was extensively practiced by the Micmacs (as opposed to the Penobscots who used these artificially brightly colored quills to wrap pipe stems). As they go about their domestic chore, the grandmother, who calls herself a chatterbox, delivers a soliloquy, mostly about her own youth. She tells of the stories she heard as a girl—stories of Glooskap (Kluskap in Micmac) and of *M'teoulino*-type individuals, stories that may sound familiar:

> One man had stomped on the ground so hard that his feet sank down into the rock. I have seen that place, where his footprints are in the rock. Others could turn themselves into animals.... My father's brother described two men who fought underwater. They could stay there for as long as they wanted, like fish....[10]

Then, she talks of the health care side of special knowledge, a field apparently not exclusively the province of shamans. "I learned to make medicines from water arum, goldenrod, ginseng, balsam, butternut, black cherry, lady's slipper, moosewood, and sweetflag, and from beaver and seal. We could save lives with those medicines...." Another facet of women's work she then describes was butchering game—flaying a moose, cutting the meat, carrying heavy slabs of it back to the wigwams, and preparing feasts, of which there were many. Her special memory is of one on the coast, after the end of the winter hunt and the arrival of spring. They boiled water in birchbark pots. They gathered mussels, scallops, clams, and lobsters. Her father harpooned a sturgeon; others supplied porpoise, seal, and turtle. Her mother had the children make moose butter out of the fat from boiled moose bones. She and her cousin painted each other's faces and braided each other's hair, decorating their tresses with red-dyed eelskin and copper ornaments. Her father oiled his skin and "shone like a great hunter" and her mother dressed up in decorated furs of seal and otter and beaver.

It was in the wigwam of the *saq'maw* (sachem) or chief that the feast was held. The men ate first; then, the women had what was left. Afterward, the men smoked pipes and told stories. The afternoon drifted slowly by. Fires flickered in the approaching dusk.

Dancing started. A certain young man from another village caught her eye and she his. He was young but he had already killed his first moose. So then the grandmother completes the tale for her granddaughter of how her grandfather had come into her life. Two years later, she agreed to marry him. But not without some qualms.

I had much to think about. I knew that if we were married, we would live in his village with his brother and brother's family. I would miss everyone, and I thought about this.... But I wanted to go.[11]

This idyllic interlude ends with the elderly woman, her dye job and reminiscences finished, saying: "I enjoy sitting here, basking like an old seal in the sun." The two of them happen to be by the ocean. The grandmother spies canoes out to sea, headed for land. "I wonder if they have found swordfish or whale," she says. There is a feeling of timelessness and utter peace.

This is a subtle bit of re-creation, subtle in its unspoken contrast of arcadian adaptation to nature with the modern world existing in the same space today. A lost paradise humanized. And included, too, a perhaps unintended subtlety about another feature of this Native American tribal life in 1400: how an intuitive sense of these nonscientific people dealt with the problem of interbreeding. In the family bands of the Penobscots and possibly of the Micmacs, one had to marry outside the group. Bear could not marry Bear. And the grandmother of the year 1400 story has to go to another village to live. In addition, tribal and even racial purity was not essential. Prisoners were often adopted, frequently taking the place of a family member lost in battle. After the white man appeared, they could become Indians, as well, and spawn their own mixed families.

The tranquil Micmac scene by the Atlantic coast necessarily skirts some of the rougher edges of this pre-European indigenous lifestyle. Prisoners, if they weren't adopted, were likely to be tortured to death, or tortured badly and then burnt alive. (Lest we forget, the Europeans of this era were likewise burning people at the stake: heretics, accused witches, and certain non-Christians, such as Jews—and in considerable numbers.) The warfare of the Abenakis and the Mohawks is replete with ugly incidents.

Frank Speck tells of a particularly gruesome one when a group of old Penobscot women were camped on a large boulder jutting out into Passadumkeag Stream, while their husbands and sons were hunting. A war party of Mohawks fell upon them, killed them, scalped them, impaled their bodies upon sharp stakes, and fixed their mouths and eyelids open so that they appeared alive.

Under the leadership of a war chief and shaman named Mandoamek, the Penobscots extracted their revenge. Discerning that a large band of Mohawks were descending the Penobscot to attack Old Town, he bided his time. One day, several canoeloads of young Penobscot boys fishing upriver returned to their Indian Island village carrying the heads of a certain fish, the black chub, fastened on sticks. To Mandoamek, it was a sign the Mohawks were near. He approached their camp with his men and sang a magical medicine song that put the enemy to sleep, whereupon the Penobscots went in and cut off the heads of the Iroquois. These were mounted on sticks, like the chubs, and fixed with mouths and eyes open, like the martyred women.

But there were horrors worse than these. They are encapsulated in another entry in the Wabanaki resource book. This time, it is a woman of the Kennebec tribe, speaking to her daughter who is ill, maybe dying.

The year is 1650. Invisible demons, far worse than the

Chenoo, the ice cannibals, have beset these Wabanaki. The mother, in her expressed thoughts, describes how her husband, also ill, confronted the French priest in the village and accused him, as a European, of coming to America to kill all Indians:

> Your father held a hatchet in his hand, but he did not raise it, and when he came back to the wigwam he collapsed on the ground, bleeding from his mouth and nose, his skin spotted and blue. Within a few hours he was dead. Then my son died. Now, daughter, it is you.... The village is deserted. Everyone is gone who could go, except for the sick, who moan in their wigwams, and the dead who lie where they died because there is no one to bury them. Only the black robe [the priest] still walks around. He is strong and nothing bothers him.[12]

The woman has asked her uncle, a *M'teoulino*, to help. But he has gone and left behind his medicine bag and drum and rattle, the tools of his trade. His dreams are no longer true, he told her. In other words, he is powerless against the disease the Europeans have brought.

Her dilemma, as a Native American whose familiar belief system is under intolerable siege, is heightened when the priest enters her wigwam. He places a cross on top of her supine child's chest and recites a prayer in a language the mother doesn't understand.

"Child, I have to choose. Do I permit the cross to rest on your heart or do I carry you to the canoe?"

Approximately 150 years had elapsed since the first recorded contact with the strangers from across the Atlantic. In 1501 a Portuguese, Gaspar Corte-Real, landed in Newfoundland and kidnapped forty-seven Beothuk Indians whom he took back to the Continent. The native people as described by some of the earliest explorers were uniformly healthy and fine physical specimens. European germs changed all that as the contacts continued. The tribes had no resistance to measles, smallpox, or plague. Their medicine men were helpless. Although it didn't happen overnight, the Wabanaki world—one of the first to encounter these invaders—was turned upside down.

NOTES

1 This particular description is taken from *The Wabanakis of Maine and the Maritimes,* a resource book prepared for and published by the Maine Indian Program of the American Friends Service Committee (Bath, Maine, 1989). Fannie Hardy Eckstorm, in *Indian Place Names of the Penobscot Valley and the Maine Coast,* has a different geographical section of the river spawning the name Penobscot. She says it is between Treat's Falls and the Old Town Great Falls and means, literally, "at the descending rock."

2 *The Wabanakis of Maine and the Maritimes,* page D-23.

3 Frank Speck, *Penobscot Man.* Orono, ME: University of Maine Press, 1997 reprint.

4 Ibid., page 312.

5 Ibid., page 311.

6 Fannie Hardy Eckstorm, *Old John Neptune and Other Indian Shamans.* Orono, ME: University of Maine Press, a Marsh Island Reprint, 1980.

7 Ibid., page 6.

8 Ibid.

9 Ibid., page 48.

10 *Wabanakis,* page C-29.

11 Ibid., page C-30.

12 Ibid., page C-33.

SIX

Meanwhile, in Europe

TIME, IN THE WABANAKI mind-set, was circular. Their calendars are still portrayed as wheels, with the months (or moons) displayed along the outer rim. The names are descriptive of what nature is doing at the moment. August for the Penobscots is the "moon of fall fish or white chubs"; for the Micmacs, "the birds shed feathers moon." Correspondingly, the Penobscot January is the "moon that provides little food grudgingly," and the Micmac first of the year, the "frost fish [tomcod] moon."

Across the Atlantic, time had become linear. The underlying sense was that it was headed somewhere, had a purpose, not just going endlessly round and round. Therefore, it had measurable value, a sentiment we were to inherit in the notion "time is money," a concept the American Indians would have found unfathomable.

As for the months, the West Europeans went in for Roman antecedents — January, out of Janus, the God of Beginnings, able to look in two directions at once with his back-to-back faces; August, from Augustus, the first and one of the greatest emperors; as well as July for Julius Caesar, his nonimperial predecessor; March derived from Mars, God of War; and September through December represented Latin numbers.

Rome was always an intellectual underpinning as the Old World inched out of the Dark Ages into the fifteenth century's dawning Renaissance. The universal Roman Catholic Church was one of its bequests. Another was the example and lasting dream of world empire, kept fitfully alive in an institution derided by historians as "neither Holy nor Roman nor an Empire." Nations were being born out of the feudalism that had followed Rome's destruction by essentially tribal entities, mostly of Germanic or Scandinavian origins. Crusades had been undertaken without success against the Moslems who hemmed them in, particularly in Eastern Europe and the Middle East but also in Iberia.

It was perhaps no accident that Gaspar Corte-Real arrived in Newfoundland as early as 1501. For the Portuguese, commencing in 1415, led Europe's counterattack and launched the great maritime adventure that helped the continent break from its isolation. Actually, the sparkplug was a young prince, half Portuguese, half English, known to history as Henry the Navigator. He was the son of King Joao I and Phillipa of Lancaster, daughter of John of Gaunt, and also the sister of King Henry IV of England. Under Prince Henry's command, Portugal, having just fought off an invasion from Castile, full of national pride and restless energy, crossed the Straits of Gibraltar and assaulted the Moorish stronghold of Ceuta in a sort of minicrusade. Then, fired with the idea of further conquest and exploration of the African coast, Prince Henry subsequently retired to a small fishing village called Sagres and established a school of navigation, collecting the best mapmakers, ships' captains, and nautical experts of the day. Succeeding Portuguese kings kept up his efforts until their ships reached India and the Far East. Joao II, intent on this effort, turned down a chance to bankroll Columbus. Once Spain, formed by the merger of Castile and Aragon, had rid itself of Moors (and Jews), it did back Columbus and, rather than compete with Portugal, devised a breathtakingly arrogant compromise. The two persuaded the Pope to divide the world between them and at a sleepy town in Old Castile called Tordesillas, signed a treaty to that effect.

The reaction of other budding nation-states was best summed up by the French monarch François I. He said he would "like to see the clause in Adam's will" that left the planet to the two Iberian powers. It was clear there would be challenges, particularly in areas not clearly staked out, like North America.

The English actually beat the French to the punch. Three years after Tordesillas, in 1497, King Henry VII, another descendant of John of Gaunt, sent an expedition to the New World. Its leader was an Italian, from Columbus's hometown of Genoa, who had settled in Bristol, a budding seaport on England's west coast. His name was Giovanni Caboto and we know him as John Cabot. We also know his goal was the same as that of Columbus—to seek the rumored "Northwest Passage" to the riches of the Orient.

Cabot reached Newfoundland and possibly Cape Breton Island at the outermost tip of Nova Scotia. But his explorations inland were, in the case of Newfoundland, effectively stymied by the Beothuk Indians. He dared not go much beyond crossbow range of his ship. The hostility of these natives actually preceded by four years the outrageous kidnapping of their people by Gaspar Corte-Real. What experience of whites had left them so jaundiced? Vikings were in Newfoundland centuries earlier, as the excavations at L'Anse aux Meadows have confirmed, and the Basques allegedly had been fishing for cod in their waters since the year 1000. So extensive was the Basque pursuit of cod that in one of their folk-tales a medieval fisherman pulls up a codfish talking in Basque, a tongue no one else in the world speaks. It is also recorded history that seventeen years before Cabot's first voyage, two merchants in his adopted city—Thomas Croft and John Jay—sent ships west-ward looking for cod. A recent discovery by British scholars of a letter dispatched by Bristol merchants to Columbus, himself, showed he knew or should have known they had been to America before him.

In any event, Cabot, whose trip had been funded by Bristol merchants as well as the English crown, never discovered the fabled highway to Asia. Still, he was impressed by the abundance of the cod fishery and even more so by the many sites on the rocky coast and islands just offshore for salting and drying the fish. He claimed this "new found land" for England and went back to North America the following year on a trip during which he vanished.

His son Sebastian, as a youngster, may have been on the first voyage but certainly not on the second. Sailing for the English in 1506, he reached Hudson's Bay. Later, he was to head his exploring efforts in a different direction, going east to Russia and eventually becoming governor of the Muscovy Company, devoted to trade with

The Interrupted Forest

that region. Yet, despite these early Cabot voyages, England's initial advantage was never fully exploited.

François I, who sat on the French throne from 1515–47, moved into the vacuum. Another Italian mariner was hired, this time by the French, and in 1524 Giovanni da Verrazano sailed across the Atlantic, also seeking a shortcut to the Far East. He avoided the northernmost climes, made landfall around North Carolina and proceeded up the coast, entering New York Harbor (where a prominent bridge bears his name), and ending his exploratory mission in Maine. He traded with some Abenaki natives, but they were difficult if not openly hostile. "We found no courtesy in them," he reported. Exchanges could only be carried out by Verrazano's men from a small boat anchored behind the breakers, tossing fishhooks, knives, and other sharp metal objects ashore by a rope and retrieving Indian trade goods the same way.

Not to be outdone, the Spanish, by then well en route to becoming the world's greatest power, also entered these north regions. In 1525, a year after Verrazano's fairly fruitless trip, the Hapsburg Emperor Charles V, who was also King of Spain, likewise chose a foreigner to do his exploring. This sailor was a Portuguese, Estevão Gomes, who usually appears in history books by his Spanish name of Esteban Gomez. He, too, was instructed to find the "Northwest Passage." He'd already participated in finding a "Southern Passage" as a crew member under his countryman Magellan (real name, Fernão de Magalhaes) when the latter, too, was sailing for Spain. But although Gomes scouted the entire Atlantic Coast from Newfoundland to Florida, he was as unsuccessful as his predecessors. However, he has left some traces of his presence in Spanish names he gave to certain features of Maine's geography, like the Bay of Fundy, (originally *Bahia Profundo*—Deep Bay) and Casco Bay (from *casco*, the word for helmet), which had struck him as helmet-shaped.

France's François I, never a monarch to sit by idly, reinvolved himself heavily nine years later by launching a sustained effort. The leader he chose for it was an experienced seaman from Brittany, a native of St. Malo, Jacques Cartier. From this busy port on the English Channel, Cartier took three voyages to the New World, two

subsidized exclusively by the king and the third by a wealthy nobleman. His trips had important results, among them his reaching the
Gulf of the St. Lawrence and traveling up its mighty river into the
interior as far as Hochelaga, now Montreal. Other sites in eastern
Canada he claimed for France included the Gaspé Peninsula, New
Brunswick, Quebec, and Prince Edward Island. He traded not only
with the Wabanakis but even with the distant Iroquois, and from the
former received the very furs they were wearing: "...all went back
naked without anything on them, and they made signs to us that
they would return in the morrow with more furs." Another native
group Cartier encountered was the Montaignais, far northern
mountain people, "who came as freely on board our vessels as if they
had been Frenchmen." These Indians were accustomed to Europeans from their dealings with fishing vessels in the Gulf of St.
Lawrence.

Cartier's book, *Relation Original du Voyage de Jacques Cartier au
Canada en 1534*, made fascinating reading for his contemporaries. He
talked of seeing birds that "bite like dogs" (these were gannets) and
of hunting the now extinct great auk. This bird was the size of a
goose, just as good eating, and so abundant Cartier's crews salted
down four to five butts for each ship besides what they ate fresh.

On Cartier's third trip (1541–42), financed by the Sieur de
Roberval, the motive was to attempt a colonization scheme. It failed,
nor did the voyage gain much new geographical information.

That the Spanish were worried about this first French initiative has been revealed by a document in their archives. It is a report
from a spy sent by the Spanish Council of the Indies to Samalo de
Lila (St. Malo de l'Isle). Their object was to stop these "French cor-
sairs," whom they feared had designs on their empire, but they
lacked the financial resources to do much about Cartier and his
activities.

The trail the St. Maloan had blazed was not forgotten in
France. The earliest New World voyage exclusively to obtain furs
was organized by French investors in 1569. Hitherto, they had been
solely interested in the fishing prospects. Merchants from St. Malo,
Rouen, and Dieppe did extremely well in procuring pelts during a
series of voyages starting in 1581. By 1583 a Rouen merchant

named Etienne Bellenger had established a trading and missionary post. Although he eventually abandoned it, his profits from furs were 1,000 percent. In 1585 French businessmen sent ten ships to Canada.

The Englishman Richard Hakluyt, on a trip to Paris, saw with his own eyes furs worth 20,000 crowns. This was one of the goads for an extensive effort, in which Hakluyt played a pivotal role, that made England into a colonizing power.

Equally as important as economic gain, if not more so, in the promotion of overseas expansion by the English was the feeling they had to catch up with the French and Spanish. As Lesley B. Cormack has written in his interesting study of the genesis of English imperialism:

> Until the sixteenth century, England had been marginal, both on the Ptolemaic map as an insignificant island on the edge of the known world and in the political and intellectual life of Europe.[1]

Cormack's thesis is that the intensive study of geography at the country's two major universities, Oxford and Cambridge, and the dissemination of this knowledge through the ruling classes, helped create Britain "as a true imperial power, portraying itself as the preeminent Protestant nation." The English and Scottish peoples of this realm soon forged a hard belief in their right to extract what they needed in economic wealth wherever they found it, as well as to extract homage from people they considered inferior. Associated with that prejudice was a strong faith in the superiority of Protestantism over Catholicism.

King Henry VIII had broken with the Pope in 1533. One of his daughters, Mary, ruling for five years, had brutally tried to bring back the old religion and earned herself the nickname "Bloody Mary." But her half sister Elizabeth, true to the Anglican Church of England, then ruled for forty-five years, a period during which England changed profoundly. Although a "Protestant Succession" would not be totally settled until the defeat of Bonnie Prince Charlie in 1745, the hearts and minds of the British had long since turned away from Rome. The vast bulk of their religious energy, even to the extent of leading them into a civil war, was devoted to fighting about what kind of Protestants they would be.

The Elizabethan era saw not only theological conflict but nationalist rivalry based on religion: Protestant England versus, above all, Catholic Spain, especially under its most powerful of rulers, Philip II, who had been the husband of "Bloody Mary" before her death. He claimed the throne of England and actually tried to get it by proposing —in vain—to Elizabeth. Then, he tried to conquer it with his Armada—again in vain. In the same period, France, too, underwent an internecine Protestant-Catholic struggle. The Catholics won out after the Protestant leader, Henri of Navarre, declared, "Paris was worth a Mass" to justify his conversion. As long as he sat on the throne as Henri IV, there was equanimity between the two faiths. His assassination by a Catholic fanatic was soon followed by the revocation of the Edict of Nantes and a wholesale exodus of Huguenots.

Of the men who moved England onto the world stage, some had started as soldiers in these sixteenth-century battles: Sir Walter Raleigh, Sir Humphrey Gilbert, Sir Francis Drake, Sir Ferdinando Gorges—men from the West Country who had fought on the Continent against the French and on the seas against the Spanish and in Ireland against Catholic rebels. In the latter area, Raleigh and Gilbert (his half brother) gained a thorough sense of colonialism. Large estates were given them in Munster and Cork on which they settled their coreligionists and suppressed any insurgent natives without mercy. A description exists of Sir Humphrey Gilbert receiving visitors in his field tent whose entrance is lined by twin rows of severed Irish heads.

On the gentler side of the imperialism promoters, but no less deadly in the long run, were the academics, Oxford and Cambridge dons. The most prominent was Thomas Harriot, a mathematical geographer who also had a taste for action. He went on one of Raleigh's early expeditions to Virginia and lived to write about it in his *A Brief and True Report of the New Found Land of Virginia*. Others not as noted were nevertheless intellectual giants of their time: men such as John Dee, consultant in navigation to explorers like Raleigh and Gilbert and to political powers such as Sir Francis Walsingham, Queen Elizabeth's secret service chief; or the Oxford professors

Henry Briggs and Thomas Allen, the latter having been Harriot's teacher; and Edward Wright, the preeminent geographer and associate of that strong supporter of exploration, Henry Percy, the ninth Earl of Northumberland.

Linking these various pockets of interest was the very visible figure of Richard Hakluyt. He has been described as a diplomat, spy, and churchman." He was in Paris as a chaplain to the English ambassador and one of his parishes was in Bristol where as Prebendary of St. Augustine's Cathedral, he had time to get to know the business community and become a strong influence on promoting overseas voyages from that city. He was also a fellow of Christ Church College, Oxford, and lectured there for many years. His enduring opus is his book *The Principal Navigations, Voyages, Traffiques, and Discoveries of the English Nation,* which encouraged the English to see themselves as leaders in exploration and trade, already ahead of rivals like the Spanish, Portuguese, French, and Dutch. This work has been called "the prose epic of the English nation." The son of a merchant, Hakluyt was a principal investor in Raleigh's South Virginia Company; "many of his unpublished manuscripts were explicitly promotional of the plantation of North America and any attempt to discover a Northwest Passage...."[2] After his death, his assistant Samuel Purchas published a number of these pieces in a work called *Purchas, His Pilgrims.*

Another towering figure among these early English internationalists was actually a teenager. However, he also happened to be the heir to the English throne. Prince Henry Frederick Stuart, the firstborn of King James I, represents one of the great might-have-beens of history, British or otherwise. He was ten years old when his father, previously King James VI of Scotland, traveled south to assume the English crown after the death of Elizabeth in 1603. There had not been a royal child for the British people to cluck over since Elizabeth, herself, had been a girl. The three Stuart youngsters, Henry, his brother Charles, and his sister Elizabeth, were heartily welcomed but no one was more taken to their hearts than Henry.

He was a handsome and precocious young man, adept at sports and so dedicated to the princely ideal of chivalry that he participated avidly in mock medieval jousting tournaments. A new King Arthur, perhaps, and a Protestant one, for his father had split the religious training for his two boys. Henry, who would someday head the Church of England had been raised an Anglican; Charles, an Anglo-Catholic.

Henry was indulged; Charles supervised strictly.

It wasn't long before Henry, who did not like his father's court, had a minicourt of his own at Richmond Palace. Once staffed by lackeys of the king, it soon became Henry's private reserve when he appointed his own men.

It did not matter to Henry that James had imprisoned Sir Walter Raleigh (basically for being too anti-Spanish). While still a boy, Henry had had his mother take him to visit the distinguished adventurer in the Tower of London and, in time, Raleigh became like a father to him.

Other heroes of Henry's were the French king, Henri IV, who'd remained in his eyes the gallant knight champion of the Protestant cause in France despite his conversion, plus that doughty fighter for Dutch freedom from the Spanish in Holland, Prince Maurice of Nassau.

These were men of action and action was what young Henry wanted. He had no patience with his father's policy of accommodating Spain and favoring peace at almost any price. Those Englishmen with military aspirations—a "Protestant War Party'—gathered about the crown prince. "Henry embodied for them all that was necessary to make England the pre-eminent power of Protestant Europe and perhaps of the world."[3] The young prince has also been credited with bringing the Italian Renaissance to England. He collected works by Michelangelo and Raphael and introduced Italian architecture. His political platform seemed to have three goals: 1) the renewal of Merry Old England; 2) to connect England to Europe, especially Italy; and 3) to promote geographic investigation of the New World.

There might well also have been in his mind, in regard to the latter effort, a look back to his distant ancestor, Prince Henry the Navigator of Portugal. For Richmond Palace became another Sagres, where "...a court of geographical protégés provided Henry with a plan for imperial expansion and an image of himself as a conquering prince."[4] The poet Michael Drayton celebrated this situation in effulgent verse:

> Britain, behold here portrayed to thy sight
> Henry, the best hope, and the world's delight;
> He like great Neptune on the seas shall rove
> And rule three Realms, with triple power, like Jove.[5]

Those "three Realms" alluded to no doubt were Europe, Asia (the East India Company had been founded in 1602), and America. Henry wanted Britain to be a strong sea power. With the help of Raleigh, who in his prison cell at night wrote "Observations and Notes Concerning the Royal Navy," plus the support of Raleigh's cousin and bosom pal, the soldier-poet Sir Arthur Gorges, the three of them managed to get a new warship—the PRINCE ROYAL—built and launched in 1610. King James, who had once had the question debated: "Resolved, it is greater to *defend* than to enlarge the bounds of an empire," had pointedly neglected Britain's fleet.

Prince Henry's growing estrangement from James was best expressed in his famous remark about Raleigh's imprisonment: "No king but my father would keep such a bird in a cage."

Openly, the young prince consorted with the prisoner, who had been condemned to death on a trumped-up charge of treason but whose sentence had been stayed because of the king's fear of popular wrath. Henry kept Raleigh's home estate of Sherburne from being given to one of James's favorites by confiscating it himself. In 1611 he secretly smuggled out a manuscript Raleigh had written for him and saw it was given to a publisher. The work was entitled *The History of the World* and was to have a significant impact on later English history. What Raleigh wrote was the first part of a three-part thesis, whose import was not what an autocratic Stuart monarch wanted anyone to hear. For Raleigh baldly stated that God interfered in human affairs to punish rulers who abused their powers. A *divine right* of kings to do whatever they wanted did not exist. He showed through history the catastrophes that overtook kings who ruled tyrannically. In this, he was encouraged from the start by Prince Henry and assisted by Harriot, who helped him with the chronology.

It was a theme that resonated in English life in the years to come—a philosophical underpinning for the forces that later overthrew and executed Henry's brother Charles.

The Richmond Court Camelot collapsed in 1612. Henry, fond of swimming in the Thames, did so in ignorance or defiance of the filth tossed into the river. Eventually, he contracted a fever, most likely typhoid. Despite infusions of a special elixir prepared by Raleigh, he succumbed—nineteen years old—leaving as heir-apparent and subsequently king the younger sibling he loved to tease by calling him "Archbishop of Canterbury," so solemn, stiff, and unbending was Charles.

Had Henry lived to rule England, there might have been neither a Puritan exodus nor a Civil War, and the history of North America and of New England and of Maine, as well as Great Britain, would have been far different than it became.

Yet even without Henry's continued guidance, the die had been cast for British overseas expansion. The allure of North America had been enhanced by such mythical Shangri-Las as "El Dorado," "Norumbega," and, above all, the "Northwest Passage." It was the latter that enticed Sir Humphrey Gilbert on two voyages, the first sharing command with his half sibling Raleigh, and the second a fatal solo leadership effort in which he claimed Newfoundland for England and sank on the way home. That was in 1583, during Elizabeth's reign. Also then, a common seaman named David Ingram returned home after being shipwrecked in Mexico and told his drinking mates in waterfront pubs extraordinary tales. Agents of the Queen's security chief, Sir Francis Walsingham, brought the loquacious tar to the court, where he bragged about "Norumbega," a native American city paved with gold and silver, seen with his own eyes, in approximately the Penobscot region. His epic trek, he claimed, had taken him from Vera Cruz all the way to Canada. Raleigh, who had already looked for "El Dorado" in Guiana, was released from the Tower after Prince Henry's death and returned to South America on another attempt to find that city of gold; unfortunately, an attack by one of his associates on a Spanish vessel led King James to reinstate his treason sentence and have him executed.

Ironically, one of Raleigh's most dogged persecutors, Sir John Popham, ultimately the Chief Justice of England, played a key part in the first effort to colonize Maine. The area by then was considered simply "North Virginia." Two "companies" had developed from a massive royal land grant of the entire American East Coast between 34 and 45 latitude to a group of importuning nobles. This vast region, named "Virginia" at the *Virgin* Queen's insistence, was divided north and south, with some overlap. The bottom half went to the "London Company;" the top to the "Plymouth Company." The latter organization included kinsmen of Raleigh, like Sir Ferdinando Gorges and Raleigh Gilbert, son of Sir Humphrey, but they collaborated with Sir John Popham, "a rough, coarse, and brutal man," in financing several exploratory trips to New England. The names of Gosnold, Waymouth, and Pring were associated with these ventures.

Captain Bartholomew Gosnold left first, on March 25, 1602. Among his crew was another son of Sir Humphrey Gilbert's— Bartholomew. Their landfall was north of Massachusetts Bay and they next headed south, rounding Cape Cod, discovering and naming the Elizabeth Islands before finally landing on the westernmost of them, Cuttyhunk. Although Captain Gosnold carried colonists and built a small fort on Cuttyhunk, they refused to stay and were carried home to England, along with a valuable cargo of sassafras, the flavorful root from which root beer is made, but prized because it was believed to cure plague, fever, and syphilis.

Shortly after Gosnold, Captain George Waymouth departed on May 2, 1602, in the first of his two voyages to the New World. He was sent by the East India Company with instructions to find a "Passage to Cataya or China or ye backside to America." No more successful than anyone else, Waymouth was later commissioned to embark on another trip that had more momentous, if unintended, consequences than one more failed search for an Asian route.

Meanwhile, Captain Martin Pring sailed on the first of his two trips. With a pair of ships, the SPEEDWELL and the DISCOVERER, loaded with trading goods such as colorful hats, toys, beads, bells, looking glasses, and thimbles, he touched shore in Casco Bay, yet soon sailed south, seeking sassafras in and around Cape Cod, where he tangled with the local Indians, using mastiff dogs to disperse them.

Next, in 1605, Waymouth's second trip occurred. Its importance centered on the five Indians he kidnapped from the mouth of the St. George's River in Maine. Four were Wabanaki, members of the Wawenock tribe; the fifth, a visitor from southern Massachusetts. Indians had been abducted from North America before; most have left no trace. But in this case, three of the natives were sent to live with Sir Ferdinando Gorges, the other two with Sir John Popham. Once they learned some English, their wild tales of the riches of their homeland fired up the already bestirred enthusiasm of both men for colonizing this part of the world.

Two more voyages were then dispatched. Captain Henry Challons and Captain Martin Pring were to take different routes and meet near the entrance to Penobscot Bay and choose the site for a new colony. Pring made the rendezvous, carrying on board Nahanada, one of the Indians transported by Waymouth, then cruised the Maine Coast and found all the rivers and harbors he'd been told to investigate. Challons never showed. Blown off course, he'd been forced to the West Indies and seized by Spaniards at Puerto Rico. The lateness of the season finally led Pring to return to England. His favorable reports spurred Gorges and Popham to prepare another expedition, slated for 1607.

The story of the Popham Beach colony often has been told. Excavations currently conducted by the Maine State Museum continue to reveal new details of this pioneer effort, located below Sabino Head in the present-day town of Phippsburg. Led by George Popham, Sir John's nephew, and Raleigh Gilbert, the settlement effort lasted through a winter with only one death and, in the spring, relief ships appeared with fresh supplies. But the one death was that of George Popham, and the ships from England brought news that "Admiral" Raleigh Gilbert had been summoned back to succeed his deceased older brother as head of the family. Daunted by lack of leadership and fear of troubles with the local Indians, the would-be settlers evacuated the site, taking with them the ship they had built in North America, a 30-ton pinnace, the VIRGINIA.

That settlers had been in Maine even earlier was a fact they most likely didn't know. Farther north, in 1604, a French expedition had wintered over on an island in the St. Croix River. Its leader was a French Protestant nobleman, the Sieur de Monts, a close friend of King Henri IV. The second-in-command, the far more famous Samuel de Champlain, was a Catholic. At this stage of French history, cooperation between the two religions was still possible. But the harsh weather conditions and inability of the French to combat scurvy as the Indians did (by drinking tea made from hemlock needles) led to terrible casualties. Their toehold in Maine was abandoned and so was any French physical presence to the south, despite de Champlain's exploratory sails as far as Cape Cod. These first Europeans to set foot in force on what today is Maine retreated to Nova Scotia and set up headquarters at Port Royal. Why they did, passing over such attractive sites as Penobscot Bay and Portland and Boston Harbors, has never been quite explained. They kept up much of their claim of land at least to the Kennebec, but let the English take possession of everything below that river.

To the Wabanaki, only beginning to feel the intrusion of these invaders at this point, it hardly mattered. What was happening in Richmond Castle or at Durham House (Raleigh's headquarters when he was not in jail) or in the Parisian court of Henri IV or in Rome or Ireland or Madrid or the marketplaces of the Western world was an utter unknown, less imaginable even than the monsters of myth who peopled their forests.

But the first *plantations* had been attempted, the first germs spread, their "paradise" penetrated.

And a faster pace of change was imminent.

NOTES

[1]Lesley B. Cormack, *Charting an Empire, Geography at the English Universities 1580–1620*. Chicago: University of Chicago Press, 1997. Page 12.
[2]Ibid., page 62.
[3]Ibid., page 209.
[4]Ibid., page 212.
[5]Michael Drayton, from his poem "Poly-Olbion," in *Poems*.London: W. Stansby for John Smethwicke, 1619. From a 1969 reprint.

SEVEN

Earliest Settlement

IN THE SPRING OF 1605, Samuel de Champlain left St. Croix Island, after the horrendous winter the De Monts expedition had suffered, and explored southward. Somewhere on the Maine Coast, he encountered a party of Indians and was informed of a shipload of foreigners not far off who had killed five Indians. This was the first—and inaccurate—intelligence of Captain George Waymouth's infamous kidnapping episode. It has been alleged that the date Champlain departed St. Croix, June 18, was the same day Waymouth sailed treacherously away with his captives.

Those abductees came back, but not all at once. Nahanada accompanied Martin Pring on his second voyage, returning to his tribe and the status of sachem. Their chief encampment was on the Pemaquid peninsula, close to the one chosen by the Popham settlers, and with them was another of the kidnapped Mainers—Skitwarroes, who had also boarded at Sir Ferdinando Gorges's manor. He had come with the Popham group, decamped at Pemaquid, and left them without an interpreter-guide when they decided to situate elsewhere.

The most famous of the quintet was Tisquantam—better known as Squanto—and he was the unfortunate visitor from "Away" whose adventures homeward bound (kidnapped again and sold into slavery in the West Indies) kept him from Massachusetts almost until the arrival of the Pilgrims.

The other two kidnapped Indians are lost to history. They were on the ill-fated Challons voyage and, captured by the Spanish, they were most likely enslaved, too, but unlike Squanto did not somehow get to Spain, subsequently to England, and at long last to New England.

The presence in England of these native Americans as house guests of two influential noblemen has often been cited as an important catalyst for later events. Did Shakespeare meet them? It has been said that, in writing *The Tempest*, he had Cuttyhunk in mind, not Bermuda, and a clairvoyant view of what was in store for these Indians.

The Tempest had its premier performance before King James in 1611, while Raleigh and Prince Henry were still alive. Whether it was Bermuda or Cuttyhunk that inspired the Bard, the play is set on a New World island dominated by Prospero, an exiled Italian duke whose brother has usurped his position. Prospero has fled to this remote island with his daughter, and he himself, (he has magic powers) has usurped control from the original natives, symbolized by one Caliban (a Shakespearean anagram for "cannibal").

Prospero, otherwise a kindly and good man, treats Caliban with the harshness of a master who feels aggrieved that his benevolent treatment has been met with ingratitude and rebelliousness. "Thou most lying slave, whom stripes may move, not kindness! I have used thee, filth as thou art, with humane care...." One senses the latter-day imperialist, bewildered that the "white man's burden" he has assumed has been greeted with a demand to pack up and go home.

Miranda, the daughter, scolds the slave, reminds him of her "pains to make thee speak" and that before, he "wouldst gabble like a thing most brutish."

To which Caliban saucily replies: "You taught me language, and my profit on't is I know how to curse. The red plague rid you for learning me your language."

But the displaced native's greatest complaint is that he was once his own king. "This island's mine...which thou tak'st from me."

Not only did Shakespeare's insight extend into feelings exotics like Tisquantam and Skitwarroes and Nahanada might have toward the English, but he also, while providing comic relief, sets up a preview of how ordinary Englishmen might act as settlers in these new

surroundings. Thus, Trincalo, a jester, and Stephano, a drunken butler, aspire to take charge and become kings of the island, themselves,
by overthrowing Prospero. This "revolt of the masses," encouraged
by Caliban and fortified with frequent gulps of wine, ends in farce,
but in a sense presages the phenomenon of upward mobility that
overseas emigration was to mean for class-ridden societies in
Europe. Shakespeare had it right that a new dynamic was at work
in these new climes Europeans were entering, despite the fact his
play's denouement, a return to legitimacy, was meant to please such
a true believer in autocracy as James I.

The roster of those who constituted the Popham colony
exhibits the hierarchical nature of English society at the time. On
top, "Gentlemen of Quality," separated into "Council Members" and
"Other Gentlemen." The former included *Captain* George Popham,
President, and *Captain* Raleigh Gilbert; Admiral, as well as *Captain*
James Davies, Captain of the Fort; *Captain* Edward Harlow, Master of Ordnance; *Mr.* Robert Seaman, Secretary; and *Mr.* Gome
Carew, and another Raleigh and Gorges relative, as Chief Searcher
(for mines, gold, etc.). The second category of *Gentlemen* was com-
prised of the *Master* of one of the ships, the chaplain, Richard Sey-
mour, and an Edward Popham. Next in the pecking order were
"Notables," among them the doctor, whose name was Turner, and
John Hunt, draftsman, who left an amazingly accurate map of the
fort they built. Then came "Other Persons," mostly ship's officers.
Bringing up the rear was the category "Commonalty, Landsmen,
Planters." These were approximately a hundred people, ranked in a
descending order of soldiers, craftsmen, farmers, traders, and
riffraff.

The last named may be an editorial comment by Jeffrey Brain
who includes this entire listing in his monograph *The Popham Colony*.[1]
That "the gaols of England" provided candidates for colonization
was a well-known fact and Sir John Popham, in Parliament, had
been instrumental in passing legislation to make "banishment
beyond the seas" a punishment for vagrancy.

The social and economic condition of England in this period is
a study in itself, but must be touched upon for a fuller understanding of the early settlement of New England and Maine. The coun-

try, since the reign of Henry VII, had been emerging from its feudal, medieval past and nowhere was this pattern more disruptive than in the matter of landownership. Under the old manorial system, land was divided into self-sufficient estates and the lord of each, who might be anyone from a king to a bishop to a baron or any lesser noble, held title and loaned out parcels in return for services and dues. Among their tenants were some who had a manorial title to their bit of land. This was called a copyhold. In addition, there was a commons—land that was open to all in the community for various purposes. As Christopher Hill writes in his book *Liberty and the Law:*

> Traditional rights to collect fuel, fruits and berries from
> the waste, to pasture cattle and birds on the commons,
> to glean after harvest, meant the difference between a
> viable life and starvation to villagers who had no assets
> but their labor.[2]

The operative term for the method by which various powerful individuals took private control of these commons and squeezed out their traditional users is *enclosure.* For decades, if not several centuries, the process of divesting the lesser people of their property rights continued apace and its consequences, as they accumulated, were momentous. Some of the stouter yeomanry were able to hang on as tenants of the great landlords. The idea of the latter was to convert copyholds into leaseholds, with rents that were arbitrary and could be "racked" or raised at any time, without recourse to any relief. Hundreds of thousands were driven from the land, whole villages destroyed. Vagabondage increased (although punished), highwaymen infested the roads (Sir John Popham, the quintessential hanging judge, was said to have been such a mobile footpad in his youth), and innumerable candidates for overseas banishment, primarily as indentured servants, were created.

Contemporaneous with this fundamental counterrevolution in landownership was a growth of agriculture (now more efficient when done in larger consolidated areas) and industry, which had a vast pool of cheap labor to draw upon. Idleness was equated with lawlessness and ferociously counteracted. The poor were supposed to be morally obligated to work for starvation wages and never complain.

Some poets, however, voiced their woes for them. John Taylor had a stinging rebuke in verse for enclosure landlords who comported themselves like kings:

One man now in garments he doth wear
A thousand acres on his back,
Whose ancestors in former times did give
Means for a hundred people well to live
Wear a farm with shoestrings edged with gold
And spangled garters worth a copyhold:
A hose and doublet, which a lordship cost ·
A gaudy cloak (three manors' price almost)
For which the wearers are feared and abhorred.[3]

John Clark summed it up in a couplet:

Enclosure came and trampled on the grass
Of labor's rights and left the poor a slave.

Michael Drayton, who so admired Prince Henry, also entered the lists, describing a "ravenous lord" who:

Raising new fines, redoubling ancient rent,
And by the enclosure of old common land,
Racks the dear sweat from his laborer's hand,
Whilst he that digs for heath out of the stones
Cracks his stiff sinews, and consumes his bones.[4]

It was little wonder the ancient tales of Robin Hood achieved a new popularity in England during the 1600s. Game laws were another burden for the common folk. As Christopher Hill writes, "Of all the laws which the lower classes regard as contravening their liberties, the most conspicuous and the most resented were the Game Laws...."[5] Robin Hood's hold on the English imagination derived in part from a nationalistic antagonism—that of native Anglo-Saxons versus a foreign invader, the Normans. Not shooting the forest's deer, as they had in the past, was an economic hardship on the nonaristocratic inhabitants—and the revival of interest in this theme after the advent of the Stuarts was, in part, because they, too, were from Away (from Scotland) and usurped ancient hunting rights. James I's Game Laws of 1603 and 1605 started by taking away hunting rights from copyholders. The extension of the Royal Chase under Charles I took those rights even from higher gentry, who were no longer allowed to hunt on their own property. When Charles was advised his expansion of a Royal Forest into one particular parish had burdened it with poor relief for people who'd lost their grazing rights, he suggested they build a workhouse—at their own expense.

Both of the first two Stuarts were profligate monarchs who had continual problems balancing their budgets. Sales of forests and of hunting rights helped buoy their royal exchequers, but often wreaked havoc on the forests, which were cut down, and on the wildlife, which was slaughtered. Dispossessed by deforestation and Royal edict were "cottagers"—settlers in those regions, some perhaps squatters, others with limited rights lost because of legal manipulation. They sometimes rioted. King James wasted no time in alerting Parliament to their unwanted presence and he laid it on thick, telling the M.P.s such cottagers "…are breeders, nurseries, and receptacles of thieves, rogues, and beggars and other malefactors and disordered persons."

Sir John Popham died in June 1607, a little more than a week after the departure of the expedition he and Sir Ferdinando Gorges had sent to Maine. His son and heir, Sir Francis Popham, had raised most of the money for it but with the death of the father and Sir Francis's failure to recoup his losses through fishing fleets sent to New England, the task of furthering the colonization of "Northern Virginia" fell to Gorges.

On his own, Sir Ferdinando spent the next forty years after Sir John Popham's death promoting the populating of Maine.

His concept of colonization fit the style of his times and his class. The pattern had been set in England, itself, as great lords enclosed properties, turning copyholds into leaseholds and enriching themselves from the rents, and also in Ireland, where lands were taken from the Irish and granted to English favorites, like the 12,000 acres in Munster which Elizabeth gave to Sir Walter Raleigh. Gorges would do much the same in America. In a quasifeudal pecking order, where he actually became the "Lord Palatine," with rights to a *Province of Maine* only slightly less regal than those of a king, he would (for a fee) dispense *patents* to would-be settlers, and they, in turn, could sublet or simply establish their own tenants.

It was not to be a democracy. Gorges would choose who was to govern and, in some instances, these would be his relatives—a son, a cousin—and in others, agents who worked for him. Religion would be provided exclusively by the Church of England and solely strong Royalist supporters of the King's prerogative would be allowed to settle.

Or so it was supposed to work.

On July 23, 1620, Gorges's original Plymouth Company was re-chartered by King James, who issued an enormous land grant to the newly constituted Council of New England. "Northern Virginia" had a new name, thanks to the famous Captain John Smith, who had coined "New England" and publicized it in a best-selling book after his trip to Maine in 1614.

The new company had a highly distinguished set of incorporators, in addition to Gorges. It also had possession of all land between 40 and 46 degrees of northern latitude "together with the seas and islands lying within 100 miles of any part of the said coasts of the country...."

Like today's "200-mile limit," this latter stipulation bestowed exclusive fishing rights—a privilege soon to be highly contested, particularly by the other Virginia Company. The English settlers at Jamestown, who sent ships north to fish, wanted no part of paying license fees to Gorges and Co. An action of theirs in 1613, when their Captain Samuel Argall had destroyed a French settlement near Mount Desert Island, ironically had kept Maine safe for the English, in general, and the Council of New England, in particular.

In the summer of 1622, the Council of New England made a major land grant to two of its leading members: Sir Ferdinando Gorges and an ex-governor of Newfoundland, Captain John Mason. They received "all that part of ye maine [*sic*] land in New England lying upon ye seacoast" between the Merrimack River and the Sagadahoc (or lower Kennebec) "to ye furthest heads of ye said rivers" and 60 miles inland. Eventually, Gorges and Mason would divide their property, the former taking what became Maine and the latter New Hampshire.

The Council's first real paying customer was a protégé of the Duke of Buckingham named Christopher Levett. On May 5, 1623, he paid them £110 for a patent to 6,000 acres he was to choose for himself within the Council's domains. A native of the city of York in northeast England, he had proposed to Gorges and Co. to build a city in New England and call it York. Levett was not an aristocrat; his father had been an innkeeper, his mother one of the lesser gentry, and he, himself, had worked for a living—as a "King's woodward" (forest ranger) in Somersetshire, Sir Ferdinando's home county. Despite his origins and no doubt because of his loyalty, he had strong support from figures close to King James, such as Buckingham. As a result, Levett had enough men and resources to leave England by the fall of 1623.

He touched first at the Isles of Shoals, then landed in New Hampshire near the Piscataqua River. Actually, by then, the Council of New England had also sent over a governing body for its holdings, including Sir Ferdinando's son Robert as governor and lieutenant general.

Levett met Robert Gorges and was sworn in as a member of his Governor's Council. Then, he headed Down East, past Agamenticus (soon to be Gorgeana, Sir Ferdinando's capital), past Cape Porpoise, past Old Orchard Beach, and into Casco Bay.

The place where he decided to locate his settlement bore the strange name of Quack. True to his intent, Levett called it York. Some local Indians were still there, and the Englishman, who styled himself "His Majesty's Woodward of Somersetshire and one of the Council of New England" was urged to stay by Cogawesco, the sagamore of Casco. After building a house and fortification and exploring the entire region between Cape Elizabeth and Sagadahoc, Levett returned to England. He left behind ten of his men and aimed to raise more money and recruits; to that end, he wrote *A Voyage into New England*, which was published in August 1624.

Addressed to the Duke of Buckingham and other notables, it began with the wonders of his voyage—"strange fishes which we there saw, some with wings flying above the water, others with manes, ears, and heads, and chasing one another with open mouths like stone horses in a park," and ended with several chapters arguing the benefits of an investment overseas, both tangible business profits and a more intangible public good that would accrue.

Levett's encounters with the natives afforded a vivid glimpse of the relationships in this clash of cultures. And he also received an insight into the lack of control possible from the home country, due to distance, the slowness of communication, and the character of the exploiters. At Quack, Levett visited Cogawesco and found two other sagamores, plus wives and children—some fifty natives, as opposed to seven Englishmen. But it was a genial gathering, with gifts exchanged, including a beaver skin from "the great sagamore of the east country...which I thankfully received and so in great love we parted."

Traveling north to "Cape Manwagan," Levett noted nine ships fishing off it and he stayed four nights in a Wabanaki encampment, meeting sagamores of note, such as Menawormet, his old friend Cogawesco, and Somerset (maybe Samoset)—"one that hath been found very faithful to the English."

Trade, or "truck," as it was then called, was apparently already well developed. The Indians had brought beaver coats and were intending to go to Pemaquid and barter with a Mr. Withebridge, a ship master. When Levett said he would *truck* with them, they declined at first but Somerset, calling Levett his cousin, said he should have all their beaver. They traded until the Indians were left with only a coat and two skins but that night, these were stolen. Levett allowed the distraught natives to search his ship and, although the goods weren't found, the two groups departed in peace.

Commenting on his receiving permission to settle at Quack, Levett said he "was glad of this opportunity, that I had obtained the consent of them, who as I conceive hath a natural right of inheritance, as they are the sons of Noah, and therefore do think it fit to carry things very fairly without compulsion...." But at Quack, which was visited by English fishing vessels, he soon saw evidence that his fellow countrymen had different intentions not only toward the natives but toward all authority.

Referring to "an evil member in the harbor," who was unscrupulous in dealing with the Indians, Levett wrote:

And it is no wonder he should abuse me in this sort, for he hath not spared your lordships and all of the Council for New England.

This man—he was the captain of a ship—gave as his justification "that the lord had sent men over into that country with commissions; to make a prey of others," and that although the Council had forbidden him to trade "yet he would have all he could get; in despite of who should say to the contrary, having a great ship with seventeen pieces of ordnance and fifty men."

Then, in an action that did not bode well for the future, he had his men beat up Somerset and another sagamore who wouldn't trade with him. The bruised chiefs, "in a great rage…said they would be revenged on his fishermen at sea."

Before taking leave of his Indian friends, Levett ran into more cross-cultural misunderstanding. Shocked that the Englishman's wife wouldn't emigrate to Quack on her own, they told him to beat her, amazed she wasn't there to work for him. Told King James had only one wife who had died, they wondered who did all the King's work. Thus, Levett could write:

Their wives are their slaves, and do all their work; the
men will do nothing but kill beasts, fish, etc.

This was a very English misreading of Wabanaki culture, and an example of their own cultural biases intervening. For in England, hunting wasn't work; primarily, except for poachers, it was the recreation of the rich. Life didn't depend on game, the way it did for the Indians. To Europeans, this looked like "idleness" and became one of the excuses used for confiscating Indian land: *they didn't work it.*

So home went Christopher Levett, leaving behind those ten of his men who, he told his Wabanaki friends, had instructions to "kill all the Tarrantens [*sic*] they should see." He also told them to look for his ship and then send word to all the sagamores in the country "that poor Levett has come again."

Unfortunately, his reception in England was not what he hoped. The pamphlet he wrote did not produce results. Robert Gorges had come back before him with fairly discouraging reports of the Council's progress in New England. "Poor Levett" had to take a job in a naval expedition to Cadiz that ended disastrously. The King even asked the churches in the country to take up a collection on his behalf. But voluntary measures were not effective and special taxes for overseas development politically unthinkable.

Christopher Levett did return to New England, but is not recorded there until 1630. Apparently he was in Salem and seen by the Puritan leader, John Winthrop, who noted the event in his writings. On the return voyage, Levett died and was buried at sea. He had already disposed of his patent for Quack-York-Casco Bay to several merchants back in England.

That last glimpse of Christopher Levett leads to another aspect of the Council of New England's contribution to Maine settlement, albeit taking place in Massachusetts. Without the Puritans, American history can hardly be imagined as it unfolded in the northeast. They were there because of a grant from the Council of New England, which did not foresee what such action might mean. The next round of settlement would have some astonishing results.

NOTES

[1] Jeffrey Brain, *The Popham Colony*. Salem, MA: Peabody Essex Museum, 2000.

[2] Christopher Hill, *Liberty and the Law*. London: Penguin Books, 1996. Page 31.

[3] John Taylor, *Works*. 1630. Vol. I, page 32.

[4] Michael Drayton, *Poems*. London: W. Stansby for John Smethwicke, 1619. From a 1969 reprint. Page 417.

[5] Hill, page 34.

EIGHT

The Puritan Influence

PURITAN WAS INITIALLY a dirty word in England—in a political sense—much as certain American conservatives have tried to make "Liberal" instantly pejorative or as "Communist" or "Red" was before the collapse of the Soviet Union. But because politics and religion were so intertwined in the sixteenth and seventeenth centuries, calling someone a Puritan was also akin to saying he or she was a dangerous heretic.

John Whitgift, 1530–1604, has an unusual surname, but not one well known to Americans. He was the Archbishop of Canterbury—and thus the leading prelate of the Anglican Church—late in the reign of Queen Elizabeth, when congregations began questioning the institution's authority and practices. Dipping back deep into Christian history, he likened such dissidents to past challengers of Christian orthodoxy. Whitgift harped particularly on the *Cathars* in France (we call them *Albigensians*) who were wiped out in a thirteenth-century crusade. The archbishop argued:

This name Puritan is very aptly given to these men [the recalcitrants in his own church]. Not because they be pure, no more than were the heretics called Cathari; but because they think themselves to be more pure than others as Cathari did...."[1]

This similarity three centuries later of a search for purity included a rejection of the very idea of church hierarchy. In words that equaled the ferocity of the priests of the Cathars, against the pope of Rome, the blast against Archbishop Whitgift, himself, by one Martin Marprelate Senior (a pseudonym), in a secretly printed pamphlet, was absolutely vicious:

> I do protest that the entering in of this cursed man John Whitgift and of all others our bishops in England, is not an entering into the Church of God by the door Christ Jesus. Wherefore I affirm all of them to be thieves, robbers, wolves, and worriers of the flock, therefore not true shepherds.[2]

Seven issues of these pamphlets were distributed in the country, their basic point that "our church government in England by lord archbishops and bishops is a government of maimed, unnatural, and deformed members serving for no use in the church of God."[3]

Nor were these mere wars of words. Just as most of the Cathar leaders had been burned alive, Whitgift saw to it that some of the early, antihierarchical Puritan preachers he could lay his hands on were tried for sedition by the Church's High Commission Court and hanged in April 1593.

Before his death, one of them, Henry Barrow had written a book entitled *Four Causes of Separation*. Among those questioning the monopoly of the Anglican Church, a debate arose: to separate or not? Here is the distinction we Americans often fail to make between Pilgrims and Puritans. Though both factions wanted to change the structure of England's religion, the Pilgrims elected to do it from outside while the Puritans wanted to take over from within.

The small body of Separatists who fled to Holland from the village of Scrooby in Nottinghamshire have more than made their mark on history. In 1604 their minister, John Robinson, had been expelled from a parish at Norwich for "preaching." Seeing the sermon as a weapon against it, the Anglican hierarchy fought its use, preferring to saddle religious communities with pastors who performed sacraments but were otherwise "dumb dogs," as they were called behind their backs. Robinson's ideas were considered anathema. A most vexing argument of his was: to maintain the Church would suffer without bishops and archbishops, rather than stay in the hands of its congregation, was "to act in the spirit of those who

The Interrupted Forest

enclose the commons of their poorer neighbors...."[4]

Another point of contention with the established religion was observance of the Sabbath. Anglicans used it for leisure and sports, in particular, and in 1618 James I issued a "Book of Sports" and decreed it must be read aloud in every church. One reason the Scrooby exiles in Holland thought of leaving was that the Dutch did not keep Sunday sacred. Thus, when Thomas Weston, a London businessman, arrived in Leyden and told them of "sundry Honorable Lords" in the home country who had received a large royal grant in the "more northerly part" of what had been Virginia and "wholly secluded from the Virginia Company" and now "called by another name, viz. New England," they were interested.

Previously, they had experienced difficulty negotiating with the Virginia Company. The main trouble had been religion. Attempts to elicit a guarantee of tolerance from the Jamestown Anglicans had been rebuffed. Yet in the end, they sailed anyway with a patent from the Virginia Company, secured by John Peirce, one of the "Merchant Adventurers" who invested in their expedition. All along, the Pilgrims may have had in mind a bit of sleight of hand—that is, landing far north of the Virginia Company territory and applying for their patent retroactively from Gorges. In any event, this was exactly what happened.

Once again, John Peirce acted as their front man, but now with the Council of New England. His and Thomas Weston's inclusion underscores the business nature of the enterprise, as opposed to its religious purpose. Weston, a cloth merchant, initially assembled the key businessmen who backed what to them was primarily a profit-motivated venture, although some had sympathies with religious dissent.

Paying off the debt owed these gentlemen in England became the top priority of the "Plimouth Plantation." Their need for furs to sell led the settlers at New Plymouth not only to set up trading posts nearby—at Buzzards Bay and in Dutch Connecticut—but soon had them headed north to Maine.

Once their agriculture flourished, they had a surplus of corn and learned they could trade it with the northern Indians. A single trip to the Kennebec in 1625 netted them a whopping haul of beaver

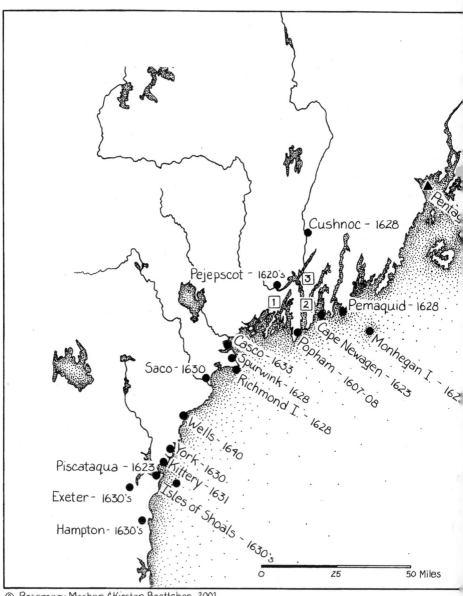

Cushnoc – 1628

Pejepscot – 1620's

Penta̶...

3

1   2

Pemaquid – 1628

Casco – 1633
Popham – 1607-08
Monhegan I. – 162...

Saco – 1630
Spurwink – 1628
Cape Newagen – 1623

Richmond I. – 1628

Wells – 1640

Piscataqua – 1623
York – 1630.
Kittery – 1631

Exeter – 1630's
Isles of Shoals – 1630's

Hampton – 1630's

0   25   50 Miles

© Rosemary Mosher & Kirsten Boettcher, 2001

Early Settlements

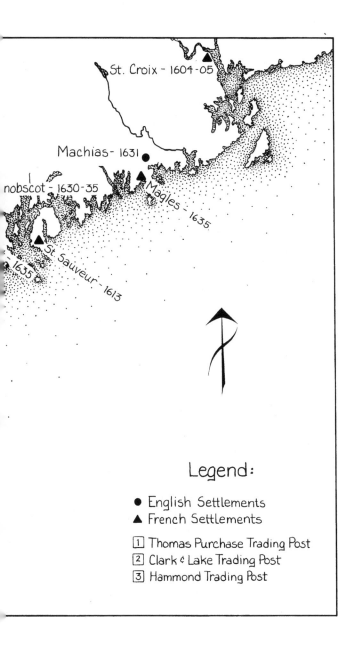

St. Croix - 1604-05

Machias- 1631

nobscot - 1630-35

Magles - 1635

St. Sauveur - 1613

1635

Legend:

● English Settlements
▲ French Settlements
1 Thomas Purchase Trading Post
2 Clark & Lake Trading Post
3 Hammond Trading Post

pelts—700 pounds. They had ascended the river as far as they could go—to the falls at Cushnoc (Augusta) and here they decided to establish a trading post. As insurance they would not be molested by "interlopers," they sent Governor William Bradford's assistant, Isaac Allerton, back to England to seek a patent for Kennebec land from the Council of New England, and he was successful! This entryway into the great Maine North Woods with its treasure-trove of fur-bearing animals, was theirs—a section of the river, 15 miles deep on either side, from an unidentified point called Nequamick to Cobbosseecontee Falls. The Pilgrims of New Plymouth intended—with armed men on site—that it was to be *exclusively* theirs.

The threat was from fellow Englishmen like Levett's sea captain, greedy for gain and willing to try to horn in. One who did was stubborn, pugnacious John Hocking, shipmaster, in the pay of a Puritan nobleman, Lord Say and Seale. With the arrogance of having an aristocrat behind him, he sailed straight to Cushnoc, anchored, and prepared to trade, himself, with the Indians. Seeing a man on shore trying to cut his anchor line, Hocking picked up a musket and shot Moses Talbot dead. Moments later, a ball fired from the riverbank felled the "interloper."

Two deaths, recorded in history as "murders," the first of non-Indians in Maine, had a wider impact than simply an isolated incident in the bush. The Puritans had just established themselves in Boston. They were not quite ready to admit they had no jurisdiction in Maine nor that a servant of Lord Say and Seale's could be slain with impunity. So they arrested John Alden of Plymouth when he happened to be in their town and held him responsible. Although he hadn't even been present at the shooting, it took a hurried visit from his friend Myles Standish to get him out of jail.

Farther Down East, at the mouth of the Penobscot River, the Pilgrims established another trading post, basically to preempt competition, this time from one of their own, Isaac Allerton, allied with London merchants. Today, we call that location Castine, but it has had other names like Pentagoët and Majabagaduce. Unfortunately for the Pilgrims, Castine remained a headache. Its first manager was Edward Ashley, described by these godly folks disapprovingly as "a very profane young man who…lived among the Indians as a savage and went naked among them and used their manners." When Ashley was discovered selling guns and ammunition to the Wabanaki, they had him arrested and shipped back to England.

So, well before the "Great Migration" of Puritans to Massachusetts had begun in 1630, their "cousins," so-to-speak, in religious nonconformity, the New Plymouth Pilgrims, had peppered New England, including Maine, with satellite outposts. John Winthrop, Sr., the Massachusetts Bay Colony's governor, complained the Separatists had taken the best places. From the Dutch in Connecticut, the Pilgrims also had learned the efficacy of *wampum* as a cheap medium of exchange. These strands of shell beads were especially prized in Maine since the *Venus mercenaria* clam that produced the purple and white material for the beads grew mostly in warmer southern waters. A pattern of economic activity, based largely on continued demand in Europe for beaver hats, had been set in motion prior to the massive Puritan influx.

A new king on the English throne and a new Archbishop of Canterbury had conspired to convince many Puritans it was prudent to leave the home country. The king was Charles I, essentially a closet Catholic, married to a Frenchwoman who practiced her papist religion within the royal palace, while he, as titular head of the Anglican Church, ruled in quintessential autocratic style. His appointment of William Laud to the top church administrative position presaged an energetic attack on Puritanism. Realizing they were unable to make their ideas prevail from inside the Church of England, the dissenters now looked to remove overseas and construct their own society. Significant numbers, from all walks of life and most regions of England, found themselves willing to depart.

The trick was to organize them. An advance guard, inspired by the Reverend John White of Dorchester, reached Cape Ann, Massachusetts, as early as 1626, and set up a "pious fishing community." It failed in less than two years. But from the experience, Reverend White helped to construct the New England Company, supported by sympathetic Puritan merchants—men with influence and deep pockets.

A King's Charter in 1629 turned the New England Company into the Massachusetts Bay Company and added special powers of governance over any settlers in the area granted by their patent, which covered from the Charles River north to the Merrimack. Already, a small Puritan group led by John Endecott had established itself at Salem.

The big boatloads that created Boston, Charlestown, Cambridge, and other settlements were about to come. Two weeks before Charles rather inexplicably gave these Puritans a real green light — their Charter — the quirky monarch had dissolved Parliament and begun the more frightening aspects of his dictatorial reign.

At the core of the Massachusetts Bay Company was a body of East Anglian Puritans whose leaders had ties to the Earl of Lincoln. John Winthrop, Sr., a squire from Groton, took charge, following a momentous decision made the night of October 20, 1629, during a secret meeting of the company at Emmanuel College, Cambridge University. It was nothing less than the birth of self-government. But to those present, who constituted the company's General Court, the vote just seemed somehow logical, rather than revolutionary. Their Charter would not rest in England; neither would their General Court. Their company would operate completely in Massachusetts.

The unintended consequences of this simple act have been well summed up by Richard S. Dunn in his book, *Puritans and Yankees,* a study of the Winthrop family. Armed with the Charter, which was physically carried across the Atlantic, the elder Winthrop "defied regulation by either Charles I or Parliament and achieved virtual independence...."[5]

This Charter, so artlessly gained from a distracted monarch, would be a bone of contention in transatlantic English politics for at least another sixty years. The Massachusetts that Winthrop and his fellow Puritans fashioned would be as far removed from English normality as could be imagined. That it loomed larger on the political scene than tiny New Plymouth was due, unsurprisingly, to its much greater size. After a dozen years, more than 24,000 Puritans had arrived in Massachusetts — a prodigious number — and their families were increasing. Their style of government was not democracy. Winthrop argued there "was no warrant in scripture for one" — but it bore seeds of greater equality. To Winthrop, they had "a mixt aristocracy." For example, their method of land distribution reverted to town governments who parceled out lots to inhabitants—lots they could own and not have to pay rent to great lords. But to vote and to participate in town government, one had to be chosen a freeman; to be a freeman, one had to be elected a church member. These members governed the church in the name of the congregation, yet were but a small minority of the inhabitants, all of whom had to attend church and pay for the upkeep of the minister and meetinghouse. Moreover, certain officials were magistrates who received more acreage in the division of land. Later, when certain Puritan-minded nobility, including Lord Say and Seale, wanted to emigrate to Connecticut, their petition was rejected; what they wanted was a real aristocracy, hereditary and feudalistic, not the mixed halfway variety invented by the Puritans.

Winthrop's biblical fundamentalism set the tone for the "godly commonwealth" converted out of a trading company. He, himself, believed God personally had selected Massachusetts Bay for their plantation and the proof was that the Indians had been swept away by illness within 300 miles of them. Their settlement was to be, in his words, "the city upon a hill," a religious beacon to the world. Church and state were to have no separation, nor was there tolerance for any other way of thinking. As they had been persecuted for their nonconformity, so, too, would they punish dissension within their ranks. A common theme was to keep these ranks together, to resist spreading into new settlements. Yet geopolitical reality immediately intervened. Winthrop's own son, John, Jr., soon had to be sent north to Agawam (Ipswich), creating a town there as a buffer against the northern Indians.

Another less noticeable feature of the Puritan migration was its preponderance of people from a particular region of England, namely East Anglia. Along with certain local customs, accents, and architecture, honed by centuries of use, the East Anglians brought with them the town meeting form of government. Selectmen, as local government officials, had long existed in East Anglia. Townspeople, called townsmen in that eastern part of England, gathered annually and voted on their municipal laws. In 1636 the Massachusetts General Court established the town in statute as the basic governing element. This action later proved invaluable when their system of granting land was legally challenged. In the words of Professor David Hackett Fisher in *Albion's Seed, Four British Folkways in America:*

> This system was unique to New England and nearly
> universal within it. It was the combined product of
> East Anglian experience, Puritan ideas, and the Amer-
> ican environment.[6]

Research has shown that landholdings in East Anglia were more egalitarian than elsewhere in England, and in Massachusetts this degree of equity was actually exceeded. A typical distribution was that of the town of Billerica, where 115 men received land by 1651, with a median holding of 60 acres. "No family was enormously rich, few were entirely landless. Tenancy was uncommon and in some towns entirely unknown," Fisher writes.

When Massachusetts moved its influence and many inhabitants north into Maine some two decades later, their East Anglian folkways were to clash and then meld with the West Country-dominated population already there. A good deal of Maine history and culture derives from this interaction, played out over several centuries. Inasmuch as the ruder, colder, wilder border country of Maine had served as a refuge for Massachusetts's own nonconformists, the first shock of the collision was all the greater.

It was a rough society in Maine, hardly godly, and characterized by adventurous fishermen who often doubled as unscrupulous traders. Tempestuous John Oldham was one of them, "a mad jack in his mood," driven from Plymouth and ultimately killed in Connecticut by Indians he had cheated. Visitors to Maine were warned not to start drinking with these types "for when wine in their guts is at full tide, they quarrel, fight, and do one another mischief, which is the conclusion of their drunken compotations."[7] The above is a quote from "An Account of Two Voyages in New England" by John Josselyn, Gent., whose brother Henry has been described as "prominent in Fernando Gorges's politics."[8] The latter had settled at Scarborough, where his literary sibling visited him. An Anglican, a Royalist, son of a nobleman, "courtly" Henry Josselyn fought off the Puritan encroachment into Maine for as long and as hard as he could.

It was on April 3, 1639, that Gorges, now seventy-two years old, received the king's charter for his very own domain in New England. Even by feudal standards, it was a large slice of land, all the way from the north bank of the Piscataqua River opposite New Hampshire to the Sagadahoc River, or where the Kennebec enters the ocean at Bath.

The old knight had been at the game of colonizing for more than a quarter of a century—with not much success. The politics had been complicated and, at times, furious. He had had a huge fight on his hands after his Council of New England gained a monopoly of fishing rights off the Maine Coast and Parliament attempted to rescind it. Only the king's shutting down of Parliament had saved this privilege for him.

Since the early 1630s, Gorges had watched with growing concern the growth of the Puritan commonwealth in Massachusetts. So he tried sabotage—having their Charter taken away by the king—but friends of the Puritans in high places, like the Earl of Warwick, were able to thwart the move. In 1635, trying a new tack, Gorges and his associates disbanded the Council of New England, so the king could reestablish his control over all New England, including New Plymouth and Massachusetts Bay. Subsequently, the king named Gorges the overall "Governor of New England," an appointment that met with implacable resistance from the Puritans. In the end, Sir Ferdinando had to be satisfied with his official Charter, or full proprietary grant, making him sole owner of the Piscataqua-Kennebec area, henceforth identified as the "Province of Maine."

What seemed at last a permanent arrangement in this corner of the New World has been aptly described by Maine historian James Phinney Baxter:

> Thus we have before us two neighboring governments
> founded upon sharply antagonistic principles: the one
> of the people, by the people and for the people; the
> other of the lord proprietor, by the lord proprietor, and
> for the lord proprietor.[9]

Sir Ferdinando became "an uncrowned monarch in a little kingdom of his own," to quote Charles Banks, the author of a two-volume history of York, the community chosen by Gorges to be his capital city. This was not the York, formerly Quack, on Casco Bay, but was the York which lies forty miles to the south, and originally was called Agamenticus and then Gorgeana. Sir Ferdinando never set foot there nor anywhere in his "Palatinate." The ship he had constructed to carry him across the Atlantic sank upon being launched, a happenstance in which the devout Puritans saw the providential hand of God. However, in 1640, he sent a cousin, Thomas Gorges, to govern his territory. Sir Ferdinando had been an indefatigable booster of Maine for many years, extolling all its features, and when Thomas Gorges reached the site where his cousin planned a cathedral city with a bishop, there was no reason for him to think Maine wouldn't someday outstrip Massachusetts. The Puritan colony had already fought its Pequot War against southern Algonquian tribes while Maine had nothing but peaceful relations with the northern Wabanaki. "Maine had larger fishing grounds, more fur pelts, and better stands of timber than Massachusetts," writes Emerson "Tad" Baker, archaeologist and historian.[10] The only problem was Maine's lack of population.

Thomas Gorges settled into a manor house built for Sir Ferdinando on the local river. This projected shire town had been inhabited since 1630. A saw mill was already operating, to take advantage of "the stately cedar, lofty pines, sturdy oaks, and walnut trees" Thomas had cited in one of his letters, and likewise, a grist mill existed to grind the wheat raised by the settlers. There were only twenty-eight households when Thomas arrived, hardly enough to staff the elaborate government Sir Ferdinando had envisioned, with a lord mayor, councilors, aldermen, sergeants of the White Rod, etc. Recent research has shown that only a minority were from the West Country. Much of England seemed represented and Thomas, who had Puritan sympathies, was not particular about whom he let live in Maine. He was quick to allow the Reverend John Wheelwright and his followers—Puritans but expelled from Massachusetts as schismatics—to have land in Wells, even though they weren't and never would be Anglicans.

His stay was brief. The Civil War in England broke out and by 1643, Thomas Gorges was back home, fighting on the opposite side from his cousin Sir Ferdinando.

In hopes of attracting more settlers, sub-grants like that to John Wheelwright continued to be made. But most were to business speculators. A huge tract of midcoast Maine, 30 square miles, was given to John Beauchamp, an original investor in the Pilgrims' venture, and Thomas Leverett of Boston. Called the "Muscongus Patent," it stretched from Pemaquid to the Penobscot and later was a source of considerable litigation. Smaller but still large grants of 12,000 acres between the Muscongus and Damariscotta Rivers went to the Bristol merchants, Robert Aldworth and Giles Elbridge. Grants of 1,500 to 2,000 acres dotted the Maine countryside at places like Scarborough, Cape Porpoise, and Cape Elizabeth (Richmond's Island).

John Winthrop, Sr., from Boston, had his eye on what was happening north of Massachusetts. Contrasting its development—or lack of same—with his own booming colony, he commented on their mode of settlement in his journal, sure the Puritan method was superior:

> Thus this and other gentlemen in England get large circuits of land, etc., in this country, and are very ready to grant them only to such as will become tenants, and to encourage them, do procure commissions, protections, etc., which cost them nothing, but will be at no charge in any right way of plantation, which should be by coming themselves or sending some of their children, etc.; but now, as they adventure little, so they are sure to lose nothing but their vain hope.[11]

More than a decade would elapse before Massachusetts would establish itself in Maine in 1652, taking over what seemed like a failed enterprise, but in turn inheriting avenues of change in its own manner of existence.

They—both types of Englishmen—would then have twenty years of peace to merge themselves before the crisis of a full-scale Indian war was upon them. Both types of Englishmen were confined in their footholds to the coast or riversides close to the sea. Had Rudy Engholm flown his plane back in time over the land from Cape Cod to Aroostook, one big woods would have been all that was seen, except for pinpricks of settlement and smoke from a few

Indian encampments. That wilderness did not look like much of a setting for all of the drama about to ensue.

NOTES

1 John Whitgift, *Works*. Cambridge, England: University Press, 1851–1853. Page 43.

2 *Theses Martinianae*, Pierce edition.

3 Ibid.

4 Christopher Hill, *Society and Puritanism in Pre-Revolutionary England*. London: Penguin Books, 1964.

5 Richard S. Dunn, *Puritans and Yankees*. Princeton, NJ: Princeton University Press, 1962.

6 David Hackett Fisher, *Albion's Seed*. New York/Oxford: Oxford University Press, 1989. Page 199.

7 John Josselyn, *An Account of Two Voyages in New England*. London: G. Widdows, 1674.

8 In the Foreword to the Massachusetts Historical Society's 1972 reprint of Josselyn's *New England Rarities Discovered*.

9 James Phinney Baxter, *Sir Ferdinando Gorges and the Province of Maine*. Boston: The Prince Society, 1890.

10 Emerson Baker, "The World of Thomas Gorges," in *American Beginnings*. Lincoln, NE: University of Nebraska Press, 1994.

11 James Kendall Hosmer, ed., *Winthrop's Journal*. New York: Charles Scribner's Sons, 1908.

NINE

Life Becomes Complicated

T HE WABANAKI TRIBES of the Northeast no doubt had scant knowledge of and little interest in the political concatenations of the Europeans who had appeared in their domains. In time, they learned to tell the difference between French and English. Whether they could distinguish between Massachusetts Bay and New Plymouth and the Province of Maine is less probable. The English were the English, and they were coming into traditional hunting grounds, cutting down trees, planting crops, building stone walls, and raising livestock. Of Roundheads and Cavaliers fighting pitched battles for control of the English homeland from 1642 to 1646, they probably knew nothing. Puritans and Royalists certainly must have looked the same to them. That Massachusetts was steadily encroaching northward, taking over New Hampshire settlements by 1643 and starting on Maine in 1652, was a historic movement beyond their ken. Their discussions of current affairs were most likely to be of the "truck houses," the trading posts they frequented, how fair were the traders, what price they got for their pelts in terms of trading goods or wampum, and what effect the foreigners and their domestic animals were having on the game they needed for survival.

Cheating the natives might seem easy, but it had consequences. "Great Walt"—otherwise Walter Bagnall—chased to Maine after the Puritans shut down the infamous "Merrymount" colony near present-day Quincy, learned the hard way. He was killed by an Indian on Richmond's Island in revenge for his abuse of them. If provoked strongly enough, the Wabanaki would strike back.

But in the first decades, once Massachusetts incorporated most of inhabited Maine, life went on placidly enough.

Originally, the Puritans had not wanted anything to do with Maine. John Winthrop, Sr., explained why, when in 1643, the northern colony had been left out of a confederation pieced together by Massachusetts with Plymouth, Connecticut, and (a separate) New Haven for military purposes. "Those of Sir Ferdinando Gorges, his province beyond Pascataquack, were not received nor called into the confederation because they ran a different course from us both in their ministry and civil administration," the Puritan leader stated in general terms. Then, he became more explicit: "...for they had lately made Accomenticus [a poor village] a corporation and had made a tailor their mayor and had entertained one Hull, an excommunicated person and very contentious, for their minister." But since 1639, the Massachusetts Bay Colony had been gradually extending its upper border northward, absorbing the four settled New Hampshire communities—Dover, Hampton, Portsmouth, and Exeter—and reaching the southern banks of the *Pascataquack* (Piscataqua) River.

This mini-imperialism of the Puritan commonwealth was, in some respects, a defensive reaction. For almost a decade, they had been under siege from forces in England, incited by enemies such as Sir Ferdinando Gorges and Archbishop William Laud. The former had failed, in 1632, to have the king's Privy Council revoke the Massachusetts Bay Charter. The latter proved a more obdurate foe. Laud, as chair of the Privy Council, began by trying in February 1634 to stop—unsuccessfully—twelve boatloads of Puritan emigrants destined for Massachusetts. Then, he demanded that Matthew Craddock, a Puritan leader, surrender the Massachusetts Bay Charter to him. Craddock replied truthfully that he didn't have it in his possession—Winthrop did, in Boston. Laud used a subcommittee at the Privy Council, "the Commission for Regulating Plantations," to sue in the Court of King's Bench to repeal the Massachusetts Bay Charter. In 1638 and 1639, Laud's lackeys made repeated demands for the return of the Charter. Defiant Massachusetts went so far as to fortify the defenses of Boston and Charlestown—against an English attack!

The outbreak of the Civil War in England put a temporary end to this threat. For all intents and purposes, the Puritans now had a free hand to do what they wished.

Earlier, the Pequot War of 1636–37 had given them a taste of expansion. Although the ostensible *casus belli* for the Puritans was several murders committed by Indians, there seem to have been other hidden agendas. Following the battle, one of the Puritan military leaders openly declared: "Thus was God pleased to smite our enemies and to give us their land for an inheritance." Richard Drinnon, author of *Facing West, Indian Hating and Empire Building*, insists upon this point, stating: "On the economic level, that is exactly what the Pequot War was about: the acquisition of Block Island and Connecticut."[1]

The climactic event of this conflict was a nighttime attack on June 5, 1637, that caught the Pequots completely by surprise. With the English were Narragansett and Mohegan allies who took part in the resulting massacre. The Pequot wigwams were put to the torch and many tribespeople, including women and children, burned to death. John Winthrop, Sr., wrote that Miantonomo, the chief of the Narragansetts, had "acknowledged that all of the Pequot country and Block Island were ours...." The Pequots were obliterated as a tribe and their name declared extinct by the Connecticut Assembly.

The next Puritan aggression was bloodless. A labored interpretation of their Charter served as the pretext. They construed the language in the document describing their northern boundary — "three English miles northward" of the Merrimack River — to mean three miles north of the source, not the mouth. This placed their border in a line between Lake Winnipesaukee and Casco Bay. Therefore, every settlement below was fair game to be added to Massachusetts. Once New Hampshire fell, the north side of the Piscataqua River beckoned and Cromwell's victory in England assured the Saints (i.e., the Puritan leaders) they would not be hindered if they advanced into Maine.

Technically speaking, by then (the early 1650s), *Maine* consisted solely of three towns: Kittery, Gorgeana, and Wells. A "loving letter and friendly" was first sent to Kittery and, at a gathering of the inhabitants, local citizens were induced to abandon their ties to Sir

Ferdinando Gorges and accept the jurisdiction of Massachusetts Bay. Similar actions occurred at Gorgeana (which was renamed York to honor a recent Cromwellian victory) and Wells. By July 5, 1653, the Saints had gained control of not only the truncated "Province of Maine," but had actually invaded the adjoining "Province of Lygonia" and snapped up Saco (with Biddeford), Cape Porpoise, and Arundel (the Kennebunks). Five years later, Scarborough, Spurwink (Cape Elizabeth), and Casco succumbed.

Although accomplished in stealthy and protracted fashion, the Massachusetts takeover was the first watershed historical event in the eventual formulation of today's Maine. For almost 170 years afterward, there was no independent legal entity called Maine. The immediate governing center was Boston, in charge of a vast, indeterminate territory that, using the Calvinistic Pilgrim-Puritan vernacular, was a "waste," a "howling wilderness." Until the American Revolution, London overtopped Boston as the mecca in which to conduct one's ultimate politicking, but the appellate relief the English capital offered was frequently tenuous and unreliable. Witness the problems of Edward Godfrey, the last governor of the "Province of Maine" when it consisted of Kittery, York, and Wells.

One of the first changes Massachusetts instituted in the towns it had conquered was how land was distributed. Less than three weeks after York capitulated, a town meeting was held which made nine grants of 100 acres each. For the average Englishman, 100 acres of arable land and 50 of pasture was a dream of riches. Historian John G. Reid in *Maine, Charles II, and Massachusetts* has stated the case that "a substantial body of the inhabitants of Kittery and Agamenticus clearly preferred Massachusetts rule, with its prospect of the release of land from the grip of the patentees."[2]

Godfrey was one of those patentees. His worst nightmare had come true. In 1651, after Kittery had been approached, Governor Godfrey sent frantic missives to London, appealing to an indifferent Parliament against the Puritan encroachment. In York, when he saw the odds against him were too great, he, too, initially agreed to accept Massachusetts rule. But when he was not allowed to keep all his land—only a house lot of 35 acres, 500 acres of river marsh, and 200 acres of upland—he went into opposition again.

Letters to the General Court in Boston were of no help. So in 1655 Godfrey went back to England seeking redress. He was soon among those, after the Restoration of Charles II, leading the charge against Massachusetts for its violation of property rights. "When the Ministers and Deputies [i.e., of Massachusetts] enter on men's estates and land as they have done...and subjugate all other Patents and make them townships"—this was an unmitigated atrocity, he argued. But Godfrey was too much of a small fry in this game of transatlantic real estate. He never ended up as the "armigerous" (coat-of-arms bearing) land baron he dreamed of becoming. Instead, he died in an English debtors' prison.

The Puritans, when they invaded Maine, had now been in the New World for a full generation. The sons had easily departed from the fathers in the question of spreading out from "the city upon the hill" and acquiring land.

John Winthrop, Jr., was a prime example. His acquisition of large Connecticut properties on former Pequot land is cited as typifying "the second generation's increasingly pronounced drive for property, which was supplanting the first settlers' religious impulse."[3]

By the third generation, all restraint was gone. John, Jr.'s sons, Wait and Fitz John, were deep into land acquisition, but none more so than his son-in-law, Richard Wharton, a "large-scale overseas trader and internal land speculator," with huge projects in Maine.

North of Casco Bay, pockets of English settlement existed, as well. The farthest reach of the Bay Colony's pretensions to owner-ship ended around the present-day Portland suburb of Falmouth, Maine. By the late 1650s, Yarmouth, Brunswick, New Meadows, Pejepscot, Boothbay, Arrowsic, Wiscasset, Damariscotta, and other places all the way to Pemaquid were variously occupied. Probably the largest landowner was Thomas Purchase. When his widow's deed was later published (she had sold her land to Richard Wharton), her holdings included all of Georgetown, Arrowsic, Phippsburg, Bath, West Bath, Brunswick, Harpswell, Topsham, Bowdoinham, Lisbon, Durham, Lewiston, and Auburn, plus parts of Freeport and Yarmouth.

The Pilgrims still had their outpost on the Kennebec. Despite the fact that fur trading at Cushnoc had diminished almost to nothing by the early 1640s, the elders in New Plymouth were not ready to cede their property, either de facto or de jure, to Massachusetts. In fact, in 1653, they applied to England for a patent to the whole Kennebec region. A year later, their request was granted and so the straggling settlements in the Sagadahoc watershed and those few along the Kennebec River came into Plymouth, not Boston, hands. In May 1654 the Pilgrims' special emissary, Thomas Prence, convened sixteen local settlers to sign an act of submission in a scene reminiscent of what had happened in Kittery and York.

The land situation in this "north country" was indeed confusing. Local Indian chiefs were also in the habit of granting territory, often in conflict with grants made overseas by England. Robinhood was a sachem whose deeds have survived, unlike those of his father Mentaurmet, who deeded the English all of his lands in the Sheepscot area. In 1639 Robinhood sold to Edward Bateman and John Brown the whole of Woolwich, or Nequasseag, between the Kennebec and Sheepscot Rivers. A recorded deed of January 20, 1652, has this same Robinhood, along with his equally colorfully named colleagues Dick Swash and Jack Pudding, granting a neck of land on the Sheepscot "from the burnt islands...to a freshet called by the English 'The Oven's Mouth'...." On June 14, 1659, another deed confirmed that Nanuddemaure sold to John Parker a six-mile parcel on the southwest side of the Sagadahoc River, but there is no indication Nanuddemaure was a sachem, with special authority to sell land. In any case, chiefs had no right to dispose of tribal land without the concurrence of the tribe, and Indian ideas of relinquishing land were different from those of the English. Permanent occupation was a foreign concept to the natives who principally felt they were selling hunting privileges.

English occupancy, if only in small patches, reached as far as the Pemaquid peninsula. There, a settlement had been established by the two absentee landlords from Bristol, Robert Aldworth and Giles Elbridge. Their man in Pemaquid was Abraham Shurt, a former Bristol businessman, who served them for nineteen years; after their deaths his accounts were questioned and he left for Boston. The Pemaquid colony, in its exposed position at the end of the English line of settlement, lived a precarious life. In 1632 it was the object of a pirate raid in which £500 worth of furs were taken by Dixie Bull, a young Englishman of good family turned buccaneer. Reputedly, he became an outlaw to recoup losses he'd suffered from French raids on the trading post at Castine. Plus, the very nearness of the French was a seemingly permanent threat, although William Bradford claimed there was often collusion between the two sides. "In truth, the English themselves have been the chiefest supporters of these French...the plantation at Pemaquid...does not only supply them with what they want, but gives them continued intelligence of all things that pass among the English...."

Such communication could be two-way, as in 1636, when Shurt advised Governor Winthrop of an impending French attempt to occupy Pemaquid. The word had come from an English captive encountered on a French fishing smack. That the invasion never took place has been attributed to two factors: the French inability to incite the Wabanaki and Shurt's adroit wooing of one of the French factions then engaged in a power struggle—the famous La Tour-D'Aulnay civil war.

Immediately past Pemaquid was a sort of no-man's-land between the two European powers. Chief Samoset of the Muscongus River area had given several grants to Englishmen, including John Brown. The French referred to Brown's house at New Harbor as *"La maison de Jean Brun qui fait la limite des terres de son Majeste d'avec celles de la Nouvelle Angleterre."* ("The house of John Brown that marks the limit of the lands of His Majesty [the French king] from those of New England.") Here, in their minds was the exact boundary between New England and Acadia.

English penetration beyond occurred, but was ephemeral. Richard Foxwell, a Massachusetts Puritan, acquired a plantation near St. George but the Boston government could not guarantee him protection and he withdrew under French pressure. Briefly in the 1650s, a pioneer settler named Philip Swadden tried living past the line. He vanished when the French took physical possession of St. George in 1656.

The two English outposts established farther Down East—the primitive "truck houses" at Castine and Machias—were subsumed, too, by the French. Once Edward Ashley was arrested and sent back to England in 1631, Thomas Willett took charge of Castine for the Plymouth colony. Under him were seven assistants and all did a brisk business trading with the Indians for furs. Then, in the summer of 1632, a French ship appeared, seemingly needing to repair leaks but actually bent on robbery. Willett was away, gone to Boston. Departing with their loot, which included Dixie Bull's valuables, the marauders told the unharmed employees to inform their boss that "some of the Isle of Ré gentlemen had been there." The Isle of Ré was a notorious haunt of privateers on the west coast of France.

For another three years, the tiny Pilgrim settlement lived a tranquil existence. But in 1635 the French came in force, took Willett's goods, and evicted the English.

Their invasion had come at the tail end of a string of events with international implications. In part, the ownership of Nova Scotia and much of Down East Maine was at stake. On September 10, 1621, James I gave the Scottish nobleman, Sir William Alexander, the Earl of Stirling, an immense grant of the Maritimes plus the nearby Maine Coast, notwithstanding a conflicting claim by King Henri IV of France years earlier. By 1628 Alexander was ready to bring Scottish settlers. Nailing down British pretensions to this land was a naval expedition the next year under Admiral David Kirke that effectively conquered "New Scotland." Soon added to Alexander's settlers were Frenchmen, led by a self-proclaimed Huguenot, Claude La Tour, who received a large property on the southern Nova Scotian coast near Cape Sable.

But Charles I had become king of England, with a French wife, Henrietta Maria, and to mollify her, he returned the whole region to France. Sir William Alexander was ordered to evacuate his Scots and "demolish the fort that was builded by your son there…to remove all the people, goods," etc., and leave "the bounds there altogether waste and unpeopled" as it was when young Alexander arrived.

The Treaty of Saint-Germain-en-Laye confirmed the French possession, which they insisted extended all the way to Pemaquid and the Kennebec. Isaac de Razilly, acting for a group of French developers, ordered the coast to be cleared of all English within their claim.

It was Razilly's chief lieutenant, Charles D'Aulnay, who led the assault on Majabagaduce, whose name was changed by the French to Pentagoët (and only much later to Castine).

The Pilgrims attempted to fight back. A Boston ship captain, Richard Girling, owner of an armed 300-ton vessel, was engaged and Myles Standish and a contingent of twenty soldiers were brought aboard for an amphibious operation. But arriving off Pentagoët, which was lightly defended, Girling refused to bring his craft close enough for a landing, content to stand offshore and fire his ship's guns until he was out of powder. This vain naval bombardment, to quote Wilbur D. Spencer in *Pioneers on Maine Rivers* , "…was the first of the kind recorded in the annals of the state, and if its object had been attained might have advanced the English development along the northern coast and changed the whole history of Maine."[4]

As for Machias, set up by Isaac Allerton to be a rival trading post to the Pilgrims, its history was brief. The claim was now made by Claude La Tour that his grant from Sir William Alexander extended to Machias; also, the so-called French Protestant was secretly acting for France. So when some Englishmen ignored his prohibition against building a station at Machias, La Tour attacked, killed three of the defenders, and as William Bradford curtly recorded, "This was the end of the project."

The defacto border between the French and the English had perforce become John Brown's house at Pemaquid. Had it remained so permanently, there obviously would be no *Maine* North Woods, as such, today.

The next several decades were fairly quiescent for the English colonists, Puritans, and others. John Winthrop, Sr., briefly embroiled Massachusetts in the fight between La Tour and D'Aulnay, backing the so-called Protestant, but this semicomic, semitragic opera was over by the early 1640s. By then, too, England's Civil War was in full flower and the Saints in Boston were left alone to expand. They went west to Springfield, south to Connecticut—which became something of a satellite—and, as we have seen, north to Maine, up to Casco Bay, at least. But in 1660, the Stuart monarchy was restored. Charles II, son of their great enemy Charles I, was on the throne. It was payback time!

That the Puritan Commonwealth survived an extremely serious assault was due to luck, stubbornness, and an opponent essentially more preoccupied with higher priorities. The enemies of Massachusetts in the mother country did all they could to foment trouble. Sir Ferdinando Gorges was dead, but his grandson of the same name was loudly demanding the return of his property. A Royal Commission containing a vehement Puritan foe, Samuel Maverick, arrived with an armed escort and, among other acts, installed a royal government in Maine. The section north of Casco Bay, referred to as Sagadahoc, was entirely separated and bestowed by the king on his brother James, the Duke of York, as the "Duke's Province" or "Cornwall County." Later, it would juridically become part of New York, recently captured from the Dutch.

The Puritans stonewalled these outsiders at every turn. When the commissioners, after a few months, sailed back to England, the Saints, with "a troop of horse and foot," simply reoccupied Maine. They released those Massachusetts partisans imprisoned under the temporary Royalist government and reestablished the status quo. Finally, to solidify their control absolutely, they cleverly bought out the Gorges family for £1,250. Charles II was furious. It had been done behind his back. But he took no further action.

If, as Puritan consciences were wont to do, they could see God's hand in every possible event, and if their insubordination to the king might be deemed a cause for divine punishment, there was ample evidence the Almighty had become wroth with them. Their greatest trial was soon at hand—one involving their very survival. King Philip's War!

NOTES

1 Richard Drinnon, *Facing West, Indian Hating and Empire Building.* New York: Schocken Books, 1980. Pages 46 and 48.
2 John G. Reid, Maine, *Charles II and Massachusetts, Governmental Relationships in Early Northern New England.* Portland, ME: Maine Historical Society, 1977.
3 Dunn, *Puritans and Yankees,* page 107.
4 Wilbur D. Spencer, *Pioneers on Maine Rivers.* Portland, ME. Page 384.

TEN

King Philip's War and Other Calamities

JOHN JOSSELYN MADE his second visit to Maine in 1663. On his earlier trip in 1638, he had described the Maine Coast from Biddeford Pool to Saco as "one scattering town of large extent, well stored with cattle, arable land, and marshes and a saw mill." A quarter of a century later, the New England he saw was flourishing far more, the grip of English settlers even on a remote corner like Maine visibly solidified. In the parts of Maine under Massachusetts authority, a Puritan "look" was emerging: less *scattering*, the homes clustered close to a spired church, a commons, a communal center.

A metaphor deeply imbedded in the Puritan mindset and often referred to by their ministers in sermons was the "Hedge." Taking this most English of boundary markers as God's form of protection—a "Hedge of Grace"—they saw the necessity of crowding together, a chosen people in a well-tended countryside, while beyond lay nothing but wilderness.

Afraid in England that their "Hedge" was disintegrating, they had fled to the New World, which was nothing but a wasteland, yet also a potential New Eden.

Therefore, they carved out their niches and placed around them the New England equivalent of the bushy, briarpatch hedgerows of the home country—the quintessential stone walls of their farmsteads. The dark forest beyond, as they imagined, was the abode of Satan and the Indians who dwelled there were his bond slaves, "trapped in the snare of the Devil." If they were paranoid— and they were—it was from the fear that Satan would combine against them not only his Indian minions but also the "Episcopals," the bishop-loving Anglicans endeavoring to destroy their church.

While John Josselyn was staying at Black Point, the settlement in Scarborough where his "only brother" Henry was the squire, he remained long enough (eight years) to witness the tug of war between the two types of Englishmen. Maine, then, in his words, had a mixed population, "some be Royalists, the rest perverse spirits..." (i.e., partisans of Massachusetts) and also a mix of "planters and fishers." Shortly after the author went home in 1673, the outbreak of King Philip's War in Maine would help blend these diverse peoples into a single unified defense.

John Josselyn had plenty of opportunity to observe and write about the local Indians. On his pages they come across as human, not as "bond slaves of Satan." They are "a tall and handsome timbered people, black-eyed, which is accounted the strongest for sight and generally black-haired...." Also "Tatarian-visaged," speaking a language he describes as "Tatar" or close to "the Turkish tongue." In his small book *New England Rarities Discovered*, focusing mostly on natural history and natural remedies of the region, he devotes a section to "A perfect Description of an Indian Squa [*sic*] in all her Bravery...." Indian men, he says, are somewhat horse-faced, "but the women, many of them, have very good features, seldom without a *Come to me*...in their countenances...broad-breasted, handsome straight bodies and slender"—although he says, too, "plump as partridges."

That John Josselyn was physically attracted to these Indian maidens seems evident. That he shared at least some of his countrymen's scorn for native people is plain, as well. They may not be "bond slaves of Satan," but he likens them to the Irish, whom the English considered savages. Echoes of Shakespeare's Caliban reverberate when Josselyn accuses the Wabanaki of cannibalism, as "were formerly the heathen Irish." He records the cruelty of Indian to Indian in the graphic description of two captive Mohawks tortured to death, but also dwells on the evils rum trading by both English and French have caused. King Philip is mentioned, but only in the context of adorning himself with wampum on a trip to Boston.

King Philip, of course, was not this Wampanoag Indian

leader's real name. He was Metacom, son of the Pilgrims' friend Massasoit. Why he went to war in July 1675 has been the subject of fierce polemical discussion for hundreds of years. Was he justifiably goaded or was he of "a subtle and mutinous temper?"

Indians weren't blind. They could see the changes the white men were bringing to their way of life. A predecessor of Metacom's, and a neighbor, the Narragansett chieftain Miantonomo, had said as early as 1642:

> ...our fathers had plenty of deer and skins, our plains
> were full of deer, as also our woods, and of turkeys,
> and our coves full of fish and fowl. But these English
> have gotten our land, they with scythes cut down the
> grass and with axes fell the trees; their cows and horses
> eat the grass, and their hogs spoil our clambanks, and
> we shall all be starved.[1]

William Cronon, who reports this speech in his ecological study of colonial New England, *Changes in the Land*, sees Miantonomo as a pioneer pan-Indian leader, preaching unity against the white man. "For so are we all Indians as the English are...so must we be one as they are, otherwise we shall all be gone shortly," Cronon quotes him as saying. In addition, he proposed they kill all the English "men, women, and children but no cows," and then use the bovines as food "till our deer be increased again."

These statements bear reexamination in the light of facts presented by Francis Jennings in his *The Invasion of America: Indians, Colonialism and the Cant of Conquest*.[2] As the title suggests, Jennings takes a strongly pro-Indian tack. For example, he insists that in Indian warfare, prior to the "invasion," women and children were never killed and that the English commenced this style of total warfare during the Pequot War, in which Miantonomo played a role, but as an ally of the white man. Therefore, Jennings's theme is that the Indians had no intention of uniting against the English and all of their hostilities were predicated upon defending their own shrinking pockets of turf. He labels King Philip's War the "Second Puritan Conquest," the first having been the Pequot War. He maintains "the first mobilizations and first attacks were made by the Puritans."[3] King Philip's War could not have been a *war of extermination* between two races because of the Indians, since the Mohegans and the Mohawks fought alongside the English.

As for the goals of the combatants, the Indians never for a moment aspired to drive out all the English or hoped for mastery over them. Their purpose was to salvage some measure of self-government in secure territory.[4]

Both "King Philip's War" and the "Second Puritan Conquest" are pejorative terms, intended to prove a propaganda point. The argument over whose land this America is continues on to this day in sotto voce fashion, although the issue seemingly was settled long ago. By 1675, the year the conflagration burst forth, the Puritans had obviously burst far beyond their "Hedge." The lust for land beyond what a man could cultivate had taken hold. It was resisted in New England, "where the founders feared the rampant power of land wealth," and in Massachusetts between 1631 and 1656, only 100 large grants were made and few were as large as 3,000 acres, but that ethic was breaking down. Ten years after King Philip's War, Richard Wharton would own a quarter of a million acres in Maine.

The logic in regard to Indian possession was implacable and self-evident. As Douglas Edward Leach writes:

To English husbandmen, who thought of land in terms of well-tended farms, it was preposterous to suggest that valid titles to thousand of acres of unimproved wilderness rested in the hands of mere roving savages.[5]

That some lingering doubt, however, may have troubled the minds of settlers then is aptly expressed in a novel of King Philip's War with the following dialogue between a mother and daughter during an Indian attack on their homestead.

"Surely, we are here rightfully," says the daughter. "I have heard my father say that when the Lord made me a present to his arms, our valley was a tangled forest, and that much toil only has made it as it is."

"I hope that what we enjoy we enjoy rightfully," says the mother. "And yet it seemeth that the savage is ready to deny our claims."

"And where do these bloody enemies dwell? Have they, too,

valleys like this, and do the Christians break into them to shed blood in the night?"

"They are of wild and fierce habits, Ruth, and little do they know of our manner of life...."

The stilted dialogue may have identified the author of these lines as James Fenimore Cooper. The work is an obscure one from the pen of this prolific writer, among our first to delve into Americana as a subject for fiction, and its odd, cryptic title is *The Wept of Wish-Ton-Wish*.

Cooper was the son of one of the largest land speculators in pre-Revolutionary America, William Cooper, founder of Cooperstown, New York. In the *Wish-Ton-Wish* epic ("wish-ton-wish," says Cooper, is local Indian for "whippoorwill") he is describing Puritan-origined pioneers 150 years earlier in the Connecticut wilderness as they battle the natives.

Metacom appears in Cooper's story, a sinister but magnificent figure. In line with Josselyn's description of his fondness for wearing wampum, he has a "gay belt" of the shellfish jewelry wrapped around "his head in the form of a turban." His harangue to a group of captured English touches on his motivation for going to war, and at the bottom of it all *is* the land question:

> Why hath the Great Spirit made thy race like hungry wolves?... Why is the mind of a Yengheese so big that it must hold all that lies between the rising and setting sun?... We have taken up the hatchet, that the land which the Great Spirit hath given might still be ours.... We listen to hear in what manner the hunting-grounds of the Indians have become the ploughed fields of the Yengheese.... Why have the people of the Yengheese lost themselves on a blind path? If the country they have left is pleasant, cannot their God hear them from the wigwams of their fathers?... Now what the Great Spirit hath made for a red man, a red man should keep. They whose skins are like the light of the morning, should go back toward the rising sun, out of which they have come to do us wrong.

The reply of the spokesman for the colonists, lame and

abstract as it might seem, was still the heartfelt justification these New Englanders gave for their presence in America. "God hath otherwise decreed," the Englishman answered. "He hath led his servants hither, that the incense of praise may arise from the wilderness."

While Francis Jennings may attribute sheer calculated imperialism to the Puritans' battles with Philip, it could equally be argued they were religiously brainwashed. Cotton Mather, the famed Boston minister, put forth a dogma in his masterwork "Magnalia Christi Americana" and as paraphrased by Barrett Wendell, who wrote a biography of the Puritan priest, it is as follows:

> In the view of the Puritans, the Indians were the wretched remnant of a race seduced to the Western Hemisphere by the Devil himself that he might rule them undisturbed by the rising light of the Gospel. The landing of the Pilgrims was an invasion of the Devil's own territory.... The outbreak of the Indian was his natural retort; every arrow, every bullet, every war-song and magic chant, of the expiring natives of New England was a missile armed by Satan himself against the power of Christ. The laity met the attack with gunpowder; the clergy were no less active with prayer. To which should be attributed the final victory—a victory not so much over Philip and his followers as over Philip's satanic master....[6]

The conflagration about to engulf almost all of New England began as an incident in Plymouth—a murder, to be exact. The victim was John Sassamon, a Christian Indian with some Harvard training, who also happened to be King Philip's interpreter and confidant. Allegedly, he was killed because he was on the verge of betraying Philip's battle plans to the English. Three fellow Wampanoags were seized as his murderers. The superstitious mind of the Puritans is well revealed by Cotton Mather's description that Sassamon's corpse gushed forth blood when touched by one of the accused, a sure sign of guilt, and that the plot was thus revealed. Conventional wisdom holds that Philip went to war only after the kangaroo court-type trial and grisly execution of his men, hostilities he began with a fierce attack on Swansea, a Pilgrim satellite community whose installment on his territory the Wampanoag chief had vainly resisted.

Plymouth's alliance with Massachusetts, Connecticut, and New Haven soon brought in those colonies, plus their Indian allies, while Philip enlisted other tribes to join his own, in particular the Narragansetts, and later several of the Wabanaki groups in Maine.

Francis Jennings describes the opening gun differently: Plymouth turning down a mediation effort by the deputy governor of Rhode Island and the death of an Indian on Aquidneck Island for which the natives exacted revenge. But the final outcome was probably never in doubt. Although Philip was even able to take the war into New York, almost as far as Albany, he failed against superior forces (including the Mohawks), was hunted down back in his own territory, and ultimately killed. The toll was grim: by October 1676, the colonists had suffered losses of 600 men, £150,000 in expenditures, 1,200 houses burned, and 8,000 head of cattle killed versus 3,000 Indians dead—and the battle still raged in Maine.

Refugees from southern tribes such as the Wampanoags and Narragansetts fled north and individuals among them took part in some of the Maine fighting. Yet nothing might have happened above the Piscataqua had not a sort of "last straw" for the natives occurred. This was the famous tragedy along the banks of the Saco River, fomented by a bunch of drunken English sailors. These boozing tars were determined to test a bizarre theory: that Indian babies instinctively could swim from birth. They upset the passing canoe of an Indian mother and child. The babe sank. Retrieved, he died nevertheless. *He* was the son of Squando, the local Sokoki chief. Thus, three months after Metacom went on the warpath, Maine was afire.

Typical of the English myopia of how their actions impinged upon the natives was a statement from the Reverend William Hubbard regarding the sailors' horrendous act. Blithely, the Puritan cleric dismissed it as "some little color or pretense of injury" and "...only an occasion to vent the mischief they formerly had conceived in their hearts," before adding: "Surely, if their hearts had not been secretly filled with malice and revenge before, they might have obtained satisfaction for the wrong done."

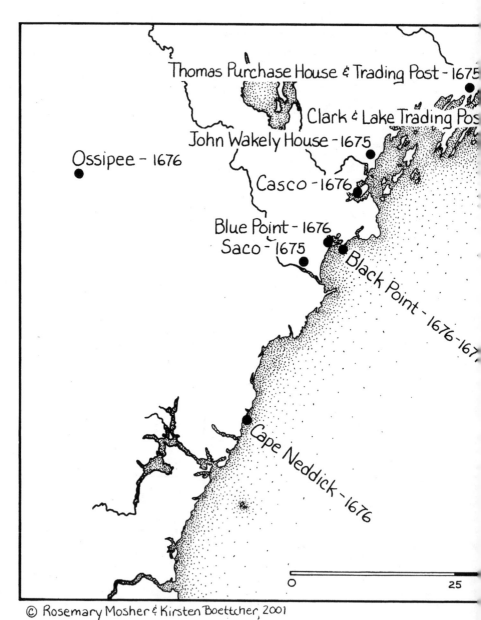

Thomas Purchase House & Trading Post - 1675

Clark & Lake Trading Post

John Wakely House - 1675

Ossipee - 1676

Casco - 1676

Blue Point - 1676

Saco - 1675

Black Point - 1676-167

Cape Neddick - 1676

25

© Rosemary Mosher & Kirsten Boettcher, 2001

King Philip's War—Major Attacks in Maine

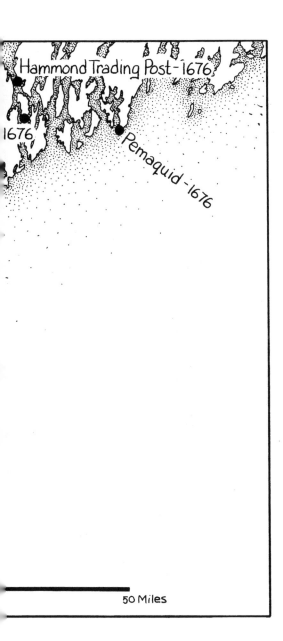

Hammond Trading Post - 1676

1676

Pemaquid - 1676

50 Miles

145

Yet Hubbard, with a dash of double-think, was able to condemn "those scattering plantations in our borders," such as on the Maine frontier, where the inhabitants, resistant to Boston officials and clergy, existed almost in "the manners of the Indians they lived amongst." Their lawlessness and mistreatment of those Indians were the tinder a spark like the senseless death of Squando's son could ignite.

Initially, it was the Sokokis (Sacos) and the Androscoggins who went to war in Maine. The Kennebecs and the Penobscots did not join in until negotiations with Massachusetts broke down. A key element here was the English refusal to sell the more northern tribes powder and shot for their guns, on which they'd become dependent for hunting. The English made it plain they didn't trust *any* Abenakis and also declined responsibility for *any* English who had harmed them. Consequently, during the summer and fall of 1676, on a broad sweep from Pemaquid in the north to the Piscataqua River in the south, all of what was then Maine fell under attack.

Fighting flared at Pejepscot, at Falmouth (where seven members of one family were slain), at Saco, at Scarborough, at South Berwick, at Cape Neddick (part of York), and at Biddeford Pool, etc. The day before King Philip was slain in the swamps of Rhode Island, a Wampanoag named Simon led a raid on Casco Bay, and the next day Richard Hammond's trading post at the mouth of the Kennebec was torched, Hammond killed, and sixteen of his people made prisoner. Then, the same war party destroyed the Clarke and Lake Company garrison at Arrowsic, and Thomas Lake, its founder, lost his life. The whole of the Sagadahoc region was soon abandoned by the English, and assaults continued in the Scarborough area, especially at Black Point, where the Kennebec chief Mogg captured Henry Josselyn. A year later, Mogg was shot to death in another battle at Black Point.

Not until yet another year of warfare passed was a treaty signed to halt the bloodshed. The damage to the north country had been devastating. If there were the slightest bright side, it was that much of the internal friction—the dichotomy between Massachusetts newcomers and original Mainers—seemed ended. The Bay Colony, which had sent troops to help drive off the Indians, was now an important bulwark against exterior threats. And such were not long in coming—from the French and from their own government in England!

The year 1677 saw the provincial government in New York take possession of Sagadahoc, which now, by Royal fiat, was under its jurisdiction. Theoretically, this immense territory stretched from the Kennebec to the St. Croix—a vast wilderness, much of which was also claimed by France. In August 1677, New York Governor Sir Edmund Andros signed a separate peace treaty with the Wabanaki and persuaded the Indians to stop all of their hostilities in the Duke of York's province. An aristocrat from the Channel Islands, Andros had landed in America three years earlier to receive New York back from the Dutch and, arriving with him had been a company of English soldiers—the first "regulars" to be sent over—an ominous sign the home government was determined to take more control of the colonies. The haughty, overbearing yet capable Andros soon proved a far greater threat to landholding and property rights in New England than either King Philip or Count Frontenac, the formidable French leader in Canada.

Another peace treaty, in 1678, signed by Massachusetts and the Maine Indians, was a patchwork affair satisfying no one. The Wabanaki recognized English property rights and the Puritans admitted an underlying Indian sovereignty in Maine by agreeing to pay an annual quit-rent to the tribes of a peck of corn for each settled English family.

Tensions, though, continued to mount: the quit-rent wasn't paid; settlers blocked migrating fish with their nets; English cattle repeatedly trampled the Indians' unfenced fields—and so yet another treaty was signed—with the Pennacooks, Sacos, Androscoggins, and Kennebecs in 1685. It was no more successful than the others.

Farther north, tribes like the Penobscots felt the pressure of the encroaching English. Expressing it well is a fictional excerpt from the Wabanaki resource book, postulating "A Penobscot Boy's Thoughts: 1685." In the story, he and his father are forced to travel to Pemaquid to trade their furs with the English since Baron de Castin, the Frenchman in charge at Pentagoët, has no goods to offer them:

As we paddled out into the ocean, I glanced back at the English village. My father noticed this and spoke to me. He said that when he was a boy, it had been a good place. It had been possible to live well there right through the summer. But even the good English, he said, ruin the land, so that we cannot use it anymore. The game leave. When we share with them, he said, the land becomes useless to us.[7]

The next tale in the resource book is entitled: "English Cousins Have a Talk in Pemaquid: 1685." Cousin Jonathan has come from Boston to visit Cousin Miles. Several themes emerge from their discussion. First and foremost, what to do about the Indians. Their mere presence, Jonathan says, is a temptation to the "worst sort of English, who covet their land and furs...." But his solution is chilling: "It may be best to get rid of the Indians, so that the temptation is gone. In Massachusetts, we killed most of the Indians and the rest we forced to submit to our will. I think the same thing will have to be done here." Then, there is the question of confused property rights. Miles explains about the deed from Samoset to John Brown of the entire Pemaquid peninsula and how it conflicts with the Council of Plymouth's grant of the same acreage to Aldworth and Elbridge and how both conflict with the land given the Duke of York. Jonathan predicts the original John Brown purchase, on which the local settlers base *their* ownership, will never "stand up against the deeds of the Council or the King."

With the advent in 1686 of Sir Edmund Andros to the governorship of the "Dominion of New England," the possibility of such dispossession became very real—nowhere more so than in Massachusetts. The Bay Colony had finally seen its hallowed Charter taken away by legal action in England in 1684. When the Duke of York became James II, this crypto-Catholic authoritarian tightened his rule both on the home country and overseas. The unruly provinces from Sagadahoc to Delaware were arbitrarily thrust into a single government and Andros put at its head. A whole flood of Royalist carpetbaggers, exemplified by men like Edward Randolph, now came to the fore, expecting jobs and land—and land to be held in the manner intended by Sir Ferdinando Gorges: greater and lesser lords and under them, tenants paying quit-rents. Andros declared all land titles in Puritan-controlled areas like Massachusetts and Connecticut were invalid, since they had been conferred by *towns* — and there was no provision in English law for towns; therefore, they had no authority to disburse land. And Indian deeds were invalid, too. All property owners must now reregister their estates, pay fees, and receive them back on a tenancy basis. Among the sullenly rebellious Yankees, not many came forward.

When James II's own tyranny and ever more open Catholicism became too much for the English people and he was overthrown in the Glorious Revolution of 1689, the rebellion in New England turned violent. It was like a dress rehearsal for the events of 1775. A "Committee of Safety" directed the uprising in Boston that jailed Randolph and his fellow placemen and ultimately Governor Andros, himself. They were all shipped back to England to await the pleasure of the indisputably Protestant William and Mary who had been placed on the British throne.

In terms of landownership and the assurance of property rights, which the economist Mancur Olson sees as the absolute prerequisite for democracy, the Glorious Revolution was a seminal event, both in England and America. "The democracy established by the U.S. Constitution was influenced by the political settlement in Britain in the Glorious Revolution of 1688–89," Olson writes in his book *Power and Prosperity*.[8] Through the efforts of this bloodless revolt against the Stuarts, an independent judiciary, a bill of Rights, and a carefully constrained monarchy were put in place so that Englishmen, in Olson's words, "came to have a relatively high degree of confidence that any contracts they entered into would be impartially enforced and that property rights, even for critics of the government, were relatively secure."[9] So at home, so overseas. Landowners in Massachusetts and Maine and all over America need not fear another Andros or Randolph appearing and jeopardizing their titles.

Yet there were still dire threats hanging over Maine settlers.

As one of his last official acts, Governor Andros had led an expedition Down East into Acadian territory he claimed was English and ransacked St. Castin's property at Pentagoët. Because this French ex-soldier and future baron was married to the daughter of

Madockawando, chief of the Penobscots, the event triggered a reprisal raid on Pemaquid. Andros's overthrow by the colonists, when it became known to Madockawando, offered a perfect opportunity to strike now that "the land was in confusion." In August 1689, the Penobscot chieftain and his son-in-law spearheaded the attack on Pemaquid, destroyed its fort, killed most of the garrison, captured others, and left a mocking message:

> Sir Edmund Andros is a great rogue and nearly starved us last winter, but he is now a prisoner and we do not care for New England people. We will have all their country by and by.

NOTES

1 William Cronon, *Changes in the Land*. New York: Halland Wang, 1983. Page 162.
2 Francis Jennings, *The Invasion of America: Indians, Colonialism, and the Cant of Conquest*. Chapel Hill, NC: Institute of Early American History and Culture, University of North Carolina, 1975.
3 Ibid., page 299.
4 Ibid., page 30.
5 Douglas Edward Leach, *The Northern Colonial Frontier, 1607–1763*. New York: Holt, Rhinehart and Winston, 1966. Page 39.
6 Barrett Wendell, *Cotton Mather, The Puritan Priest*. New York: Harcourt Brace and World, Inc., 1963 (first published 1891). Page 21.
7 *Wabanakis*, page C-38.
8 Mancur Olson, *Power and Prosperity: Outgrowing Communist and Capitalist Dictatorships*. New York: Basic Books, 2000. Page 36.
9 Ibid., page 37.

ELEVEN

War, War, and Some Peace

A FAULT-LINE WAR is a term Harvard professor Samuel P. Huntington either invented or co-opted in his study, *The Clash of Civilizations*. Writing about the post Cold War world, he zeroes in on conflicts between cultures—dire, protracted battles that can last for decades. The seventeenth- and eighteenth-century warfare between Europeans and Indians in Maine certainly fits this category.

Huntington's criteria include:

> Fault-line conflicts are communal conflicts between states or groups from different civilizations.... Fault-line conflicts sometimes are struggles for control over people. More frequently the issue is control of territory.... Fault-line wars are off-again, on-again, wars that can flare up into massive violence and then sputter down into low-intensity warfare or sullen hostility only to flare up once again.... Fault-line wars are almost always between peoples of different religions.[1]

These fault-line wars, he also warns, can bring additional partners into the fight.

The colonial wars that wracked eastern America and Canada from 1689–1762 played a critical role in determining the ultimate future of Maine. At their core was the land hunger of the English. The independence of the Wabanaki tribes, which meant the natives would control the land, could not long be tolerated. Moreover, *they* were the "Heathen," instruments of Satan, believers in pagan gods. Christianize them? Why, they couldn't be trusted, and in King Philip's War, the Reverend John Eliot's Protestant converts were

deported en masse from Natick to a concentration camp on Deer Island in Boston Harbor, held for several years, and their land in Natick taken away. Worse still, the French were converting the Maine Indians to Catholicism.

It was during the first of these new wars, following King Philip's, that the French entered the picture in full force. Four wars were structured enough to be given actual names and usually invoked formal declarations by the belligerent governments in Europe.

King William's War led off, named for the Dutch monarch who took England's throne from James II. It started in 1689 and was ended in 1697 by the Treaty of Ryswick.

Queen Anne's War followed in 1703 and the Treaty of Utrecht put an end to it in 1713. Anne was James II's daughter and Mary's sister, but an avowed Protestant.

King George's War erupted after a hiatus of more than three decades. In the interim, numerous irregular battles were fought in New England (sometimes referred to collectively as *Governor Dummer's War*), several of which broke the power of the Wabanakis in southern and western Maine. King George's War, itself, began in May 1744 and was concluded at Aix-la-Chapelle (Aachen, Germany) in 1748.

Finally, after continued sporadic warfare, there was the *French and Indian War*. It lasted from 1756 until 1762 and was capped by the culminating Treaty of Paris of 1763 that ousted the French from Canada.

Had the French won (and it was not preordained they would lose), the hold of the Indians on their lands might have been equally loosened, but gradually, not as brutally and rapidly as under the English. The French settled land, too, but in a different mode from most of the English. Large grants were made by the king to *seigneurs* —people of importance—and they populated their *seigneuries* with tenant farmers called *habitants*. The size of these seigneuries were enormous, the average at least a dozen square miles and some of 100 square miles. The system mimicked the feudal laws of France—annual rents in money or in produce or in work done for the seigneur. As in La Patrie, the seigneur's manor and the parish church formed the heart of the community, and for the habitants, life seemed little different from their peasant existence in France, yet actually not as harsh. Despite this fact and that certain of the French immigrants, like the *coureurs de bois*, led wild and free lives, there was no great rush to Canada and Acadia. In 1689 their combined numbers were around 13,000, and by 1715 had not even doubled to 25,000. The rival English, in the same period, had just doubled their collective population—but the figures were from 200,000 to 400,000.

The elegant diplomats sent to parley in those Dutch cities of Ryswick and Utrecht, or who drove through the cobblestoned streets of Aachen and Paris, had scant knowledge of the colonies whose fates they were deciding. To them, these were mere pawns on an international chessboard. Acadia, for instance, was exchanged back and forth nine times between Britain and France. Admittedly, Acadia's borders were vague, comprising Nova Scotia, New Brunswick, and big chunks of northern and eastern Maine. At Utrecht in 1713, the British finally took Nova Scotia for good (including New Brunswick and Newfoundland) while the French held onto Cape Breton Island and still maintained their Down East claim all the way to the Kennebec River.

A counterclaim against France arose out of political events in England, as the new William and Mary government grappled with the problem of establishing a status for the ever-troublesome colony of Massachusetts Bay. Another Royal Charter replaced the one abrogated in 1684 and defined the commonwealth's jurisdiction seemingly once and forever: it added Plymouth and Maine to the Puritans' other existing territories. The hated Dominion of New England was dissolved, and Sagadahoc, that no-man's-land from the Kennebec to the St. Croix, was removed from New York and made part of Massachusetts. Indeed, the Bay Colony's boundaries now included "the country or territory commonly called Acadia or Nova Scotia."

Ironically, the Massachusetts General Court had once considered selling Maine, practically as soon as they'd bought it from the heirs of Sir Ferdinando Gorges. A majority of the legislators thought "it should be sold again to the highest bidder toward reimbursing the expense of defending it, which they computed at £8,000...."[2] The lawmakers in Boston voted to have a committee undertake the sale, then reconsidered the action. Several decades later, the responsibility of *protecting* Maine was totally theirs juridically.

The person most responsible for the new Massachusetts Charter was the Reverend Increase Mather, the father of Cotton Mather. As pastor of Boston's Second Church, Increase Mather had fought against Governor Andros until, in the middle of the night, he'd had to flee to England to avoid arrest. The "Glorious Revolution" gave him a chance to lobby hard in London for a replacement of the old Charter on favorable terms and he mostly succeeded, although some critics carped at the provision for the king to appoint their royal governor, instead of allowing a popular election, as before.

However, the elder Mather was able to influence the initial choice. It was a man his son Cotton had actually baptized after a later-life conversion, a Maine man, born and raised on the northern frontier, a fighting man: Sir William Phips.

This rough-hewn native of Woolwich was no aristocrat. His knighthood had been earned when he'd located and salvaged a sunken Spanish treasure ship in the Caribbean, north of today's Dominican Republic, and shared his loot with the monarchy. The events of 1689—the overthrow of Andros and the devastating French-Wabanaki attack on Pemaquid—found Phips in Boston and, in March 1690, he agreed to head up a planned counterstroke to capture the French headquarters in Acadia—Port Royal.

Phips had, so to speak, "beginner's luck." His first command was his most successful. A lightly defended Port Royal surrendered without firing a shot in May 1690. The Protestant English forces "cut down the cross, rifled the church, pulled down the high altar, breaking their images...." and plundered the town before returning to Boston. It was a cheap victory and Phips's reputation profited, but militarily it had no effect. Less than two weeks later, Wabanaki and French forces destroyed Fort Loyal in present-day downtown Portland. By the second week in June, the Massachusetts General Court ordered an expedition against Quebec and made Phips its obvious commander. This ambitious attack, involving more than 2,300 New Englanders, accomplished between August and November 1690, turned out to be an unmitigated disaster.

Yet William Phips continued to be lucky. His apologists, Increase and Cotton Mather, convinced their fellow Puritans that God's displeasure with their worldliness had caused the fiasco, not Phips's poor leadership. Consequently, Increase Mather was able in London to secure a political plum for his Maine-born protégé.

As chief executive, Phips had his hands full. The war with the French and Indians continued, emptying the Massachusetts treasury. His native Maine was all but deserted—nobody English left north of Wells, while adjoining York was utterly destroyed in the "Massacre" of January 1692. The Salem witchcraft trials craze had erupted, fanned by his friend Cotton Mather. Plus Phips had lots of enemies in Boston, put off by his ill-bred manners and humble origin, his mistakes in Canada, and the fact he hadn't been elected.

Phips was convinced that the future of Massachusetts lay to the northeast, in Maine and Nova Scotia. The region's furs, its timber, and its available land were resources he constantly touted to the English government—and he had no compunction about exploiting them, himself. In 1693 he convinced Madockawando to sign a peace treaty. It was a diplomatic coup, in that the Penobscot sachem and his allies—Kennebecs, Androscoggins, and Sacos—acknowledged "obedience unto the Crown of England on behalf of all Indians… from the Merrimack River to the most easterly bounds of Massachusetts…." In addition, regarding land, the English were to enjoy "all and singular their rights of land and former settlements and possessions."

This treaty was signed at Pemaquid, which Phips had restored to English control and where he was building a massive stone fort, not the usual wooden blockhouse. While there in person, the governor also made a private deal with Madockawando, buying thousands of acres from him in the St. George River area. In return, Phips allegedly gave the Penobscot chief a large number of silver coins and elaborately entertained him aboard his flagship in Pemaquid Harbor. Phips next petitioned his friend William Blathwayt, the powerful secretary of the Lords of Trade in London, to give him an exclusive monopoly of the fur trade from "Saco eastward to the utmost bounds of Massachusetts," citing in part his need to make up financial losses suffered at Woolwich during King Philip's War.

Years afterward, following Phips's death, his adopted son Spencer Phips swapped Madockawando's deed for a 10 percent interest in the famous Muscongus Patent, which originally had been granted the same land.

The governor's self-seeking soon brought scathing complaints. Nor did the Indian raids cease, as a faction led by the warlike Chief Taxous of the Kennebecs stirred resistance. Other outrageous actions by Phips—such as physically beating up officials who disagreed with him, were likewise reported to London. He was recalled to the home country to explain himself and died shortly after his arrival. Although always controversial, Sir William Phips handled the transition from the Dominion government to a more self-governing Massachusetts with a strong sympathy for protecting rights previously threatened. He approved laws affirming freedom from arbitrary imprisonment and, most importantly, where land was concerned, backed a measure giving uncontested ownership to any tracts in a settler's possession for three years.

King William's War ended with the Treaty of Ryswick in 1697. But only a brief truce resulted. Five years later, Queen Anne's War commenced.

Out of a quarter of a century of warfare, dating back to King Philip's time, the Northeast colonials had come to several interlinked conclusions. Implicit was the idea the Indians had to be subdued, if not entirely eliminated. Explicit was the voiced opinion the French had to be driven from the continent, for it was the French, the English believed, who were stirring up the natives.

Several of the major incidents during these next eleven years of hostilities were offensive thrusts against Canada. In 1704 Colonel Benjamin Church, the renowned Indian fighter whose forces had killed King Philip, was sent to capture Port Royal. Now sixty-five years old and so fat he had to be pushed up hills by his men, Church mostly caused troubles for the Indians, burned Grand Pré, and did not even try to take Port Royal. But six years later, a much more serious expedition did. Colonel Francis Nicholson was brought from New York and given command of a mixed force of New England colonials and British marines. Port Royal surrendered to him without a fight. Then, Nicholson was assigned to a far more ambitious project—the reduction of Canada, itself. He was ordered to attack Montreal, while an amphibious operation sailed up the St. Lawrence and attacked Quebec. Unfortunately, this latter task force ran into bad weather. Eight of its transports foundered on the rocks with a loss of almost 1,000 men, and Admiral Hovenden Walker lost his nerve and retreated.

The peace treaty at Utrecht in 1713, however, salvaged something for the English. This time, Acadia was not given back to the enemy. England's claim to the Nova Scotian mainland, plus Newfoundland and Hudson's Bay, was recognized. Yet the French were allowed to keep Cape Breton Island, which commanded the entrance to the St. Lawrence. The fortress they built at Louisbourg became a serious problem for the New Englanders. And the status of the Maine portion of Acadia remained undetermined, whether English, French, or Wabanaki.

The English signed their own treaty with the Indians in the same year, meeting at Piscataqua (Portsmouth, New Hampshire). While the Indians maintained the French had had no right at Utrecht to sign away their land and asserted their independence, the New Englanders insisted they were English subjects.

After Queen Anne's War, a single purpose predominated for Massachusetts. The colony wished to exploit Maine's rich resources and was determined that neither the Abenaki, nor the French would stand in its way. Massachusetts knew that the tribes would oppose settlement but justified its actions with powerful rationalizations: Indians were naturally treacherous, unwilling to abide by legal agreements, and susceptible to baneful French priests.[3]

Thus, Kenneth Morrison paints a picture of English determination not only to move back where they'd been in Maine but to extend their reach wherever they could. A major instrument for doing this was the General Court, their legislature in Boston. It had established a "Committee for the Settling of the Eastern Parts," before which came such items as that Edward Hutchinson and John

Watts had ten families "gone and ready to go" to Arrowsic "to make a settlement there and asking for a Serjeant [*sic*] with nineteen sentinels from Casco Fort" to assist them.

This request was reported in May 1715. The following month, the committee received the proposal of Thomas Hutchinson and John Wentworth (of New Hampshire), both esquires (members of the gentry) — "in behalf of themselves and partners...for the settling of towns forthwith in a regular defensible manner."

One town had "lands platted" from Pejepscot Falls to Macquoit in Casco Bay — six miles square — and this became Brunswick; the other, "in a square of a mile to the eastward of Ambroscogging River [*sic*] fronting to Merry Meeting Bay" — six square miles, as well — was to be Topsham.

The busy legislators did all they could to encourage such activity: freeing these towns from provincial taxes for five years; authorizing the stone fort near Pejepscot Falls to be repaired and fifteen men, a sergeant, and officers to man it; dispatching another twenty men to Arrowsic at the behest of Edward Hutchinson; laying out a survey for a road from Wells to Pejepscot Falls; and drafting an act "for settling and quieting the titles of the lands that are to the eastward of the Piscataqua River."

Edward Hutchinson did establish his foothold on Arrowsic Island, for in August 1717, in its community of Georgetown, another treaty was negotiated with the Indians.

Governor Samuel Shute sailed to this parley on the HMS SQUIRREL. Beforehand, he had the Indians given a British flag to bring "in token of their subjection to His Majesty King George," and the head canoe of the Indian flotilla *was* flying the Union Jack as it approached the British warship. Meeting on land, the governor gave the tribesmen an ox for dinner and Indian and English bibles. Chiefs from the Kennebecs, the Penobscots, the Pigwackets (a branch of the Sacos), and the Androscoggins were present. Several members of the Governor's Council also attended, as did John Wentworth. Shute opened by reminding the natives they had met with Governor Joseph Dudley at Piscataqua four years earlier, accepted submission, ratified agreements, and agreed "that this great, good, and wise Prince George is their King, as well as ours." The governor told them, "If you behave yourselves well, I shall use you kindly." The flavor of the dialogue that followed repeats itself in many of these Anglo-Indian confabs.

Wiwurna of the Kennebecs spoke for all of the Wabanaki:

Wiwurna: "We will be very obedient to the King, if we are not molested in the improvement of our land."

Shute: "You shall not be interrupted in the improvement of your lands and the English must not be molested by you in theirs.... You must desist from any pretensions to lands which the English own."

Wiwurna: "...And we now return thanks that the English are come to settle here and will embrace them in our bosoms that come to settle on our lands."

Shute: "You must not call it your land, for the English have bought it of you and your ancestors."

Wiwurna: "We desire there may be no further settlements made."

Shute: "Tell the others they must be sensible and satisfied that the English own this land and have deeds that show and set forth their purchase from your ancestors."

Wiwurna: "We are willing to cut off our lands as far as the mills and the coasts to Pemaquid.... It was said at the Casco Treaty that no more forts should be made."

Shute: "Forts are not made for your hurt but for your security and that of the English since we both are subjects of King George."

Wiwurna: "We can't understand how our lands have been purchased. What has been alienated was by our gift."

The governor then read aloud to the argumentative Kennebec chieftain the contents of deeds of sale to land on the Kennebec made by six sagamores to Richard Wharton. Wiwurna countered he couldn't speak for the west side of the Kennebec but was sure nothing had been sold on the east side. Shute offered some standard complaints about Indians killing "young cattle" and that they should muzzle their dogs when they came on English land. Still contesting it was *Indian* land, the Kennebec Indians produced a letter to Shute written by their Jesuit priest at Norridgewock, Father Sebastian Rasle, relaying information that the King of France had been asked by the governor of Canada if he had ever given Indian land to the English and the King had said no. Furthermore, he would help the Indians if their lands were encroached upon. Governor Shute testily replied the letter wasn't worth his regard.

The conference might have ended in a complete stalemate but the next day, the other chiefs disavowed Wiwurna, accepted the English conditions, and gave a wampum belt to seal the agreement. A key element in their retreat seems to have been their dire need for English provisions and ammunition.

An ominous note, perhaps, was that upon departing, they neglected to take their British flag with them.

Of all the "baneful French priests" the English railed against, none seemed more threatening to them than Father Sebastian Rasle. This frail, partly crippled intellectual Jesuit from the Franche Comté, the mountainous frontier of eastern France next to Switzerland, lived with his Wabanaki flock in their village near Norridgewock on the Kennebec River. He was, to put it mildly, a controversial figure—a saint to his charges, a scholar and martyr to his countrymen, a warmonger to his English enemies. At the very least, he was part and parcel of the uncertainty that hung over the New Englanders as they started to repopulate Maine, where not a single new town had been founded between 1675 and 1715. At the worst he was, in their words, "the Chief Fondater of the war"—that is, Dummer's War—the fault-line war flareup that wracked northern New England throughout the early 1720s.

Rasle has been a figure of deep interest to several poets, as well. William Carlos Williams, in a book of poetically literary essays, *In the American Grain*, devotes an entire chapter to him. He was, writes Williams:

> ...a spirit, rich, blossoming, generous, able to give and
> to receive, full of taste, a nose, a tongue, a laugh, endur-
> ing, self-forgetful in beneficence—a new spirit in the
> New World.[4]

He shared his Indians' lives, ate well when they did, and went hungry like them during the months of scarcity. He spiritualized an already spiritualized people, acting as a sort of super-shaman. Yet in another sense, he was a field general and a bit of a foreign minister. They saw him as a living, infallible, paternal parent in their midst. When Phillipe de Vaudreuil, governor of New France, wanted all Maine Wabanakis to relocate to French-held Cape Breton Island after the Treaty of Utrecht, Rasle led other priests in fighting him. His country's strategic goal, Rasle argued, should be to bolster the independence and territorial integrity of the tribes against the English. Thus, after Wabanaki warriors attacked and burned newly settled Brunswick, the latter put a price in sterling on Rasle's head. His response:

> *...ni leur mauvaise volenté pour moi, ni la mort dont ils me menacent ne pourront jamais me se parer de mon cher troupeau....*

(...neither their ill will toward me nor their death threats will ever separate me from my dear flock....)

Maine poet Robert Chute made Père Sebastian Rasle the centerpiece of a set of poems, *Thirteen Moons*, celebrating the last year of his life.

It was August 1723, and he and his *troupeau* were in *Wikkaikizoos*, the moon of many eels upon the sand and, ordinarily, they would be going to the seashore, but:

> The English stand between us and the sea. Their forts
> rise to block us from the sun.

Forts the Wabanakis at Arrowsic asked them not to build. The natives were feeling encircled. Already, English militiamen had been to Norridgewock, but the Kennebecs were warned in time and whisked their priest to safety.

It was September 1723:

> The corn is good. Acorns fall. Smoked eels hang like
> greasy hair from many poles. Pale salmon come....

But soon, hunger will come, too, with the March moon.

> Where can we hunt?
> Where can we fish?
> The English stand like sharp stones
> And we must turn away.

June 1724.

We may not go southward to the sea. The English swarm around...and beat their drums.[5]

Then, that fateful late afternoon of August 14, 1724, arrived and the English caught them by surprise in a daylight raid. Leading the attackers were officers from York. One of them, Captain Jeremiah Moulton, had seen his parents killed before his eyes as a four-year-old during the "massacre" of 1692. Yet he didn't want Father Rasle killed. He was furious with Lieutenant Richard Jacques for shooting the priest through the head instead of capturing him for a show trial in Boston. The British version of the Jesuit's death was that Jacques had rushed into his house to find him with a captive English boy who had been tortured or abused and, in his rage, had fired. The French version was that Père Rasle had rushed to the center of the village, stood next to the cross drawing English fire so the women and children could escape, and that his body had been hideously mutilated. The English rebuttal: Rasle was a cripple and had been since his youth when he'd broken both his legs and they hadn't healed properly; besides, his death was tit-for-tat, since the French and Indians had murderously shot down the local minister at York in 1692.

What was not in dispute, nor defensible, was that this man of God had been scalped and the horrid hairpiece displayed in the streets of Boston where the conquering heroes were greeted with "great shouting and triumph."

It was the end of the Kennebec tribe's power. The refugees fled north and west, some to Canada, others to mingle with their Penobscot and Passamaquoddy kin.

In Chute's postscript entitled "The Last Moon," a Norridgewock survivor mourns:

We are gone now....
Search if you will.... Where are the leaves
that fell before the English came?
We are gone like the leaves and scattered....
The land is not ours. We have lost our prayers
The river no longer runs to the sea.

NOTES

1 Samuel P. Huntington, *The Clash of Civilizations: Remaking of World Order.* New York: Simon and Schuster, 1996. Pages 252–53.

2 Thomas Hutchinson, *The History of the Colony of and Province of Massachusetts Bay.* Cambridge, MA: Harvard University Press. Vol. I, page 278.

3 Kenneth Morrison, *The Embattled Northeast: The Illusive Ideal of Alliance in Abenaki-Euramerican Relations.* Berkeley, California: University California Press, 1984. Page 166.

4 William Carlos Williams, *In the American Grain.* New York: New Directions Publishing Company, 1956. page 120. The spelling of Rasle's surname confounds historians as much as his presence did the Yankee colonials. Rale, Ralle, Rasles, even Racle, as well as the more common Rasle, were used.

5 Robert Chute, *Thirteen Moons.* Brunswick, ME: Blackberry Press, 1998.

TWELVE

The Inexorable Turning of the Tide

THE SIGHT OF A PRIEST'S scalp on display in Boston may not have been so shocking, after all. It was said of the renowned Indian fighter John Lovewell that he "not only paraded scalps through the streets of Boston, he also wore a wig made of Indian scalps."[1]

In another decisive action of Dummer's War, on May 7, 1725, Lovewell immortalized himself by getting killed in a battle near present-day Fryeburg, in which the Pigwacket chieftain Paugus was also slain. Under ordinary circumstances, this battle in the western part of Maine might have been considered a draw. There were about forty-five men on each side and both forces were shot up pretty badly in a firefight around the shores of Saco Pond (later renamed Lovewell's Pond). But what made Lovewell's clash with Paugus so memorable and seemingly decisive was that afterward, the Pigwackets packed up and left for Canada, never to return.

On two fronts, then—along the Kennebec and in the western Maine foothills of the White Mountains—Indian resistance had cracked. It was only a matter of time before land-hungry English settlers would be on their way.

That the Western Abenaki within Maine—Pigwackets, Sacos, Androscoggins, Norridgewocks, Kennebecs—were exiled to Canada following Dummer's War has long been an item of faith among some Maine historians, but is now under challenge. Evidence exists that many returned and pockets of them, never officially recognized, existed around places such as Bethel and Moosehead and South Paris until recent times.

Like Captain John Lovewell, Captain Jeremiah Moulton, and

Moulton's commander, Colonel Johnson Harmon, Colonel Thomas Westbrook also served as an Indian fighter during Dummer's War. His theater of offensive operations was from the Kennebec to the Penobscot, and his mobile force of rangers roamed as far as Mount Desert, harassing the Wabanaki. Part of his mission, as well, was to defend new settlements created by the Massachusetts General Court and private land speculators in Mid-Coast Maine. Westbrook was a speculator, himself, in "eastern lands." His martial reputation has never been quite on a par with his above-mentioned colleagues; the Indians he fought didn't flee to Canada or seemingly disappear. But his name has survived due in good measure to his postwar involvement and important role in the mast trade.

The mast trade! Westbrook's career helps illustrate the transition at this critical juncture of developments in Maine. From a military man's worries about survival to a businessman's concern focused on economic growth, he embodies the turning of the tide that insured a permanent English presence north of the Piscataqua. With the Indians pushed back, spaces in Maine abandoned a generation earlier quickly filled. There was suddenly the leisure to argue about peacetime affairs, and foremost among the thorny issues, debated in Boston, fought in the courts, and even occasioning violence, was the practice of procuring masts for the Royal Navy.

One of the clauses of the 1691 Massachusetts Charter specified once and for all that trees large enough to be masts for the Royal Navy belonged by law to the king. It didn't matter where these great pines grew, although a caveat in the Charter language exempted private property owned before 1691. For entrepreneurs, particularly those with newly acquired land in Maine, this meant the uncompensated loss of some very valuable resources. (One tree, alone, might be worth £100, a small fortune in those days.) Hatchet-marked with the king's broad-arrow sign under the watchful eye of the King's Surveyor of the Woods, such monarchs of the forest could then be removed by a gang of men hired by those who had a monopoly of supplying the British navy. These none-too-gentle woodsmen might also destroy a quantity of other trees in order to get to and get out the monumental "pumpkin" pines, some said to be a 1,000 years old and to weigh 1,000 tons. The injustice of the system has been adjudged a contributing factor to the alienating of Americans from the home government, or at least starting them on the road to independence.

The official English attitude can be summed up in the words of Richard West, Esq., the attorney for the Board of Trade in an opinion rendered in 1718. Said West: "Maintaining the royal prerogative in relation to naval stores in America is of the utmost consequence to the kingdom."

Britain's power was dependent on its navy. The navy's ships needed sturdy, reliable masts. They could obtain excellent ones from the Baltic, but the supply was not always ensured. The Danes had more than once blockaded access from the North Sea. So, although transportation from America took three times as long, the naval commissioners as early as 1654 sent three ships to New England for pine masts. Their quality was immediately appreciated. "The gift of two cargoes of great masts from the General Court of Massachusetts Bay to the King was particularly acceptable," the Puritans were informed in 1677. They were trying to appease Charles II's anger over their buying out the heirs of Sir Ferdinando Gorges behind his back. Thus, the English idea that it was a patriotic duty for the colonists to *give* the navy their best trees had a long tradition.

That it rankled Yankee settlers more and more as the eighteenth century progressed was partly because more and more of them owned land and partly because of an unwise choice of enforcement personnel by the administration in London. No poorer choice for the earliest "Surveyor of Pines and Timber in Maine" could have been made than Edward Randolph, Governor Andros's flunky—an "active, unpopular, and often unscrupulous supporter of royal authority." In 1688, a year before he was arrested and deported, Randolph traveled as far Down East as Penobscot Bay, conducting an official survey of the Maine woods. Under William and Mary, the Navy Board sent John Bridger in 1696 on an investigatory tour and nine years later, established him as the first real surveyor general. A former shipwright, Bridger's position, competence, and energy, rather than an obnoxious personality, led to his eventual ousting in 1718.

Bridger was a go-getter. One of his first acts was to get the New Hampshire legislature to incorporate the 1691 Charter's language in legislation of their own—that "all trees of the diameter of 24 inches and upwards at 12 inches from the ground..." were the king's. Then, at Bridger's urging in 1711, Parliament passed "An Act for the preservation of white and other pine trees for the masting of Her Majesty's Navy." This act expanded the restrictions on cutting pine to other colonies as far south as New Jersey.

The issue was creating such political sparks in Massachusetts that in his annual message to the General Court in 1716, Governor Samuel Shute saw fit to dwell upon it:

> I am further to observe to you, that notwithstanding there was an Act passed in England in her late Majesty's reign, for encouraging the importation of naval stores, and another for the preservation of white and other pine trees, growing in Her Majesty's colonies of America; yet nevertheless, His Majesty hath been informed that great spoils are daily committed in his woods in the Province of Maine and other parts of Massachusetts, by cutting down and putting to private use, such trees as are or may be proper for His Majesty's Royal Navy.[2]

The governor, as he spoke, might well have been casting an accusatory eye at one member of the General Court, Elisha Cooke, Jr., leader of the "popular party." This Harvard graduate and practicing physician had followed his father, Elisha Cooke, Sr., as a dedicated foe of anything smacking of the king's prerogative. Their antecedents were pure Puritan and Pilgrim and both were effective political agitators.

But for Elisha, Jr., there was more than populism in this issue. He had, along with various partners, bought into the Muscongus Patent in Mid-Coast Maine, a 1,000-square-mile tract including hundreds of thousands of acres of the best timberland. According to *Sibley's Harvard Graduates*, he "offered them for sale with the understanding that they would fix the local courts against convicting poachers on the King's Woods." John Bridger complained the settlers in Maine were "being persuaded that His Majesty had no right to the woods in this country by Elisha Cooke and on that opinion they will act next winter they say."

The ingenious, if specious, argument Cooke had concocted was the king had no claim to the Maine Woods because of the purchase Massachusetts had made in 1677. When called before the Governor's Council, Cooke declared: "...that the Province of Maine being granted by the King to Sir Ferdinando Gorges and the title and right of the said Gorges derived to the Massachusetts Colony, the timber therein belongs to them and King George may not take it away." The controversy exploded in the house after the council refused to act upon a complaint by Cooke against Bridger.

A group of Maine representatives joined him, saying inhabitants of their towns had been threatened by Bridger, who warned them they couldn't cut wood without permission from him or his deputies and that they were, in their own words, "deterred from following their lawful employment."

A committee chosen to look into the Cooke-Bridger affair finally reported the allegations made by the surveyor general against the legislator-doctor-speculator "are not supported by the papers laid before us." Those allegations included Cooke's buying up worthless old grants but laying them out in the best pine forests, using his influence to get them confirmed, and selling them for a handsome profit. Moreover, the king's man groused, "The King's right was never called into question until Mr. Cooke (that incendiary) with unparalleled insolence...endeavored to poison the minds of his countrymen, with his republican notions, in order to assert the independency of New England."

Unimpressed by such vituperation, the General Court Committee proclaimed Bridger "had obstructed the inhabitants of this Province in their just rights and privileges of logging by his arbitrary and unwarrantable demanding of money of them for liberty to improve their rights."

Then, like the good politicians they were, they stated they wanted to take "some effective care" to secure His Majesty's rights to mast trees but also to see His Majesty's "good subjects" did not have their privileges and properties invaded and for the governor to proclaim such a delicate balance to be government policy.

Then, they voted to put Cooke and William Pepperrell on a committee to look into the cutting of trees in Maine, which was tantamount, as the old pols' saying goes, to putting the fox in charge of the henhouse. Pepperrell, then Kittery's representative and later to become the largest landowner in colonial America, was a major poacher of mast trees.

Governor Shute, an ex-army colonel who had fought with Marlborough, retaliated by vetoing Cooke's election by his peers to be speaker of the house.

In the tone and content of this dispute, there can already be detected intimations of the much greater political battles to come. The charge that demagogues were seeking to arouse the Massachusetts colonists to break away, the accusations of British venality, the money involved (two big white pine trees were worth the same amount as John Bridger's yearly salary), the hallowedness or hollowness, depending on the point of view, of the king's prerogative — these themes would echo and expand for decades. Elisha Cooke, Jr., would eventually be labeled the Sam Adams of his generation.

But a Sam Adams with oodles of land. The politics surrounding the Muscongus Patent's claim, in which Cooke was a major shareholder, had a long reach — not only into the Boston establishment but also to the highest echelons of London, and antecedents deep in the New England past, as an outgrowth of the grant by Gorges's Council of New England to Beauchamp and Leverett in the seventeenth century.

Connected with it, too, was that most notable of Elisha Cooke, Jr.'s, confederates — Samuel Waldo — a name firmly imprinted on the saga of the peopling of Maine.

Samuel Waldo was from "Away" in the sense that he kept his domicile in Boston and never moved to the lands he had acquired in Maine. Born in England, he was brought to Boston when four years old by his father Jonathan, educated at the Boston Latin School and, as a young man, went into partnership with his brother, Cornelius, dealing in naval stores and lumber — Maine products — that they sold to the West Indies and Europe.

"Soon after entering active business, he [Samuel] became connected with a landed interest of great magnitude."[3]

In these words, a Maine Historical Society monograph introduces the most critical turning point in Waldo's life—his relationship with the Muscongus Patent.

From the original grantees, this vast property had descended ultimately in 1714 to John Leverett, the president of Harvard. He not only added to it the tract Sir William Phips had bought from Madockawando, but reorganized the company to settle families on the grant once the Treaty of Utrecht had made peace possible. He put up ten shares for sale to ten "Proprietors" who procured twenty "Associates." Among the latter were Samuel Waldo's father and brother; hence his initial interest.

During Dummer's War, Indian attacks caused the Muscongus landowners considerable damage, although warriors were unable to overcome two blockhouses built in Thomaston, despite a siege of thirty days.

But far more serious danger arose following the resumption of peace in 1726. A powerful group in England began asserting that the original patent was null and void, and these would-be usurpers included some real political heavyweights, like Thomas Coram, a rich London merchant whose ambition was to turn the territory between the Kennebec and Nova Scotia into a brand new province, separate from Massachusetts, and also Colonel Martin Bladen, one of the leading lights on the Board of Trade. Their argument to the king was practical as well as legalistic: in a new province, there would be no problem about exclusive royal possession of the mast trees.

To back this promise, they chose as their man in America the successor to John Bridger as surveyor general of the King's Woods—David Dunbar, a choleric, bullheaded, Scots-Irish ex-army colonel. Sent to Maine, he commenced by wreaking havoc with local settlers, driving the lumbermen from their homes, seizing their timber, and burning their sawmills. Supported by a recommendation in May 1729 from the Board of Trade to the Privy Council that the province of "Georgia" should be created, Dunbar hastily rounded up a hundred impoverished "Irish" families in Boston and shipped these countrymen of his to Pemaquid, his projected capital. With Gaelic canniness, he renamed the town for Frederick, Prince of

Wales, and laid out six more towns, all named for big-shot leaders of the ruling Whig Party in Parliament.

Samuel Waldo entered the picture at the behest of the Muscongus patentees, led no doubt by Elisha Cooke, Jr. If he would sail to England and use his and his family's influence to quash this takeover attempt, the proprietors would give him half of their 600,000 acres. And this is finally what happened. By April 1730 Waldo was able to convince the Board of Trade to drop its support of "Georgia" and, two years later, he got the Privy Council to order Dunbar to vacate the proposed new province altogether. Maine, up to the Nova Scotia border, remained an inseparable part of Massachusetts—a position the governor of the Bay Colony, Jonathan Belcher, had emphasized by sending the sheriff of York County to arrest some of Dunbar's people in Frederick Fort who had seized and roughed up two Massachusetts men.

The troublemaking Dunbar did not disappear from the scene. As a sop to his powerful friends, the Crown appointed him lieutenant governor of New Hampshire. From this post, he could stir up mischief for Governor Belcher (nominally his superior) and other enemies, and he was still the surveyor general of the King's Woods!

In his book *Revolutionary New England*, Boston Brahmin historian James Truslow Adams characterized a phenomenon of "Americanization" that has bedeviled conservative elitists since our history began. His opinion, if not its genteel expression, could equally have been David Dunbar's:

> The frontier always and everywhere breeds squatters'
> doctrines and individualism. The speculator in a new
> land and the settler in the wilderness ever tend to dis-
> regard vested interests, distant authority, and any
> restraint placed upon their individual exploitation of
> the natural resources about them.[4]

Adams then haughtily asserted these woods owners weren't patriots defying royal tyranny when they destroyed masts. "They were merely thoroughly characteristic frontiersmen defying all restraint."

David Dunbar, in the eighteenth century, put it this way: "Any man that behaves any different from the crowd, stinks of the prerogative. This expression is common with them."

His contempt for the settlers and his pugnacious methods led to more than resentment. In 1734, in Exeter, New Hampshire, a group of Dunbar's men, sent to seize cut lumber, were set upon by "Indians"—of the same sort who later would dump tea in Boston Harbor and harass surveyors in the Maine woods. Retreating to the vessel that had brought them down the Squamscot River, the fugitive king's men embarked only to discover the ship's hull had been stove in, causing them to sink. Back ashore, they huddled shivering in the bulrushes all night before trudging back to Portsmouth on foot.

Nor were ruffians and Robin Hoodish scofflaws alone in play here. The future Sir William Pepperrell, Jr., of Kittery not only was deep into the unauthorized mast business, he was also the judge before whom the surveyor general had to bring his cases or defend his employees from being sued, as in the famous lawsuit of *Frost* versus *Leighton*. The defendant in this instance was Dunbar's man against whom John Frost of Berwick sought an action for entering his property and removing seven pine trees. Although Leighton had a perfect right to do so under the revised White Pine Act of 1729, he had also cut four beech trees, four hemlocks, one maple, and sundry other growth to get at the pines. Pepperrell fined him £120. An appeal to the Privy Council in England reversed Pepperrell's ruling and Frost was ordered to return the money and pay costs, but the Massachusetts General Court refused to enforce the decision.

An interesting twist in these mast trade battles was the role of Samuel Waldo. Formerly an arch foe of David Dunbar's, he now found himself on the same side. His very success in warding off the challenge to the Muscongus Patent had made him a large landowner, which might have allied him with the likes of Pepperrell and Cooke, but in England, Waldo had made a cozy deal with Ralph Gulston and his brothers, the exclusive Crown agents for New England white pines. Waldo actually hired the lawyer who defended Leighton before the Privy Council, the barrister William Shirley, and also later lobbied successfully to have him made governor of Massachusetts.

Waldo's stake in the mast business, in which he collaborated with Colonel Thomas Westbrook, was not his sole interest in Maine. Like other great landowners, he was anxious to add value to his property and the best way was to open it for settlement. In 1734, an ad appeared in a Boston publication:

"Samuel Waldo of Boston, Merchant" was looking to settle two towns of 40 families each on a "tract of land, to which his title is indisputable..." on the west side of "a navigable river, the St. George's, in the Eastern Parts of this Province." All interested families should come to his house in Boston March 17 to 24, and he would give each "that shall agree with him to settle..." 100 acres. "The better to accommodate the settlement, a double sawmill will... be erected on said land...." And, he, Waldo, would personally be on the site from April 10–30 to lay out the lots.

He even appealed to Dunbar's countrymen, the poor Scots-Irish in Boston, and induced forty-five of them to settle in Warren, giving each a hundred acres for a token quit-rent of "one peppercorn per annum lawfully demanded," apparently a legal stratagem to preserve his feudal claim in the Waldo family.

Waldo's mother, it was said, came from Germany, and he decided to seek immigrants from the Rhineland Palatinate where Lutheran Protestants were experiencing discrimination from the majority Roman Catholics. As his agent, Waldo employed a German-Swiss, one Sebastian Zuberbuhler, who recruited some 200 locals from around the city of Speyer. The appropriately named community where they settled in Maine — Waldoboro — still boasts an old German cemetery.

The Muscongus Patent (from now on known also as the Waldo Patent) was not the only large-scale operation trying to develop Maine. Other major companies had formed, too, around the kernel of an original grant from the Council for New England, such as the Pejepscot Proprietors, owners of Richard Wharton's former property, and the Kennebeck Proprietors, who had the early Pilgrim grant around Cushnoc.

Like Waldo, the men involved in these ventures were powers in Boston. Thomas Hutchinson, Sr., Adam Winthrop, and Steven Minot, some of the principals in the Pejepscot Company, had impeccable Masachusetts credentials. The Kennebec Proprietors had their heavy hitters, as well, including James Bowdoin and Thomas Hancock (the very rich uncle of John). It should be noted that those two great American patriots, James Otis, Jr., and John Adams, at one time or another served as legal counsel for the second group.

There were proprietors with a small *p* who entered this development game, in addition to the combines. Some were lone individuals such as William Pepperrell and William Vaughan, who became big in their own right. Pepperrell, it was said, could mount a horse at his home in Kittery Point, ride to Scarborough 30-odd miles away, and never leave his own land; Vaughan bought all of Bristol, Bremen, Damariscotta, Nobleboro, most of Newcastle, and parts of Jefferson and Waldoboro.

But ownership with a very, very small *o* was also encouraged by the General Court, which had been given the power in the 1691 Charter to confirm land transactions. Since the French and Indian threat had receded, not vanished, defense, even after Dummer's War ended, was still uppermost in the Boston lawmakers' minds. It became legislative policy to create a line of settlements across Maine, spreading east and west.

Consequently, we find in the House on November 20, 1734, two members from Marblehead introducing a bill to provide "A Tract of Land for a Township for such persons belonging to said Town of Marblehead as will settle thereon."

This was a standard practice for towns in overcrowded Massachusetts and once the General Court acted, and the township was surveyed, the lots laid out, and the plan accepted, the town would call a meeting. In Marblehead, this happened eight months after the process had been initiated. Townspeople and outsiders at the gathering bought lots and, if they didn't use them to settle, resold to others who would. In time, New Marblehead sprang up in Maine. Today, it is the community known as Windham, an exurb west of Portland.

The same year, York County was moving west, too. Sanford, initially called Phillipstown for its founder, Major William Phillips, was first settled in 1734.

Rewards to veterans were another spur to settlement inland.

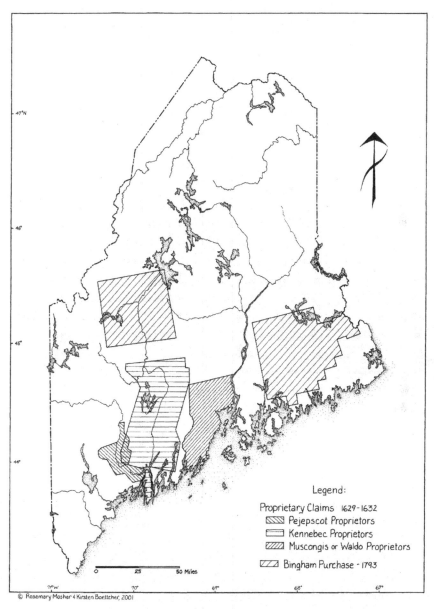

Legend:

Proprietary Claims 1629-1632
▨ Pejepscot Proprietors
▤ Kennebec Proprietors
▨ Muscongis or Waldo Proprietors

▨ Bingham Purchase - 1793

© Rosemary Mosher & Kirsten Boettcher, 2001

Lands of the Great Proprietors

175

The Narragansett grants were given to veterans of King Philip's War. Narragansett #1 became Buxton; Narragansett #7, Gorham. There were also the Canada grants, for those who had joined Phips's ill-fated expedition against Quebec. Sudbury Canada, now Bethel, is the most notable in Maine; others were in New Hampshire. On one occasion, when a grant to a Maine man turned out to be in New Hampshire, he (Captain William Raymond) received a new tract and thus we have Raymond, Maine. Often, these grants weren't taken up and their certificates, handed down to family members, were purchased by speculators years later.

Politics in the government halls of Boston and London in this period (the 1730s, 1740s, and 1750s) had a profound effect on the ultimate composition of the land that finally became Maine.

Jonathan Belcher, son of a prominent Boston merchant, was chosen governor of Massachusetts by the Crown on the argument made by his supporters that, as a native-born Massachusettsan, he could somehow deal with the unruly Yankees. But part of conciliating his countrymen was to be "soft" on enforcing the mast tree laws. As a result, Belcher created a fearsome enemy in Samuel Waldo, to add to others like David Dunbar, the Wentworths in New Hampshire, and mast king Ralph Gulston in London. William Shirley, who had come to Boston and actually been given an Admiralty Court job by Belcher, was an even more deadly foe. He was out to get Belcher's job.

Waldo went to England to promote Shirley's candidacy. This was a bit of desperation on his part, for Belcher had openly challenged his claims to the Muscongus Patent and was encouraging the Indians in the region to accuse Waldo of having cheated them of their lands.

In the picturesque language that was always his trademark, Belcher lambasted Waldo in letters he sent to his friends. His nickname for his enemy was "Trinkalo"—no doubt an allusion to the Trincalo in Shakespeare's *The Tempest*—a buffoonish jester with grandiose ideas of becoming a king. "The grand affair of a new governor is almost out of sight," he wrote to a supporter in New Hampshire. And whenever Waldo returned to Boston, he added, it would be as "a sort of beheaded puppy.... We have a squadron of deaths, writs, arrests, and judgments…that would make him clap his tail between his legs and leer like a dog."

Belcher's correspondence is sprinkled with caustic nicknames and invectives. Benning Wentworth was "Don Granada" because of his Spanish grandee airs. Mrs. Frances Shirley, who was in London conducting her own effective lobbying effort for her husband, was "Mrs. Gypsy." David Dunbar was "the bullfrog of the Hibernian fens." William Pepperrell, who stayed neutral during this fracas, was simply "Kittery." William Shirley, whom he'd originally befriended, drew special venom. "Shirley is a mean, false, ungrateful beggar.… That ingrate…that quondam impoverished lawyer."

In the end, Belcher was ousted. It aided the plotters that a new ministry took office in Whitehall, headed by the Whig political boss, the Duke of Newcastle, who was William Shirley's patron. During the spring of 1741, an elaborate shakeup occurred in New England. Belcher was dismissed and Shirley appointed in his place. Simultaneously, New Hampshire was totally severed from Massachusetts and allowed its own governor. Somewhat later, Jonathan Belcher was mollified with the sop of the governorship of New Jersey.

A new era can be said to have commenced in Massachusetts with the accession of William Shirley. Not that all internal squabbling stopped. Yet Shirley was shrewd enough to know that focusing on an external enemy was a tried and true way to create at least temporary unity. He was an imperialist. Beefing up defenses against the French and Indians was good politics because it was good for business; even better was going on the offensive against them. The opportunity arrived in March 1744, when England and France officially declared war against each other.

Two months later, on May 24, 1744, "King George's War" erupted in North America. French forces on Cape Breton Island crossed the narrow strait separating their territory from British Nova Scotia and overran an outpost at the tiny settlement of Canso. The small fort was burned, the captured garrison removed to the French fortress at Louisbourg and, symbolically, the gauntlet thrown down to the ambitious, bellicose governor in Boston.

Shirley's response was nothing less than breathtaking. He proposed that the New Englanders, by themselves, if need be, would capture Louisbourg, the seemingly impregnable super-fort Louis XIV had built at immense expense. The "mad scheme," as its critics scornfully dubbed it, was, amazingly enough, adopted and, even more astoundingly, carried out successfully almost entirely by the colonials under William Pepperrell. Coming when British successes in what was essentially a world war were few and far between, the capture of Louisbourg in 1745 had an incredible impact. Equally negative was the impact on New England three years later when the Newcastle government, for petty political reasons, handed the awesome redoubt back.

More transatlantic politics led to Shirley's replacement within another decade. The man who succeeded him as governor of Massachusetts, Thomas Pownall, played a crucial if not entirely conscious role in adding a large portion of the northern woodlands to Maine. The crucial event was his expedition to the Penobscot in 1759.

Nathaniel Hawthorne writes of Governor Pownall: "He was a gay and fashionable English gentleman who had spent much of his life in London, but had a considerable acquaintance with America." This is part of a dialogue between an old Bostonian and his grandchildren in "The Whole History of Grandfather's Chair," a Hawthorne sketch.

"Did the people like Pownall?" asked Charley.

"They found no fault with him,'" replied his grandfather. "It was no time to quarrel with the governor when the utmost harmony was required in order to defend the country against the French."

Pownall had come to America in 1753 ostensibly as the secretary to Sir Danvers Osbourne, the newly appointed governor of New York. For ten years, young Pownall had worked for the Board of Trade, run by his older brother John, but now he also acted unobstrusively as their observer, quietly gauging the status of the struggle against the French and Indians. Like many a younger son of a well-placed English family, Pownall was in the New World, too, to seek his fortune.

Before long, because of Sir Danvers Osbourne's suicide, he was, in effect, the de facto governor of New York—a position that led him into the political intrigue of the day, putting him in eventual conflict with William Shirley, on leave from his Massachusetts governorship to become overall commander of the British forces in the French and Indian War. This was the era of Washington's surrender at Fort Necessity, of Braddock's horrendous debacle, the loss of Fort William Henry at Lake George in New York, and the crushing Oswego defeat. When Shirley was called home to England in disgrace, Thomas Pownall supplanted him in the top job in Boston, no doubt with the help of his powerful brother.

The idea of an expedition to place a fort at the mouth of the Penobscot River had been suggested previously by Governor Shirley and likewise by Samuel Waldo. In any event, by January 1758, Pownall was writing as chief executive in Massachusetts to Prime Minister William Pitt:

> A fort at the Penobscot River would be of utmost importance.... It would take possession of this very fine country, which the Indians never dispute when done in war. It would effectively drive off the remains of the Norridgewock and Penobscot Indians as it would break their hunting and fishing. It would be taking possession of the finest bay in North America.

Initially, the General Court balked at funding such an undertaking, but Pownall was persistent. In his message of February 1, 1759, to the legislators, he reminded them: "You know that as long as an Indian has any claims to these lands, the French will maintain a title to them." The fort, he insisted, "Will root up the seeds of another war and secure the title of these lands to the subjects of this province."

A week later, the General Court accepted the report of its Committee on the Governor's Message, signaling a green light for his project to proceed.

On May 8, the forces gathered in Maine at Falmouth (Portland), 333 men strong, left by sea, and made their first stop early the next day, bivouacking at Fort St. George, which had been erected by the proprietors of the Waldo Patent almost forty years before. Accompanying Governor Pownall was Samuel Waldo, himself— General Waldo—from his service in the Louisbourg campaign.

Two days later, Pownall sent out his first scouting party. It was led by a company commander, Captain James Cargill of Newcastle, a renowned and notorious Indian fighter. A descendant of the Scots-Irish immigrants David Dunbar had lured to Mid-Coast Maine, Cargill was that type of home-grown frontiersman, expert in woods warfare, like Robert Rogers, Jeremiah Moulton, John Lovewell, and others who had learned much from their Native American foes. Four years earlier, in the same St. George's location, Cargill had killed a peaceable Indian, his wife, and child during a time of truce, a murder for which he'd been arrested but—to no one's surprise—acquitted after two years in jail. So here he was in 1759, heading a commando of a dozen men for Governor Pownall on the east side of the St. George's River.

Once more, Indians were killed. Encountering an Indian camp, Cargill called to its occupants: "Come in at good quarters," i.e., surrender peaceably. The Indians cried out: "No quarters. No quarters," and, as Cargill claimed, fired upon the English. Their shots were returned; the Indians ran and two fell, one of them then staggering into a swamp. The other dead "proved to be an old squaw."

Following this inauspicious start, Governor Pownall instituted a meeting with various Indian representatives. He was tough. When they told him they did not consider themselves subjects of King George, he said they had broken treaties they, or their forebears, had signed and therefore had "forfeited their lives, their liberties, and their lands." But if they *came in* (surrendered), he would protect them.

Furthermore, Pownall said to them:
Tell your people that I am come to build a fort at Penobscot and will make the land England. When I have built my fort and set down at Penobscot, if ever an Englishman is killed by your Indians…you must all from that hour fly from the country.[5]
Incentives Pownall offered the natives to become English subjects were they would have wigwams and planting ground near the fort and "may hunt as usual.… But the English shall hunt also." There would be an English Justice and an Indian Justice, under

English law. "You shall have a free market for your furs and the price shall be set by agreement."

Then, the expedition moved on and at the harbor at Fort Point on Cape Jellison in Stockton Springs, they found an ideal location. "I never yet saw so well suited a site for a fort," the governor exulted.

Setting the construction work in progress, Pownall continued upriver to about two miles below present-day Bangor. They went ashore on the east side of the Penobscot because it was Waldo's land and he had gone with them.

Pownall describes what happened next:

Brigadier Waldo, whose unremitted zeal for the service had prompted him at the age of sixty-three to attend on our expedition, dropp'd down just above the Falls of an apoplexy, and notwithstanding all the assistance that could be given him, expired in a few moments.

Reportedly, Waldo took a step toward the riverbank and announced, "Here is my bound," before he dropped dead.

His body was brought back to Fort Point and buried near the flagstaff with the full honors of war. Later, his remains were removed to the King's Chapel Episcopal burying ground in Boston.

After a trip Pownall took with Captain James Cargill and twenty men to Pentagoët, which they found abandoned and took possession of in the name of King George, the governor returned to Massachusetts where he received a hero's welcome.

In his view, he had firmly established the Commonwealth's claim to "a large and fine tract of land in the dominions of the British Crown belonging to this Province, but for many years a den of savages and a lurking place for some renegade French."

The claim was legitimized, he maintained, by his planting of a leaden plate on "the east side of the river about three miles above marine navigation." The site has been identified since as Treat's Falls in the town of Brewer. The text read: "May 23, 1759. Province of Massachusetts Bay. Dominions of Great Britain. Possession confirmed by T. Pownall, Governor." He, himself, wrote later, "I buried said plate at the root of a large white birch tree, three large trunks springing from the one root. The tree is at the top of a very high piked hill...." A flagstaff was erected there and they ran up the Union Jack and saluted.

At the time, Thomas Pownall could hardly know that within four years, the French would be driven from Canada, nor that a dozen years afterwards, the colonists would revolt. (Back in England by then, as a member of parliament, Pownall was one of the Americans' strongest supporters.) Neither could anyone foresee the future of the Waldo Patent and the direction the brigadier general's heirs would take, which would have such an impact on Maine and its woods.

This expedition, despite its few moments of drama, must have seemed fairly routine for the times. But its importance was immense.

NOTES

1 Colin G. Calloway, ed., *Dawnland Encounters*. Hanover, NH, and London: University Press of New England, 1991. Page 167.

2 "Governor Samuel Shute's Message, November 7, 1716," *Journal of the House of Representatives of Massachusetts*. Boston: Massachusetts Historical Society, 1919. Vol. 9.

3 Joseph Williamson, *General Samuel Waldo*. Portland, ME: Maine Historical Society Collections, 1887. Vol. 9.

4 James Truslow Adams, *Revolutionary New England*. Boston: Atlantic Monthly Press, 1923. Page 121.

5 Joseph Williamson, "Journal of the Voyage of Governor Thomas Pownall from Boston to the Penobscot River," *Maine Historical Society Collections*. Series 1, vol. 5.

THIRTEEN

Goodbye to France, Goodbye to England

FROM HIS TRIPS, Governor Thomas Pownall gained an appreciation for the Maine Woods that he was able to express effectively. For example:

> The general face of the country, when one travels it along the rivers through parts not yet settled, exhibits the most picturesque landscapes that imagination can conceive, in a variety of the noblest, richest groups of wood, water, and mountains. As the eye is led on from reach to reach at every turning of the courses, the imagination is in a perpetual alternative of curious suspense and new delight, not knowing at any point and not being able to discover where the way is to open next, until it does open and captivates like enchantment.

Perhaps, too, he had a glimmer of understanding that the tide had turned against the French and the long dreamed of goal of the colonists—to expel them from the continent—was in the offing. Before setting out for Penobscot, he already knew Louisbourg had been recaptured, Quebec was under siege, and the building of his fort would close the enemy's last river route to the Atlantic. A scant three and a half months after his expedition, Quebec fell to the English. Montreal was taken the following year.

Pownall left Massachusetts in 1760 for a supposedly more lucrative governorship in South Carolina. He was succeeded by an Oxford-trained lawyer, Francis Bernard (later *Sir* Francis) who was to be as disliked by the New Englanders as Pownall was liked, although at first he was received cordially.

He had come from New Jersey, where he'd been governor, and since he had had to pay the Crown for his new post and assume higher personal expenses, one of his immediate acts was to ask the General Court for a reimbursement. The penurious Yankees weren't willing to part with any cash, but came up with an ingenious solution. One thing they had in abundance was land, so they granted His Excellency one-half of Mount Desert Island and to cloak this give-away, stated it was for his "extraordinary services."

Actually, Bernard *had* helped the Commonwealth by preparing a lawyer's brief on Massachusetts's title to the lands between the Penobscot and the St. Croix—in order to repulse a challenge from Nova Scotia. This legal duel pitted them against the Earl of Stirling, heir of the first recipient of Nova Scotia, and the province's existing governor. But by digging into distant and recent history, Bernard was able to "out-argue" his opponents, citing among other facts that the Massachusetts Charter of 1691 had literally included Nova Scotia in the Bay Colony, that Phips's expedition of 1690 had given effective control of the area to Massachusetts, and that "Governor Pownall with a large armed force erected a very respectable fort on the Penobscot and took formal possession of the country in the right of Massachusetts." The Lords of Trade and Plantations did finally side with Bernard.

The Massachusetts General Court had not waited for the Peace Treaty of 1763 before dealing with this newly legal addition to their domain. By 1760 they included it in Lincoln County, one of two counties they carved that year out of Maine's single previous existing county of York. Lincoln's shiretown was Pownalborough (now Dresden) in the heart of the territory claimed and being set-tled by the Kennebec Proprietors. But settlers soon were heading even farther Down East—a movement accelerated by the General Court when, in 1762, it created thirteen townships in today's Hancock County—six between the Penobscot and Union Rivers and six east of the Union River. The first six were referred to as the David Marsh Townships, named for their leading speculator. An important stipulation of these grants was that they had to be confirmed by the Crown within eighteen months in order to be valid.

Rumor had it that another reason for giving Governor

Bernard his generous helping of Mount Desert Island was his influence with the King's government to assure prompt recognition of the claims. Many Boston lawmakers were eager to speculate, themselves, in these lands. However, they were to be disappointed and Bernard subject to deep embarrassment when the bureaucrats in England dragged their feet, though the lack of confirmation of grants did not leave those territories unpopulated.

Bernard plunged right ahead, sailing from Boston to visit his Mount Desert property as early as September 1762. In advance, he dispatched two surveyors, John Jones and Barachias Mason, to lay out his lines. After a brief stop at Fort Pownall, he arrived in Southwest Harbor on October 2 and joined the surveying party, while also doing some duck and partridge hunting. On October 7 he met Abraham Somes, originally of Gloucester, who had been there since 1761 in a "log house, neat and convenient, though not quite furnished, and in it a notable woman with four pretty girls, clean and orderly." On a piece of birch bark, Bernard wrote a pledge to Somes and his neighbor James Richardson that they could stay in their homesteads.

Francis Bernard was a bit of a loose cannon. He had lots of ideas—but not many of them politically salable. He had once referred to the provinces in America as "republicks" and so offered suggestions for making them more amenable to monarchy. Thus, in Massachusetts, which had a popularly elected House of Representatives and an upper body, the Council, chosen from their ranks, Bernard proposed restructuring the latter group to bypass the popular assembly and give the king total control.

His geopolitical proposals were no more welcome than his government reform. His notion was first to dissolve the provinces of Connecticut and Rhode Island: Connecticut west of the Connecticut River would be joined to New York; its eastern part combined with Rhode Island and New Hampshire, and joined to Massachusetts. Western Sagadahoc, up to the Penobscot, would become the new province of Maine, with Falmouth as its capital; the rest of old Sagadahoc, from the Penobscot to the St. John, plus Nova Scotia, was to be a third new province but known as Nova Scotia, and the thirteen townships created by the General Court divided between it

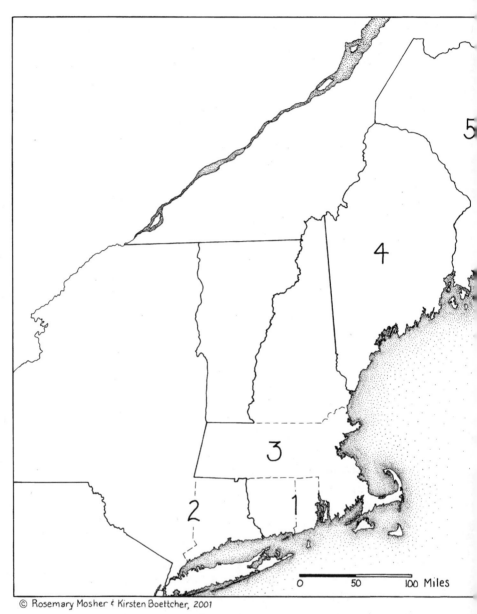

Governor Bernard's Proposal

Bernard's Proposal:

1. Dissolve border between Connecticut and Rhode Island
2. Join western Connecticut to New York
3. Combine eastern Connecticut, Rhode Island, New Hampshire, and Massachusetts
4. New Hampshire border to Penobscot River becomes the Province of Maine
5. Penobscot to St John River combine with part of Nova Scotia into new Province of Nova Scotia

and Maine. An interesting sidenote to these vain political fantasies is that in 1765, Bernard received a grant from the governor of Nova Scotia of 100,000 acres, including Moose Island (Eastport) for himself and his associates.

His plan to settle 1,000 Acadians in Maine wasn't all that bizarre. They had been kicked out of Nova Scotia and were seeking a home and the governor wanted to see them in eastern Maine. He was even willing to find them a Catholic priest. Word came back from London that there would be no "Papist colony on any part of the eastern shore" (i.e., Maine).

It was Francis Bernard's bad luck to be in the governor's chair in Massachusetts when the Stamp Act passed. His attempts to enforce it, plus his seizure of John Hancock's sloop LIBERTY in 1768, earned him unmitigated enmity. Sam Adams led the charge and the General Court weighed in by questioning his Mount Desert grant. James Otis, Jr., whom he had vetoed as speaker of the house, was a member of the investigating committee. The British government, seeing the handwriting on the wall, let Bernard know they were "pleased to grant him discretionary leave to be absent from his government," made him a baronet (the lowest order of nobility), and brought him home in the summer of 1769.

In Massachusetts the press reported the public was rejoicing "that the King had been graciously pleased to recall a very bad Governor." Bernard was described as someone "who for nine years had been a scourge to this Province, a curse to North America, and a plague to the whole Empire." As soon as his ship was underway, according to the *Boston News-Letter*, bells were rung and "the cannon at the Castle were fired with joy...fired incessantly until sunset," etc. His successor, Thomas Hutchinson, although a native Bostonian, became, believe it or not, even more unpopular.

We are now on the cusp of the American Revolution. To understand the ways that conflict affected Maine—above all the northern and eastern reaches—it is necessary to touch upon population movements already begun as French power waned, and which continued in greater force after 1763. "How they swarmed into this new country, both Maine and the present Nova Scotia, to take possession of the land wrested from the French is an epic story," Fannie Hardy Eckstorm writes.[1] This noted Maine historian had as her subject an official survey undertaken by that indefatigable would-be developer, Governor Sir Francis Bernard, to promote another of his quixotic schemes—in this case, to push a 400-mile road through the wilderness between Fort Pownall and Quebec.

In 1760 a British officer, Colonel James Montresor, had already explored a route south from Quebec to the West Branch of the Penobscot, thence to Moosehead Lake, the Kennebec, Fort Halifax (Winslow). and back. The party Bernard assembled, headed by John Preble, a well-known Indian interpreter, and Joseph Chadwick, surveyor, was to go, more or less, in reverse fashion. Chadwick, who kept the journal that Mrs. Eckstorm annotated and republished, started with the immediate problem they faced in employing Penobscot guides, underscoring the fact they would still be very much in Native American territory:

> The Indians are so jealous of their country being exposed by this survey, as made it impracticable for us to perform the work with accuracy.... Which after two days dispute, the result was that I should proceed with this restriction that I should take no draughts (make no maps) of any land but only writings.

Yet leaving Fort Pownall, Chadwick could note the extent of English penetration already reaching Frankfort Township to the north, commenting that it was *owned* three-fifths by the heirs of Samuel Waldo, one-fifth by Governor Bernard, and one-fifth by Colonel Thomas Goldthwaite, commander of Fort Pownall and agent for the Waldos.

Farther up the Penobscot, the Indian presence remained strong at Old Town and Mattawamkeag where fields planted to corn were noted. En route to Quebec, they passed Katahdin. Confirming the Indians' awe of the mountain, he reported they told him Indians could go no farther up than the tree line, that an Indian who did go higher was never seen again.

On June 20, 1764, the surveying party arrived in Quebec City and on the return trip, explored the Passadumkeag River, gateway to the Down East Machias, Narraguagus, and Union Rivers country. As for a road to Quebec, Chadwick was brief: "Reported that it was not practicable to make any road."

However, Governor Bernard seemed pleased with their work, for Chadwick adds the following memorandum:

> Sir Francis Bernard said that he had now effected what he had taken a great trouble to settle. viz. The boundary line between this province and the government of Halifax, and the dividing line is the River St. Croix, called by the French Petite St. Croix and by the Indians Magaguadavic, which falls into the grand Bay of Passamaquoddy.

Mrs. Eckstorm adds that this statement was apparently not known to those negotiators in later years, arguing about the exact location of the St. Croix, as they struggled to establish the U.S. and Maine's precise frontier with Canada.

In the 1760s this land could almost have been viewed as juridically seamless. The outbreak of the Revolution would find communities in Nova Scotia as resolutely Yankee in thought and custom as any in Massachusetts, Connecticut, New Hampshire, or Rhode Island. If the New Englanders from the south who headed into these wilds were too individualistic to stop midway in lands being promoted by big developers like the Kennebec Proprietors or Waldo heirs, they came to roost in places like Mount Desert, Ellsworth, Gouldsboro, and Jonesboro—or Maugerville and Fort Cumberland, which were in the part of Nova Scotia now New Brunswick.

When Machias was reoccupied in 1763 by sixteen settlers from Scarborough, they first mistakenly applied to Nova Scotia for their grant. Their subsequent petition to the Massachusetts General Court in October 1766 stated they had originally thought they had settled on Crown lands, but since had learned Machias was in the Bay Colony. They had made improvements at great cost, they added, and wished to have their community incorporated as a town.

Not hearing from the General Court, they reapplied with a petition from "Ichabod Jones and others," that was finally read and accepted on June 15, 1767. The supplicants were given a six-square-mile township—subject to the usual conditions of a General Court land grant—a survey to be made, lots for schools and church laid out (and in this case, one for Harvard), sixty Protestant families recruited and established, sixty houses built, etc. Originally given six years to obtain the king's approval, "Ichabod Jones and others" were later given an extension in 1770. The outbreak of the Revolution made His Majesty's confirmation, which still had not been forthcoming, a moot point.

Machias, scene of the first naval battle of the Revolution, turned out to be a strategic stronghold for the Americans during the war and a key to their retention of the area during the peace negotiations that followed.

The flood of emigration into the North Country was not viewed with favor by everyone. Establishment types and large-scale land developers were not happy about the sense of freedom of choice that it provided. Professor Alan Taylor in his book, *Liberty Men and Great Proprietors*, describes an orthodox Andover, Massachusetts, minister's sermon at the start of this era that excoriates the direct access to natural resources in the "Eastern Country" as leading to the indiscipline of the poor:

> Too much land has proved more inconvenient than too little. Through such a plenty of land, numbers are supported by the spontaneous products of nature with little labor...by men of desperate fortunes and idle habits...[which]...perpetuates idleness, intemperance, ignorance, a savage temper, and irreligion...[such men forget] the submission they owe to civil rulers and gratitude to them for their care and protection.[2]

Here we are, far beyond the "hedge" of the Puritan divines, worried about spiritual straying, and deep into the thinking of early capitalism, hoping to fix the poor in place to become low-wage workers. But while the Reverend Thomas Barnard's description might certainly apply to some who went to settlements like Machias and Gouldsboro and Maugerville, in a larger sense it pertained to a majority of Americans whose ancestors sought religious freedom at first but also the economic and personal freedoms they were losing in England. Once those freedoms—such as owning property and choosing leaders—were threatened by overseas and home-grown elites, the path to rebellion was opened to far more than a minority of "men of desperate fortunes and idle habits."

News of the explosion at Concord and Lexington traveled fast throughout Massachusetts, even to remote corners like Machias.

The community on the Machias River that had grown up since 1763 was no longer just a resuscitated trading post nor a squatters' haven. It had a Congregational church, a tavern, and sawmills capable of producing a million and a half board feet of lumber a year. It even had a somewhat structured society, with Ichabod Jones, sawmill owner and transplanted Boston merchant, at the top. Jones, later to be accused of Toryism, was probably more a cautious businessman than a diehard reactionary. His 1770 petition to the General Court for incorporation of the town carried the following assurance, expected from any upright, law-abiding citizen:

> That as this township is remote from the center of the
> Province and at a great distance from His Majesty's
> Surveyor of Woods and Timber, that the said petition-
> ers take special care not to cut or destroy any of His
> Majesty's timber on or about the said township.[3]

Jones had brought his family from Boston to Machias in 1774 and, as a shipowner, was in the habit of sailing back and forth between the two points, carrying lumber south and much-needed provisions north. When he arrived in Boston in the spring of 1775, shortly after Concord and Lexington, he was aware Machias was desperate for supplies. That and the need to transport the rest of his personal possessions sent him right back, but because of the outbreak of hostilities, he had to obtain British permission. Vice Admiral Samuel Graves gave it to him, but only if he would bring them lumber needed to build barracks. To see that Jones kept his promise to do so, the British naval commander assigned the armed tender MARGARETTA to accompany the merchant.

The political climate back in Machias boded ill for a quiet reception of the king's vessel. Upon the news of Concord and Lexington, the townspeople had erected a "Liberty Pole." Their leaders were actually local businessmen and sawmill owners like Benjamin Foster and George Stillman, while the most fiery spirit of all, as if in a rebuke to that Andover clergyman, was the establishment minister, the Reverend James Lyon, chair of the Committee of Public Safety.

A ten-day period of tension commenced after the docking of Ichabod Jones's vessels: the UNITY, the POLLY, and the MARGARETTA. True to form, the young British naval officer in charge, Midshipman James Moor, ordered the Liberty Pole cut down, precipitating a prolonged crisis. Benjamin Foster, agitating for action against the British, created a niche for himself in Maine folk mythology by designating a stream to be crossed by those volunteering to fight, which forever became "Foster's Rubicon." A motley mob, armed with every rustic weapon conceivable and hailing from as far away as Jonesboro, then were led by Foster and Jeremiah O'Brien in Jones's sloop UNITY to capture the MARGARETTA at sea. In the firefight on board, young Moor was fatally wounded; so, too, was an innocent bystander, Robert Avery, and one American, the intriguingly named Coolbroth Smith.

Under Jeremiah O'Brien's command, the renamed MARGARETTA (now MACHIAS LIBERTY) and other captured craft became "the beginnings of the Massachusetts State Navy." He and his brother John eventually became noted privateers, harassing British shipping all along the Atlantic Coast. Captured off New York and imprisoned in England, Jeremiah added to his fame by succeeding in a daring escape, returning to Maine, and indulging in more anti-British naval adventures.

There was a good deal of bravado in Machias. The Reverend James Lyon wrote to the Massachusetts General Court in September 1776:

Some members of the Court consider the eastern country as a moth (costs more than it is worth and would be wise to let it suffer and sink). Should your honors believe the east to be a moth, dispose of it, and give us the right of dominion. We shall then become an independent state ourselves and we shall think of Nova Scotia as worth annexing to our dominion.

In reality, Nova Scotia did seem vulnerable. In the Cumberland County towns of Truro, Onslow, and Londonderry, it was said only five persons could be found willing to swear allegiance to the Crown. The Maugerville town meeting of May 14, 1776, passed a series of anti-British resolutions, one of which stated baldly: "...it is our minds and desires to submit ourselves to the government of the Massachusetts Bay and we are ready with our lives and fortunes to share with them the event of the present struggle for liberty."

Moreover, there was now a military man in Machias, a landowning squire from Onslow but originally out of Norton, Massachusetts, "Colonel" Jonathan Eddy, who was organizing an army to go back into Nova Scotia, arouse the inhabitants, and attack the main English garrison at Fort Cumberland.

An American thrust against Canada had already been tried on an ambitious scale in the fall of 1775—the famous, ill-fated Benedict Arnold expedition—up through the middle of Maine, following a combination of routes explored by Montresor and Chadwick to reach Quebec. Expectations that the Canadians would rise up to depose their English overlords were not fulfilled, but those were French, Eddy could argue, not good Yankee stock.

At the end of March 1776, Eddy was in Cambridge, talking to George Washington, whom he was unable to sway. Undaunted, he went on to Philadelphia to lobby the Continental Congress, but again with no success. Described as "neither a demagogue nor a megalomaniac," he was certainly a most stubborn gentleman.[4] In his home district on the Chignecto Isthmus, he had been popular enough to be elected to the Nova Scotian Assembly, and during the French and Indian War in the 1750s he'd fought under Colonel Robert Monckton and John Winslow in a joint British-American force that had captured the very fort he proposed to take.

Returning to Machias in the summer of 1776, Eddy began to organize an attack. He set forth with only twenty-eight men and a schooner, despite attempts to dissuade him by another exiled patriot from Nova Scotia, a neighbor and a colleague of his in the Halifax Assembly, the Scottish-born John Allan, a man who was to play a far greater role than Eddy in the struggle over this corner of North America.

Jonathan Eddy's "expedition" into Canada was equally as futile as Benedict Arnold's, but nowhere near as tragic. For one thing, his force never amounted to more than 150 men (Arnold had 700), his casualties were few and historians have generally dismissed his aborted raid as a farce. In his own defense, he afterward

194   *The Interrupted Forest*

argued they "did capture fifty-six British soldiers, two captains, one surgeon, one chaplain, besides thirteen killed, plus seven deserted to us..." and, more importantly, they had kept 2,000 British soldiers at Halifax and out of His Majesty's troops then blockading New York.

Yet ominously, once more, the Canadians had not risen to join the Americans in any numbers; despite a shared Anglo-Saxon heritage, most weren't rushing to shed their allegiance to the Crown and there were complaints that some of Eddy's men had not been averse to plundering the locals.

John Allan, son of a career British Army major, had fled his home near Fort Cumberland in the spring of 1776 with a price on his head. He had had to leave precipitously, abandoning his wife and children, at the tail end of a conference with the local Micmac Indians where he had urged them to support the American cause. He, too, went to Massachusetts and Philadelphia, seeking help for the area. Near Trenton, on December 22, 1776, he dined with George Washington. When he left for Machias in February, it was with commissions for himself as a colonel of infantry and as superintendent of the Eastern Indians.

He also brought letters with him, signed by George Washington, for the local Indian chiefs; one to "my good friend and brother Perre Thommar [*sic*]" of the Maliseets and another to "Brothers of the Passamaquodia," both admonishing them "never let the King's wicked counsellor turn your heart against me." In the constant struggle for the allegiance of the Native Americans in eastern Maine, there were many reversals of loyalty but, overall, the Penobscots and Passamaquoddies sided with the Americans and the Maliseets split—Washington's "good friend and brother," Pierre Thomma, generally leaning to the British, and a second Maliseet leader, Ambroise Bear, sticking with the Americans. The latter and his men joined Colonel John Allan in the spring of 1777 when he, too, attempted an incursion into Nova Scotia—to the St. John River, intending to occupy its lower valley. Like Eddy's foray, it was woefully undermanned and ended in as ignominious, if less freebooting, a retreat. Pouring back into Machias were Indian allies, refugee Yankee sympathizers from Nova Scotia, and a chastened John Allan, now on the defensive.

A British counterattack was not long in coming. Two months later, an impetuous British admiral, Sir George Collier, sailed into Machias with a force of marines. They swept aside the small boom Colonel Eddy had placed at the mouth of the Machias River and proceeded up the waterway, but not before receiving intense musket fire from a detachment led by some of those heroes of the MARGARETTA affair: Benjamin Foster, George Stillman, and Stephen Smith. The British brig HOPE, the only one of their vessels with a shallow enough draft to navigate the river, was bombarded by cannon fire directed by Colonel Phineas Nevers, another Nova Scotian refugee. Indians, whooping and hollering, also fired at the British ship, continually pelting the attackers with shot until they finally retreated, and then fled. Still, Sir George Collier claimed an English victory, saying his action had frustrated another planned American invasion. Jonathan Eddy, conversely, crowed the British had suffered seventy casualties and the Americans only two.

Shortly after the battle, though, Jonathan Eddy left Machias, having turned his men over to Major George Stillman, and retired to his birthplace of Mansfield, Massachusetts.

John Allan stayed in Machias for the rest of the war, playing a pivotal role in maintaining an American presence Down East. It was a heartbreakingly difficult task and the importance of his impact on the history of northern Maine is due to his efforts to keep the Indian tribesmen loyal and a revolutionary fighting spirit intact in the face of dispiriting odds. He had little help from either the Continental Congress or the patriot government of Massachusetts. There were strong and clever British officials ranged against him, with the enemy's influence growing after they occupied Castine, followed by the repercussions of the disastrous American defeat on the Penobscot when their massive effort to retake Castine ended in the worst U.S. naval defeat prior to Pearl Harbor.

Through it all, John Allan somehow persevered. His people were hungry and ill-supplied from Massachusetts, a particularly acute problem since the British offered the Indians more goods and even inveigled some into signing a treaty of neutrality.

But why focus on this tiny pocket of American resistance in a remote, unimportant wilderness spot? It has none of the heroic drama of an Alamo. Machias was little more than a symbolic American presence, albeit a steady one, mostly.

Well, for one thing, the British were contemplating their *New Ireland* scheme.

When an amphibious operation under Admiral Sir George Collier and Brigadier General Francis McLean bloodlessly occupied Castine in mid-June 1779, the official position of the invaders was that they were simply back on British soil. Nor was the Penobscot area necessarily to be considered as belonging to the former Province of Massachusetts Bay or Nova Scotia. If certain pro-English politicians had their way, they would be in New Ireland, a separate province created for the special purpose of rewarding American Loyalists.

Allegedly, this plan was the brainchild of a foreign office bureaucrat named William Knox, himself a Tory exile from Georgia, who had received encouragement from fellow exiles in London to persuade his colleagues at Whitehall of the necessity of a sanctuary on American soil for the king's supporters. True, there was no doubt Great Britain would prevail and bring its rebellious subjects to heel, but if ever there had to be an evacuation, here was a goodly chunk of territory that could be salvaged. The first royal word on the subject even included almost all of Maine—at least from the "Sawnko" (Saco) River to the St. Croix.

It was in the language of an order approved by the British Cabinet and by the king on August 10 and 11, 1780. We have the testimony of the arch-Tory of them all, former Massachusetts Governor Thomas Hutchinson, that he had an interview with William Knox two years earlier in which he was told the Penobscot district was "to be erected into a new province to be given to the refugees...as a recompense for their sufferings...and to ease Government of the expense it is now at for their support." Note that the date, which was September 3, 1778, preceded the actual capture of Castine. Hutchinson, although appalled by the idea of breaking up Massachusetts, kept his mouth shut. He said he was reminded of a story about a friend of Lord Shaftsbury's who, after secretly marrying, asked for the Lord's opinion of his bride, but received no honest answer, because although Shaftsbury thought his friend had made a preposterous match, it had already been done. Even later, when Hutchinson was sounded out by Knox about being New Ireland's governor, the arch-Tory kept his counsel, but no doubt went on trying to sabotage the plan behind the scenes.

Among those lobbying heavily for New Ireland were two ex-Bostonians, Dr. John Calef (pronounced *calf*), a physician and onetime representative in the General Court, and John Nutting, a building contractor. Before the revolution, both had speculated heavily in Down East Maine lands, yet had never received confirmation from the Crown. Certainly, they hoped New Ireland would clear up their titles. Additionally, the type of province proposed was calculated to warm the cockles of any monarchist's heart, with its elitist structure and vivid departure from democratic Massachusetts.

For example, it would have an established Episcopal church, with its hierarchy of bishops, and top-down command. The provincial government would also be stacked in favor of the Crown. There would be no elected assembly and so, in line with Governor Bernard's thoughts, the legislature would be appointed by the Crown and hold their seats for life, unless removed by the king. All lands in New Ireland would have quit-rents attached to them, payable to the Crown, which the legislative body could use for paying expenses. "Distinguished Loyalists" could be exempted from these quit-rent taxes. Every inhabitant would have to swear an oath of allegiance to the king. Land distribution would be done to "lay the ground of an Aristocratic Power"—that is, "large Tracts to the most Meritorious" who could then lease "to the lower People in manner as has been practiced in New York, which is the only Province in which there is a Tenantry and was the least inclined to be Rebellious...." In short, New Ireland would serve as a model for what the U.S. would have been like had it stayed under British rule.

This Royalist paradise, its founding document declared, "may with great propriety be called New Ireland, especially as the era of its establishment is coeval with that of opening the trade of Ireland with the American Provinces."

The *coup de grâce* to this scheme was given, most historians say, by an attorney general's ruling in Great Britain. Alexander Wedderburn, in his capacity as the king's lawyer, issued an opinion that the scheme was illegal, a violation of royal charters granted to Massachusetts, whose government and boundaries remained intact despite the rebellion. William Knox later grumbled that Wedderburn, unhappy he'd been passed over for a peerage, blamed Lord George Germain and therefore, in revenge, killed a proposal supported by Germain. Thomas Hutchinson's work behind the scenes remains a titillating historical mystery.

New Ireland or no New Ireland, the Penobscot bastion remained a magnet for Tory refugees from all of the thirteen colonies. John Calef continually advertised their plight in letters to British officials—such as his story of John Perkins, Joseph Perkins, and Mark Hatch, original owners of much of the Majabigwaduce (Castine) peninsula, persecuted by a Colonel Cargill who headed a mob that had seized their vessels and robbed them of their cattle. Or of old Shubael Williams, "near seventy years of age," whipped with 500 lashes for transporting provisions to the British troops.

But in the end, Calef was told by Lord North, the British prime minister, "Doctor, we cannot make the Penobscot the boundary. The pressure is too strong."

Regarding the boundary that ultimately marked the final shape of Maine, the U.S., and Canada, the scene now shifts from the dense forests, primitive settlements, and rocky fringes of the Maine Coast to that most cosmopolitan of Old World cities, Paris, France. I well remember spying a plaque one day on the front wall of an edifice next-door to my Left Bank hotel and feeling a real patriotic thrill. At 56 Rue Jacob, presently a nondescript office building, a bilingual inscription is matter-of-factly displayed:

EN CE BATIMENT
JADIS HÔTEL D'YORK
LE 3 SEPTEMBRE 1783
DAVID HARTLEY
AU NOM DU ROI D'ANGLETERRE
BENJAMIN FRANKLIN,
JOHN JAY, JOHN ADAMS
AU NOM DES ÉTATS-UNIS D'AMÉRIQUE
ONT SIGNÉ LE TRAITÉ DÉFINITIF DE PAIX

RECONNAISSANT L'INDÉPENDANCE
DES ÉTATS-UNIS

IN THIS BUILDING
FORMERLY THE YORK HOTEL
ON SEPTEMBER 3, 1783,
DAVID HARTLEY
IN THE NAME OF THE KING OF ENGLAND
BENJAMIN FRANKLIN,
JOHN JAY, JOHN ADAMS
IN THE NAME OF THE UNITED STATES OF AMERICA
SIGNED THE DEFINITIVE PEACE TREATY
RECOGNIZING THE INDEPENDENCE
OF THE UNITED STATES

Why such a world-shaking treaty was signed at such an obscure locale a block from the Seine, and not at glittering Versailles, the seat of the French monarchy, has been explained as the result of David Hartley's instructions—he was not accredited to go to Versailles. It may also have been a demonstration of the French government's pique, particularly the annoyance of France's foreign minister, Count de Vergennes, that the Americans made their deal with the British without consulting him or obtaining his permission. By acting in this way, Franklin, Jay, and Adams also ignored their orders from the Continental Congress, which Vergennes had been at some pains to engineer through his agents in Philadelphia.

The dramatic story of how the U.S. consolidated its independence through diplomacy after the battle of Yorktown is perhaps as obscure to most Americans as the Paris venue of its signing. The actions of the three principal commissioners—Franklin, Jay, and Adams (there was a fourth, Henry Laurens, who played a minor role, and a fifth, Thomas Jefferson, who never participated)—were nothing short of miraculous in winning almost all of the American points and dodging the bullets their allies, as well as their English enemy, tried to fire at them. The French, whose help was considerable, were not pouring troops, supplies, and money into the thirteen colonies out of the kindness of their hearts; they desired the U.S. to be an independent republic in order to weaken the British, but

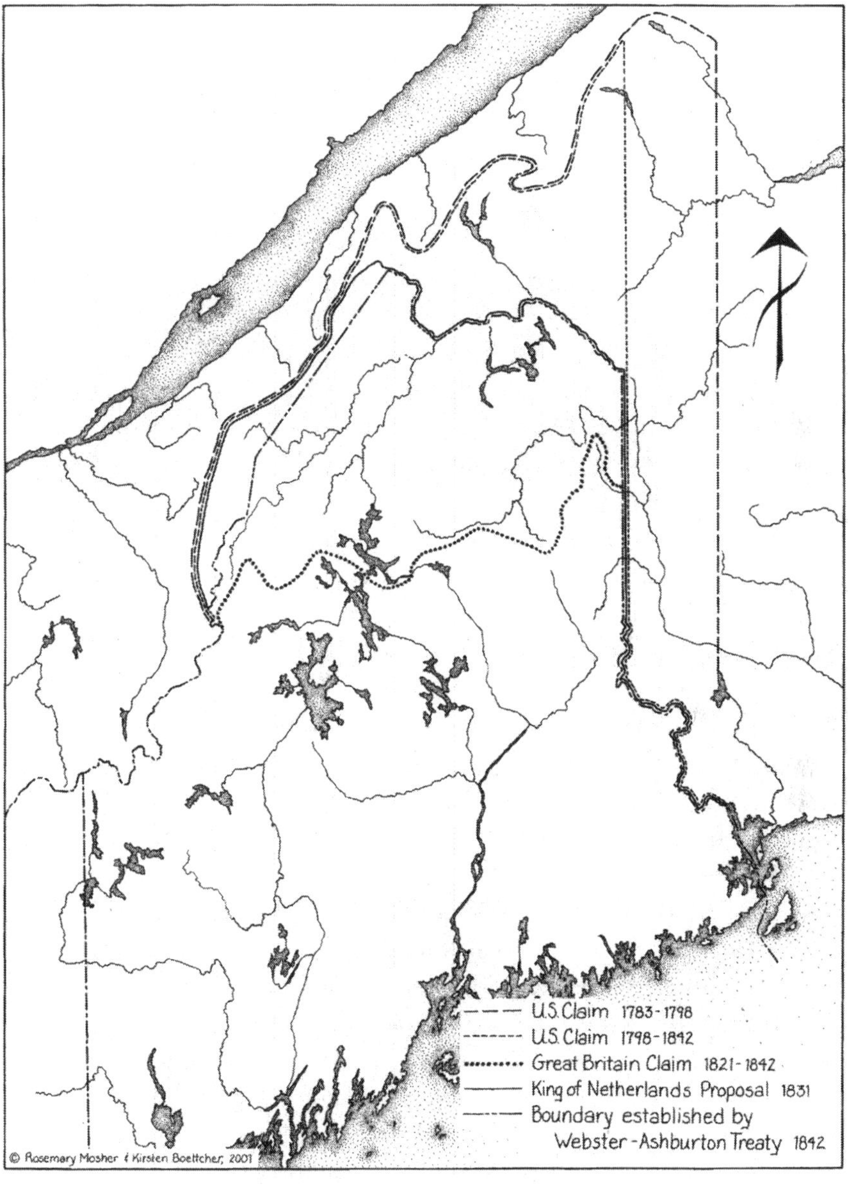
U.S. Claim 1783-1798
U.S. Claim 1798-1842
Great Britain Claim 1821-1842
King of Netherlands Proposal 1831
Boundary established by
Webster-Ashburton Treaty 1842
© Rosemary Mosher & Kirsten Boettcher, 2001

United States Borders

wanted a *weak* republic, dependent upon France. Therefore, Vergennes favored leaving Canada in British hands and closing off the thirteen colonies at the Appalachians. Spain, another American ally, had even less love for a powerful U.S.; their chief minister, Floridablanco, wanted control of both banks of the Mississippi and a ban on any American shipping to New Orleans, plus ownership of Florida and the Gulf Coast. Furthermore, the Spaniards refused to sign any peace treaty until Britain returned Gibraltar to them. Holland, the third U.S. ally, was mostly interested in the Far East and Indonesia.

Tucked into this welter of global issues, the question of the northeast border of Maine or, indeed, the fate of Maine, itself, seemed of small import. But here is where John Adams proved his mettle.

During some of the early discussions with David Hartley's predecessor, Richard Oswald, who had done land speculating in America, the issues of Canada and of Maine were raised—Franklin at first suggesting, probably facetiously, that Britain cede all of Canada to the new United States; then Oswald made a claim for all of Maine. This latter demand, not so facetiously, was eventually backed by a clerk named Roberts from the Board of Trade and Plantations, with "huge volumes of…original records in order to support their incontestable claim to the Province of Maine." But John Adams came to the rescue. He astonished Roberts by producing still more impressive records of Massachusetts's claim to Maine. Among them was the proof of "Governor Pownall's solemn act of burying a leaden plate" where he did, "the laying out of Mount Desert, Machias, and all the other towns east of the River Penobscot," the grant by James I to Sir William Alexander that bounded Nova Scotia by the St. Croix River, and, as he wrote in his memoirs, "that I was possessed of the authorities of four of the greatest governors the King of England ever had, Shirley, Pownall, Bernard, and Hutchinson, in favor of our claim and of learned writings of Shirley and Hutchinson in support of it."

Adams told Vergennes, whom he didn't like or trust, that their talks with the British were hung up on two items—"the Tories and Penobscot" and, in a sense they were linked, since King George III was adamant about helping the Americans who had stayed loyal to him. A fairly unsung hero working to unsnarl these complications was a private English citizen named Benjamin Vaughan, a friend of Lord Shelburne, the prime minister, and of Benjamin Franklin, as well. He was also the brother of one of John Adams's employers, Charles Vaughan, a Braintree lawyer who had represented the Kennebec Proprietors. Shuttling back and forth between London and Paris, Benjamin Vaughan pushed for a compromise on the treatment of the Tories and a successful formula was worked out. The U.S. federal government would recommend to the states that they compensate those who had lost their property and give them twelve months to return unmolested and make their claims. With this and other thorny matters settled, the only loose end was the exact demarcation of Maine, which they left to be decided by a commission. To critics of their signing of a document they hadn't cleared with the Count de Vergennes, John Adams had a pithy Yankee response: "...that he [Vergennes] meant to keep his hand under our chin to prevent us from drowning, but not to lift our heads out of the water."

The momentous event in the building at 56 Rue Jacob most likely did not seem so momentous at the time. No one could have predicted the great world power thus unleashed. It was an absolutely brilliant piece of diplomacy. Yet its one flaw, the vagueness of the northeast boundary, would cause continual problems for the new nation and, in particular, for the new State of Maine, which thirty-seven years later would come into being.

NOTES

[1] Fannie Hardy Eckstorm, "History of the Chadwick Survey," *Sprague's Journal of Maine History*. Vol. 14, no. 2.

[2] Alan Taylor, *Liberty Men and Great Proprietors: The Revolutionary Settlement on the Maine Frontier, 1760–1820*. Chapel Hill, NH, and London: University of North Carolina Press, 1990. Page 32.

[3] Records of the Massachusetts House of Representatives, April 3, 1770. Vol. 4, part II.

[4] George Rawlyk, *Nova Scotia's Massachusetts*. Montreal and London: McGill-Queens University Press, 1978. Page 238.

FOURTEEN

Goodbye to Massachusetts, or Almost

WHILE THE 1783 PARIS Peace Treaty put an end to the sporadic, hit-and-run warfare that had plagued the Down East region, it also bequeathed a heritage of uncertainty. The British did not even evacuate their garrison from Castine until the following year. The Tories went with them, to be sure, but where did they land in large numbers? Right next-door in Nova Scotia. The buildup of Loyalist refugees this close to the unestablished border so unnerved John Allan that he wrote to John Hancock, asking that Massachusetts move against them, particularly in their growing settlement of St. Andrews. It was here, on a peninsula jutting into Passamaquoddy Bay opposite Robbinston, that most of the evacuees from Castine settled. They called themselves the Penobscot Association. Joined with them was the 74th Association, who were Scots of the Argyle Highlanders, taking their discharge in Nova Scotia rather than going home. Other Loyalists, some from North Carolina, were spread out on the same peninsula.

Yet the bulk of the émigrés, initially sailing from New York in the spring of 1783, headed to the St. John River area more than 3,500 strong. By November 1783, most of this exodus had been completed.

Also, there was something of a split among the Loyalists in the Maritimes, characterized by the terms Canadian historians use for them: *Refugees* —those who came away first, as early as the evacuation of Boston in 1776; and *Provincials* —soldiers in organized units of the British forces who stayed in America until the last minute. A political tug-of-war over where to put these demobilized Tories was one cause of disenchantment with the provincial authorities at Halifax, where Governor John Parr tended to favor the earlier arrivals and also members of his own government who had speculated in land along the St. John. The Royal Fencible Americans, DeLancey's Brigade, and others were assigned to settle in less favorable regions upriver, north of Sunbury County.

So, well before Maine began thinking seriously about breaking off from Massachusetts, the newcomers to Nova Scotia were undertaking to remove themselves from Halifax.

The British system of top-down government allowed them to secede much more easily and far more quickly than Maine was able to do. If any one leader can be credited with creating New Brunswick, it was a quintessential Yankee named Edward Winslow, self-exiled from Plymouth and a scion of the famous Pilgrim family. He had been Muster-Master of Provincial Troops for His Majesty in America and had political contacts in England. So did his former deputy and fellow Harvard grad, Ward Chipman, and the two of them teamed up to secure the approval of the government in London. The great distance to Halifax was put forward as the major reason for secession, and the name originally suggested for the new province was none other than New Ireland, it being considered good strategy to offer a name that had once received the king's blessing. When the British powers-that-be, in remarkably short order, agreed to let the area north of the Bay of Fundy govern itself, they, however, declared it would be called New Brunswick, for reasons best known to themselves.

In less than a year after the great Loyalist migration, New Brunswick was a going concern, with its own governor, council, and (rather powerless) elected assembly. Winslow, who had hoped for the key position of secretary of the province, had to be satisfied with a seat on the Governor's Council.

The presence on the map of New Brunswick by August 1784 had to act as a constant reminder to the populations of eastern Maine of the failure of Massachusetts on the whole to support and protect them during the war. Raids by the Tory refugees had been no less a threat of death and injury than the Indian assaults of earlier days. The seventy-year-old Shubael Williams of North Haven, whom the British claimed to be a victim of Yankee cruelty, was in reality a Patriot, as the Americans told it, whipped for his loyalty to the Revolution. British commandos had daringly penetrated as far south as Thomaston, kidnapping General Peleg Wadsworth, grandfather of the poet. For a full flavor of the coastal Maine settlers' fear of Tory refugees in the Revolution, a fictional account—Ben Ames Williams's novel, *Come Spring*—paints a vivid picture of the terrors haunting the wilderness pioneers (based on historical figures) who established the town of Union in Mid-Coast Maine. Rumors were rife of Indians, Tories, and British Regulars combining to drive them off the land.

A real-life petition of the inhabitants of Lincoln County asking the Massachusetts General Court for an abatement of taxes following the disastrous Penobscot expedition may have laid it on a bit thick about their troubles, but its graphic tone undoubtedly derived its intensity from personal experience:

> The failure of the late expedition to Penobscot has already laid desolate a number of very hopeful settlements in these parts: the inhabitants, men and women, having fled through the wilderness to the western parts of the state, leaving behind their stock, provisions, crops, and all they had....

Which exposed them to:

> ...an insolent and triumphant enemy who avows the design of treating the country as a conquered one and its inhabitants as persons taken in actual rebellion.

Some who were required to take oaths and work for the British, constructing forts and performing other tasks, were:

> ...subjected to be cudgeled, kicked, and abused by every petty officer set over them.

The document was signed by such coastal leaders as Militia Generals Samuel McCobb and James Cargill and selectmen from inland Kennebec towns such as Winslow, Vassalboro, Winthrop, and Hallowell.

The General Court ordered the Lincoln County officials to furnish aid to those dispossessed and, in turn, swore to reimburse them.

Pressures like these contributed to the fact that Massachusetts ended the Revolutionary War in a parlous fiscal condition. "...her people borne down with the weight of taxes—her treasury empty—her credit that of a bankrupt—her paper-money currency worth, in the market, scarcely 10 percent of its normal value—her commerce next to nothing...and no resources for the payment of her debts created by the war, except what might possibly be derived from the sales of her wild lands, or from direct taxes on the people...." The writer then conceded the political impossibility of taxes. Land sales, he intimated, "seemed to promise some relief."[1]

Thus was created the Committee for the Sale of Eastern Lands in Lincoln County, where the Commonwealth's greatest acreage of public land existed. Its prestigious members were Samuel Phillips, Jr., president of the senate (and the founder of Phillips Academy, Andover); Nathan Dane, a former member of the Continental Congress; and Nathaniel Wells, a future Massachusetts chief justice from the town of Wells. Except for the U.S. government, no other state in the country had as much land at its disposal. Although the District of Maine's northeastern extent was still vague, there were in this region upwards of 17 million to 20 million acres potentially available to bring in much-needed cash.

The committee members had very little idea of what they had to work with, so a first order of business was to conduct a survey. A military man, General Rufus Putnam, was sent to explore the mostly uncharted land between the St. Croix and the Penobscot. Leaving Boston in August 1784, he began with the lands bordering Passamaquoddy Bay and was back within four months with a preliminary study. The committee was so pleased by Putnam's work that he was made superintendent of surveys. The next spring, Putnam went Down East with a twenty-one-man team and stayed until December.

An interesting incident on this second trip was the surveying party's encounter at Pleasant Point with a hermit-like lone settler who turned out to be former Governor Sir Francis Bernard's son. Of John Bernard, the comment was voiced: "Poor fellow. We pitied him. He had probably never done a day's work in his life." Now, accompanied only by "a little dog," he was cutting trees, trying to lay

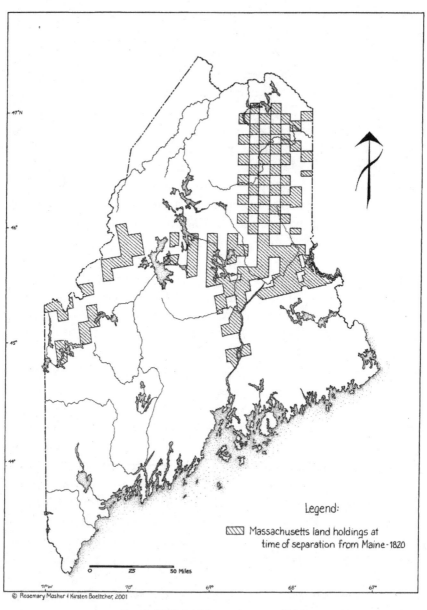

Legend:

Massachusetts land holdings at
time of separation from Maine -1820

© Rosemary Mosher & Kirsten Boettcher, 2001

Land Held by Massachusetts, 1820

claim to land he believed to be in his father's grant, extending from Mount Desert Island to the St. Croix.

Poor fellow, indeed. Because he had never shown Tory tendencies and had remained in America, the General Court could state they "had ample testimony of the uniform consistence and propriety of his political conduct previous to and during and since the late war..." and grant him half of Mount Desert Island, plus other property. These lands he promptly mortgaged and, with the money, went back to England, claimed his father's baronetcy, and lived the life of an English nobleman far from the wilds of Maine.

In its report to the General Court in June 1785, the committee also revealed it had sales contracts for about 79,000 acres with, among others, those two Revolutionary leaders on the northeast coast, Colonels John Allan and Jonathan Eddy. They alerted their colleagues to their belief that the rate of sales would be "greatly expedited" if they could settle a boundary dispute between the Kennebec Proprietors and the Pejepscot Proprietors, plus ascertain what lands should continue to be held by the Penobscot Indians. On the latter issue, their logic was that "the lands on the Penobscot River and between that and the Kennebec River...appear by the application of purchasers for them to be much more salable than any other lands in that county."[2]

Accordingly, "commissioners" were sent to treat with the Penobscots to see how much of this valuable property they could inveigle from the natives. There were three of them, led by General Benjamin Lincoln, a hero of the Revolution and actually the first secretary of war of the United States. A hulk of a man, with a pronounced limp from a bullet that had shattered his ankle, Lincoln has been described as "gracious, having a kind and amiable expression, with a lack of military pomp, prolixity, and tediousness, who spoke with brevity and gentle wit." In the negotiations he and his two colleagues, General Rufus Putnam and Doctor Thomas Rice, conducted with the tribal chiefs on August 28, 1786, General Lincoln started off genially enough, discussing the "kind intentions" of the Massachusetts government to settle the Indians' land claims to "mutual satisfaction" and congratulating them on "the happy close of the war in which you had been our faithful friends and brethren."

The setting was Kenduskeag (an early name for Bangor) and the four chiefs—Orono, Orsong, John Neptune, and Neptonboyett—sat on an "elegant" green lawn near the river, with the rest of the Penobscots standing behind them.

As to their "claim," the natives were quite specific. "We claim down to a small stream below Oldtown, one mile above Colburn's. If the English come nearer, our dogs will do them damage and make a quarrel."

This was not what the commissioners wanted to hear. The Indians were reminded they had relinquished all of this part of the country to Governor Pownall. That they were still here was by the sufferance of the Provincial Congress of 1775, which had met with them at Watertown and granted them six miles on either side of the river from the head of tide. "On this you all now rest your claims." The argument followed that if the tribe gave up that claim, they would be given a larger tract upriver and two islands in Penobscot Bay.

The Indians replied they didn't "think it right to remove further up the river." The commissioners said: "You have our proposals from which we shall not depart." The Indians' retort was that if they moved, they expected to be paid. The commissioners: "We do give you more land and better for hunting. What further consideration do you desire?" The Indians: "Blankets, powder, shot, and flints."

In the end, it was agreed the Penobscots would have 350 blankets, 200 pounds of powder, and shot and flints "in proportion"—to be delivered when they signed the ratification. Four witnesses to the Indians' consent were then introduced by General Lincoln—the Reverends Daniel Little and Seth Noble, Colonel Jonathan Eddy, and William Colburn.

So it seemed a deal had been struck, sealed with handshakes, and a feast provided by the commissioners. On October 4, Governor James Bowdoin reported to the General Court that the Indians had acquiesced in relinquishing all their lands on the west side of the Penobscot 43 miles upriver to the Piscataquis and on the east side 85 miles up to Mattawamkeag, keeping only their Indian Island home at Old Town and some other islands in the river.

Two years later, when Massachusetts moved to consummate

the pact by delivering the agreed-upon blankets and ammunition, sending the Reverend Daniel Little as their emissary, difficulties arose. The first was merely a diplomatic wrangle over where they would meet, the Indians rejecting Kenduskeag and wanting the event held at Indian Island. Reverend Little initially "was in doubt" but eventually caved in, fearful there would be no "conference" if he didn't. Thus, on June 21, 1788, Little and his party met with the sachems in one of their bark-covered houses and the firing of a cannon announced the start of the conclave. Little opened by reminding them of their promise to General Lincoln, stating he was ready to hand over the blankets, and other items, and a parchment containing the government's "gift of land" as soon as they signed. Orson Neptune was the Penobscots' spokesman. He argued: "If anybody takes any land from us it must be King George, for the General Court and General Washington promised we should enjoy this country," adding the tribe had "not a right understanding of matters at Kenduskeag" and had been "pressed to make that treaty contrary to our inclinations."

Not only was Reverend Little sent away without a signed document but also with a personal dig. Neptune asked the interpreter: "Is not Mr. Little a minister?" Answered in the affirmative, he shot back: "Brother, ministers ought not to have anything to do with public business."

Eight years later, the Penobscots did relinquish territory of 200,000 acres, and more was pried from them afterward. No one could have known in 1806 what colossal irony had attended the natives' innate stubbornness. By sending the Reverend Little packing, they had unconsciously set the stage 200 years into the future for the epochal Indian Land Claims case of the 1970s (which will be discussed subsequently) as one of the most important events ever in Maine land history.

Aggravation from the Indians (even though their lands were eventually just about all taken) and the need to raise tax money weren't the only issues facing the General Court then. General Benjamin Lincoln, in a 1786 letter to Governor Bowdoin, touched on a problem that would bedevil the Commonwealth for decades—how to deal with settlers whose title to the lands they occupied was dubious or nonexistent. Lincoln warned the governor about people who had "set themselves down on public property in the eastern part of this State." He felt they should somehow be accommodated:

> The Commonwealth has wisely, I think, established a
> rule for quieting those who so settled before the first of
> January 1784. No provision has been made for those
> who have taken up such lands since that date. This, sir,
> I think will be a source from which great discontent
> will flow hereafter.[3]

A month later, the General Court received a petition from the Penobscot region clearly illuminating the problem. It was from a Stephen Bussell and others who had settled on Township 10, known then as Colonel Eddy's Township. They were worried because they had heard that the General Court planned to sell all unappropriated land in Lincoln County. "We trust your Honors do not wish to deprive us of our labours, without making us some compensation," they wrote. What they asked for was a grant of 100 acres each, "where we have improved and settled." Bussell, himself, had already been there thirteen years, Patrick Monney the same, and Thankful McMahan ten years.

Others, on the west side of the Penobscot, like Benjamin, John, Edwin, and Israel Smith, Reuben Newcomb, John Crosby, and others, were also beseeching the lawmakers that since "we have settled on land to which we have no other title but possession," they hoped the legislature would not let "any individual man or company...dispossess or take from us that which has cost us so many years' hard labor." They reminded the authorities in Boston that when the Americans had tried to retake Castine, they had joined General Lovell's army and, with the failure of the expedition, they and their families were exposed to the British enemy and "the revengeful temper of the Refugees.... Some of us have suffered stripes and imprisonment and have frequently lost our sheep and cattle...." At the very least, they concluded, if they couldn't be given the land outright, they wanted "the preference of purchasing our lots, which contain 100 acres each, at the same rate other lands are sold at."

Grants to Revolutionary War veterans were common, but offi-

The Interrupted Forest

cers seemed to get preference. Colonel Eddy, in June 1785, received almost 10,000 acres in Township 10, without having to pay anything. General Benjamin Lincoln, even before his mission to the Indians, was allowed to buy more than 50,000 acres in the Dennysville, Perry, Pembroke area of Washington County. Colonel John Allan got a whole township—33,000 acres—near Whiting for a mere £300. General Peleg Wadsworth paid almost that much for only 7,800 acres, but in a more developed place—Hiram, in southern Maine. And General Henry Knox received land in the vicinity of Bangor to make up a deficiency in the Waldo Patent, which he had secured through his wife's inheritance. Not until 1801 did Massachusetts grant free bounty land to ordinary soldiers.

The land sale program of the Commonwealth was not a howling success. In 1786 a new approach was tried—a lottery. The prizes were 50 townships surveyed between the Penobscot River and Passamaquoddy Bay and 2,720 tickets were issued costing $200 apiece. The goal was to make half a million dollars and apply it to paying down the debt.

The result: a measly 437 tickets were sold, only $87,400 brought in, with a disposal of no more than 165,280 acres.

Thus, when the other expedient to stave off bankruptcy—taxing the citizenry—was tried, the consequences were dire. In western Massachusetts, armed revolt broke out when the courts attempted to foreclose on tax-delinquent landowners. History knows this event as Shays' Rebellion and as a catalyst for the creation of the U.S. Constitution. A year after Kenduskeag, General Lincoln was in the saddle again, leading a militia force against Daniel Shays and his followers. General Rufus Putnam was with him once more, too. The rebels were dispersed and, partly at Lincoln's urging, treated with clemency. Some scattered to Maine and found a ready audience for their discontent in the squatters of that wilderness section of Massachusetts.

But before taking up this colorful chapter in the saga of the Maine North Woods, General Henry Knox—the principal target of the squatters' wrath and the ultimate symbol for the large-scale land dealings that occurred—has a story worth telling to place these events in context. There is also an intrinsic link here to the political movement that eventually, after a thirty-four-year struggle, separated Maine from Massachusetts.

Knox was a Bostonian of Scottish ancestry who started adult life as a bookseller, married well, and became a military hero and a confidant of George Washington. His wife Lucy (née Lucy Flucker) was a granddaughter of Samuel Waldo. After the war, through her, and Knox's astute buying up of other heirs' portions of the estate, the entire Waldo Patent came into his possession.

Big as this land area was, it apparently did not satisfy Knox's ambition. Serving as secretary of war under both the Articles of Confederation and the Constitution (1785–94), he became part of a Federalist elite in Philadelphia, many of whom (Washington included) were engaged in large-scale land speculation. One of the bigger operators at the time, a promoter of the Scioto Company that invested in Ohio lands, was a naturalized Englishman and former congressman named William Duer. While working as an assistant secretary of the treasury under Alexander Hamilton, he and Knox did business together and, in partnership, they decided to buy "not less than one million nor more than four million acres of land" in Maine. As front men for them, they hired two other associates from their staff days with Washington—General Henry Jackson of Boston and Royal Flint of New York.

Their instructions to the pair for conducting negotiations with the Committee for the Sale of Eastern Lands were rather explicit in their deviousness:

It may, however, be necessary to remark that it has been intimated to us that the Committee are not disposed in favor of large purchases—from a jealousy of monopoly.... In this case names may be made use of to obtain the whole land we want by different applications varying in some instances in order to avoid suspicion of combination....[4]

Knox and Duer had pegged their highest price at twelve cents an acre, although hoping to pay as low as six cents. Jackson heard from the committee that they wanted fourteen cents an acre and would sell no more than one million acres to any one customer. But either Jackson was a superb salesman or the committee was really anxious to unload its land, for on June 23, 1791, they agreed to sell two million acres at ten cents an acre. A week later, Jackson, acting as Knox and Duer's straw, had a contract. Although Knox still thought he wanted four million acres, in the long run he settled for three million—two million "on the east side of the Penobscot River," including all of the ungranted lottery townships—and the other million on the Kennebec. In all, the partners bought $400,000 to $500,000 worth of land, with a down payment of only $10,000, with $25,000 due on the first of their three contracts within 60 days after a survey was done.

Note that during all of this, Knox was still secretary of war and Duer remained in his important treasury post.

Then, in March 1792, Duer failed and ended in debtors' prison. The federal government went after him, too, for unbalanced items in his treasury accounts.

Knox, strapped for money, began looking for an angel to help bail him out. An important businessman named William Green appeared to be a prospect, but eventually backed away. It was at this point that a prominent member of the Philadelphia Federalist elite, U.S. Senator William Bingham, well known to Knox, entered the scene. He was the land speculator par excellence, reputedly at one time the largest property owner in the United States.

A graduate of the University of Pennsylvania, Bingham had begun his career when the Continental Congress appointed him their agent on the French West Indian island of Martinique, where he was helpful in supplying the American cause. Back in Philadelphia after four years, he married a sixteen-year-old beauty, Ann Willing (later called the "most beautiful woman in America"), a daughter of the banker Thomas Willing, who was in partnership with Robert Morris, the main financier of the Revolution. In the 1790s Bingham and Morris were described as the two most active land traders in the country, and their wealth and ostentation made them members of "this new Republican court" that held sway in Philadelphia as long as it was the capital. Not only did Bingham own huge tracts in Pennsylvania and New York (Binghamton is named for him), but he had also entered politics—in Congress under the Articles of the Confederation, then in the Pennsylvania legislature, where he became speaker, and in the U.S. Senate. By 1792 he was in discussion with Henry Knox about Maine lands. In November 1792, Knox was asking his jailed partner, William Duer, if he would accept Bingham as a purchaser.

Whereupon, Duer began creating difficulties. He said no to Bingham and wanted Knox to negotiate with a man named Theophile Cazenove, who was working for a Dutch land company which would take two million acres at six cents an acre off their hands. Out of the deal Duer was to receive $50,000, with a $15,000 advance that would presumably be sufficient to release him from debtors' prison.

However, Knox eventually convinced Duer to accept Bingham, not Cazenove, as their rescuer and four days later, on December 20, 1792, the former secretary of war signed a memorandum of understanding with the U.S. senator. After an all-night work session with their lawyer, they then dispatched their emissary, Major William Jackson, to New York with $50,000 in notes to persuade Duer to sign off, which he did.

Elements of the agreement between Knox and Bingham were that the latter would guarantee the former one-third of the residual profits from the venture, that Bingham would take over Duer's share and also advance the money Knox still owed on the original contract.

In the third week of January the following year, 1793, William Bingham traveled to Boston to conclude the arrangements. He stayed almost three weeks, visiting Governor John Hancock, among others, complaining jokingly about the excessive wining and dining he had to undergo yet noting jocularly that if he ate enough Boston fish and venison, he would be so invigorated that he'd be able to produce a son and heir (his first two children were girls, Ann and Maria).

His time in "the Hub" wasn't all social. The Committee for the sale of Eastern Lands, in return for the money he gave them, presented him with sixteen deeds, encompassing two million acres of Maine land, half on the Penobscot, half on the Kennebec.

Since Bingham's contract with Massachusetts required the placing of a certain number of settlers by a certain date, a first order of business for him was to hire an agent. In General David Cobb, a one-time speaker of the Massachusetts House, he found his ideal candidate and recruited him with a lot at Gouldsborough of 2,000 acres, profits promised from 20,000 more, a hefty $1,000 advance, and a $1,500 annual salary. Instructed to buy mill sites and curb timber stealing, Cobb set forth, while Bingham bought additional property, including a feudal French grant on Mount Desert Island, and also advertised openly for customers.

One technique he employed was to piggyback on a pamphlet General Benjamin Lincoln had originally issued in 1789, no doubt to promote his own lands in Washington County. Major William Jackson may have been the go-between, since he had been Lincoln's aide-de-camp during the war. Bingham's pamphlet, published in the spring of 1793, was entitled: *A Description of the Situation, Climate, Soil, and Production of Certain Tracts of Land in the District of Maine and Commonwealth of Massachusetts.* In it, he addressed forty-four questions to the general; among the answers were that the wood near the sea could be transported to different seaports for fuel; that there was timber for export to the West Indies and Europe; that hard-to-transport wood could be burned to create pot and pearl ashes; that lots of fish were available (salmon, shad, alewives, sturgeon, herring, cod); that the people—descendants of English, Irish, Scottish, and German stock—were "a strong, robust race of people, capable of enduring much fatigue...." As for the cold, the General answered coyly: "I have suffered as much from the cold in Carolina as I ever experienced in Maine."

This public relations campaign did not have the desired effect. Settlers did not flock to the Bingham-Knox lands. Part of the problem was the attraction of lands in other parts of the country. "The rage of speculation and emigrating into York State is beyond conception," a would-be land buyer, Dr. Ebenezer Hunt of Northampton, Massachusetts, wrote to Henry Knox, and even lower down in Maine, there was fierce competition. "Kenduskeag [Bangor] will be the Philadelphia of this country," land speculator Oliver Leonard wrote David Cobb. Yet Cobb had his own more-close-to-home ideas about why they didn't have a better market. Illegal cutting of trees was the root cause:

...for if a people who live by lumbering are indulged in cutting the forests wherever they please, they will have but little more estimation of the value of the soil than the savage who hunts them for his living.... Prevent depredation and you may raise the prices of land to what you please.[5]

Bingham recognized the problem. In a communication to Cobb in November 1795, he stated:

The country will never turn its attention to agriculture
until lumbering is discouraged, which must be effected
by throwing every difficulty in their way.[6]

A legislative solution was suggested: "...heavy impositions in favor of the rights of the proprietor of the soil."

In the same year, Bingham also recognized his pockets were not inexhaustibly deep and he, too, began to look around for an angel. Eventually, he turned to Europe where one of his partners had established contacts with Henry Hope and Company in Holland and the Baring Brothers, John and Francis, in London. These banking and investment operations had close ties and one of the younger Barings, Alexander, had been sent to Amsterdam to apprentice with Hope and Company. The two firms, acting jointly, decided that investments in American land looked promising and Alexander Baring, then only twenty-one years old, was sent across the Atlantic with a letter of credit for £100,000 and the leeway to spend £25,000 more.

He arrived in Boston at Christmastime, 1795. Cobb was sent from Gouldsborough to meet him and deliver a personal letter from Bingham. Then, he escorted Baring to Philadelphia via New York, where they were entertained by Knox, and eventually Baring was deposited with Bingham. On the 27th of January, 1796, all concerned attended a dinner party at President Washington's home and a few days later, Bingham confided to Cobb that Baring had admitted coming to America with the intention of buying Maine lands — that is, if the price was right.

There was still a good deal of dickering to be done. Bingham wanted $560,000 and Baring would only offer $401,000 for most of the Penobscot land (Baring apparently had a "prejudice" against the

Kennebec tract). The negotiations were strung out, but pleasantly. In the summer of 1796, Bingham, his beauteous wife, his equally gorgeous teenaged daughters, young Baring, his friend John Richards, and others all traveled together as a "party of pleasure" to Maine, where the women boarded at Knox's palatial home in Thomaston while the men went on to Gouldsborough and points farther Down East. The Knox mansion, incidentally, had been named "Montpelier" at the suggestion of Mrs. Bingham. Also, Alexander Baring was smitten by daughter Ann Bingham. He would later marry her, and his brother would marry Maria Bingham. Impressed by Maine, Baring consummated a deal with Bingham a year later for close to 600,000 acres, paying $263,901, allegedly a bargain price.

All this land buying was occurring at the same time several other actions underway were affecting lands in Maine. Jay's Treaty of 1794 was a momentous, if relatively unknown, event in American history, credited with causing the formation of political parties when Jefferson and Hamilton split over our relations with Britain and France. The part related to Maine, however, was innocuous enough, merely creating a joint U.S.-British Commission to establish which river Down East was the true St. Croix.

Colonel John Allan had been right to fear the presence of a nearby Canadian province inhabited by former Tories. With no defined official border, there was territory both sides could claim and, as early as 1785, problems were developing over Moose Island, on which the community of Eastport was eventually situated. On November 24, 1785, Governor James Bowdoin sent a message to the Massachusetts General Court that the American inhabitants of Moose Island had been notified by the sheriff of Charlotte County in New Brunswick to send jurors to that county's court "on penalty of forfeiting their estates in case of refusal." A protest from Governor Bowdoin to Governor Carleton of New Brunswick had produced no relief but only "an implied declaration" that Moose and several other islands were within the Canadian province. This was followed by news that the same Charlotte County sheriff had tried to arrest a U.S. excise deputy officer on Moose Island, that Moose Island was being included for legal purposes in the Seventh Parish of Charlotte County, and that two American ships had been seized.

It was incidents like these that the Jay Treaty's Commission had been designed to eliminate. The British claim fancifully argued for a line drawn from a point in the then so-called Schoodic River northwest of St. Andrews straight toward Florida, lopping off a goodly chunk of Washington County. The U.S. position, equally untenable, clung to the Magaguadavic River as the actual St. Croix, which would have done similar damage to New Brunswick. The discussion lingered on for four years until the Schoodic was declared the right river, but without the line the Britons wanted. Yet Eastport, incorporated as part of Massachusetts that same year (1798), was still not safely in the U.S., nor would it be until 1818.

The other principal land controversy of the time concerned the Indian lands. The whites were unrelenting in their efforts to get their hands on them. They succeeded with the Passamaquoddies in 1794, but Alexander Baring wrote to his home firm in 1796: "The Penobscot Indian lands are not yet sold, nor is any arrangement with the Indians made as yet." David Cobb stated: "I reckon our back tract worth twice as much when the Indians are removed than before." It was actually in 1796 that the Penobscots finally succumbed, ceding riverfront land on both banks of their river for 30 miles upstream of head-tide, receiving in return the usual mixture of blanket cloth, powder, shot, and rum. A seasoned surveyor, Park Holland, who had been Down East with Rufus Putnam in 1784, was then sent to map nine townships north of Bangor thus opened to settlement.

Holland was an ex-militia captain who had participated with Generals Putnam and Lincoln in suppressing Shays' Rebellion. He had also surveyed Bingham's "back tract" and, in 1795, reported to the great land speculator in Philadelphia as "the only really trustworthy source" on what was in it. He was a tough but diplomatic woodsman who, before the Penobscot Treaty was signed, had had to face down an Indian at Old Town threatening to shoot him if he went upriver. The same resistance met him at Mattawamkeag from natives fearing that, in their prescient words: "...bye and bye the poor Indian would have no land and no moose meat."

Possible starvation on one of Holland's northward treks has accounted for a bit of folklore—the story of the "little yellow dog."

A companion of the surveying party, the dog was about to be eaten when they ran out of food—but it rousted out a porcupine, which they devoured instead.

Holland, in his surveying, which he continued until 1820, was possibly the first American to hike through to the French Acadian settlement in the Madawaska region, writing about the Gallic exiles he found in the wilds of northern Aroostook and understanding their history and plight:

The British gave their American soldiers [the Loyalists] land upon the St. John's [*sic*], where these [French] people had settled, sixty or seventy families in number and who in their anger, moved upriver, determined to have no communication with them.

Twice uprooted, the Daigles, Cyrs, Heberts, Violettes, Theriaults, and others Holland encountered were among the original French settlers of Nova Scotia, driven from their homes by the English in 1755, resettling (those who didn't go to Louisiana and elsewhere) on the lower St. John, only to be displaced again. In the wilds of the upper St. John, they were to live even longer and in even more uncertainty about their nationality than the Yankees of Moose Island.

Uncertainty about land tenure was not confined to those on the borders. In *Come Spring*, Ben Ames Williams has Joel Adams, a member of the first Board of Selectmen of Union, telling his wife Mima the fears he has for their title. The scene occurs at the end of the Revolution before the town was incorporated:

"Then there might be land troubles. I bought from your father [Philip Robbins] and he bought from Doc Taylor. Taylor bought from Flucker [Thomas Flucker, the father of Henry Knox's wife Lucy] and Flucker claimed to represent the Waldos, but he was drove out for a Tory. He agreed to protect Taylor when he sold to him; but I don't know as he agreed to protect anyone Taylor might sell to.... S'pose the Waldos claim Flucker hadn't any right to sell to Taylor? Taylor won't stand up for us. I don't know what it will come to."

Wife Mima responds:

"You can't scare me, Joel. This is our land. It's not ours because we bought it. It's ours because we've worked on it and loved it, and we're going to keep it...."[7]

The same sentiment was being expressed all over Maine with the exception, in many cases, that unlike the Adamses and Robbinses, the occupants of the laboriously cleared ground and self-erected cabins had never paid a penny for their homesteads. They truly were "squatters."

A vivid description of such people has been left in the unpublished diary of Joseph Sewall of Bath, a land surveyor, active in western Maine in the early 1800s. On a trip in March 1808 to survey a half township west of the Bingham Kennebec purchase, granted to Bath Academy, Sewall spent a night en route at Norridgewock. "Nothing more interesting than dialogue with some squatters," he writes. These folks were on their way to Farmington:

> He was a squatter if one might judge by appearance. His face had not suffered washing since Christmas; his hair had not known a comb since the peace of '83, and all things about him equally careless. His woman had a handkerchief hauled about her neck so as to secure a piece of dirty cloth over her head and shoulders resembling a cloak—one child on her hip, her stockings about her ankles as she walked. Two children on foot...four to six...without shoes, having stockings worn through the heels and two on their sledge together with all the effects they could call their own, drawn by one old horse that could hardly walk....

The dialogue touches on land issues then heating up, beginning when Sewall says the Bath Academy property would probably be on sale by June, at $1 an acre, with the best timberland going for $2 an acre. The squatter interjects, "the State sells land for 50 cents a naker [*sic*]." Sewall explains, "the land was given to us for the purpose of creating a fund to support an academy in Bath" and no price was set in their deed. The squatter asks if the state has more land "up that way" and the surveyor cites a number of townships for sale between Bingham's million acres and the New Hampshire border, going for 50 cents to 75 cents an acre. Then, the squatter says:

"Twoodent do for you to run land here, I guess." The reason: "There is so many Indians about."

Now, these are a peculiar kind of Indian, eventually referred to as "White Indians." Sewall admits he feels for these people who settled on land they didn't own. "They want to get their land for what it was worth when they took it up. That is impossible. They do not conceive what will follow such conduct as they are now pursuing"—such conduct being the terrorizing of surveyors and other agents of the landowners. Sewall is sure the Commonwealth will crack down on them. The squatter replies, "But they can't catch them. You can't see 'em a days and a nights they'll come out as thick as the musketors." Sewall persists in believing their cause is doomed. "The killing of a few horses we view as trifling, but to see so many good citizens spending their time in painting and dressing like Indians, in watching and notifying each other...must in the end reduce them to poverty."

Unmolested, Sewall did complete his work for Bath Academy, bothered only by the cold and fatigue of working in the wilderness, whose beauty he nevertheless fleetingly praised: "Farewell ye venerable elms whose spreading branches poets never sang. Farewell ye purling streams meandering through the plain. Ye lofty pines that tower the forest.... Ye Mountains Kanabaga and Bigelow...." He continued his surveying westward in the years to come, being selected for, among other tasks, to work on the Canada Road, slated to link the Kennebec to the St. Lawrence.

Maine was spreading out. The inland west, relatively peaceful since Lovewell's Fight in the 1720s, was attracting settlers, too. The only incident of the Revolution to affect it was a brief Indian raid in 1781 on the isolated outpost of Sudbury Canada (Bethel), led by a white-hating Androscoggin chief named Tomhegan. Three men were killed and three taken captive. After the war ended, the latter three (Lieutenant Nathaniel Segar, Lieutenant Jonathan Clark, and Benjamin Clark) returned to this Androscoggin Valley area the Indians claimed they'd never ceded and picked up their lives again, as other settlers advanced downriver to Rumford. A fourth captive, who'd escaped Tomhegan, Captain Eleazar Twitchell, became the first local lumbering magnate, sending "huge quantities of white pine" to Brunswick to be shipped to the West Indies.

One of those who left the Bethel area and moved downriver early on, even before the Indian attack, was Jonathan Keyes, a settler originally from Shrewsbury, Massachusetts. He cleared land on a grant that had been given to Timothy Walker, Jr., and a number of other inhabitants of what is now Concord, New Hampshire— "proprietors" who joined Keyes in a settlement they called New Pennacook (Pennacook was Concord's Indian name). Tomhegan's raid frightened them, as well, and they departed for a safer section of Maine, but returned like the Bethel evacuees and picked up stakes in a community they renamed and had incorporated as Rumford.

While the exact motive for the use of this latter name is murky, or at least the subject of much debate, its connection to an extraordinary historic personage named Count Rumford is, if not indisputable, certainly fair game for any author's speculation. For Massachusetts-born Benjamin Thompson, who became a bonafide count of the Holy Roman Empire, was married to the sister of Timothy Walker, Jr., and allegedly chose his title of Rumford in her honor, since Rumford was yet another name for Concord, New Hampshire, where he met and wooed her (she was then a widow, fourteen years older than the eighteen-year-old Thompson). The count's adventurous life might make a dandy movie. Treated as a Tory, he was forced to leave America, only to be heartily welcomed in England, made Undersecretary for the Colonies, knighted at age twenty, then was off to a career with the Elector of Bavaria, who gave him his title of nobility, and on to a second career as a world-famous scientist who wanted nothing more than to go back to New England and procure "a little quiet retreat near his old home," something the American government would not allow him to do.

The town of Rumford was incorporated by the Massachusetts General Court on February 21, 1800.

With the Indian menace gone, the Revolutionary War over, and the eighteenth century having passed into the nineteenth, the only hostiles left in Maine were the White Indians.

Henry Knox wrote to William Bingham on February 22, 1796, about "Some little uneasiness" arising on the Waldo Patent twenty miles from his home, instigated "by one Samuel Ely...a sort of clergyman, the most factious scoundrel on the face of the earth." Ely, he informed Bingham, had been run out of Massachusetts for his part in Shays' Rebellion and there was now a warrant out for him in the District of Maine. He had raised an armed mob and, although it had not happened on Knox's land, Knox was worried that Baring might hear of it and be scared off from buying their lands.

Samuel Ely was no unwashed, uncombed squatter. His degree as a minister had come from Yale and he was a skilled writer. The pamphlet he published and disseminated in Maine in 1797 entitled *The Deformity of a Hideous Monster, Discovered in the Province of Maine, by a Man in the Woods Looking after Liberty* served as a bible for the White Indians or Liberty Men. The "monster" was Knox. By harping back to New Englanders' hatred of tenancy, Ely struck a nerve with his charge that the General Court was selling lands to proprietors as part of a plot to reduce the settlers to tenants by driving up the price of land prohibitively.

The problem did not disappear in Maine, despite the power of the Commonwealth. Indian-garbed settlers had actually been harassing proprietors since as early as 1761 when a mob so-clad had routed Dr. Sylvester Gardiner, the principal Kennebec Proprietor, from his residence in Pownalborough. The first appearance of Samuel Ely was in April 1793 when he led a crowd at Ducktrap Plantation (Lincolnville) in destroying a mill dam belonging to George and Philip Ulmer, supporters of Knox. Four months later, the clergyman, armed with a club, beat Job Pendleton, another Knox man, and the following January, a mob loyal to him did the same to Prince Holbrook. In July 1800, surveyors working for Knox were shot at in Thorndike and three men wounded. The *Eastern Herald and Gazette* ran the story as follows:

Eastern Settlers Not Quiet

On Friday last 25, Messrs. Bradstreet Wiggins, Nathan Smith, Peter Smith, and Abel Wheeler were employed in surveying land on Knox's patent and running a line between Belfast and 25-mile Pond settlement, they were fired upon by a number of armed men, who lay concealed in ambush. Mr. N. Smith was very severely wounded in the groin and is now in this place, under the care of Dr. Mann. Mr. P. Smith and Wiggins were slightly wounded. The number of guns discharged appeared to be 8 or 10. No persons were seen by the surveyors.[8]

One could understand the desperation behind these actions. The same newspaper subsequently printed an official notice from James Stubbs, tax collector of nearby Frankfort, wanting $60 in taxes on 20,000 acres of undivided, unimproved land in the town and if he didn't get it by a certain date, "so much of said land as will discharge the same will then be sold at public vendu to the highest bidder at the house of Capt. Tobias Oakman in said Frankfort."[9]

And there was worse violence to come. On September 8, 1809, at Malta (now Windsor), White Indians led by an Elijah Barton ambushed a continued attempt by an Isaac Davis to survey for the Kennebec Proprietors, and one of the chainmen, a Paul Chadwick, was shot and killed. In October, 200 White Indians marched on Augusta to liberate the prisoners accused of murdering Chadwick, but were driven off by the militia. The violence slowed down when Maine became a state but did not entirely subside until 1825.

The movement for "Liberty" this continued agitation spawned has been seen as one of the strongest contributing factors in Maine's breaking away from Massachusetts. The seeds of separation had long been in place and, in 1785, meetings were already being held. The original supporters were far from scruffy backlanders anxious about property rights. Future Federalist bigwigs like General Peleg Wadsworth and his son-in-law Stephen Longfellow, were in the vanguard of the secession effort. The first vote, held on May 7, 1792, was disappointing, a defeat, 2,074 to 2,524. Yet five years later, Alexander Baring was reporting: "It is expected that the District of Maine will be formed into a separate State.... The constitution will be modeled after that of Massachusetts and I have no doubt that our friend Knox will be made Governor...."

His timing was off by twenty-three years and the man who became governor was William King. A self-made wealthy merchant and shipowner, King had changed his political party from Federalist to Jeffersonian Democrat-Republican, and his championing of the "little people"—the backcountry settlers and squatters, as a representative from Bath in the General Court—won him great support, both for himself and separation. The accomplishment that most endeared him was his successful maneuvering of a "Betterment Act," which required any settler evicted from land he didn't own to be reimbursed for any improvements made. Another key impetus for separation came from the inaction of the Federalist governor of Massachusetts, Caleb Strong, during the War of 1812 when the British once again occupied Castine, Eastport, and most of the coast to Belfast, even raiding Bangor, while Boston wouldn't lift a finger to help, despite the pleas of William King, as commander of the Maine Militia. The drama of the down-to-the-wire acceptance of Maine as a Free State by Congress, coupled with Missouri as a Slave State, in 1820, has often been told. Less examined has been the separation agreement between the two entities. It's doubtful many Maine people know that part of the deal was allowing Massachusetts to keep and sell half of the unallocated land in Maine. Thus, for more than thirty years, until the lawmakers in Augusta finally bought out those remaining rights, the Commonwealth maintained a land agent and a presence in the Maine North Woods.

NOTES

[1] "History of the Wild Lands of Maine," *Seventh Report of the Forest Commissioner of the State of Maine.* Waterville, ME: Waterville Sentinel Publishing Company, 1908.

[2] *Collections of the Maine Historical Society.* Portland, ME: Fred L. Tower Company, 1916. 2nd series, vol. XXI, pages 13–14.

[3] Ibid., page 246.

[4] Frederick Allis, Jr., ed., *William Bingham's Maine Lands, 1790–1820.* Boston: The Colonial Society of Massachusetts, 1954. Page 44.

[5] Ibid. Cobb to Bingham, October 5, 1795.

[6] Ibid. Bingham to Cobb, November 7, 1795.

[7] Ben Ames Williams, *Come Spring.* Union, ME: Union Historical Society (republished edition, 2000). Page 667.

[8] *Eastern Herald and Gazette.* Portland, ME: January 25, 1800.

[9] Ibid., March 6, 1800.

FIFTEEN

The Lumber Capital of the World

I CAUGHT MY FIRST SALMON (landlocked) at Grand Lake Stream in 1954. I was not a stranger to Maine, having gone to summer camp in Casco throughout World War II, but I was certainly a stranger to its history. Wandering around this remote corner of Washington County when I wasn't sitting in a boat with a fishing rod in my hands, I had no idea of the antecedents of what I was seeing.

Even the Maine Indians I was viewing (for the first time) when we landed near the Princeton "Strip" (I had no way of knowing they were of the Passamaquoddy tribe) seemed entirely in the present. I did not need the pejorative comments of the local guide's assistant to know they lived in poor and downtrodden conditions. That was all too visibly evident.

How could I know that Grand Lake had been the scene of epic warfare between Mohawks and Passamaquoddies before the white man had impinged? Or that next to Grand Lake Stream Plantation was Indian Township, left to them after they had surrendered most of the rest of their land in 1794, and, at 23,000 acres, the largest single landmass then belonging to Indians in Maine? Or that these same Passamaquoddies had fought for the Americans in the Revolution (and in all the wars since)? Or that the picturesque site where we had fished was originally in Township 3, Range 1, which became Hinckley Plantation after Judge Samuel Hinckley of Northampton, Massachusetts, paid off Titus Goodman's note to Massachusetts and took possession on February 7, 1811?

Lumbering had actually begun there in 1810, but it was not until 1820 that a David Cass came to settle with his family, followed by a Baxter Smith. Both were on a 3,000-acre piece that was part of the land Massachusetts had reserved for itself after the separation. The Commonwealth sold its share in 1827, some of it to Judge Hinckley, who in 1835 sold the whole township to Colonel Nehemiah Marks of St. Stephen, New Brunswick, son of a Connecticut Loyalist. Neither Hinckley nor Marks lumbered; they were most likely speculators, hoping the price of land would go up. But those who followed as owners—a succession of good old Anglo-Saxon surnames like Copeland, Sawyer, Murchie, Boardman, and Todd—were engaged in shipping the area's pines to Milltown on the St. Croix and the lumber made from them to Europe or elsewhere in the U.S.

This brief community tale, except for its setting so close to the Canadian border and the presence of Indians nearby, could have been duplicated just about anywhere in Maine after 1820. The anonymity of the countless Copelands, Sawyers, Murchies, and others merely emerges now and then in local histories that preserve a few memories of them. Even big shots, like Judge Hinckley or Colonel Marks, flash before us and are gone. And David Cass, as the first settler, might have had no more notoriety than of a soon-forgotten trailblazer had he not been the half-brother of the famous Lewis Cass—U.S. senator from Michigan, secretary of war and the Democratic presidential candidate in 1848. David Cass was also an "unforgettable character," a legend in the woods. Called "the General" and much feared (all 380 pounds of him), he was married to "Aunt Nellie" (all 105 pounds of her); they both eventually died in the state asylum.

At Cass's home, gangs of lumbermen would gather to drink whiskey with him. A favorite and sadistic antic of theirs was to catch the dog, dip it in a barrel of caulking tar, and then roll the beast in wood chips and let the poor thing run around. Using only his bare hands, Cass could move a log that a yoke of oxen couldn't budge, and he would employ both huge paws to pick up a pair of antagonists—sometimes Indians, sometimes law officers who'd arrested him—and hold them underwater or jam their heads through railings. A trapper and farmer who cleared 100 acres and sold stumpage on 300 more, he was the outsized version of many another hard-drinking, hard-working pioneer in these Down East woods, as wild as the wild lands themselves.

Hinckley Plantation has remained obscure, but one similar Maine community, arising out of a wilderness just as complete, did begin to grow and shine in the same era and come to dominate imaginations. These early years of the nineteenth century saw Bangor emerge in a starring role—the gateway to the heart of the vast, untapped, northern Maine forests—first as a town, then a city that, for a while, was uncontested as "the lumber capital of the world."

Certain names dominate others here, too. As Bangor "lumber barons" of this period, the two names most frequently heard are Rufus Dwinel and General Samuel Veazie, while David Pingree is most often named as the biggest of the large landowners who succeeded Henry Knox and William Bingham. Yet despite the notoriety of these gentlemen, the historic record they left behind is patchy enough so that at least the two aforementioned appear most vividly in fictional works, such as Ben Ames Williams's *The Strange Woman* and Ardeanna Hamlin's *Pink Chimneys*. Then, too, there is Fan Jones, who shows up in one disguise or another in these novels, the real-life madam of a real-life bordello (reportedly with blue chimneys) that was a striking feature of Bangor during its heyday as an entrepôt for the vast amounts of timber being harvested in the Penobscot River watershed.

A name that emerges from the very earliest days of Bangor is one mentioned before—the Reverend Seth Noble. This peripatetic Massachusetts-born clergyman moved around; driven from Nova Scotia because of his pro-American sentiments, he physically took part in the battle of Machias, then came to the Penobscot area with his fellow exile from Canada, Colonel Jonathan Eddy, and like Eddy, attended negotiations with the local Indians. By 1788 he had left Eddington to become the first minister at Kenduskeag Plantation, which, as a rough frontier settlement, was willing to put up with some of his idiosyncrasies. These included his moving in with the Widow Emery after his wife's death and waiting awhile to marry her, plus an open fondness for liquor. In spite of his hard drinking, he was entrusted by his parishioners to go to the General Court in Boston and present their petition to be incorporated as a town.

Incorporated with what name? Apparently, "Sunbury," a suggestion of Noble's to commemorate the county where he had lived in New Brunswick. The possibly apocryphal tale still told is that the absentminded cleric instructed the legislators to call the town *Bangor* from a hymn by that title he'd been whistling in the statehouse. Given his predilection for rum, his contemporaries back home probably winked at each other when he tried to explain he'd thought the lawmakers had been asking the name of the tune.

There are those who claim the whole story is pure legend and point to a petition presented the General Court May 18, 1790, from forty-five families on "the property of what is commonly called Kendeskeag [*sic*] Plantation" who "labour under many disadvantages for want of being incorporated with town privileges" and wanted the Massachusetts government to "incorporate us into a town by the name of Bangor."

At any rate, Bangor it became—on February 25, 1791—just another collection of cabins in clearings hewn out of the woods. The place had pretty much been abandoned during the Revolution, but people began coming back—people like Robert Treat, a fur trapper, who by 1791 was flush enough to have a boat built to transport lumber to Liverpool, England.

Another who returned was James Budge, the "first big lumber operator," who floated masts to Castine.

Accredited as the first settler was Jacob Buswell from Salisbury, Massachusetts, a cooper by trade, called by one of his enemies "an old damned grey-headed bugger of hell."

There had been pre-Revolutionary sawmills. Now, William Hammond and John Dudley built a new one at the head of tide on the Kenduskeag. Some businessmen from Boston came in 1800 with capital to invest. But in 1800 only 279 people lived in Kenduskeag; nearby Hampden and Orrington had 904 and 786.

In 1801 a William Crosby wrote: "I went to Bangor, but to my astonishment, I could see no village." He turned around and headed home. A like experience was recorded by Deacon Eliashib Adams in 1803. "Walked to Bangor from Bucksport. So disgusted—went to spend night in Orrington."

Yet in 1835, a visitor wrote:

What was once a little, dirty, insignificant village, without character and without name, was now Bangor, which lifts its head in justly anticipated greatness and speaks of Boston and New York as sisters.[1]

The city's population growth, gauged from 1800, was almost fourfold in the next decade, to 851, reaching 1,221 in 1820, and more than doubling by 1830 to 2,867. The next decade of the 1830s to 1840s was fairly spectacular. It saw Bangor change from a town to a city in 1833, ending with 8,621 inhabitants in 1840, becoming 14,432 in 1850, and slowing to 16,407 by 1860.

Lumber was the driving economic engine—lumber that at times was considered legal tender and "would buy any goods and pay any debts." Major Robert Treat, who also owned a store, wrote in his ledger: "A remarkable feature is the incredible amount of 'rum' and 'toddy' which the old fellows of that day could carry off and *pay for*," and a goodly portion of that payment was in shingles and boards.

The scope of the excitement engendered by Bangor's growth in this period shines through the prose of one of Maine's illustrious but still not-well-known sons, Hugh McCulloch, secretary of the treasury under Presidents Lincoln, Johnson, and Arthur. In his memoirs, *Men and Measures of Half a Century*, he makes this bald statement: "The wildest speculation that has ever prevailed in any part of the United States was in the timberlands of Maine," and then describes how the word spread throughout New England and, "The desire to speculate became so great that a courier line was established between Boston and Bangor by which orders first to buy and subsequently to sell were transmitted and for months little was talked about but Maine lands."

This feeding frenzy is further elaborated upon with a gentlemanly sense of disapproval by a man of such solid fiscally responsible reputation as McCulloch:

Brokers' offices were opened in Bangor, which were crowded from morning until night and frequently far into the night by buyers and sellers. All were jubilant, because all, whether buyers or sellers, were getting rich. Not one in 50 knew anything about the lands he was buying, nor did he care to know as long as he could

The Interrupted Forest

sell at a profit. Lands bought one day were sold the next day at a large advance. Buyers in the morning were sellers at night. The lands were bought and sold over and over again, until lands which had been bought for a few cents an acre were sold for half as many dollars. As is always the case when speculation is rampant and inexperienced men become speculators, dishonesty was in the ascendant.[2]

The ultimate anecdote symbolizing this land fever, printed in a Baltimore newspaper, was of two paupers who escaped the Bangor almshouse and before their recapture the next morning had each earned $1,800 from investments in the forests. No names were given but these rascals might have been Pat and Mike—to reflect the Irish-Catholic immigration becoming conspicuous there, even well before the Potato Famine. These impoverished Irish were drawn to Bangor to work in the woods and later to build railroads; they drew the hostility of the Anglo-Saxon population not only because of their religion but also for their defiance of the growing push for temperance. Soon, a "Peppermint Row" of saloons catering to loggers and sailors arose in a downtown section dubbed the "Devil's Half-Acre." One bumptious saloonkeeper, Pat Moran, raised hackles by turning a Methodist meetinghouse into a rum shop he archly christened "Moranbega," mocking the sedate "Norumbega Hall" of the gentry.

Resentment against the newcomers was predictable. The mob destruction of a building used for a Catholic church in 1833 actually led to Bangor's change of status from a town to a city. The more responsible citizens decided they needed the leadership of a mayor and a more structured government to avoid such unruly (and unflattering) incidents.

On July 3, 1834, Ralph Waldo Emerson made his first visit to Bangor. The author of essays such as "Self-Reliance" and "Nature" had a mixed reaction to the spectacle of the woods operation then at full throttle in the Penobscot River sawmills. American industrialization had a certain attraction for him; here were the self-reliant Yankees making use of their resources and their ingenuity.

July 7, Rode up the river to the Mills. Noble sight is the sawmill of ten saws—the servitude of the river. It floats the timber down; there by the application of machinery, the river hands up the reluctant log into the mill as I have seen a halibut hauled into a ship; the river saws the logs into boards, then floats the raft into Bangor; then floats the brig or ship that receives the boards onward to the ocean....

Inserted, too, in Emerson's writing is a note of regret about the object of these procedures. Emerson referred to "The pride of the forest—white pines of four-foot diameter, which it cost a hundred years of sun and rain and cold to rear, must end in a sawmill at last."

Emerson stayed around Bangor for several days, hosted by a distant relative, William Emerson, who took him to visit Indian Island. Again, his impressions were two-edged: "...wretched people—300 in the tribe—Neptune [probably John Neptune] an able man.... Women all squatting on the ground—listless and filthy yet good faces...." Then, a bit of self-reliant Yankee tut-tutting: "They own all the islands in the Penobscot above Old Town and cultivate none."

The Concord Sage's comments on other matters also help give a sense of that time and place. He noted there was talk of a charter for a railroad from Bangor to Old Town and plans for a 200-mile line between the St. John River and Bangor. He cited people who owned five or six townships despite the Mainers' prejudice against large landholdings, and told of cases of great land sales where neither the buyer nor the seller ever saw the property involved.

The overriding role of the Penobscot River was immediately clear to him and he rather poetically expressed his insight that it was:

...the source of all the present and prophet of all the future greatness of this great country. Every ripple is a cupid. The ideas of the people are habitually enlarged by the activity of the creation around them.

The railroad grant mentioned by Emerson may not have been the earliest in Maine. The first charter was given in 1833 to the organizers of the Bangor and Piscataquis Canal and Railroad Company, led by Moses Greenleaf, a name that still resonates in Maine history. As a surveyor, Greenleaf was on a par with Joseph Chadwick,

Rufus Putnam, and Park Holland, but he went them one better by publishing a number of books, including his memorable *A Survey of the State of Maine* which came out in 1829. Greenleaf was a tireless promoter of opening up eastern and northern sections of Maine, even boosting Aroostook County before it had any English-speaking settlers. Bangor was to be the hub for various of his projects — one, a railroad or canal linking Bangor to the slate deposits in Williamsburg, where he lived (today's deorganized Williamsburg Township bordering Brownville Junction and Katahdin Ironworks Township), and another, a railroad from Bangor via Moosehead Lake to the St. John River. His concerns for encroachments from New Brunswick were evident in his 1829 book. With some fairly vitriolic language he tried to arouse his countrymen, railing against British "unblushing finesse and chicanery" and the "grasping cupidity" of the New Brunswick "provincial agents and subalterns." Dying in 1834, Greenleaf never lived to see the outcome of the border dispute.

His nephew, the future Maine railroad impresario, John A. Poor, declared he owed his interest in railroads to his uncle. "He was my teacher and my most valued friend to the time of his lamented death...."

The questions Greenleaf liked to pose to his contemporaries to spur their development efforts were: "Whether our Siberia may change to an Utopia?" and, if "The bug bear terms, 'wilderness,' 'savage,' etc....will be remanded to the place from whence they came, there to dwell with 'ghosts,' 'hobgoblins,' etc....in 'old women's' notions?"

That wilderness had retreated before the onslaught of civilization was seen clearly enough in the Bangor area by Henry David Thoreau in the several decades after Emerson's early visit. As a matter of obscure fact, Thoreau first came in 1838. Looking for a teaching job, but finding none, he lingered to talk hunting and fishing with an old Penobscot man at Indian Island and then returned to Concord. On subsequent, more publicized trips, he was to describe Bangor as:

> ...the principal lumber depot of this continent with a
> population of 12,000, like a star at the edge of night,

still hewing at the forest of which it is built.

And in which:

> The mission of the men there seems to be, like so many
> busy demons, to drive the forest all out of the country,
> from every solitary beaver swamp and mountainside, as
> soon as possible.

He had gone to see some of General Samuel Veazie's sawmills. Instead of the ten saws at which Emerson marveled, Thoreau now saw "sixteen in a gang, not to mention circular saws…the trees were literally drawn and quartered there."

Veazie owned 52 local lumber mills out of 242 in the whole greater-Bangor area.

Nor was that all that was going on. A vast enterprise centered on the Penobscot River country. Upriver and to the west and east, attuned to the rhythms of nature, individual entrepreneurs were cutting pine, an activity particularly suited to the colder weather when the earth froze and when "twitch" roads to the riverbanks could be iced so oxen could haul those long logs and leave them until the meltdown in the spring. With the "freshet," or flood water, the "drive" was underway, down tributaries into the branches of the Penobscot and on to the mills of Old Town, Orono, Bradley, Bangor, and smaller towns, but stopping first at the "booms" to be sorted.

Until 1825 there weren't any booms. Each lumberman drove his own logs to the Bangor area mills. But with so many different owners and their logs, this soon caused mass confusion. Therefore, in 1825, the Penobscot Boom Corporation was chartered to construct a boom at Costigan Island which would catch the logs and get them to their correct destinations, using the owners' distinctive marks on the felled trees like cattlemen cutting out branded cows from a herd. When Rufus Dwinel bought the whole operation, he charged 38 cents per 1,000 board feet for the service. Then, in 1833, he sold out to Veazie, who built another boom, the Argyle. In time there were four major Penobscot booms—the Argyle, the Nebraska, the Mexico, and the Pea Cove—and all were essentially crib-work piers, filled with rocks, where floating logs were directed, identified, made into log rafts for each owner, and delivered to the mills.

In 1846 the lumbermen decided on more such rational cooperation. They formed the Penobscot Log Driving Company (the P.L.D.) and consolidated the effort of getting the logs downriver, letting them be run by one cooperative outfit, under a single master driver. Other rivers in Maine made similar arrangements.

The boom business, when it was a monopoly, as under Samuel Veazie, could stir more than controversy—such as a march to Augusta by those seeking to lower the general's tariffs. In 1844 a compromise was reached between the contending parties to establish a rate of 36 and a half cents per 1,000 board feet for 10 years instead of the prevailing rate. "Said corporation assents as a measure of compromise of my just rights for the cause of peace," was the statement to which Veazie, a notoriously tough businessman. put his signature, no doubt with gritted teeth. He afterward sold out to David Pingree.

Others were also trying to get into the business. An interesting document of September 18, 1847, reveals leases made by the Penobscot Indians of some of those islands that Emerson had complained were not being put to use. The agreement was not exactly between the tribe and the lessees, but between its obviously non-Indian agent, a man who signed as A. Hayford, and the Henry Campbell and Company. These leases, which allowed the building of booms and piers the Indians couldn't remove, gave strips of land around the entire perimeters of Islands 44–57. For this concession, the tribe was to receive $60 a year.

At the end of the drive, ready to receive the products of the mills, were ships that had sailed up the Penobscot from its mouth at Castine to berth at Bangor, 100-ton schooners, sometimes as many as 2,000 or more a year and so closely packed it was often said you could walk from Bangor across to Brewer on their lined-up decks. Steamboats, too, began going up the Penobscot as early as 1824. Eventually there was even one named the GOVERNOR NEPTUNE.

Much of the entertainment in the city of Bangor in the 19th century revolved around the lumber trade.... Whenever the drive came in, the city declared a holiday and all went to greet the river drivers. Cannon were fired, races were held to determine who could arrive with the first stick, and competitions for canoeing, log twirling, sawing, and chopping were often held.[3]

So writes Professor David Smith, a respected historian of the Maine lumber trade, bringing the real past to life with apt description.

Here is fiction by Ben Ames Williams about the Bangor of those days, doing pretty much the same thing:

> The river was well sprinkled with slabs and bark and edgings, refuse from the mills above, and once or twice they broke through solid rafts of this drift, floating in a loose assembly acres in extent. Sawdust filled the water everywhere, changing its color. Some of it was on the surface while the rest, saturated and waterlogged, was carried in solution as it slowly settled toward the bottom. In the narrow shoal channel above Hampden the water was full of it, constantly churned by passing bottoms and racing tides...and then they began to see the vessels massed in river off Bangor town.[4]

We also see imagined glimpses of actual major figures in this part of Bangor's history, like General Samuel Veazie:

> He was at this time in his middle forties. He had a huge, blocky head, and his jutting, clean-shaven jaw and his clamped lips testified to the driving force in him, while his eyes, the right narrowed and piercing, the left wide open and with a questioning lift to the lid, showed the shrewd ability which marked his career.[5]

Or Rufus Dwinel:

> His eye was large and bright and keen, but hard and steady and with no mirth in it to match the quizzical line at the corner of his mouth. His hair was dark and naturally a little curly, and he wore a luxuriant side whisker in front of each ear.... Dwinel had a violent temper but tonight nothing occurred to rouse it and he was genial and pleasant, even to General Veazie whose loud voice and dogmatic pronouncements might sometimes strike sparks from the mildest man.[6]

These were two quintessential sons of Maine, arisen from the hardscrabble bedrock of the state, self-starters, endowed perhaps with a tad more Yankee shrewdness than their competitors and no doubt more energy and grit. Other Bangor men made their mark in the lumbering trade, as well, but Veazie and Dwinel are those most noted by historians, nor were their affairs entirely restricted to the woods.

Veazie, originally from Portland, began his business life as a common sailor traveling to the West Indies, from which he could bring back goods to sell. Soon he opened a store in Topsham and also became a cigar manufacturer. The War of 1812 brought him into the military and he emerged a general in the militia. By 1826 he was in Old Town and bought the Jackson Davis mills. Next he bought every sawmill in sight and, after six years in Old Town, moved to Bangor, built an elaborate home, and later built another in a northern ward of the city that became the town of Veazie.

Rufus Dwinel was a farmboy from Lisbon, one of sixteen children, and he came (with brother Calvin) to Bangor, likewise in 1826. He, too, first ran a store, then got into sawmills by building some at Great Works (Bradley). Also, he bought the Penobscot Boom, which he sold to Veazie in 1833, and like most Bangor businessmen, speculated in timberlands. James Vickery writes: "Of all the so-called 'lumber barons,' Dwinel did more with less capital than any other of his contemporaries, which included such men as Veazie, H. E. Prentiss, Amos M. Roberts, and Samuel F. Hersey."[7] Dwinel was Bangor's second mayor and he had real estate interests, plus a part ownership of the Bangor House.

Both Veazie and Dwinel were investors in the early railroads that used Bangor as a hub. Both Veazie and Dwinel were heavy users of the courts, especially against each other. Their mutual litigation, primarily on the sawdust and other wastes Veazie was putting into the Penobscot, lasted throughout their careers.

The "Telos War" of 1846 gave Rufus Dwinel his greatest notoriety, more so even than the lynch-mob raid he led in Bangor during the Civil War to destroy a "Copperhead" (pro-Southern) newspaper. As wars go, Telos was a pretty tame occurrence, but organized—as opposed to individual—violence in the Maine North Woods presented a memorable spectacle. Besides, the whole thing ended up in the legislature.

The Telos venture began as a nifty bit of engineering and a sly trick on the Canadians, with whom Maine people were having their problems. What started in 1840 at Telos and Webster Lakes in the heart of the great Penobscot watershed was nothing less than a plan to turn river waters in a different direction. Normally, those lumbering the region would have tipped their logs into the Allagash, the nearest large river, which flowed north toward the St. John and Canada but the Canadians were playing games and taxing American logs, despite treaty obligations not to do so. A woodsman named Shepherd Boody was sent by Bangor lumbermen Amos Roberts and Hastings Strickland to "see if the waters would come this way." Boody said yes and proposed a set of dams and a canal at Telos to run the Allagash through an old stream bed and ravine into the East Branch of the Penobscot. Thwarted by the Maine legislature in an attempt to incorporate the canal, Roberts and Strickland "went private," buying the entire township, T6 R11, owned jointly by Maine and Massachusetts, and proceeded to build. By 1842 they had a going operation, charging a toll of 50 cents per 1,000 board feet for all the logs passing through. Roberts, who'd bought out Strickland, sold the operation to Dwinel in 1846.

Around 1843 or 1844, David Pingree had entered the scene, buying townships for lumber around the Allagash lakes. Here was a character cut from the same cloth as Veazie and Dwinel. Born in Bridgton, he, too, had migrated to seek his fortune, but to Massachusetts and the seaport of Salem, where he prospered as a merchant and shipowner and, like Dwinel, served a term as mayor. When one of his clerks borrowed money from him to speculate in Maine land in the Allagash region and couldn't pay him back, Pingree ended up by circumstance as a landowner in his native state. Less circumstantial was the involvement of Ebenezer S. Coe, an engineer and New Hampshire native, whom Pingree sent north to evaluate this land and whose recommendation was to buy more. In time, the two men became partners and owners of "possibly the largest tract of pine timber in the world."[8]

But they eventually had to drive their wood through Rufus Dwinel's toll gate at Telos and pay his rate of 36 cents per 1,000 board feet. When Pingree screamed bloody murder over the tariff,

Dwinel calmly raised it to 50 cents.

But Dwinel soon predicted that Pingree, as stubborn a Yankee as himself, would try to force his logs through Telos.

The Bangor *Daily Mercury* on April 28, 1846, started a series of somewhat tongue-in-cheek articles, speculating in a mock-heroic style, with the names of the principals not very carefully disguised:

> The battle will be fought at the west end of the Telos Cut. The Natives under the banners of old Naumkeag [Pingree, *Naumkeag* having been Salem's Indian name] will attack the cut with a force of 141.... The number of the foe who, under Sir Harry [Dwinel] will dispute the passage, is not yet ascertained....
>
> Should Sir Harry succeed in repelling the Natives, he is to be made Viscount Telos. But if Victory shall perch on the Naumkeag banners, the leader of the forces will be created Earl of Number Seven and Baron of the Eleventh Range.

On May 5, the *Daily Mercury* printed actual news of rumors that Pingree's lumbermen would refuse to pay. It was stated that Rufus Dwinel had sent men to prevent any passage unless the tolls were paid. The satire then continued:

> There are men of great daring upon both sides...there may be quite a brush before the matter is settled.... We think there will be more words than blows.... Few men on either side are willing to die for the value of a few dollars.

And then on May 8:

> Advices from Viscount Telos have been received in the city, by arrival of Sir Harry, from which we learn that he has gained a bloodless victory. Naumkeag, we believe, surrendered at discretion.

What happened in real life was described by Pingree's sub-contractor, Henry Cotton, whose job was to get his logs past the toll. Cotton had arrived, expecting to pay Dwinel's 36 cents, only to be told it *was*, indeed, 50 cents!

> When we got to the cut we found 50–75 men there, a large part of them had belts and sheathed knives, not a

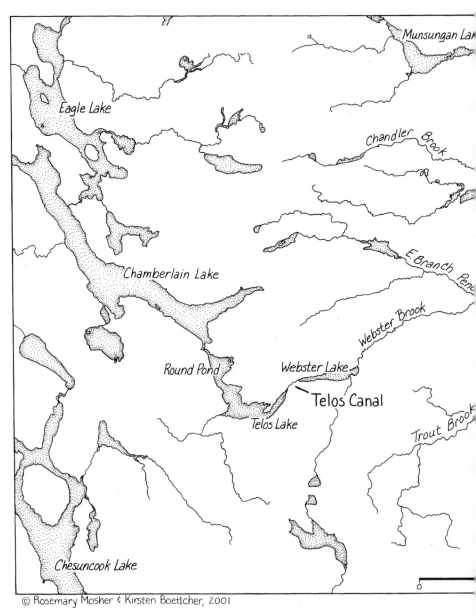

Eagle Lake

Chamberlain Lake

Round Pond

Telos Lake

Webster Lake

Telos Canal

Munsungan La[k]

Chandler Brook

E Branch Pen...

Webster Brook

Trout Brook

Chesuncook Lake

The Telos Area and the Telos Canal

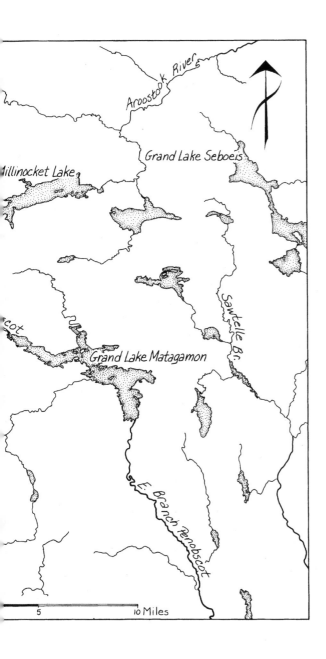

243

common thing for lumbermen to carry such knives. Some of the men said they came from Bangor. Don't know much about the men. Some were said to be State Prison graduates.

Another of Pingree's men, Samuel Hunt, referred to the riffraff Dwinel had collected in the Devil's Half-Acre as a "posse" and that a "Mr. Head was the principal man." Not only did the Pingreeites have to pay 50 cents per 1,000 board feet, but half of the expenses of the "posse," besides.

The drama finally shifted to Augusta when Pingree sought redress from the legislature. Dwinel, in his defense, harped heavily on a Maine nationalism theme, that "David Pingree, Esq., a wealthy individual" was simply a rich interloper from *Away*, buying up five out of six townships, and local lumbermen on Pingree lands felt they could use force because they were "under a rich man like Mr. Pingree," and "Mr. Pingree is troubled with dreams he must thereafter sell his timber 50 cents less per 1,000 than he would receive if he could pass my canal toll free," and would they "justify" letting the state land agent set traps by which Maine citizens "are to be caught by individuals of another state and fleeced?"

His chauvinistic rhetoric didn't fly. The lawmakers gave Rufus Dwinel two choices, both unpalatable. They passed an act that Dwinel could incorporate his canal under a state charter, but charge no more than 20 cents per 1,000 board feet, and if he didn't accept these dictated terms by a certain date, another bill would become law, allowing the incorporation of the Lake Telos and Webster Pond Sluicing Company, which would open the canal free to all.

Hotheaded though he was, Dwinel was even more clear-headed as a businessman and he conceded.

Another larger-than-life figure in the lumbering circles of that day was Colonel John Black. He was not a Bangor man, but lived in Ellsworth, where his elegant mansion home has been turned into a museum. As the son-in-law of General David Cobb, Black inherited the position of agent for the Bingham lands. He has been credited with helping to originate the frenzied land speculation of the 1830s by selling his lands in odd lots to small buyers, disposing of land he bought at 12 cents an acre for as high as a dollar an acre.

Like Veazie and Dwinel, Colonel Black had his own sawmills; one at Mariaville (named for William Bingham's younger daughter Maria) was in operation as early as 1810. By 1828 his mills there and at Ellsworth were putting out close to four million board feet a year. A quarter of a century later, Ellsworth had thirty-one sawmills at work on the Union River.

Born in England, John Black came to the U.S. as a seventeen-year-old trained accountant, hired to work for Cobb at Gouldsborough; he married Mary Cobb and succeeded his father-in-law in 1820. He, too, had a store, run by his sons, William and George, and his account books are full of homely items like "Joseph Tillinghast, 1 axe, 1 handle," "Joseph Hinckley, 1 jack knife," "Mrs. Boyd, needles, thread." His colonelcy came from the local militia and he was town clerk of Gouldsborough before his 1810 move to Ellsworth.

Although naturalized as an American in 1804, he seemed very much the English country squire. One gets the sense of a tenant approaching a lord of the manor in a letter to him from a Joseph Spaulding, Jr., of Caratunk, dated August 31, 1827. This servile-sounding petitioner was waiting to hear about a surveying job he and Black had discussed in Bingham the previous March, "but perhaps you have abandoned the idea of having me do any for you." If that was so, Spaulding then asked to be given the job of making a "country road" for Black and added bleakly, "...if I should be denied the privilege of both, it would be quite a disappointment to me for I am very anxious to pay for my land and have no other means to pay for any but my two hands...." He wishes to hear some news soon, "for now I'm between hope and despair." Nor was Spaulding alone in his penury, which seemed the norm in this corner of western Maine. He finished his letter by saying: "There are a number of my neighbors who would be very glad to work on the road to pay for their lands, otherwise they shall have a long day."

Black was also relentless in the war he waged on trespassers who cut on the Bingham lands. Complaining that local juries would not give "proper damages," he nevertheless caught such interlopers and confiscated their logs and logging outfits. Finding logs marked *R*, which he knew were taken from his Township 32 in the South

Sunkhaze Stream area, he simply commandeered them and changed the *R* to a *B*.

No doubt the colonel was less cavalier in his dealings with another of the surveyors he did hire, "Squire" Eleazer Coburn of Bloomfield (now Skowhegan), to do work on the Bingham heirs' Kennebec lands. The Coburns, father and sons, were to become another legendary force in the Maine Woods and one son, Abner, was not only later a governor of Maine but allegedly the state's "first millionaire." It may have been Abner for whom Eleazer billed Colonel Black $18 — "18 days of my son at 1 dollar a day" — in the bill he presented for 36 days of survey at "No. 3, 3rd Range, perambulating the East Million line." We also find E. Coburn hired to do more work on "Number 3 range in the Million Acres on the east side of the Kennebec" because there were thirty settlers anxious to have the township surveyed and he, Black, wanted it done while the streams and ponds were still frozen.

One of the ways in which Abner Coburn amassed his holdings was to buy up certificates given to Revolutionary War veterans and their families for land in Maine. For example, in February 1829, the General Court appropriated Township 4, Range 2, north of the Bingham Kennebec Purchase (NBKP) as an area to provide bounties for veterans or their widows and children. In effect, these were like promissory bonuses the grantees could sell, since few if any of these now aging soldiers or their kin intended to move Down East. T4 R2 NBKP happened to be what is now Moose River Plantation in the Coburns' home Somerset County and it had been surveyed by Eleazer Coburn. Within four years, Abner was there, buying a 100-acre lot for $50, and presently he had deeds for 64 grants in the township. By the time this game of Monopoly in Moose River ended, Abner Coburn had 131 lots and everyone else 85.

Sara J. Cowan, in her Master's thesis on "Revolutionary War Bounty Lands in Maine," states the obvious aim behind such activities, which were being practiced all over Maine. "Most of the benefits," she wrote, "were derived by alert lumbermen and their agents to whom it presented an opportunity to buy good timberland at bargain prices."[9]

Yet Eleazer and Abner and Philander Coburn were not considered crooks or unprincipled speculators but highly respected business people. The testimony of a Boston merchant has been quoted in a biographical sketch of Abner:

> I knew the Coburns when I was selling goods in the Kennebec Valley in the forties. There was hardly any money in the region, but it seemed to me that nearly every local storekeeper and well-to-do farmer had a piece of paper signed A and P Coburn, which they held to be as good as money, and which had been given for produce for the lumber camps.[10]

From logging to river-driving was a natural progression for businessmen like the Coburns. In 1835 the Kennebec Log Driving Company, similar if not identical in structure and purpose to the Penobscot Log Driving Company, was formed. Apparently, none of the Coburns were among the initiators of this cooperative arrangement to float logs from as far upriver as the Forks and Caratunk Falls down to the boom at Gardiner. Abner Coburn first appears in 1842 when chosen a director. The next January at the KLDC's annual meeting Abner Coburn, Esq., was named moderator, but asked to be excused. The members "voted not to excuse him." Three months later, he was elected their president. At the March 1844 meeting, Abner was made moderator, director, and president and also placed on a committee "to attend to the Rafting bill now before the Legislature and see that it is restored to its original draft as regards price." In 1849 he gave up the office of president but remained moderator year after year until 1857, when he became president again.

These same leadership qualities were evidenced in his role in railroads. Initially, the line for which he raised money was the Somerset and Kennebec Railroad Company, which was to service his Skowhegan home area. When it was leased to the Portland and Kennebec, he became that company's president, and the same thing happened when the P & K merged with the Maine Central, where he was president from 1875–88.

In banking, politics, and education, Abner Coburn also rose easily to the top—the presidency of the First National Bank and the Skowhegan Savings Bank, state representative (and on the Committee on State Lands and State Valuation), on the Governor's Council, a founder of the Republican Party, heading Maine's electoral ticket when Lincoln was elected, one of the wartime governors, president of the Board of Trustees of Colby College for eleven years, and the same for the State College of Agriculture and Mechanical Arts, which became the University of Maine.

Not every Mainer thought Abner Coburn was the cat's meow. John W. Haley of Saco was an infantryman in the 17th Maine and when Coburn came to Virginia to review his unit, the comments in his diary were scathing: "Governor Coburn is, without exception, the most wretched speechmaker that ever punished the cushion of the governor's chair. He acted more like a great blubbering schoolboy.... The sum total of his remarks was the sum of all flattery, piled so thick it fell off in great chunks."

Abner Coburn was en route to Augusta in 1884 to vote as an elector for James G. Blaine when he was taken seriously ill, dying shortly afterward. This millionaire shared a home with his brother, Philander, and neither of them ever married.

Other examples of such homegrown "tycoons" cropped up elsewhere all over Maine, known more locally than Veazie, Dwinel, Pingree, Coe, and Coburn—people such as Dr. Moses Mason in Bethel or Milton Gilman Shaw in the Moosehead region or Shephard Cary in Houlton or Isaac Farrar in Bangor. The list can be stretched nearly ad infinitum. A final act—the Webster-Ashburton Treaty of 1842—rounded out the borders of Maine, incorporating thousands of acres more of timber open to cutting, offering new names to the roster.

How these Aroostook lands came into Maine's possession is a story often told—but not always from the vantage point of the exiled Acadians who settled the Madawaska territory on both sides of the St. John River and were like an advance edge of settlers pushing into Maine wildlands, except doing it from a different direction.

Madawaska, during French times, had had a distinct identity as the *Seigneurie de Madouesca*, a feudal holding belonging to *Sieur* Charles-Aubert de la Chesnaye. Whether in British times Thomas Carleton, governor of New Brunswick, or his brother, Guy Carleton, Lord Dorchester, governor of Quebec, had the right to bestow it on others was never determined, but the Acadians and a few "Canadians" (i.e., *Quebeçois*) were ensconced there by 1785. They were not exactly living under the old French system of seigneurs and tenants, nor did they operate on the New England principles of settlers forming town and state governments. As Charlotte Lenentine writes in *Madawaska—A Chapter in Maine-New Brunswick Relations*:

> The Madawaskans, descendants of transplanted Frenchmen of the seventeenth century, had no tradition of self-government nor interest in local governing bodies. They had no voice in the government of the province.[11]

At the most, they had a church warden and a local man who kept in touch with the provincial government, and conflicts were settled by the priest and two assessors, one from each side. Most of these early Madawaskans were illiterate, so all contracts were verbal and a man's word was his bond. To *perde sa parole*—break your word—was unforgivable.

Nevertheless, questions of governance and security arose and led to requests to Lord Dorchester to appoint militia officers who could also act as law officers. The Acadians sought Quebec's help because law officers in New Brunswick had to take the "test oath" in that Protestant province and abjure any allegiance to the pope. This was a foretaste of the far more serious jurisdictional fights that would develop with their Maine neighbors. For the next thirty years, Madawaska peacefully developed in isolation, oblivious to developments beyond the fringe of settlement in this northern wilderness.

Once the St. Croix line had been settled through Jay's Treaty, Edward Winslow, the American Loyalist, could exult: "We lose not a single British settlement," only "a few miserable Frenchmen at Madawaska on the route to Canada...." In fact, Winslow, as one of the British negotiators, had been trying unsuccessfully to swap Madawaska for Moose Island.

The war of 1812 briefly touched Madawaska when a British infantry unit passed through. With memories of their expulsion from Nova Scotia and then the lower St. John, the Acadians worried the soldiers might uproot them again. But the troops simply marched on to the coast.

The next disturbances were smaller scale — individual Americans arrived, seeking timber.

The Madawaskans were farmers, not lumbermen. When Nathan Baker arrived from Kennebec County in 1817 and set up a sawmill at the mouth of Meriumpticook Stream 15 miles north of Madawaska and John Harford and his son did the same 15 miles even farther north, these did not immediately seem to be worrisome incursions. But when Baker claimed the territory for the U.S., American surveyors mapped the north bank of the St. John, and the Yankees tried to form a town, the concerns expressed reached all the way to the British ambassador in Washington, who protested to President John Quincy Adams.

The northern border still had not been delineated and the rival claims of the U.S. and Britain were literally miles and thousands of acres apart. Then two events in the next few years further aroused the political sleeping dogs.

One was the arrival of John Baker, Nathan's brother, in 1820. A native of Moscow, Maine, he married his brother's widow, plunged into the lumbering trade, and belatedly displayed an American chauvinism that gained him national recognition. The other was the joint action of Massachusetts and Maine in instructing their land agents to convey deeds to American settlers in the Madawaska Territory. James Irish, the Maine agent, and George Coffin, the Massachusetts agent, traveled into the region. Ironically, their first contact was with John Baker, whom they intercepted en route to Fredericton, where he had planned to be naturalized as a New Brunswick citizen. They easily talked him out of it and gave him the legal title he'd been seeking for his property.

It was Baker's famous celebration of the Fourth of July two years later that really inflamed the situation. The backwoods lumberman was arrested by New Brunswick authorities for "trespass and intrusion and high misdemeanor" — the latter charge related to his running a New Brunswick constable off his land. As Baker departed with his captors by canoe for jail in Fredericton, he ordered his wife to fly an American flag.

Sentiment was whipped up in Maine and the U.S. by the image of Baker rotting in a New Brunswick "dungeon." In actuality, he was out on bail in Fredericton, sprung by his friends among the local merchants to whom he'd sold lumber. But the political climate was heating up and reaching a state where the U.S. government sent federal troops to Houlton and a military road was hastily constructed from Bangor. However, a truce was reached and the boundary matter submitted to a neutral arbiter, the king of Holland.

When the Dutch monarch's Solomonic decision was rejected by both sides, Maine acted unilaterally and legislatively incorporated the town of Madawaska. The governor of New Brunswick, Sir Archibald Campbell, promptly arrested all the officers of the "town." But that particular crisis petered out and tension did not flare up again until 1837, when Ebenezer Greeley, an American census taker, was arrested while counting heads in Madawaska.

The segue into the "Aroostook War" came two years later. Maine had a feisty new governor, John Fairfield of Saco, and he told the legislature that New Brunswick "trespassers" were stealing timber on Maine land to the whopping tune of $1 million. The aroused lawmakers in Augusta voted $10,000 to send a posse northward under Rufus McIntire, a former sheriff of York County. McIntire and his men proceeded to seize New Brunswick lumbermen, their ox teams, and the cut timber. In turn, McIntire, himself, and several of his men were surprised in the night, seized, and carted off to the Fredericton jail.

An aroused Maine threatened to go to war alone if the federal government didn't intervene. The local Solons voted $800,000 for an expeditionary force. Promoting the issue nationwide, but in a mock-serious style, was Seba Smith, a Maine journalist who had created the fictitious character of Major Jack Downing of Downingville, Maine. Smith wrote dispatches to the *New York Mirror* depicting the impact of the Aroostook War on Downingville.

The first matter was to select twenty Downingville men out of eighty to join the militia company being raised to march north. Inside a bowl were placed sixty white beans and twenty black beans to be drawn by a sergeant.

Seba Smith focused on a certain Peter Livermore, secretly a coward, who drew a white bean that exempted him, but who boastfully showed his bravado in expressing disappointment:

"...It wld've been fun alive to a gone down there and had a brush with them...New Brunzickers. My old fowling piece wld a made daylight shine thru 50 of 'em in half an hour's fighting...."

Then, Livermore *was* chosen, having to take the place of a declared coward. And *he* didn't stay silent:

"But Captain...it seems to me like presumption to go throwing myself into danger, when it wasn't my lot to go...."

That captain, who presumably cut Livermore no slack, was Jack Downing, "sent home [from Washington, D.C., where he'd been an aide to the President] with a captain's commission to collect forces to cope with the trouble in Madawaska."

Seba Smith's whimsical satire fitted well the comic-opera sense of this bloodless contest (one man supposedly was killed accidentally), settled amicably enough by General Winfield Scott, sent from D.C. to do just that, and by his old 1812 antagonist, Sir John Harvey, governor of New Brunswick. No shots were fired between these peoples who had "ties of common blood, language, civil liberty, laws, customs, and manners and interests," as Scott put it in one of his letters to Harvey. It then remained for the politicians to settle the northeast boundary between the U.S. and Canada and this was finally accomplished by Secretary of State Daniel Webster and Lord Ashburton, who was none other than Alexander Baring.

That Webster-Ashburton transaction is a tale in itself, full of intrigue about hidden maps and secret slush funds, but on August 9, 1842, the treaty was signed in the old State Department building at 15th Street and Pennsylvania Avenue. Lord Ashburton, who'd been worn down by the oppressive D.C. heat, could finally go home and, although he was criticized for giving in to the Yankees, and Webster was criticized for giving away a chunk of Maine to the Brits and even investigated for bribing Maine officials to accept the compromise, the sectioning has stood the test of time.

Madawaska was split—those on the south bank became Americans and citizens of Maine, which acted promptly to legalize their land titles. Thousands of acres of forest were added to the state (the British had wanted to cut off Aroostook at Mars Hill) than otherwise would have been the case.

Opening the *Bangor Daily Whig and Courier* all through the spring and summer of 1842, you would have seen a running ad placed by George W. Coffin, who was still the land agent for Massachusetts, which still had title to half of Maine's wildlands:

Timberlands by the township, half townships and quarter townships, in various parts of the State of Maine, situate on boatable waters, are offered for sale, so as to suit all persons who may be disposed to purchase for lumbering operations and will be sold on liberal terms of credit.

There was also land suitable for agriculture and for settlement and "For prices and terms, apply at the Land Office in the State House, Boston...."

The "Panic of 1837" had put only a temporary halt to the feverish land speculation of the 1830s in Maine. On July 8, 1842, the Bangor paper reported that the northeast boundary had been agreed upon, townships were being resold, the price of lumber was up, "the good people of Boston need not stop building for fear that lumber will fail them this year," and the pages of the *Whig and Courier* were full of ads for saws and axes.

Lumbering would remain a giant in the Maine economy.

NOTES

1 As quoted in *Woodsmen and Whigs* by Abigail Ewing Zolz and Marilyn Zoidis. Virginia Beach, VA: The Donning Company, 1991.

2 As quoted in *A Financial History of Maine*, by Fred Eugene Jewett. New York: Columbia University Press, 1937.

3 David C. Smith, *A History of Lumbering in Maine, 1861–1960.* Orono, ME: University of Maine Press, 1972. Page 31.

4 Ben Ames Williams, *The Strange Woman.* Boston: Houghton-Mifflin Company, 1941. Page 153.

5 Ibid., page 191.

6 Ibid., page 294.

7 James Vickery, ed., *Illustrated History of the City of Bangor.* Bangor: Bangor Centennial Committee, 1976.

8 Lew Dietz, *The Allagash.* New York: Holt, Rinehart and Winston, 1968.

9 Sarah J. Cowan, "Revolutionary War Bounty Lands in Maine." Master's thesis, Columbia University, 1954.

10 Augustus Freedom Moulton, *Memorials of Maine.* New York: American Historical Society, 1916.

11 Charlotte Lenentine, *Madawaska: A Chapter in Maine-New Brunswick Relations.* Ph.D. thesis for the University of Rochester, published by the Madawaska Historical Society, 1975. Page 17.

SIXTEEN

The Romance of the Woods

W HEN JOHN S. SPRINGER'S 1851 book, *Forest Life and Forest Trees*, was republished in 1971, the introduction by that legendary Portland bibliophile, the late Francis M. O'Brien, called it "the great classic of the Maine Woods...." In O'Brien's view, it superseded Thoreau's *The Maine Woods*, which he claimed was influenced by Springer's work, and "in some ways" was better since "it was the first of its kind to detail the great lumbering operations of the Maine woods, from timber cruising and felling the trees to the great river drives in the following spring...."

Pointing out that Springer always capitalized the word *Pine*, O'Brien declared "...and if there is a god-hero of the book it is the Pine tree," and, "As the god-heroes of antiquity were humbled and fallen, so was the fate of the ancient great Pine forests of Maine."

Thus elevated to a heroic plane beyond mere commercialization, the loggers of the Northeast moved toward the status of icons, but not quite so successfully as their counterparts in the West—the cowboys—whom they resembled in the ruggedness and danger of their work. There was violence in their world, too, and plenty of tragedy. Yet the movies have featured those Stetson-wearing, six-gun-toting buckaroos, not the red-shirted, calk-booted, axe-carrying woodsmen of the Maine forests. A 20-foot-high statue of Paul Bunyan stands in the middle of Bangor, but chances are that most Americans connect him and his blue ox Babe to the Midwest, where Mainers may have brought stories about him once they had denuded their local pine forests and headed for greener chopping grounds in Minnesota, Michigan, and Wisconsin. Besides, Bunyan was mythical and there were plenty of real role models toiling away in Maine.

Springer, who lumbered himself on the St. Croix and the Penobscot, doesn't name too many names but supplies the sense of a vigorous, romantic lifestyle to which any macho man worth his salt would be attracted. The ox teams coming out of the woods after their winter's work are vividly described:

> Accordingly, colorful pennants are displayed from tall poles fastened to the sleds and sometimes, also, to the yoke of the oxen. These are made of handkerchiefs, strips of red flannel, or the remains of a shirt of the same material, and waists are sashed with red comforters, their beards being such as a Mohammedan might swear by. Thus attired, they parade the town with all the pomp of a modern caravan.[1]

And these are drinking men, their arrival "characterized by a free indulgence in spirituous liquors and many drunken carousels.... Liquor flowed as freely as the waters which bore their logs to the mills." In 1832, Springer estimated, 450–500 men on the St. Croix had consumed 3,500 gallons of booze, mostly rum. He describes a situation at Milltown, near Calais, where drunken loggers would grab passers-by, drag them into the "toll-house grog shop," and baptize them by pouring a quart of rum over their heads. It didn't matter who was cornered, "the more distinguished the candidate, the more hearty the fun."

Down in Washington County, they had their own rum song, with its refrain of "Drink round, brave boys! Drink round, brave boys!" following each stanza's mention of the chronological steps of getting the wood from "the stump in the swamp to the ship's hold."

The sequence being:
Tis when we do go into the woods.
Now when the choppers begin to chop.
And when the swampers begin to clear.
And when we get them on to the sled.
Then, when we get them on to the stream.
And when we get them down to the boom.
So when we get them down to the mill.

After which:

> The merchant, he takes us by the hand,
> Saying, "Sirs, I have goods at your command — "
> But heigh ho! Drink round, brave boys!
> The money will foot up a "spree."

Springer's book appeared the same year Maine passed the first prohibition legislation in the U.S. (despite the ardent opposition of Shepherd Cary, a prominent lumberman).

At one point or another in *Forest Life and Forest Trees*, Springer illustrates the various phases of the lumbermen's trade, as laid out in the rum song. Going into the woods, chopping down trees — especially the great white pine — is epitomized by his story of a particular pine he felled on a brook not far from Danforth. It was a "pumpkin pine" (so named for the orangey color of its wood), 6 feet in diameter, 145 feet high, "as straight and handsomely grown as a molded candle." Springer chopped at it for an hour or so on a beautiful, calm afternoon. When the giant finally toppled, the crash, he said, "seemed to shake a hundred acres." In seeking to drive home its immense girth, the author used a comparison that later drew Henry Thoreau's scorn — because Springer wrote the stump was large enough to stand a yoke of oxen on it, the Concord iconoclast shot back how that was a stupid reason to cut down a magnificent tree. But, of course, the reason Springer chopped, as did all other loggers, was to turn that wood into money. This behemoth of a pine made five logs and they had to load a six-ox team three times. To Springer's regret, the butt log was so big and so heavy that, come spring, it wouldn't float and had to be left behind in the woods. Springer was sure it would have fetched $50.

Swamping, the next stage, is simply moving the cut timber from where it has fallen to a waterside, where it can be floated. "We have here no turnpikes nor railways," Springer writes; so roads have to be "swamped." They are engineered backwards, so to speak, from the landing on the stream or riverbank to the site of the cutting, until a ribbon 10 to 12 feet wide cuts through the forest, iced smooth in winter. Springer calls it a "serpentine highway for the 'Knight of the goad'" (the teamster directing the oxen) and says: "...no street in all our cities is so beautifully studded with trees." Waxing poetical, he reminisces (as a retired Methodist minister running a dry goods shop in Boston) how much he enjoyed his labors in the logging swamp:

> I would now with eagerness exchange my house for the logging camp, my books for the ax, and the city full for those wilderness solitudes whose delightful valleys and swelling ridges give me Nature uncontaminated—I had almost said, uncursed, fresh from the hand of the Creator....[2]

After the swampers, there are the barkers and loaders—those who hew off the log's covering and also help the teamster wrestle it onto his sled. A six-ox team hauls it to the water, Springer writing that "the bobsled, as though it were a thing of life, actually screams out at every joint as if in keenest agony beneath its ponderous load."

Descents could be horribly dangerous. Springer personally witnessed a situation where a teamster, losing control when his oxen ran downhill, was thrown and run over by his sled and was still alive two hours later, when reached, with several tons of timber on top of him. His last words were "Here I am" to his would-be rescuers.

Springer declares the next task—river-driving—is "not so agreeable as other departments of labor in the lumbering operations," although it has its own powerful mystique. He acknowledges it is the most dangerous phase and accounts for the most casualties. When a drowned body is recovered, the corpse is placed in a "coffin" made of two empty floor barrels, one passed over head and shoulders, the other from legs up, then buried at some lonely spot in the wilderness, usually without prayer and in momentary silence from his usually garrulous companions. Springer admits at such times, he has never been "so extremely oppressed with a feeling of sadness while standing over the little mound...."

Eventually, the boom is reached where the logs are sorted, and then the sawmills receive them and the finished lumber flows to its customers, whether in Boston "for building and cabinet purposes" or on the island of Cuba, which "alone consumes 40 millions of feet per annum for the one article of sugar-boxes."

In addition to his descriptions—personal, anecdotal, and even folklorically poetical—of the lumberman and his life, Springer delves into the wildlife of this vast, natural area—moose, bears, wolves, and other fauna—and anticipates the intense interest in Katahdin by including a lengthy sketch of its ascent, probably by Dr. Charles T. Jackson, Maine state geologist. The lumbering trade on each of the major rivers of the state is then covered, with statistics and prices. But these dry numbers are completely overshadowed by Springer's skill in leaving the reader, when you put the volume down, with the impression of a work style about to embed itself in immortality, kept forever alive in print and media.

It was not only the anonymous poets of the lumber camps who celebrated this lifestyle in rollicking paeans to the rum they consumed or "The Logger's Boast," exulting in how they braved the elements better than city folk "in the red frost-proof flannel we're incased from top to toe" and have much more fun than the urbanites; even such an established voice as John Greenleaf Whittier's lauded the Maine woodsmen in his poem, "The Lumbermen," which, according to Springer was recited one evening in their quarters by a certain Hobbs. Among the verses were mentions of "crystal Ambejejis" and "Millinocket's pine-black ridges," "the swift and strong Penobscot," and "glimpses given of Katahdin's sides." Whittier, an outspoken Abolitionist, also brings in that political theme in references to the "Northland, wild and woody," where:

Freedom, hand in hand with labor
Walketh strong and brave
On the forehead of his neighbor
No man writeth Slave!

Their woods work, then, their brotherhood in the forest wilderness, is the epitome, to Whittier, of that quintessentially American sweep of liberty-loving individualism and egalitarianism we also assign to our cowboys.

The melting pot was already there, too. The boys in red were not just the WASP Yankees of New England. The Irish Catholics who'd come to Bangor and Portland were infiltrating the woods, too; so were the French, trickling down from Canada, along with another contingent from the north—the "Bluenoses," or Nova Scotians, and the P.E.I.s out of Prince Edward Island. To round out the stew, particularly as river drivers, were Penobscots and other Abenaki.

By 1860 a long magazine piece in *Harper's New Monthly* by
Charles Hallock introduced Long John Boardman, old Bannoc the
Canuck [*sic*], and Jenks the Bluenose—"they three hobnobbing"—
a trio of fictional buddies, but representative of "Life among the
Loggers," set in Maine.

Here is a sample of dialogue between these ethnic caricatures:

Long John Boardman, stirring up the ashes of a campfire,
remembers he was in this same vicinity about three years previously.
"Dan Smith was along," he adds, "and a smarter chap at logging
never swung an axe."

"Dan Smeet?" interrupts Louis Bannoc. "You say Dan Smeet?
He vas certainement beau swamper. Pauvre garçon—mais he no log
encore, parceque he est mort."

"Dead?"

"Oui, he vas no been long dis one, two year. Maybe he drown
downriver."

"Did you ever hear about it, Jenks? It's news to me."

"Oh, pshaw! The Frenchman be dogged. Dan got his bobsled
and tackle and fall alongside of a woman and went and married a she
Norwegian down on Sinnamahone, in Pennsylvany. That's two
years ago come January...."

While they sit around, frying and digesting longitudinal strips
of pork and swallowing black tea, the ubiquitous beverage of the
loggers seemingly more popular than rum, writer Hallock extolls the
"freedom, pure and unadulterated" they apparently enjoy. Those
three are an advance guard, along with Tom Harris, a young teamster, Captain Hinch, the boss, and a few others.

> In full panoply of red flannel shirts, good boot moc-
> casins, and hats of felt, their visages browned by expo-
> sure, and hands hardened to toil, they stand ready to do
> battle with the giants of the forest.[3]

They clear a site, build a log house, cut a road. It is autumn
and winter will be here soon to ice it down. They hunt, going after
a moose with their dogs Tige, Brave, and Lion, who then tackle a
bear. In the struggle, Bannoc, "the jovial little Frenchman," takes a
swipe on the shoulder from a lashing paw. He is patched up and
healed by the time the ox teams arrive. Hallock, later describing

established business practices in the Maine Woods, notes that some lumbermen are employed by the route or all through the successive stages, others for part-time specialties, and that the French habitants, in all cases, get paid less.

The cutting of the trees is pictured well, with technical details supplied, like the fact that some perfectly magnificent specimens are left standing because they are identified as having the "conk" or "konkus," a cancerous disease that makes their wood worthless. The axes ring, the trees crash, the teamsters shout, the log chains clank, and the bobsleds give off their unearthly shrieks. Hallock equates the dexterous delimbing of the fallen pines with the deft beheadings by a Chinese executioner. The barkers trim, the sled tender uses tackle and fall to raise the logs onto his vehicle, and the oxen are off to the riverbank. The three hundred lumber camps in Maine are all pretty much the same, says the author, although he does join to Boardman, Bannoc, and Jenks "a cinnamon-colored Micmac or Penobscot Indian...wielding the axe as their forefathers did the tomahawk." In the evening, he has them all lounging around a campfire after supper, with almost as much smoke rising from their black-stemmed pipes as from the blazing firewood. Long John sings and Captain Hinch is persuaded to tell a tale and the winter slowly passes. They are about to leave and turn things over to the river drivers when a tragedy happens: Tom Harris, the young teamster, is killed in a typical teamster accident and buried in the usual barrels in a lonely spot. The drive completes the cycle and the drama of logs going over waterfalls is touched upon: the Kennebec, the Sebois, the Neshournehunk [*sic*], Androscoggin, and Aroostook Rivers and the granddaddy of all, the Grand Falls of the St. John, with a vertical drop of hundreds of feet. The bravado of the drivers is discussed, those who break jams and miss drowning or being pulverized by inches. Then they are at the boom, where "a small army of men, armed with pikes," guides the logs to their appropriate places. The Penobscot Boom, we are told, can be visited by rowing up the river, noting the Indian village as you pass through Old Town, and the mills, now each employing 50–100 saws, are going day and night. Without this economic mainspring of lumbering, the *Harper's* article concludes, Maine, the Pine-Tree State, "like a Yankee clock with wooden works, would cease to run...."

A special vocabulary was being created in that subconscious manner in which cultures develop over time:

To the initiated the manner of conducting lumbering operations is among the wonders. For a "green-un" to hear a company of men talk about the "swampers," "sled-tenders," "choppers," "toters" and "teamsters," of the "deacon seat," "wangan," "Spanish windlass," and "turning out," is about as intelligible as "chewing up" and "sheeting home," "hauling taut" and "belay" is to the landsman. And yet to the Penobscot lumberman all these and many technicalities not understood by "outside barbarians," have a meaning.

The lexicon of lumbering terms could fill a dictionary. In addition to some translatable ones above, like "wangan"= the camp gear carried on a scow during a river drive; also a company store; or "deacon seat" = a place where loggers could sit down in a lumber camp, often a crude bench; there are many others. A sampling might include:

"bateau" = the type of boat used on the rivers, pointed at both ends. Hosea B. Maynard of Bangor, a master driver, was the acknowledged champion manufacturer of such craft.

"alligator" = a flat-bottomed scow.

"calks" = the spikes on the bottom of loggers' boots.

"cant dog" or "cant hook" = the pike-like instruments river drivers used for guiding or moving logs.

"peavey" = a better cant dog, invented by Joseph Peavey of Stillwater.

"to hovel" = to bunk with.

"twitch" = to move logs along a woods road.

"rollway" = a landing from which logs were toppled into water.

"turkey" = a meal sack tied together for a knapsack.

"kennebecker" = a carpet bag or fancier knapsack.

"black" or "light" = the men's favorite chewing and smoking tobacco.

"Canada shag" = home-grown tobacco from French
      Canada—very strong.
      The French in the Maine Woods had their own vocabulary:
billes = logs; *drave* = drive; *traineau* = sled; *cages* = rafts; la coupee
clair = clear-cutting; *bucherons* = loggers.
      Next, throw in some very un-scientific noxious species to spice
up this wilderness lore, such as "Razor-shins," "Will-am-alones,"
"Side-hill-winders," and "Ding-balls."
      A Razor-shin is less a hostile wild creature than a spirit with a
terrible thirst for whiskey. It must be placated with a quart upon
entering its territory. Failure to pay such tribute can result in muti-
lation, cutting off your scalp with a single kick or your ears with a
saber-like slash of its shins. Newcomers to camp—"greenhorns"—
are advised to leave a jug at the door. If, the next morning, the other
inhabitants of the camp smell of alcohol and the jug is empty, then
you know the Razor-shin got it.
      The Will-am-alones are little squirrel-like beasties who drop
balls of rolled-up poison ivy into the eyes and ears of men sleeping
in camps. These cause strange dreams and visions, and often the
heaviest drinkers are affected.
      The Side-hill-winders are bigger, about the size of a rabbit,
and their downhill legs are longer than their uphill ones. They will
corkscrew right up a mountain, but can be headed off by dogs and
are easy prey when tipped over. The fat cures diseases caused by
the Will-am-alones but to eat the flesh of a Side-hill-winder causes
sudden death.
      The Ding-ball, a panther, is the biggest and most ferocious,
attacking victims with its bare, ball-shaped tail joint, which can
crack a human skull. There is no record of survival from its blow. It
sings with a human voice to lure its prey and the loggers claim it will
sing all night for a meal of Indians.
      Other wildlife in the forests of the lumbermen's imaginations
included the *hodag*, the *high-behind*, the *Dungarven-whooper*, the
Maineguyanouse, and the *lethal tree-squeak*. Nor were they less inven-
tive in the games they concocted. Like *Shove-Shove*. The men would
form a circle and whoever was "IT" would bend over in the middle
and hide his face in his cap. Each player held a woodsman's boot and

one by one would smack the victim across the posterior until he guessed correctly who had hit him. That man would then replace him. Or a favorite trick on a newcomer was to question his masculinity by taunting him he couldn't climb up a certain yellow birch. When he defiantly proved them wrong by reaching the top, they would set the tree on fire. They were famous for their "lice fights." Procuring opposing champions was no problem; two lumberjacks would lift a creature from their own bodies, crease a newspaper, place their louse on each side of the fold, and set them battling until one killed the other.

They often imitated such behavior themselves. Fights were usually more frequent outside the woods—in city bars or traveling to and fro, but could break out anytime. Robert E. Pike, in *Tall Trees, Tough Men*, describes one such donnybrook where the men got to drinking and fighting over a couple of women who'd been sneaked into a camp. Three times, they tipped over a red-hot stove, almost setting the place on fire. A woodsman named McCabe nearly killed another named Johnny Arsenault, holding him by the throat and striking him with an axe, until Johnny's dog knocked McCabe over, and another fellow named Jack drew a revolver and began shooting out the kerosene lamps.

Pike's narrator (a teamster named Vern) related:
Bullets were flying wild and Johnny and Mike were tearing into each other like a pair of wild bulls and the stove was on its side and the women were yelling in the bunk-room and there was I, cold sober, the only one in the lot who wasn't happy.[4]

Whereupon Vern, who must have been a giant of a man, picked up the two combatants and threw them outdoors, telling them: "Fight there all you please. But I'm tired of picking up that stove for you."

Bill Bunting, in *A Day's Work, A Sampler of Maine Historic Photographs, 1860–1920, Part I*, provides another anecdote of the woodsmen's pugnaciousness, this time on a train bound for Norcross, south of Millinocket:
On the platform, standing in their stockings, with their sharp-calked boots slung around their necks, they [the

woodsmen, in this case river drivers] looked as sweet as lambs. As soon as all were aboard, however, the wise old conductor locked the doors and the "river hogs" began to fight, destroying the interior of the cabin in the process. They battled the entire journey, swinging their calked shoes like medieval maces. Blood flowed copiously from scalp wounds.... At Norcross when the doors were finally unlocked and the bloodied company tallied, one man was missing, having either exited or been ejected through a window of the moving train.... Butting, eye-gouging, kicking and stomping with calks—the results of calking were termed..."loggers' smallpox"—were permitted, even encouraged. The use of knives was not.... No fighting was allowed once the drive began.[5]

Early on, the reputation of these forest workers spread back into civilization, creating an image at once attractive in its roguishness and yet frightening to the respectable. Both emotions seem to have affected Benjamin Browne Foster, son of a Bangor storeowner, who began keeping a diary at age sixteen in 1847. That year he wrote about a drama at the Atheneum Theater, written by a local man, C. H. Saunders, called *The River Driver.* Part of the plot was about a riot when "raftsmen and laborers [American] were to come to Bangor and expel thence all Irishmen and foreigners."

This stage riot, which had been inspired by the events of 1833, had its postscript in and out of the theater several nights later. A performance was canceled, allegedly because the actors hadn't been paid, and the commotion spilled into the streets as the theatergoers pushed and shoved to get their money back. Meanwhile, an amateur performer named George Buffum jumped up on the stage and entertained a crowd, composed apparently of river drivers, by dancing and shouting. *The River Driver* was followed by another piece with a sylvan setting called *Nick of the Woods.*

Ben Foster, himself, in 1848 headed into the woods, or rather to a tradingpost-type of store at Weston, in the southwesternmost part of Aroostook County. He was invited to work on a river drive—actually keep the books—at $15 a month, but declined. Sometime later he indulged in a Hamlet-like soliloquy in his diary concerning his future and his ambiguous feelings about the lumber industry:

It is a most precarious and perplexing branch of trade, forever involved in doubt and uncertainty. There is doubtless a tide in its affairs which leads on to fortune but when its "flood" is none can tell till it is past and they see the ebb.... No dependence is to be placed on it.... Then add that a lumbering country's resources are but temporary in their duration. Unlike farming or commerce, let its lumber be cut away and it is used up. I must secure *now* some other situation....[6]

In 1849, the California gold rush year, Ben was tempted to go west, like so many young Mainers. Instead, he went off to school in Massachusetts and an eventual career as a lawyer. The lure of the woods had been evanescent, and he put lumbering in a context in his diary that might resonate today to a bemoaner of the two Maines:

What a poor country is this in which we live.... The California fever is carrying our citizens away...our wheat crops and potatoes are cut off. Corn is insignificant. The lumber business is our total dependence....

Ben Foster saw then, more than a century and a half ago, the frailty of an economic future utterly tied to forest products. Much of the debate since has been how Maine should deal with this geographic given. Yet the mystique of lumbering continued to grow, fueled by the songs and stories and poetry romanticizing that rough life.

The earliest of the woods songs has been dated back to 1825, when Maine men were working in the "square timber" trade in Lower Canada, rafting this special cut of lumber to Quebec. Also called "ton timber," these squared-off, 2,000-pound logs were destined for Great Britain, but their production and transportation proved too crude and labor-intensive and did not last in Maine after 1850.

Until then, they were singing:
When we get into Quebec
We're the boys who don't forget
Our whistles for to wet

With whiskey or good wine
With some pretty girl we'll boast
Till our money is all used
We're the boys that don't refuse
To return and fall the pine.

When Bangor became the epicenter, the Canadians were attracted south and the P.E.I.s—the Prince Edward Islanders— were particularly adept at making up music and lyrics, like in "The Boys of the Island," in which historic Bangor personages deal with these cut-ups in town for a spree. They sang:

Brade Kelly will poison a man with bad whiskey
For pastime they will banish their lager and ale;
Then on the corner when he does get frisky,
They will call for Tim Carey to take him to jail.

Brade Kelly was a Bangor saloonkeeper and Tim Carey a well-known Bangor policeman. At the end of these bashes, they would collect around the old European and North American Railway depot at the corner of Exchange and Washington Streets, calked boots slung around their shoulders, "long-neckers" or bottles of whiskey in evidence, "a grimy picture of dazed, doped, half-drunk woodsmen" entraining upriver after a brief carouse on their winter wages.

With them, too, went the legend of Fan Jones and her blue-chimneyed bordello, and she also inspired a folk song:

Fan Jones she runs a cathouse
Way down on Harlow Street
And if you are a woodsman
Your friends all there you'll meet.

She was Nancy F. Jones, a sixteen-year-old farm girl from West Brooksville when she came to the big city, and by 1858 she was already a fallen woman and arraigned in court for keeping a house of ill fame. With her in the docket was John Thomas, "a notorious local rowdy," who became her lover, business partner, and perhaps husband, for sometimes she called herself Mrs. Fanny Thomas. They lived together (when he wasn't in jail) until his death in 1878. Despite her frequent brushes with the law, Fan Jones was never more than fined, and even respectable Bangorians acknowledged she performed a public service because otherwise no woman in Bangor would be safe from the hordes of loggers and sailors in town. Besides, she earned respect for keeping an orderly house and never taking in underage girls. In her later years, Fan was described as "a refined-looking little old lady with beautiful white hair," always dressed in black.

Another woman, operating in a wholly different capacity in this era, was Fannie Pearson Hardy of Brewer, more familiar to Maine as the author Fannie Hardy Eckstorm. She wrote nonfiction, but with a novelist's eye and sensibility.

Well-educated — Miss Hardy went to Abbott Academy and Smith College — she was the daughter of a fur trapper, hunter, and fisherman who knew the Maine Woods intimately as a place in which he made his living. A small Penobscot Indian community in Brewer was open to her since childhood, and her empathy for Native Americans, as exhibited in her biography of Governor John Neptune, was unusual for the age. Her view of woodsmen necessarily had to be other than that of those who saw them fleetingly in their cups on the streets of Bangor.

Her best known book is *The Penobscot Man*, dedicated to John Ross and the West Branch River Drive. "These are the tales," she wrote, "of the men who tended me in baby-hood, who crooned to me old slumber-songs, who brought me gifts from the woods, who wrought me little keepsakes or amused my childish hours. Stories…I have bound into a garland to lay upon their graves."

If immortalizing them was, indeed, her intention, she has come close to accomplishing it, particularly in the case of John Ross. He has been called "the most famous riverman who ever lived."[7] The ultimate compliment to his leadership came when Ross was contracted to take his "Bangor Tigers" to the Connecticut River to run a drive from its headwaters to Hartford under conditions no one else could master. The water level was so low that gamblers in Hartford were betting heavily the drive would fail. Yet Ross somehow blasted a channel, drove his logs through, and the 150 Penobscot men he took with him were jubilant, but not surprised. They were men he had trained himself:

Yankees, Frenchmen, Indians, Province-men, but all

Penobscot. They would follow John Ross anywhere, they would do for him what would never be believed when the traditions once have faded. He was that rare creature, the idol of his men. "The King of the River," I have heard him called by a college man who had worked on the logs in vacations and knew of what he spoke.[8]

Ross had worked on the Penobscot River for fifty years, and for thirty he was the head of the West Branch Drive for the Penobscot Log Driving Company, and its cohort, the Penobscot Lumbering Association. Under his aegis, the West Branch Drive was, in Fannie's words, "a little army, drilled and commanded by a military genius." His men came to believe "there was no place on the earth or under it that the West Branch Drive could not take logs out of, if John Ross gave the word." The author described a small boy in Old Town who would "look saucily up into your face and exclaim, 'Say I'm John Ross or I'll kill you!'"

Naturally, such a larger-than-life real character would show up in the song and story of folklore. "The Black Stream Driver's Song" is one of these:

Who makes the big trees fall kertbrash
And hit the ground a hell of a smash
Tis Johnny Ross and Cyrus Hewes
Who gives us pay for one big drunk
When we hit Bangor, slam kerplunk!
Tis Johnny Ross and Cyrus Hewes.

Or this well-known ditty, entitled "John Ross," composed by an old woodsman, Dan Golden:

Oh, the night that I was married, O,
And laid on marriage bed,
Up rose John Ross and Cyrus Hewes
And stood by my bedstead,
Saying, "Arise, young married man
And go along with me
To the lonesome hills of Suncook
To swamp them logs for me."

The youth might have been Dan Golden, himself, who worked for John Ross for thirty-six winters, starting in 1867.

In the *Minstrelsy of Maine,* Fannie Hardy Eckstorm collected these and other verses, not only about John Ross, but a whole cast of characters whose names drift in and out, like Henry K. Robinson, a Brewer lumberman, the burning of whose camp inspired a song, or "The Sandy Stream Song" about Edwin A Reed's operation near Katahdin, or John Rolland or Isaac Terrill or Bill McLean or Hunter and Slipper Sam, all mentioned in a song about a woods barber who shaves them.

"The Jam on Gerry's Rock" was said to be the most famous of the modern lumber ballads, coming to Maine from Michigan in 1904, although Gerry's Rock has been identified as a spot on the Penobscot's East Branch thirteen miles above Grindstone, where a tragedy supposedly occurred. But others declare Gerry's Rock is on the Androscoggin near Rumford Falls.

The derring-do of the Indians of John Ross's crew in taking their boats over falls is also celebrated by Fannie. There is the feat of Big Sebat or Sebbatis Mitchell, the first (except for John Ross) to run the falls at Nesowadnehunk, and the tragic denouement of another such show of bravery when Thoreau's former guide, Joe Attien, drowns and his boots are hung on the pin knot of a pine.

A different kind of heroic type surfaces in a group of young men from the Washington County town of Wesley whom she cites: Dave Fenlason, Eben Cofren, Leverett Elsmore, and Wilbur Day—alias the "Shacker band," from the shacks in which they lived and from which they poached deer.

We have here another romanticism that developed about the Maine Woods—the outlaw, à la Robin Hood, battling the new phenomenon of game laws.

In 1891, before *Penobscot Man* and *Minstrelsy of Maine,* Fannie began writing for *Forest and Stream,* one of the country's leading sportsmen's magazines. Her articles, combined as *Six Years under Maine Game Laws,* seemed an attempt to communicate the impact of the editorial policy of the publication, which had been to promote restrictions on hunting and fishing. "I am speaking for the farmers, lumbermen, explorers, guides, hunters, and all others...who may be classed as our rural population." In shades of the old squatter-proprietor struggles in the Maine Woods, she sees the state's game legislation as a "contest between rich and poor, nonresident and resident, sportsman and farmer, the game being only the *casus belli* — the excuse for the war."

Her Robin Hood was a man named Jock Darling, the "Lowell outlaw," from the tiny Washington County town of that name, who continued to hunt deer with dogs after the practice had been banned. She seemed very perturbed that Darling was entrapped by one William McNamara, a Boston detective posing as an out-of-state hunter. Reaching Darling's remote camp on Nicatous Lake, McNamara hired him to hunt deer in this illegal (and unsporting) manner, in which a deer is driven into water, then easily shot since it cannot run. Yet it seemed even more unsporting to Fannie that Jock Darling was handcuffed and imprisoned rather than simply fined.

Another real-life folk hero of this ilk was George Magoon, connected with some of that Wesley "Shacker band," and the even more notorious Calvin Graves. Magoon lived in Crawford, also on the Airline (Route 9) like Wesley. A market hunter and "hounder" of deer, he was often in jail, and a folksong has him not wanting to be let out in wintertime and telling his captors, "I'll just get another deer and come right back so why not keep me here now." Nevertheless, on occasion, Magoon did use the services of the famous Washington County attorney, politician, and writer William R. Pattangall, who also wrote a short story about him entitled "The Capture of George Maloon. Picturesque Story of Officer MacCurdy's Pursuit of a Noted Down East Outlaw in the Washington County Wilds."

Note that "Patt" Pattangall (who several times ran for governor of Maine and ended his career as the state's chief justice) used the spelling *Maloon*, not Magoon. Incredibly, there was an actual George Maloon in East Machias, a political foe of Patt's, and this was his joke on him, which he published in Lewiston and Machias newspapers.

Calvin Graves was something different — not just a picaresque rogue, but a man who killed two wardens after they tried to kill his dogs. Fannie tries to explain the sympathy in the area for Graves. Despite the seriousness of his crime, it was seen as an act of self-defense. The killing, by shooting or poisoning, of their dogs was an atrocity that utterly infuriated these back-country people. Her father, informing her by letter of Graves's deed, wrote: "What I have so long expected and foretold has come to pass and in the way I predicted — by killing dogs."

Of George Magoon, it was said that he was so destructive of game the Fish and Game Department had to hire him, so they could watch him. Whether he or Jock Darling are the models for the best piece of Maine fiction on this subject is not revealed by the author. I am speaking of *The One-Eyed Poacher and the Maine Woods* by Edward Ware Smith — short stories about the adventures of Thomas Jefferson Coongate, "a kind of Maine woods Robin Hood — a poacher of gigantic proportions, of awesome prowess and resource-fulness, for whom the violation of game laws represents an assertion of human dignity, an instinctive response to the challenge of nature, and an act of self-affirmation."[9]

This forgotten little masterpiece nails down perfectly this aspect of the romance of the Maine Woods. You can almost taste the rough whiskey and forbidden venison and moose meat.

NOTES

[1] John S. Springer, *Forest Life and Forest Trees*. Somersworth, NH: New Hampshire Publishing Company, reprinted in 1971. Page 148.

[2] Ibid., page 70.

[3] Charles Hallock, "Life among the Loggers," *Harper's New Magazine*, March 1860.

[4] Robert E. Pike, *Tall Trees, Tough Men*. New York: W. W. Norton and Company, Inc., 1984. Page 127.

[5] W. H. Bunting, *A Day's Work: A Sampler of Historic Maine Photographs, 1860–1920, Part I*. Gardiner, ME: Tilbury House, Publishers/Maine Preservation. Page 94.

[6] Benjamin Brown Foster, *Down East Diary*. Orono, ME: University of Maine Press, 1975. Page 108.

[7] Pike, page 57.

[8] Fannie Hardy Eckstorm, *The Penobscot Man*. Boston: Houghton Mifflin Company, 1904. Page 237.

[9] Edward Ware Smith, *The One-Eyed Poacher and The Maine Woods*. Rockport, ME: Down East Books, reprinted in 1955.

S E V E N T E E N

Here Comes Industrialization

ALTHOUGH BANGOR was no longer "the Lumber Capital of the World" by 1872, that year recorded the highest flow of cut timber to come through the Penobscot booms. A workforce of 125 men handled 216 million board feet equivalent, whereas during the heyday of the 1830s, the Bangor area's record was 82 million. On the river, in 1872, 2,858 vessels arrived and carried back with them even more lumber, 246.5 million board feet, worth almost $4 million.

Also, that year is remembered locally for the epic riot between French-Canadian and Irish boom workers in which, according to the local press, "The Irishmen received a bad calking from the Frenchmen."

There was no reason, then, to surmise that long-log lumbering and the colorful tradition it had engendered would not last indefinitely into the future. Yet if we follow the thinking of Alfred G. Hempstead, who did a monumental study of the Penobscot Boom and log-driving on the West Branch of the Penobscot, 1872 represented a midway point toward the end of an era.[1] Reverend Hempstead, a clergyman retired to Washington County, divided the lumbering history on the West Branch into three distinct periods.

> 1828–46: A time of completely independent activity by loggers and contractors, following the pattern set in colonial times.
>
> 1846–1903: The cooperative effort, where lumbermen pooled their resources to build dams and improve navigation for everybody. Any person who owned timber or who lumbered on the West Branch was

eligible to join the Penobscot Log Driving Company, and one vote was given for each six-ox team a member used. A "master driver" was hired by the firm to coordinate everything (John Ross began in 1864).

1903–on: "The period of corporation control." In 1903 the Great Northern Paper Company basically took over the West Branch Drive.

The 1903 divide likewise reflects a new and different use of Maine wood—no longer just lumber, it is now being used in growing quantities to make paper.

In 1732, so the story goes, Samuel Waldo and Thomas Westbrook attempted to set up a paper mill—the second to be started in what was then Massachusetts—but it rapidly failed. Its location was along the lower Presumpscot River, where Colonel Westbrook owned land. At this location, now the city of Westbrook, the first of Maine's major paper companies-to-be—the S. D. Warren Company—took shape. The exact site was at Congin Falls, which is now Westbrook's business district. A small mill had been erected there around 1845 and was sold in 1854 to Samuel Dennis Warren and Otis Daniell, whom Warren soon bought out. The paper manufactured there was newsprint made from good quality cotton and linen; brown Manila wrapping paper made from colored rags, old bags, and jute; and high-quality writing paper made from the finest bleached rags. In these days before wood pulp was employed, it has been claimed that among the rags used in Maine were the linen wrappings from Egyptian mummies.

S. D. Warren was an absentee owner who kept his residence in Boston, but frequently made trips to the mill. He was born in Grafton, Massachusetts, and began his work life with a firm of Boston paper dealers. At the age of twenty-one, he was a junior partner at Grant, Daniell and Company, traveling to Europe several times to promote their rag-importing business and learning another aspect—papermaking—when they leased a small mill in the town of Pepperell. By the time he took sole possession of "Cumberland Mills," as he called his plant at Westbrook, Warren was an experienced operator; his contacts in Europe assured him a good supply of rags, and he was quick to acquire the sources of clean water he needed in order to produce uniformly clean white paper and also supply his workers with pure drinking water. Warren became noted for his benevolence to his workers, each of whom he treated "as a personal friend and not so much bones and brawn to be minted into wealth for his personal aggrandizement."[2]

Eventually, the S. D. Warren Company turned to wood pulp, but its acceptance was slow. The earliest promulgator of the soda process for creating paper from wood pulp was Hugh Burgess, an Englishman who came to the U.S. in 1854. Twenty years later it was tried at Westbrook. Spring drives of poplar logs came down the Presumpscot River from the nearby Sebago Lake and Songo River region to be fed into S. D. Warren's chemical pulping process. By the 1890s, their mills "were 'among the most extensive of their kind on the globe.'"[3]

The other giant in Maine, the Rumford Falls Paper Company, was the brainchild of a Canadian-born entrepreneur named Hugh J. Chisholm. Coming from the Niagara area, he had early been a newsboy on the Grand Trunk Railroad (along with Thomas A. Edison), and at age sixteen bought the news business and soon had 200 newsboys working for him. The Grand Trunk, whose terminus was Portland, brought him to Maine in 1872 where he published railroad and tourism guides and specialized, too, in photo albums of beautiful New England scenery. From publishing to manufacturing paper was a short step and in 1882, he not only took over the railroad line from Portland to Rumford but established the Rumford Falls Sulphite Company and Rumford Falls Paper Company, making paper with the new sulphite process. Louis Hatch, in *Maine, A History*, describes his impact on Rumford:

> From the wilderness that marked this site before Mr.
> Chisholm arrived on the scene, there arose a thriving
> city with a speed and promptness that suggested the
> conjurer's wand.[4]

It was not exactly a "conjurer's wand," but rather a *Zeitgeist* late in the nineteenth century that supported the notion of industrial development as a pure positive good, once appropriate technology had become available.

In mid-winter 1882, as he described it, Hugh Chisholm first saw Rumford. He was driving along in a sleigh when he came in view of a half-mile stretch of falls, rapids, and granite gorges where the Androscoggin dropped 180 feet.

As the publisher of New England scenes of natural beauty, he could not help but be impressed by the sight. "The magnificence of the spectacle was not all lost on me," he admitted, but then his businessman's imagination took hold: "...very soon, I began to realize, as probably many a thinking man had done before me, the vast power that was and for countless years had been going to waste...and I pictured to myself the industrial community which might grow up there."[5]

His capitalist epiphany led him to commission an engineering survey of Rumford Falls made the following year, and it revealed more waterpower than the combined strengths of the currents powering the textile centers sprouting up in Lewiston, Lowell, Lawrence, and Holyoke. Combining that factor with the plenitude of trees in western Maine and his own professional experience led Chisholm to the notion of paper. He had already dipped his toes in these waters with pulp and paper companies at Fairfield and Livermore Falls. By 1890 Chisholm had the land and capital he needed, plus a railroad connection to the Grand Trunk Railroad and Portland. In July 1893 the first paper—a run of newsprint—issued forth from the new Chisholm enterprise.

Not content, the Canadian-born magnate went on to put together a merger of twenty paper mills in Maine, New Hampshire, Massachusetts, Virginia, and New York, which he completed in 1898, and it took the name of the International Paper Company, a giant in its field (and still one today) that soon controlled 90 percent of the newsprint manufacturing in the U.S.

The inspiration that created Rumford was concurrently at work—and on an even grander scale—in another section of the Maine wilds. The Great Northern Paper Company, arising to challenge International Paper's near-monopoly on supplying newsprint, was carved out of an even vaster wilderness, seemingly overnight, to become the dominant player, industrially and politically, in the Maine Woods.

But without the growth of railroads in Maine, this aspect of industrialization—massive projects on a breathtaking scale—would not have been possible.

Most commonly associated with railroad building in nineteenth-century Maine was another epic figure—John Alfred Poor—born and raised only a short distance from Rumford in the tiny Oxford County community of Andover. As we have seen, he was the nephew of that early mapmaker and indefatigable promoter of the state, Moses Greenleaf.

His dreams were as big, if not bigger, than Hugh Chisholm's, and he started in an earlier era. It was during the winter of 1846 that he pulled off the dramatic coup that made him instantly famous. This was nothing less than a madcap dash in a horse and sleigh through blizzards and subzero temperatures to reach Montreal in time to convince the Canadian directors of the Grand Trunk Railway to locate their Atlantic Coast terminus in Portland, not Boston. Poor, who had begun his working career in Bangor during the heady land speculation days of the 1830s, had moved south to Portland and saw its possibilities as an economic rival to the Massachusetts capital. His efforts paid off in 1853, when the Grand Trunk line—much of it going through his native western Maine—was opened.

But Poor had even more ambitious visions. In later years, he talked of a transcontinental railroad—a Portland to Chicago route—to link up with service to the Pacific Coast. Yet by 1853 he had another huge project underway in Maine with far bigger "international" implications than the Grand Trunk. He grandiosely named it the European and North American Railway, and it was slated to connect Bangor to New Brunswick, then to Nova Scotia and the old French fortress at Louisbourg on Cape Breton Island, where fast steamers would pick up freight and passengers and transport them to Ireland and ultimately London. Poor chartered his proposed project in 1850 and spent the rest of his life developing it. Initially, his major argument was the shortness of this route to Europe and later, during the Civil War when anti-British feeling was strong because of English sympathy for the South, it was the need of his railroad for national defense and protecting northern Maine. On this last score, he convinced the Maine legislature in 1864 to grant the E & NARR

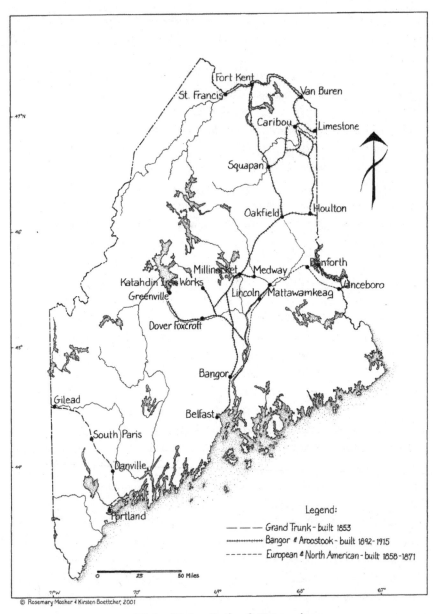

Major Maine Railroad Proposals

Legend:
— — — Grand Trunk – built 1853
·············· Bangor & Aroostook – built 1892-1915
- - - - - European & North American – built 1858-1871

© Rosemary Mosher & Kirsten Boettcher, 2001

700,000 acres of public land. Shortly before President Ulysses S. Grant traveled to Vanceboro in 1869 to celebrate the railway's reaching the Canadian border, Poor died, already having been removed from the company's management. The line did not prosper, nor did it ever reach Louisbourg, and in 1882 the European and North American Railway, a faded concept, became part of the Maine Central Railroad.

One fallout of the E & NARR's failed promise of serving Aroostook County was that Albert A. Burleigh, a onetime Maine land agent, and other Aroostook leaders obtained a charter from Augusta and built the Bangor and Aroostook Railroad.

And it was this action that help spawn the concept of erecting a huge paper company complex centered in the lake country near Millinocket Stream.

The vision originally had arisen in the mind of Charles W. Mullen, an engineering graduate of the University of Maine, who had had some experience in building a dam and a groundwood pulp mill at Enfield. Seeing the Bangor and Aroostook had completed a section of its road from Bangor to Houlton that crossed the West Branch close to the rapids and falls between Quakish Lake and Shad Pond, Mullen determined he'd found an appropriate power source for a major paper manufacturing plant in the area. With the aid of a "syndicate" of Bangor investors, he took control of the needed land, which was in Indian Township 3, part of a purchase the state had made from the Penobscots in 1833. On June 1, 1896, Mullen bought out the "syndicate" for $35,000, then sold half his rights to a partner he felt would be more effective than the men in Bangor. This person was Garrett Schenck, a New Jerseyan of Dutch origin then serving as vice-president of International Paper in Rumford. Mullen was exactly right about him. A hard-driving executive type like Schenck was absolutely required before the Great Northern Paper Company plan could work.

To start with, the fledgling company sought and received a charter from the Maine legislature for a firm to be capitalized at $1 million. Other, perhaps more substantial Bangor businessmen like Frederick and Henry Appleton and Henry and Samuel Prentiss, joined the effort, and then also Colonel Edward H. Haskell, a

Rumford associate of Schenck's, and Colonel Augustus G. Paine, a Maine-born New York industrialist.

Capital was needed in amounts Maine couldn't furnish. Schenck, never happy at IP, quit his job and went to New York to raise money. Among those he visited was Joseph Pulitzer, owner of the *New York World* and a large consumer of newsprint, but his best bet turned out to be a man he met through Colonel Paine; this was another Colonel Payne (note the *y*)—Colonel Oliver H. Payne, the former treasurer of Standard Oil and brother-in-law of William Whitney, ex-secretary of the navy.

The latter two were interested in paper companies. In fact, they already owned two sulphite mills, one in Wisconsin and one in Madison, Maine. They were both very rich men (Payne was the second-largest stockholder in Standard Oil), and they agreed to back the Great Northern project but on one condition—Schenck had to run the Madison plant, too, since it had been losing money. The final deal was put together at a March 2, 1899, meeting. Colonel Payne and his associates subscribed enough stock to finance the company, an expanded board was established, a new capitalization gained of $5 million, and an official name added: the Great Northern Paper Company. Mullen and Schenck, who controlled the land, sold it to GNP for stock, and Colonel Payne sold them the Madison mill for stock. The great enterprise had commenced.

A 1903 report of the Maine Commission of Industrial and Labor Statistics begins:

> Four years ago last May there were a farm house, a barn, and several outbuildings, with a few acres of cleared land, within the bounds of what is now the town of Millinocket. Through this wilderness the Bangor and Aroostook Railroad had been built, passing within a mile and a half of where the village of Millinocket now stands. There was a station near the crossing of the Millinocket Stream, called Millinocket, but the building was so small that, when the development of the place required larger station accommodations, it was loaded upon a flat car and hauled away. Now there is a duly organized and well-governed town

of about 3,000 inhabitants....The history of the development of Millinocket, like that of Rumford Falls, reads more like romance than reality....

The farm mentioned by the commission was the property of Charles T. Powers, who promptly sold out to GNP. Prior to Powers's ownership, it had been in the Fowler family, built by Thomas Fowler, a famed woodsman mentioned by Thoreau, who, among other things, ferried travelers between the Penobscot River and Millinocket Stream.

Great Northern bought all of Powers's land, plus all the available land between the two waterways—about 1,800 acres, enough to contain the mill and village they would develop.

The work began on May 15, 1899, and by November 1900, two initial paper machines were running; the whole plant was operational five months later. "Schenck's Folly," as rival paper companies called it, had been completed in record time.

Water power was essential and before anything else, both temporary and permanent dams had to be built, providing ponds for log storage and a constant flow to the penstocks for grinding wood and turning turbines for electricity.

The original prospectus for the company spoke of "a large water power" of about 23,500 horsepower—power enough, it emphasized, to create "300 TONS OF PAPER PER DAY." The sales pitch went on to doubt if "in the entire east, this much water power could be found or even half of it and still harder to find such power backed up by an all important element...spruce timberlands."

The company proposed to purchase 257,800 acres of such land but wouldn't "exhaust it by large cutting" because another 1 million acres of spruce existed on waters tributary to the mill. "THE SPRUCE IS FOR THE PURPOSE INEXHAUSTIBLE" this brochure also proclaims, and then compares GNP to "the Trust" (International Paper) claiming the new entity will pay four and a half times more in dividends and undersell its big competitor by one-quarter of a cent per pound, because "the Trust" has to pay 6 percent on its bonds and other capital stock.

To do much of the construction work at Millinocket, Italian workers were imported through the *padrone* system of labor contractors who brought their compatriots from Europe and supplied them to employers for a price from which they made a profit. In Millinocket, the top padrone working for Great Northern was apparently Marco Lavonia, although eventually he was overshadowed by the better known Ferdinando "Fred" Peluso, an ex-railroad construction laborer. Peluso, who also set up a store on the east side of Millinocket, prospered, becoming a bank director and Chamber of Commerce officer. The area of "Little Italy" became a distinct neighborhood of rough huts, chinked with mud and grass, full of the sounds of Italian music and the smells of Italian cooking. There was no saloon, but the Italian wine habit led to clashes with the law in dry Maine and accounted for the popularity of nocturnal visits by other nationalities.

The tasks of these laborers, who included Poles, Finns, Lithuanians, and Hungarians, were rude and difficult. They blasted ledge, moved rocks and earth, and sunk caissons for dams and mill foundations. The 1900 census listed 430 Italian-born males and one Italian wife living in Indian Township 3, which on March 16, 1901, officially became Millinocket—Maine's 467th town.

An observer noted that, although the Italians had no title to the land on which they were squatters, the town had not interfered with them. "They are not damaging the land," it was remarked, "for there is nothing there to damage."

One story out of this construction frenzy was a report of how three Italians were killed while at work on the coal dump for Great Northern, some mangled beyond recognition. Then, the number of casualties listed increased "until the whole Italian quarter was nothing but an aching void." The reason: a car had run off the coal trestle and "killed 50 natives of the land of sun and garlic." However, the actual truth was that a coal car had run into the bumper at the end of a trestle and jarred an Italian riding on the vehicle who fell off and broke his leg.

Such deflated exaggerations notwithstanding, from the day in the fall of 1900 when Garrett Schenck "sawed, barked, and conveyed to the grinder the first log," the operation, with its initial headquarters in Boston and its sales office in New York under Colonel Augustus Paine, became a major player on the national paper trade scene. In its first two years, bucking powerful competition from "the Trust," it borrowed $3 million by issuing 25-year, 5-percent mortgage bonds, but by 1903 was paying dividends. In 1906 they were already producing 104,000 tons of paper and owned 600,000 acres.

At the end of 1900, the real founding father, Charles W. Mullen, resigned, and replacing him in the procurement of the wood supply was a young Bangor lumberman, Fred A. Gilbert, who became an important factor in GNP's growth.

The stage was set for the first real flexing of GNP's muscle in Maine. Who would manage the Penobscot's water flow? Long-log lumbering and its river drive, controlled until then by the Penobscot Log Driving Company, was still very much a viable activity. As John McLeod, Great Northern's biographer, explained, the PLD "could not care less about the storage of water, except for the driving of logs." Great Northern, he wrote, "had to have control of water storage for the protection of its power development."

Bad blood between the two organizations began in 1901. The Maine legislature that year let Great Northern run the river drive, and it put Fred Gilbert in charge. The result was a disaster, a drive described as "negligently and wrongfully driven," with many logs swept out to sea and suits against GNP amounting to more than $200,000. The logging firm of Marsh and Ayer lost 1,150,000 board feet and asked for $20,000. John Ross and his company did the same. Even Charles W. Mullen, no longer with the company, sued for $6,000.

Great Northern blamed the low water level in 1901, which had made the effort so difficult. The river drivers responded it was low because Great Northern had drawn it down so much.

Feelings were no better after the 1902 drive, also conducted under legislative fiat by Great Northern.

Then, the following year, came the great collision between these two forces. By February 1903, notices began to appear in the legislative record of petitions put in to oppose the West Branch Driving and Reservoir Dam Company bill, submitted on behalf of Great Northern.

Representative Harry F. Ross, the son of John Ross, began presenting some of these petitions:

"F. W. Ayer of Bangor and 175 others."

"Stern Lumber Company and 214 others."

"A. M. Harriman, Selectman, and 68 others of Orrington."

"C. P. Webber and three others, directors of the Mattawamkeag Log Driving Company."

"James W. Cassidy and four others, directors of the Penobscot Log Driving Company."

On February 20 the *Bangor Daily News* stated: "There is a great bunch of remonstrances against passage of the bill to incorporate the West Branch Driving and Reservoir Dam Co."

Representative Ross, they added, was believed to be opposed, and this tentative declaration may have seemed either naive or sly, relating as it did to a man who had been born into the tradition of the PLD, but in the end its ambiguity proved prescient. Harry F. Ross, who was a feisty redhead, did not go down fighting. Behind the scenes, he apparently helped engineer a somewhat mysterious compromise.

The *Bangor Daily News* had sensed this might be the case. Before the opening shots were fired, its Augusta correspondent introduced the impending battle in the following terms:

> The great fight on the Millinocket bill begins next Tuesday, that is, the open fight. The scheme has been talked and talked during the past several weeks by more than a score of lobbyists but it has been done in the quiet of boardinghouse rooms or in out-of-the-way places about the state capital.

Hence, the hint of a backroom deal was in the air even prior to the moment when, in the same writer's words, "the whole case must be laid bare at the Committee on Interior Waters in the glare of public scrutiny and with the ablest skill of shrewd and capable lawyers."

On February 24 the first hearing was held and because of the intense interest, its venue was the entire house chamber, with seats for more than 150 and a visitors' gallery, rather than a mere committee room. The Honorable Charles F. Woodard, one of the shrewd and capable lawyers hired on both sides, led off for the proponents. He was immediately followed by Fred A. Gilbert who "gave evidence to the condition of the water supply in the West Branch of the

Penobscot." So did another Great Northern employee, Hardy S. Ferguson, chief engineer. "The substance of their testimony," the *Bangor Daily News* summarized, "was that more water was needed for driving logs on the river and for handling the big manufacturing plant of the Great Northern Paper Company at Millinocket...."

This initial hearing started at 3:00 PM, recessed at 7:00 PM, and continued the next day—not an ordinary event in Augusta. A major spokesman for the opponents was Patrick H. Gillin of Bangor, lawyer and sometime legislator, who also served to cross-examine opposing testifiers. Gillin closed his hour-long peroration by saying:

> Allow the Penobscot Log Driving Company to drive
> the logs and the Great Northern must get all its logs
> before we get ours. Allow them to drive the logs and we
> will not get ours as was proven in 1901. What we want
> is the right to drive the logs we cut on the West Branch.
> We want no other rights.... We want you to give the
> Great Northern Company the right to store all the
> water they can on our dam and to build what other
> dams it desires. But they have no right to our vested
> rights and we do not wish you to give them to them, nor
> do we think you will.

That plea terminated the afternoon session and when they resumed that evening, the first speaker was Fred W. Ayer, whose company had lost so much wood in the 1901 fiasco.

In the days that followed, there was continuous speculation in the press about the bill's fate. The conventional wisdom was for a divided report from the committee; Great Northern partisans saw it as a majority for the bill; the PLD forces were predicting a six-to-four split their way.

A GNP lobbyist was asked what his company would then do. "Fight," he said.

"You're not going to compromise, as has been suggested?"

"No, sir. Not unless the PLD compromises our way."

At the same time, Fred W. Ayer, the acknowledged leader of the opponents, was pictured as going around the statehouse with "smiles of pleasure illumining his face."

The word was out on March 10 that a compromise, indeed,

was in the offing, the product of a subcommittee including Harry F. Ross, which essentially would let Great Northern drive all West Branch logs to Quakish Lake by August 20, whereupon the drive to the Bangor area booms would be conducted by the Penobscot Log Driving Company. A commission independent of the two companies was also to be created to oversee the procedure.

The following day, the news was the whole legislative committee had rejected the compromise but promised to report out a bill to satisfy "every person, firm, and corporation doing business on the river."

On March 12 such a bill came forthwith and if there was mutual satisfaction, it had to be short-lived. Alfred Hempstead saw the PLD surrender of its rights above Shad Pond as a definitive change from mutual organization to corporate control, with time on the side of the latter. Four years later, he pointed out that of the 115 million board feet cut in the basin of the West Branch, 90 million was by Great Northern. Soon, GNP was controlling the entire territory. Fred Gilbert, despite his early blunders in running the drives, eventually won over the contractors by his fair treatment. He paid them promptly, put those who wished on salary, and did not try to gouge or squeeze them. Further dam building on the West Branch by Great Northern commenced in 1906, to prepare for a new major paper mill at East Millinocket, thus hastening the sense of the industrialization of the woods, so lamented by Fannie Hardy Eckstorm.

Not everyone mooned over that lost, wonderful sense of heroic individuality and enterprise epitomized by John Ross.

Echoing a sentiment that pervades the less developed sections of Maine to this day, Judge J. W. Symonds, speaking for Great Northern in the "Millinocket Bill" debate, lauded the promise of industrialization, taking for granted everyone wanted the jobs and economic benefits it would bring.

"Allow Great Northern to make its improvements," the judge declared, "and it will not be long before the Penobscot will be more than a mere highway for logs but instead a highway between a chain of prosperous manufacturing centers."

The example of Great Northern at Millinocket was appealing in the Maine North Woods. During the same era, a news item from remote Eagle Lake in Aroostook County detailed the plans of the Fish River Lumber Company, which had stopped lumbering because of a heavy snowfall. They would concentrate instead on completing their new mill, slated to open for business in the spring. Also ready then would be fifty cottages and other buildings; in short, declared the announcement bravely, "there is to be another magic city in the wilderness."

NOTES

[1] Alfred Geer Hempstead, *The Penobscot Boom and the Development of the West Branch of the Penobscot for Log Driving, 1825–1931.* Self-published in 1931, reprinted in 1975.

[2] As quoted in "Non-Adversarial Labor Relations in 19th-Century Maine, The S. D. Warren Co.," by Charles A. Scontras. *Maine History,* vol. 37, nos. 1–2, Summer-Fall 1997.

[3] Ibid., page 20.

[4] Louis Hatch, *Maine, A History.* New York: American Historical Society, 1919. Page 22.

[5] John J. Leane, *A History of Rumford, 1774–1972.* Rumford, ME: Rumford Publishing Company, 1972.

EIGHTEEN

Conservation, Anyone?

WERE OUR PREDECESSORS in early Maine entirely unconcerned about the natural resources they were exploiting? The idea we seem to have today is they believed the wilderness they'd entered was inexhaustible. No restraints, therefore, were needed. One plucked, one sawed or chopped, one shot, one netted, whatever one wanted and woe betide anyone—man or magistrate—who tried to interfere.

Yet is this picture entirely correct? A cursory look at some eighteenth-century records of the Massachusetts General Court reveals contradictions. On three separate Maine rivers, the Kennebec, the Saco, and the Penobscot, those doughty settlers are found petitioning their lawmakers for fish protection.

On June 14, 1788, the town of Brunswick, worried that seining, joining driving nets together, constructing weirs, and dipping out of season would "end in the final ruin of the fish in Merry Meeting Bay and rivers running into the same," asked to have a law already in force changed from a June 10 season start to a November 10 date. Moreover, it should ban seining, weirs, and dipping, raise the fine to not less than £10, and do everything "so as to answer the good purpose of saving and preserving the fish called salmon, shad, and alewives in the County aforesaid [Cumberland]."

From the Saco in 1790, a petition came to amend a bill passed in 1786 for regulating salmon, shad, and alewife fishing. Here, procedures were spelled out to deal with those accused of breaking the law and what to do with an illegal "Net Pot or other machine used in fishing violation of said act," and how the Justice could sell confiscated equipment.

And in January 1791 we find a petition beginning: "We the subscribers, poor distressed inhabitants on the River Penobscot in the County of Hancock," describing a stretch of dead water where salmon cast their spawn and citing how many people fish there every day, fastening from two to nine long nets together, stopping the upriver flow of the fish, dragging mother salmon out of their beds before they can spawn, and spearing salmon, too. The authorities in charge not only do nothing, the supplicants complain, but actually take part in the fishery, themselves.

These people were seeking a closed season, not just for salmon but also for shad and alewives, allowing them to be caught only between April 30 and June 30 every year, no seine dragnets or sweeps above Kenduskeag Stream, and all dams and weirs to have openings for fishways "and that all fines and forfeitures be severe." There were 117 signers, including General Jonathan Eddy.

So let us be disabused of the misconception that all conservation thought in Maine began with Henry David Thoreau's visit in 1846. There is no doubt that in hindsight Thoreau, with his line, "in wildness is the preservation of the world," has become the darling of today's environmental writers and philosophers. An essay on ecology is almost unthinkable without a bow to the Concord iconoclast. Nor is there much doubt that his first visit to Katahdin, coming as a break in the middle of his stay at Walden Pond, bowled him over, transforming the amateur naturalist who tramped around tame Massachusetts into an awestruck admirer of wildness and nature in the raw.

David Rothenberg, editor of a book of ecological articles, *Wild Ideas*, puts it this way:

It is probably on the summit of Maine's Mount Katahdin that his writing [that of Thoreau, whom he calls our *cannonized curmudgeon*], usually ornate, mannered, nearly Victorian, approaches a free wildness that approaches the timeless, animistic sense of wild wanderers from many cultures....[1]

And Rothenberg adds his own notion that, "The wild barrenness of such a mountain is chillingly inhuman but at the same time touches us deep inside."[2]

Another contributor, R. Edward Grumbine, claims: "Thoreau

was probably the first person born of modernity to recognize the grave consequences of industrial civilization's project to dominate nature and contain wildness."

It may well be wondered if Thoreau was as ideological as his latter-day admirers think or if it is his magnificent writing skill — spare, imaginative, and continually surprising — that has kept him so constantly afloat among us today. While other sojourners to Maine, writing up trips like his, have long been forgotten, there is an edge to his writing that cannot be denied, a bite, seemingly anti-industrial:

> Think how stood the white pine tree on the shore of Chesuncook, its branches soughing with the four winds, and every individual needle trembling in the sunlight — think how it stands with it now — sold, perchance, to the New England friction match company....

Or, "the trees were literally drawn and quartered there," when referring to Samuel Veazie's sawmills. Or the lyric description of a scene on the West Branch:

> As we stood upon the pile of chips by the door, fish hawks were sailing overhead and here, over Shad Pond, might daily be witnessed the tyranny of the bald eagle over that bird. Tom pointed away over the lake to a bald eagle's nest, which was plainly visible more than a mile off....

Tom was Tom Fowler and that sylvan site in Indian Township 3 half a century later transmogrified into Millinocket, the industrial foot-in-the-door in Maine's North Woods.

Thoreau was read by his contemporaries in Maine. Benjamin Browne Foster commented in November 1848 on "Ktaadn and the Maine Woods," as printed in the *Union Magazine*, quoting the famous lines about Bangor as a "star on the edge of night" and the "principal lumber depot on the continent." But he balked at what he thought were exaggerations, specifically when Thoreau writes about a moose swimming in the Penobscot becoming entangled with the shipping and being captured by foreign sailors. "This will doubtless astonish as much Bangoreans as New Yorkers."[3]

In another comment, Foster referred to "that ranting, straining, imitating, half-crazed radical, H. D. Thoreau."[4]

Nor was Fannie Hardy Eckstorm wholly a Thoreau fan. She had known some of his traveling companions like Joe Polis, one of his Penobscot guides, and Hiram Leonard, a gentlemanly hunter and inventor of a type of fishing rod. But Thoreau, in her words, "was not a woodsman…was not infallible…was not a scientist at all." Her father, Manly Hardy, a close friend of another of Thoreau's Indian guides, Joseph Attien, was her idea of a man who knew the woods. Still, she credited Thoreau with describing a landscape "all but vanished, replaced by a new forest with new customs"—the *industrial forest* of the pulp and paper industry. At least, she wrote, "Thoreau stood at the gateway of the woods and opened them to all future comers with the key of poetic insight," and she applauded him as the only one ever to "put the coniferous forest between the leaves of a book."

Other literati ventured into these woods during this era and wrote of their "adventures" for a large reading public. Francis Parkman, the sublime Boston Brahmin historian, came not so much to write about contemporary nineteenth-century Maine as to absorb background color for books he was writing on the seventeenth- and eighteenth-century French and Indian Wars. The old wilderness was his search—how to recreate it in writing—and the wilds of Maine were still extant enough for him to grasp their essence and illuminate it.

Another Boston Brahmin traveler north was James Russell Lowell, editor of the *Atlantic Monthly* and then the *North American Review*, and a marked contrast in style to Thoreau, who refused to continue writing for him after Lowell had excised sentiments against slavery from one of his articles. Lowell, also a poet and later a diplomat, tended to be flowery, sophisticated, and enamored of Latin phrases and European and Asiatic references—like this passage, while in a canoe:

The motion of the birch reminded me of the gondola
and they represent among the water-craft the *felidae*,
the cat tribe, stealthy, silent, treacherous and preying
by night.

And he admitted to closing his eyes, trying to visualize himself in Venice.

His citified, Harvard humor shows in reference to "River Driver M," who takes him moose hunting, as having an "M.A. and LL.D. in Woods College-Axe-Master and Doctor of Logs."

No doubt, Lowell felt some of the same emotions as Thoreau, but expressed them in a far more refined manner, lacking the Thoreauvian punch that has made *The Maine Woods* unforgettable and *A Moosehead Journal* a literary footnote. Here is Lowell on mountains:

> It is through one or another pole of vanity that men feel
> the sublime in mountains. It is either, How smallgreat I
> am beside it! or, Big as you are, little I's soul will hold
> a dozen of you.... To some moods it is congenial to look
> over endless leagues of unbroken savagery without a
> hint of man.

This entire piece of writing Lowell has addressed at the beginning to a friend named Edelmann Storg at the Bagni di Lucca in Italy. He ends his travelogue of Maine with a facetious attempt at insouciant whimsy: "Thus, my dear Storg, I have finished my Oriental adventures."

Another in this line of mid-nineteenth-century visiting authors, Theodore Winthrop, had an outdoorsman's enthusiasm for what he encountered and a facile, gifted pen. His account of a trip to the Maine North Woods, called *Life in the Open Air*, has a Teddy Rooseveltian ring to it—a zest for everything as hunter, fisherman, writer—having a "bully" time. Had he lived longer than thirty-three years, he might, like TR, have become a leading conservationist but he was killed in one of the early battles of the Civil War and his book was first published posthumously in 1863. Described as "a dashing bon vivant and aspiring author," he took time out from his work as a law partner to J. P. Morgan's personal advisor to go to Maine in 1856 with a companion he referred to only as "Iglesias." The joke—*iglesia* is the Spanish word for church—was that his pal, the guy with the "peaceful and creative sketchbook" (as opposed to Winthrop's "war-like and destructive gun") was the painter Frederick E. Church, a member of the famed Hudson River School, whose canvases of Katahdin and Mount Desert have become classics.

Winthrop's descriptions have a pictorial sharpness as talented as Church's brushstrokes, perceived during what the author dubbed, again à la Teddy Roosevelt, "eight days crowded with novelty and beauty and fine, vigorous, manly life." Katahdin was mentioned repeatedly:

Katahdin to the north, a fair blue pyramid.

Katahdin lost nothing by approach...as it grew bigger, it grew better.

Katahdin's mighty presence seemed to absorb such dreamy glimmers as float in limpid night-airs; a faint glory, a twilight of its own, clothed it. King of the day-lit world, it became queen of the dimmer realms of night, and like a woman-queen, it did not disdain to stoop and study its loveliness in the polished lake and stooping thus it overhung the earth, a shadowy creature of gleam and gloom, an eternalized cloud.

It [Katahdin] was still an isolate pyramid rising with no effort from the fair blue lakes and the fair green sea of the birch forest—a brilliant sea of woods, gay as the shallows of the ocean shot through with sunbeams and sunlight reflected upward from golden sands.

The Confederate bullet that felled Winthrop at the siege of Fortress Monroe in Virginia not only deprived the United States of a first-class writer, he had also made it plain that despite his enthusiasm for the adventure of the trip, he wasn't pleased "to observe the devastation wrought by overcutting in the wilderness."

On their first leg, Winthrop and Church had stopped at Mount Kineo House, a fledgling resort on Moosehead Lake—then a haven for fishermen and moose hunters and afterward a major tourist hotel complex built by the Maine Central Railroad. "Boston men haunt Kineo," Winthrop wrote, thus underscoring the fact the sportsmen coming into Maine's North Woods were apt to be well-heeled gentlemen from "Away." Yet three well-connected young college boys from Maine, itself, were to visit Kineo two decades later on a trip to climb Katahdin not dissimilar to that of Winthrop and Church and leave an interesting record of how some things had changed and some hadn't.[5]

These were the sons of George Popham Sewall of Old Town, a political figure of note in the state, who had been speaker of the

Maine House and was a close friend of Hannibal Hamlin's. One of the boys, James W. Sewall, was to become intimately connected with the Maine forest scene through his role as manager of the enormous land interests of Ebenezer Coe and the heirs of David Pingree. His son, another James W. Sewall, started the Old Town-based company bearing his name that has earned a worldwide reputation for scientific land surveying by bringing modern techniques of mapping to abet the work of foresters, which was begun once attempts at better utilization and conservation of resources entered Maine logging practices. In 1876, when the three Bowdoin men and their cousin, Ned Hunt, went from Moosehead Lake to the West Branch, the old-style cutting of pine and spruce was still in fashion. But Kineo had already changed.

No longer a rustic sportsmen's camp on its peninsula at the base of the 700-foot "mountain," it already had a hotel and grounds, and the boys mailed a letter in an "informal post-office in its barroom." They didn't see too many guests, but felt there had to be more since they saw undergarments floating from windows on the main building's fourth floor. They did see one very stout woman out strolling, "showing to great advantage her substantial proportions; lake air and diet must have agreed with her." And to add to this sense of civility, on top of Kineo they discovered a signboard warning against throwing stones from the precipice.

Tourism had come to the Maine wilds, or parts of it, although the voyage inland by the Sewalls and Ned Hunt seemed as arduous and woodsy-adventurous as any of its predecessors. One could still fish and hunt at will, and beyond Moosehead they did not encounter much in the way of human presence.

Writing about the same time, the Reverend Julius H. Ward told of traveling to the Mount Kineo House on the steamer LADY OF THE LAKE and of fishing and hunting enthusiasts who still made up the better part of the clientele. But he warned, "The fishing itself is hardly what it used to be when the lake was overfull of speckled trout."[6] However, his description of a visit to a particular trout hole, with only salt pork for bait, would turn any modern angler green with envy. The good reverend's first catch of many was a five-pounder! He spoke, too, of twenty-seven-pound togue (lake trout) taken and his guide's certainty there were monsters of more than a hundred pounds in the depths. In discussing hunting, he also talked of the impact of too much of it:

> Many people are disappointed with the hunting. They came expecting to find bears without searching for them and to kill partridges by the dozen with a single charge of buck-shot. The game around the lake has been greatly killed off, and one must go long distances to find what one wishes.[7]

Moose, he continued, had been plentiful ten years earlier. Now, they were seldom easily found except near Katahdin. Deer were numerous and likewise caribou, but the latter were "very hard to kill." Speaking of birds, he noted bald eagles were common, but not often killed. Black duck shooting was good in the fall, and only the most skilled hunters could shoot a loon. Those who stayed for a week and lived at Kineo would find the hunting out of reach, he said, but with the use of guides, other nimrods abounded until the end of October, when they were replaced in the woods by lumbermen.

Hunting, fishing, and logging thus coexisted for many years. A deer protection regulation—no hunting them between January 1 and August 1—had been on the books in Maine since 1790, but without wardens. In 1852 the governor did appoint moose wardens for every county, but again with spotty compliance. An 1870 law led the way for the flood of out-of-state sportsmen by removing a ban on hunters from "Away." Starting in 1873, the sportsmen's movement grew in the U.S; *Forest and Stream* was published and began attacking the wholesale slaughter in the woods. *Field and Stream* followed the next year. In 1874 the National Sportsmen's Association was founded. Two years later, "a few gentlemen in Machias" created the Washington County Game Association. The *Machias Union* then launched a blistering attack on those Down East poachers Fannie Hardy Eckstorm had seen fit to defend, as a:

> ...thriftless, lazy and irresponsible class, destitute of principle who adopt no moral sentiment for self-government and acknowledge no obedience to law, nor recognition of the rights of people...if the Fish Warden attempts to enforce the law...they will stone him if it be

night time, or by day they threaten to burn his property.

A leader of the conservationists in Machias was Dr. Samuel Hunter. He was particularly incensed by the market hunting going on in Washington County, with individual hunters bagging thirty to forty deer apiece and 2,500 pounds of venison saddle at a time being shipped to Boston.

In Augusta, Hunter was able to convince the lawmakers to set bag limits at one moose, two caribou, and three deer, and to appropriate $7,500 to enforce the law. His rhetoric was seething:

> Our market hunters are a peculiar class of hoodlums, made up in the great part of men without an occupation, and among then we find the skedaddler, smuggler, thief, firebug, and lazy squatter who lives from what lumber he can steal, berries he can pick, fires he can fight *after setting them*, or anything save honest labor.

This was 1883. The resentment of the locals who felt, à la medieval England, that the game laws favored the rich at the expense of the poor, has already been aired. In 1886 the incident occurred in which Calvin Graves killed two wardens trying to get at his dogs and received a life sentence. In 1893 the Maine legislature passed a bill to prevent jacking deer (i.e., stunning them with lights); in 1903 nonresident licenses were required; in 1919 resident licenses. The need to conserve a dwindling resource was overcoming the Robin-Hoodish, squatter, free-to-do-what-I-choose-in-the-woods attitude so prevalent in the past.

The Bangor and Aroostook Railroad, which had played such a key role in Millinocket's creation, was also, to use the slang of the day, a "drummer" for fishing and hunting in Maine and bringing north as many sportsmen as possible. They published a magazine called *In The Maine Woods*, which acted like a shill or carnival barker, urging the customers to come. Unlike the Reverend Mr. Ward, they saw no diminution of fishing opportunities in Moosehead Lake. To the contrary, they declared flat-out in a 1904 edition that, "there can never be any such thing as 'fishing out' Moosehead Lake." Already by 1904, the Bangor and Aroostook was advertising more than half a dozen rugged "canoe routes in Maine's Great North Country" reached by the B & A, including a West Branch trip of 80 miles, an

Allagash trip of 203 miles and a St. John trip of 231 miles.

A third recreation "hot spot" in the Maine woods was also developing to the west among the Androscoggin Lakes, as they were initially known from their position in the watershed of the Androscoggin River. Today we know them as the Rangeley Lakes. There are six of them: Rangeley, Mooselookmeguntic, Cupsuptic, Umbagog, and Upper and Lower Richardson. The latter two were named for a pioneer settler whose Anglo-Saxon surname spared a future public the effort of learning to pronounce two more tongue-twisting western Abenaki denotations, in this case for bodies of water labeled until then Lake Mollychunkamunk and Lake Welo-kennabacook. Indeed, Rangeley had its Indian title first—Oquossoc—now attached to a town in the area. The use of Rangeley came in honor of "Squire" James Rangeley, Jr., a major landowner in the region from 1825–41. His father, a Philadelphia investor with partners from New York, had bought the land, a massive grant between Bingham's Kennebec Purchase and the New Hampshire border, from the Massachusetts General Court in 1796. Squire Rangeley has been remembered as a nice man who let squatters previously on the site buy their property at fifty cents an acre and pay for the price through their work.

As early as 1840, word was out about the astounding size of the trout in those lakes. Ten and twelve pounds were not unheard of, and five to eight pounds quite common. A fishing camp, soon to become famous, called "Angler's Retreat," between Richardson and Umbagog Lakes, was established by a Joshua Rich, who arrived in 1844. About the same time, the first real vacationers from "Away," a group of Yale students, spent a summer in a rough cabin they built on an island in Mooselookmeguntic Lake.

While Ebenezer Coe and David Pingree procured much of the surrounding land and logged it, the recreation business began in earnest in 1860 with the arrival of George Shepherd Page of New York City, described as "perhaps the first proponent of fishing for trout purely as a sport in these lakes."[8] He had been brought to Maine by a native angling enthusiast, Henry O. Stanley, later a state commissioner of Fisheries. Page not only caught big fish, but took some back alive to New York (a ten-pounder and an eight-and-a-half-pounder) and tried to hatch their eggs. Although the breeding experiment was unsuccessful, the resulting publicity made Rangeley's name famous and, with the arrival each summer of more and more sportsmen, Page organized the Oquossoc Angling Association at Indian Rock in 1868, built Camp Kennebago, and, in effect, launched the Rangeleys on the same path that Moosehead and Washington County lakes were following.

Theodore Winthrop wrote about "the vocal influence of the name Androscoggin" in the same pre-Civil War book that detailed his trip to Katahdin with Frederick Church. In his felicitous style, he coined these memorable lines: "People talked as if instead of an ivory ring or coral rattle to develop their infantile teeth, they had bitten upon pine knots. Voices were resinous and astringent...."

The Oquossoc fishing club may also have had a vital influence on one of Maine's premier conservationists. As a seven-year-old boy, Percival Baxter was fishing in the lake with his father, who offered him $10 a pound for every pound of any fish he caught over five pounds. Landing an eight-pound giant shortly afterward had to have been a signal thrill in Percy's young life, even more than the $80, which he told the gentlemen in the Oquossoc Angling Association's clubhouse that evening he was going to put in the bank, and did.

Possibly the person most responsible for promoting Maine fishing in its developing phase was not even a male sportsman but a female, born Cornelia Thurza Crosby in 1854 and universally referred to by her nickname of "Fly Rod." She grew up in the Franklin County town of Phillips, not far from the Rangeley Lakes, where she first began spending summers in 1881 making use of the eight-ounce fly rod given her by Charles Wheeler, of nearby Farmington, who had made it. Her writing about fishing started with her "Fly Rod" column in the little Phillips newspaper, and her exploits — catching fifty-two trout in forty-four minutes, landing 2,500 trout in a single fishing season — were soon receiving national attention.

Far more of it came with her appearances and displays of fly-rod prowess at the national Sportsmen's Expositions in Madison Square Garden that commenced in 1895. In the national press, she was the "queen of Anglers," as much a celebrity as her friend Annie Oakley, the famed sharpshooter. In Maine she became active in fish and game affairs, and after she helped guide a law to license Maine guides through the state legislature, she was awarded license number one. In her recently published biography, author Julia A. Hunter emphasizes Fly Rod's ties to the Rangeley area, saying that one of her greatest achievements was promoting Rangeley (in part in collaboration with the Maine Central Railroad, for whom she worked), adding:

> ...her stance was that Maine was the best state in the
> greatest nation on earth and Rangeley was the best part
> of all—but all of Maine was good.[9]

Edward "Sandy" Ives, Maine's most prominent folklorist, notes in his foreword to Fly Rod's biography that she appears oblivious to two other major coeval occurrences in the Maine Woods in her formative years: the rage against game laws, such as Fannie Hardy Eckstorm documented Down East in Washington County, and the intense logging at that period even in and around Rangeley, with logs being driven to mills in Rumford and Berlin, New Hampshire, and woodsmen crowding into Rangeley and Oquossoc like their red-shirted counterparts in other Maine forests did in Bangor or Greenville or Houlton.

That Fly Rod was not an out-and-out conservationist may be surmised, although she supported catch-and-release and restricted hunting seasons. Nor was she a suffragette: just a "plain woman of uncertain age," as she described herself, in a man's world and for years the only female member allowed in the Maine Sportsmen's Fish and Game Association. She spoke of having been a fishing guide for Hugh Chisholm. She was also a friend of Percival Baxter's, having been close to his older sister Emily, who died at a young age during Percy's first term as governor. Significantly, it was to Baxter, Maine's great nature-lover rather than to any sportsman, that she left her treasured album of fishing photographs before she, herself, died at the age of ninety-two in 1946.

Striking the conservation theme developing side by side with industrialization, increasing tourism, and heavy natural resource use at the start of the twentieth century was an article entitled, "The Wild Lands, Who Owns Them," appearing in the *Bangor Commercial* in 1905. Its subhead explained the growing public argument: "Need of Proper Conservation of Forests to Insure Our Water Power—Both Sides Discussed." The *Commercial*, by the way, had been started after the Civil War by Marcellus Emery, the pro-South editor who'd almost been lynched by a Rufus Dwinel-led mob, and had ended up being owned by Harry F. Ross.

The writer repeated the opinion of a "Maine Justice" that these lands were quasi-public utilities and should be conserved, then illustrated a proper technique such as the rule of Ebenezer Coe never to cut a tree less than 16 inches at the butt. He went on to warn:

> "Pulping out" a timber tract, or, in other words, cutting everything down to the smallest, means death to the spruce for many a year. For hardwoods would come in place of the spruce and pine and then good-bye to spruce and stumpage for your life-time and mine.

Also condemned was the complacency about forest fires, which had damaged thousands of acres and reduced their value. Quoted was the Honorable J. P. Bass, a lobbyist for the landowners, who attributed much of this damage to the "careless hunter or fisherman who lights a campfire in the woods." This same gentleman also decried the state's giving away so much land years ago as "a piece of folly in which we did not participate, but for which wild land owners are not to be blamed in taking advantage of..." and how their lands pump millions of dollars into state coffers each year through the people using Maine railroads, hotels, steamboats, guides, and other resources.

Much of the article was taken up with presenting a snapshot of the great landowners in Maine in this period. The Coe and Pingree group led the list with their 1,062,000 acres. Others included the heirs of Governor Abner Coburn, 200,000 acres, "some of the most valuable holdings in the state"; then the Burleighs, including a congressman and a governor, with 200,000 to 300,000 acres; the Great Northern, which at that time had some 400,000 acres; the American Realty Company, representing International Paper, owning 300,000 acres; Elias Thomas of Portland, with 100,000 acres; and next a string of familiar names, their acreage omitted, like the Hollingsworth and Whitney Company, William H. Strickland of Bangor, the Madigan heirs, the Hinckley heirs, John Cassidy of

Bangor, the Honorable J. P. Bass of Bangor, J. Manchester Haynes of Augusta, and the Millikens of Augusta. Llewelyn Powers of Houlton, another governor of Maine, was frequently mentioned. Three years earlier, he had sold 150,000 acres, but seemed again to be buying more land.

The owners of these large tracts of forestland were concerned about fires and aware that, individually, they could not solve the problem by themselves. They felt the state should help, particularly since they were keeping their lands open to sportsmen and campers. The first order to the Judicial Committee to devise a forest protection law was signed in 1891, not coincidentally, by one of these great landowners, Governor Edwin C. Burleigh, who had formerly been the state land agent, and out of that action came the creation of a Forest Commission. In 1903, a terrible year for forest fires (200,232 acres burned, the worst until 1947), the legislators appropriated $10,000 to put wardens into the Unorganized Territories. That same year, in another move toward conservation, a Chair of Forestry was established at the University of Maine. It was assumed by Austin Cary, Bowdoin- and Harvard-educated, generally acknowledged to be Maine's first forester. Another strong influence for conservation thinking was Edgar Ring, a West Branch lumberman, who took over as forest commissioner in 1908 and successfully pushed for a Maine Forestry District to control forest fires.

When President Theodore Roosevelt, nearing the end of his second term, brought conservation-minded leaders to Washington in 1908 for what was essentially the first "White House Conference" on any subject, Maine's delegation was composed of Ring, Cary, and ex-Governor John F. Hill. Ring delivered a paper that was given wide circulation. His daughter Elizabeth, a noted historian and teacher, later wrote how he considered his participation one of the highlights of his life. The Forestry District Act had the strong support of many of Maine's leading landowners and paper companies. It was introduced by Senator Carl Milliken of Island Falls, another big landowner (who, incidentally, also became a governor). The only question about its passage dealt with its constitutionality. Could the state regulate "the manner in which private forest lands were managed and protected?" The Maine supreme court said yes.

Here, Maine was acting as a pioneer. The federal government had set up a program of grants to states that would organize fire-fighting protection for their forests, and Maine received one of the first three grants of $10,000.

Not all of this newfangled stuff—forestry, fire protection, wardens, and other conservation measures—went down well with the old-timers in the woods. Holman Day, a Maine journalist turned novelist and movie-maker, wrote several works of fiction about the lumber industry. *King Spruce* is probably his best-known work—a potboiler that would draw derisive smiles today, but serves well as a piece of history, an artifact of an era. It has been said that the "King Spruce" of the title, the fictional Umcolcus Lumbering Association, and its equally invented owner, the Honorable John Davis Barrett, was patterned on Llewelyn Powers and his Aroostook empire. When the hero, a progressive-minded school teacher, Dwight Wade, comes to Barrett's office to talk about the "science of forestry," he immediately encounters resistance.

"A man would have pretty much hard work to convince me that it is a science," Barrett replies, and as Holman Day has him comment, *with some contempt,* "As near as I can find out, it's guesswork, and poor guesswork at that."

Wade isn't to be put off; he's a pretty bumptious young man, once a star footballer, and—secretly—the boyfriend of Barrett's daughter. "I hoped," Wade continues, "that such a large owner of timberland had begun to take interest in forestry and would, for experiment's sake, put these young men [his students] upon a section of land this summer and let them work up a map and a report...."

"What do you mean, that I'm going to hire them to do it—pay them money?"

"The young men will be performing a real service, for they will plot a square mile and—"

"If there is any pay to it, I'd rather pay them to keep off my lands...."

At that moment, the real villain of the story, the Honorable Pulaski D. Britt, a state senator and officer of the company, breaks into the conversation with a diatribe against *newfangled fellers that's been studying in a book how to make trees grow.*

"Forestry," he snorts, "is getting your men into the woods, getting grub to 'em, hiring bosses that can whale spryness into human jill-pokes and can get the logs down to Pea Cove sortin' boom before the drought strikes. That's forestry!" (A jill-poke is what loggers call the one log responsible for setting up a jam and which, when it's removed, allows the rest to float downstream again.)

This antediluvian attitude toward forestry and forest protection also passed away with the change in forest ownership and usage. The paper companies saw they might need to grow trees, themselves, to ensure a steady supply of wood to their mills, and some of the large landowners realized modern forestry methods could help their bottom lines. Imperceptibly, the Dwight Wades prevailed, the John Davis Barretts saw the light, and the Pulaski D. Britts were routed—exactly as happened in *King Spruce*.

And with forestry's ascendance on the conservation scene—as epitomized by Gifford Pinchot, creator of the U.S. Forest Service and close confidant of Teddy Roosevelt, there also grew up the dichotomy within the movement expressed in the personage of John Muir, the preservationist—a dichotomy still contained today in the question: Do we continue to allow logging in our national forests or do we set large areas of them aside as roadless wilderness?

Holman Day was a good friend of Percival Baxter who, to most Mainers, is seen as the ultimate champion of a land-saving ethic in the state. In another of his novels, *All-Wool Morrison*, Day used Baxter as the prototype for the hero, but in this instance, it was Baxter the progressive taking on monopolistic industry, as Percy did, in his epic 1920s fight with the Central Maine Power Company. Percy's quarrel with CMP was not that they wanted to build a dam on the Dead River, but they wanted to do it on two public lots belonging to the state and were refusing to pay rent. He actually didn't start talking about saving land—that is, Katahdin—until 1919.

But this aspect of conservation had already appeared in Maine. The efforts of George Bucknam Dorr and his fellow summer residents at Bar Harbor to launch what eventually became Acadia National Park began as far back as 1901. The passage by Congress in 1911 of the Weeks Law that allowed the Federal government to acquire private land and set the stage for the White Mountains

National Forest also aided the Mount Desert project, which finally became a reality in 1917.

The following year, 1918, witnessed the very quiet transfer of some 33,000 more acres of private Maine land into U.S. government ownership. It is not well known even today that a portion of the White Mountains National Forest is in Maine, in the Evans Notch region, abutting the New Hampshire border in the westernmost part of the state. At one time in the nineteenth century, an unincorporated town of 300 people existed around a lumbering operation at this site on the Wild River, which had originally been cleared by a runaway slave before the Civil War. Called Batchelder's Grant, it is generally cited by the name of its post office—Hastings—after the three brothers from Fryeburg and Bethel who created the Wild River Lumber Company following the Civil War (in which two of them—Gideon and David—received battlefield promotions to major). When the Hastings' business and family line declined in the early years of the twentieth century, their holdings were sold without much fanfare, first in New Hampshire, then in Maine, to the U.S. Forest Service.

Meanwhile, a similar status was being sought for Katahdin. Or rather, the bill put into Congress in 1913 by Congressman Frank E. Guernsey of Dover-Foxcroft would have produced a combination forest reserve (the name then given to national forests) and national park. It has been said Guernsey was induced to take this action by one of his constituents, John Francis Sprague, publisher of *Sprague's Journal of Maine History*, and later a state senator. Among Guernsey's arguments in a 1916 speech, after he'd introduced his bill a second time, was the absolute necessity of saving the forests around the headwaters of Maine's rivers and streams. In language that would resonate today, Guernsey declared: "In our state is the last remnant of the virgin forest that once swept the whole Atlantic Coast. Something must, and will, in my opinion, be done to preserve it."

On this occasion, another speech by Professor Lucius Merrill of the University of Maine emphasized Katahdin and its watershed, threatened by "the axe of the lumberman and the fires which too frequently follow the axe." Lamenting that in the "Pine Tree State," he had never seen a great pumpkin pine, Merrill added, "We can construct half a dozen Panama Canals while a white pine is growing." His final comment, vis-à-vis Guernsey's bill, was: "If Congress cannot be induced to act, why should not our legislature take action and create a state reservation?"

Professor Merrill could hardly have foreseen how his wistful question would be answered. Nor could Percival Baxter when, in 1919, he first proposed *his* plan for a Mount Katahdin Centennial (state) Park to celebrate Maine's 100th anniversary in 1920. His failure to move the Augusta lawmakers was as complete as Guernsey's attempts with the Solons in Washington, D.C. A prime reason for his inability to persuade them—even offering to kick off an acquisition fund with two years of his salary—was the stiff resistance of the Great Northern Paper Company, engineered by Garrett Schenck and Fred A. Gilbert, who both had no love for Percival Baxter. The best Percy could do was get a law passed allowing the state to accept private money to buy the area and—supposedly fomented by Senator John Francis Sprague—a status of game preserve for the mountain and surrounding land.

Garrett Schenck lived out the latter part of his life as the modern-day lord of a fiefdom. His influence in the Maine Republican Party was strong, if not paramount. Schenck would send out word of his preferences among Republican candidates—Parkhurst over Milliken for governor, Hale over Fernald for U.S. senator—and it had a weighty effect. Ironically, it was Governor Frederick Parkhurst's death after one month in office that allowed Percy Baxter, then next in line as president of the senate, to become chief executive. The doughty old Dutchman not only fought Baxter on the political scene; he also refused to deal with him as a fellow businessman, when, no longer in office, Percival tried to buy Great Northern's interest in the township containing the mountain.

Schenck didn't reside in Millinocket, nor even in Maine, but tightly controlled events in the town his company had erected in the wilds. An ardent Prohibitionist, he had written into the deeds of the local houses GNP owned (most of them) that the occupants could be evicted if they sold liquor from them. In a scene straight out of feudalism, Schenck responded to the plea of one Antonio Allisio, begging not to be evicted on these grounds, by decreeing: "All right, but put him on probation."

Yet he could be open-minded, too, intervening when a teacher named Harper insulted Catholic children at a town school, making the culprit apologize to the students and the priest and putting him, too, "on probation."

Fred A. Gilbert, although lower down the company ladder as director of woods operations, was just as hostile to Percy Baxter as Schenck was. He refused even to answer the ex-governor's letters. Originally of French Catholic heritage, he is described in a biography as a 32nd degree Mason and also as "cold-blooded" and never willing to forget "anybody's pulling a fast one on him," but also appreciative of "anybody who did a good job" for him.

Garrett Schenck died in January 1928. His successor as CEO was William A. Whitcomb, formerly an International Paper vice-president, whose administration heralded a new era at Great Northern. The following year, Fred Gilbert was fired and replaced by William Hilton. In a recent interview with this gentleman's son, I was told that Gilbert was dismissed because of his "big ideas"— costly projects like a proposed railroad extension to Quebec across northern Maine and a New Brunswick power plant to be built at Great Falls on the St. John. William Hilton, Jr., was surprised to hear that Fred Gilbert had been of French-Canadian origin. He was also quick to point out that his father had an entirely different and favorable attitude towards Baxter.

With Gilbert and Schenck gone and William Whitcomb and others in the company expressing an admiration for Percival Baxter's pluck and persistence, the campaign to save Katahdin went quickly forward. On November 12, 1930, Great Northern's board of directors voted to sell 5,760 acres to the ex-governor which was the company's three-eighths undivided interest in the northern two-thirds of T3 R9, the township containing Katahdin. The agreed-upon price was $25,000.

But Baxter faced still another hurdle. The other owner was Harry F. Ross. And Harry F. Ross had no more use for Percival Baxter than Garrett Schenck or Fred Gilbert had. He resolutely refused to sell his land or even to divide it.

Baxter then took a daring gamble. Despite contrary advice from Attorney General Clement Robinson, he deeded his portion to the state. On March 5, 1931, ex-Governor Baxter's donation was publicly announced. The ploy worked. Ross took the matter to the superior court in Piscataquis County, suing both Baxter and the State of Maine. In the end, in the division, he may have gotten what he had wanted all along. "The portion owned by Harry F. Ross contains timberlands," the *Bangor Daily News* wrote on October 31, 1931. However, Ross was not a man to forgive a grudge and his animus against Percy Baxter was to come into play half a dozen years later and lead to the most serious challenge ever made to the park.

Meanwhile, the Great Depression, the advent of Franklin Delano Roosevelt, and of a Democratic governor, Louis Brann, gave an impetus to federal projects, and there began to be talk of establishing a full national forest in Maine. More than one idea was floated as cash-strapped landowners saw a potential buyer. In the fall of 1933, rumor had it that the Forest Service might buy 300,000 acres in Franklin County at the headwaters of the Moose River. But the project fell through when the feds could not get an eminent domain provision in the enabling act. An Aroostook National Forest was proposed in December 1934 under the aegis of Walter Powers, son of Llewelyn Powers. His land in Smyrna would be included plus Moro Pit, Merrill, Ludlow, Hersey, Henry Joy's own town of Crystal, and almost all of Island Falls. With some Webber family land in Haynesville and Orient, this would have made a tract of 200,000 acres. Later still, in 1935, "An Act to Permit National Forests in Maine" called for an even bigger federal set-aside: 300,000 acres in Hancock and Washington Counties, 300,000 acres in Aroostook and Oxford Counties, and even 2,000 acres in Cumberland County.

At one point, a 785,000-acre unit in Aroostook, Penobscot, Hancock, and Washington Counties was actually approved by the National Forest Reservation Commission. The only trouble was: their $12 million allocation had been exhausted.

All this activity disturbed the paper companies. Great Northern's main Boston attorney, Sheldon E. Wardwell, seemed particularly frightened. Panicky letters went to CEOs of other companies, like Hugh Chisholm of International Paper and M. Lester Madden of Hollingsworth and Whitney. To Chisholm, he wrote: "Our objection...is not a national forest as such, but to the wide-open provisions of the law which completely surrenders sovereignty to the Federal government." Wardwell's other nightmare was the loss of timber that, in his words, would "be sterilized." He expressed his fear to William Hilton that the 1933 proposal would take out 1 million acres "and drive us to New Brunswick for at least part of our supply." Hilton agreed, writing back that it might jeopardize 40,000 cords to be hauled over "King" Lacroix's railroad from Umbazooksus to Eagle Lakes.

This flurry of national forest proposals, despite support from such powerful individuals as Walter Powers and Curtis Hutchins of the Passamaquoddy Land Company, never came to any fruition.

Then, in 1936, the idea of a national park to be centered in the Katahdin area, subsuming Baxter Park, was born.

In the light of the current push for a 3-million-acre national park in the same vicinity, its story is worth telling in some detail, especially now that the Myron Avery papers have been made available at the Maine State Library.

Myron Avery, the key figure here, was in 1936 an admiralty lawyer working for the U.S. Maritime Commission in Washington. Avery, who considered himself a Maine man from Lubec, also was said to be the country's leading expert on Katahdin and held the prestigious position in the hiking world of president of the Appalachian Trail Conference (not to be confused with the Appalachian Mountain Club).

Among Avery's letters is one sent to Percival Baxter on March 13, 1931, expressing his delight in reading about Baxter's "gift of a three-eighth interest in T3 R9, the Katahdin Township" to the state. Included with this missive was a gift of his own to Baxter, a supplement to a bibliography on Katahdin and two articles on the region immediately north of the mountain. His ending could not have been more cordial. "As a citizen of the state, I wish to be one of many to express an appreciation of your very generous and far-sighted act."

Why, then, five years later, did Avery listen to Harry F. Ross and then cooperate with him on a plan to enlarge the Katahdin state park into a national park? They met in New York and Ross said he and Governor Brann had been to Washington, seeing, as Avery wrote, "about the possibility of enlarging the Katahdin Park — primarily, I suppose, through acquiring Ross's lands." The next week, Avery, back in D.C., received a letter from Ross, asking him to meet Governor Brann at the Mayflower Hotel and lobby him hard.

Avery's willingness to intervene seems due, in constant references in his letters, solely to his concern about conditions at Baxter Park, which he found "disorganized."

He wanted facilities for visitors to obtain lodging and meals of ample quality. The closing of a camp annoyed him. He fulminated against "the haphazard laissez-faire system at Katahdin" and felt the need for regulation, supervision, and authority. Otherwise, he wrote, "Katahdin, instead of the pride of Maine, will become the symbol of a state and a people which either have not the inclination or the ability to preserve their priceless treasure."

On January 12, 1937, Avery sent a letter directly to Baxter expressing his concerns. No direct reply from Baxter is included in Avery's meticulously chronologically kept correspondence, and a week later, he wrote to Ross: "What do you think of undertaking a campaign to have the federal government create a national park in the Katahdin region?" Until then, neither he nor Ross had specifically mentioned a national park. Another letter at this juncture in Avery's collection is most puzzling. It is a copy of a confidential letter from Baxter, mailed six months earlier to a Dr. E. A. Pritchard of the National Park Service, and there is no explanation of how it came into Avery's possession.

In this possibly purloined letter, Baxter is absolutely scathing toward unnamed "landed interests" desirous of selling their holdings to the Feds and "posing as being interested in parks," adding "For twenty and more years, these very people were the bitterest opponents of the Park idea in any form." Then, having cited his own park accomplishment "only after a long and tiresome contest, absolutely single-handed and in the face of abuse and bitterness that you would not believe possible," he sounds two themes he would use again and again in the ensuing debate on the national park idea: 1) that he had plans for "a large and suitable state park," which he couldn't yet reveal; and 2) that if the Park Service wanted a national park in

Maine, there was plenty of land available in Washington County and other counties elsewhere in Maine.

By March 1937, Avery and Ross not only had advanced their planning for a National Park; they had procured a sponsor for the bill needed in Congress—ex-Governor Ralph Owen Brewster, now a member of Congress. Once an ally if not a protégé of Baxter's, Brewster was now a visceral enemy. The two men had had several notorious public falling-outs—once over a contested primary election involving Brewster and then over Brewster's alleged membership in the Ku Klux Klan.

Yet as soon as Harry Ross learned that under Brewster's bill the National Park Service could not buy land but only accept it from others, he began to lose interest. A wire he sent to Avery stated: "YOU KNOW I DO NOT INTEND TO GIVE LAND TO GOVERNMENT OR ANYBODY. I INTEND TO SELL LAND."

Undaunted, Avery soldiered on alone. On March 23, Brewster put in his "Katahdin National Park" bill, which was referred to the House Committee on Public Lands. A campaign to round up support started and the first endorsement came from Avery's own group, the Appalachian Trail Conference.

Baxter may have been taken by surprise. A month later, he wrote to Brewster, saying he had received a copy of the bill and it disturbed him very much "because I have plans for the Katahdin area, which if I could disclose to you, I am sure would meet with your approval."

But the battle was on to win converts. Baxter zeroed in on the Appalachian Mountain Club. He even wrote to Avery, as if ignorant of the admiralty lawyer's part. Meanwhile, Avery tried to get *American Forests* magazine to publish an article favoring the National Park idea. He also wrote back to Baxter, leaving no doubt where he stood, and insultingly stating he couldn't understand Baxter's objection, "unless it would be that the proposed area would bear the name of Katahdin Park, as contrasted with the present Baxter State Park."

Subsequent letters between the two men dripped with this sort of invective. But Baxter, a skilled politician, soon picked up an effective issue. It was a mistake by Brewster, in a speech extolling the virtues of the National Park Service, where he spoke of the "great hotels" they would build in the region.

Baxter reminded Mainers his deed of trust for the donated land required it be kept forever wild:

> As modern civilization with its trailers and hot dog stands, its radio and jazz, encroach on the Maine wilderness, the time may yet come when only the Katahdin region remains undefiled by man.... To commercialize this magnificent area, to desecrate it with 'great hotels,' with their noisy social life, their flaming signs, the roar of motor cars and airplanes coming and going to break the peace of that great solitude would be nothing less than sacrilege....

One of Avery's allies wrote him: "Brewster seems to have spilled the beans a bit by talking about big log hotels."

The Appalachian Mountain Club, citing fears of overdevelopment, came out against Brewster's bill and the *American Forests* magazine declined to publish Avery's article. Avery's momentum was lost and he fought a rearguard action, even trying to sabotage Baxter's next gift—Traveller's Mountain, saying it was too small and too far from Katahdin. In letter after letter to Baxter, he kept repeating his charge that Percy was solely concerned with preserving his name on "Baxter Park, Baxter Peak, and Baxter Campground...." The literary contributions of James Phinney Baxter, he stated, were enough of an enduring memorial to the family.

Congress adjourned in June 1938 without taking action on Brewster's bill. After that, it was a dead letter, especially once Baxter and Brewster had a little talk and the latter agreed not to reintroduce it. Some years later, when Percy was solicited to back a Brewster primary opponent, he demurred, saying the congressman had kept his word.

For whatever reason—pride, vision, Yankee cussedness, sheer will, sense of duty—a wilderness ethic had been imprinted on the Maine North Woods.

NOTES

[1] David Rothenberg, ed., *Wild Ideas*. Minneapolis, MN: University of Minnesota Press, 1995. Page xvii.

2 Ibid.

3 Benjamin Browne Foster, "Ktaadn and the Maine Woods," *Union Magazine*, Nov. 1848. Page 152.

4 Ibid., page 232.

5 George T. Sewall, *To Katahdin: The 1876 Adventures of Four Young Men and a Boat*. Gardiner, ME: Tilbury House, Publishers/Maine State Museum, 2000.

6 Julius H. Ward, "Moosehead Lake," *Harper's New Monthly Magazine*, August 1875.

7 Ibid.

8 Edward Ellis, *"A Chronological History of the Rangeley Lakes Region.* Self-published, 1983.

9 Julia A. Hunter and Earle G. Shettleworth, Jr., *Fly Rod Crosby: The Woman Who Marketed Maine*. Gardiner, ME: Tilbury House, Publishers/Maine State Museum, 2000.

NINETEEN

The Doldrums

WHAT BOOK ABOUT Maine, no less a history of its forest lands, can do without a nautical mention? Thus, the above seafaring chapter title, which provides an apt simile for the political period in Maine affairs we are about to enter—the 1940s, '50s, and even early '60s. *Webster's Dictionary* gives one definition of *doldrums* as "equatorial ocean regions noted for dead calms and light, fluctuating winds." Maine, in the dead calm of utter Republican control and the domination of a few key industries represents in those years such an oasis of quiet, when public and economic life coasted blissfully along, buffeted only infrequently by a few squalls of controversy, soon turned back to light, fluctuating winds.

David Nevin, in his biography of Edmund S. Muskie, sets the stage.[1] In order to establish the context that made Muskie's rise to power in the early 1950s so remarkable, he describes the one-party state, dominated by a GOP that had reached its apogee. To do so, he quotes others, too.

Here is political scientist Duane Lockard:

In few American States are the reins of government more openly or completely in the hands of a few leaders of economic interest groups than in Maine.... The abundance of timber and water power had indirectly created Maine's Number One Political Problem: the manipulation of government by the overlords of the companies based on these resources. More than three-quarters of Maine is woodland and most of that terrain is owned by a few timber companies and paper manufacturers.... Developers of hydroelectric power [also] moved into politics not only to secure rights to water power sites but to protect their investment from rate cutters, competition, and controls. These two groups, combined with the textile and shoe manufacturers, have done more than merely "influence" Maine politics; "control" is probably a more accurate term.[2]

Governor Kenneth M. Curtis, a Democratic successor of Muskie's, elected in the later 1960s, is quoted as saying:

They were controlled by the paper companies, the power companies, the businessmen who run things like sardine plants. They had an overflow labor force of people who had to work for very little and they were happy enough to keep it that way. The laws that passed were those that helped these plants. These were the people, for instance, who continually defeated the intrastate minimum wage in Maine even in the 1950s when the national Republican administration was extending the interstate minimum wage.[3]

And Nevin, himself, adds:

Whole towns were...dominated by single plants which kept other plants out, by agreement or by pressure, and thus left the labor force dependent upon a single employer. The deposits of these giant firms controlled banks, which supported merchants who supported newspapers and radio stations. This interlocking at the local level corresponded to a certain interlocking at the board level among giant firms themselves, which set intractable patterns for the state. State government controlled by a party that had no reason to be responsive to the people was a willing collaborator in the system.[4]

Louis Brann, the Democrat who had slipped into the governor's seat in 1933, was reelected the following year, but proved no more than a blip. His one enduring legacy may have been a story, told and retold, about his proclivities as a backslapping, hale-fellow-well-met politico. At a gathering, he ran into an acquaintance and asked: "How's your father, Jim?" The answer was: "He died last week, Governor." By then, Brann was already shaking other hands. When his attention returned to Jim, he forgetfully asked again: "How's your father, Jim?" "Still dead, Governor" was the reply.

Brann was replaced by Republican Lewis Barrows and the total GOP dominance pattern was resumed.

Labor strife, endemic in the U.S. in the late 1930s, arrived as a brief gust in 1937 with the Lewiston-Auburn shoe workers' strike. But the weakness of Maine unions in this era has been summed up by Charles J. O'Leary, former president of the state AFL-CIO: "Organized labor in Maine in the beginning of the 1930s was small in number, spread throughout the state, parochial in outlook, and politically ineffective...." They had organized the paper industry early on, but the two main groups formed by 1904: the Pulp, Sulphite, and Papermill Workers Union and International Brotherhood of Papermakers, for many years were fierce rivals and the bitter strike of 1908 was blamed, in part, on their inability to get along. As Maine headed into the totally Republican-dominated decade of the 1940s, organized labor, itself, was headed by a Republican, Benjamin Dorsky, a motion picture projectionist from Bangor who saw the wisdom of cooperating with the powers-that-be.

The early 1940s, of course, meant a whole new ballgame for Maine and the country—World War II—and the state entered the war effort wholeheartedly. One effect on industry was a shortage of workers, as men left to go off to war; for a short space, 1944–46, more than 3,000 POW's would be sent to Aroostook—Afrika Corps veterans, *Wehrmacht* troops captured in Normandy, and Russians who had volunteered for the German forces. Great Northern, Oxford Paper, Eastern Corp., Maine Seaboard Paper, and private contractors used them for cutting wood. From October 1944 to January 1945, they were averaging 12,000 cords per month.

Since it was hard to guard them in the deep woods, some psychology was used. One German reported they'd been told "the forest was populated by wild Indians who would not hesitate to kill escaping prisoners, and we had no reason not to believe them." Probably more effective was the cold and sense of endless wilderness. Prisoners separated from their units not only didn't try to escape; they did everything they could to be found. They performed farm work, too, and it was acknowledged that without their labor, many a potato operation would have shut down. By May 1946, the last of them were repatriated. Some have come back since as tourists.

It was during the Second World War that I, too, made my first stays in Maine, as a summer camper in Casco. The North Woods or the interlocking directorate in control at Augusta were totally beyond the ken of a boy my age (starting at eleven) but the effect of the nature I encountered in the forests and on the lakes of central Cumberland County has left an indelible impression—especially memories of the fishing and canoeing we did. Out of such early emotional contacts, like the thrill of looking into limpid water and watching a school of white perch approach my bait or gazing sharply overhead on Lake Sebago to spy an eagle, are conservationists born.

That industrial negligence, insensitivity, and blindness threatened these inculcated values was as unknown to me at Camp Brunonia as it was invisible to most Mainers, unless they lived in close proximity to paper mills and dealt each day with their "smell of money," or could gauge the effect on fishing and boating in the waterways where factory effluent was being dumped.

Symptomatic of the mind-set of that era was the sad story of the village of Flagstaff. Since 1949 this Somerset County community has "slept with the fishes," so to speak, inundated by the 27-mile-long lake created when the Dead River was dammed by the Kennebec Reservoir Company. In an ironic twist, the industrial thinking so opposed to parks, wilderness, and any hint of taking land, created its own "wilderness" by wiping out a settlement that had been in existence for a century and a half. The place had derived its name from an incident in 1775 when Benedict Arnold stopped at this isolated spot on his march to Quebec and erected a flagstaff. Nearby Bigelow Mountain was named for one of his officers, Major Timothy Bigelow, who climbed to the summit and sought in vain to catch sight of Quebec City. Only miles and miles of unbroken forest met his eyes.

The view from atop Bigelow today shows a scene pristine enough to gladden the heart of the most finicky of environmentalists. But this effect was not created for its scenic beauty; its story remains one of the most egregious examples of industrial muscle-flexing at a time when there was little or no opposition to what the big companies were doing.

The Kennebec Reservoir Company was composed of the Central Maine Power Company, Great Northern, and the Hollingsworth and Whitney Company (later to become Scott Paper). The chief proponent of a dam on the Dead River was Walter S. Wyman, founder and president of CMP. He'd had his eye on a site at Long Falls since 1909 but not until 1923 did he move with determination to acquire it. In a monumental battle in Augusta that dominated the legislative session, he clashed with Governor Percival Baxter, who wanted him to pay rent for the public lots he intended to use. Such an impertinent idea earned the power company's scornful label of "Socialism." So certain were Wyman and his allies, who included Garrett Schenck, of their overwhelming influence on the legislature that Wyman actually sent a compromise bill, once Baxter had fought him to a standstill, under his own name as if he were an elected member. Before it could be passed, however, Wyman withdrew it, reputedly because the Chicago utility holding company that owned CMP was against any compromise. Four years later, with Baxter out of office, a bill went through, giving Kennebec Reservoir its go-ahead.

Yet not until 1949 were the dam-builders ready. The land was clear-cut—18,000 acres—and burned, the smoke drifting over the houses of the 200 inhabitants who were soon to be dispossessed. It was the largest engineering project Maine had ever seen. The 35-foot-high dam was 1,300 feet long, made of 650 feet of filled earth and 650 feet of concrete, able to impound 12 billion cubic feet of water.

Sometime later, other major dam proposals, like Dickey-Lincoln, surfaced, but since these were "public power" projects, the private power interests adamantly opposed them. When the Long Falls dam was erected, these sorts of issues seemed long since buried—like the defunct Quoddy Dam idea to harness Down East tides, which had flared up briefly in the '30s under FDR and then been killed by Congress. Seen from our present-day climate—Maine has become the first state in the union to remove a major existing dam (the Edwards Dam in Augusta) against its owner's wishes—the destruction of Flagstaff village looms like an antique ghost of unthinkable public policy. But in the 1940s, no one—even the residents of Flagstaff, unhappy as they must have been—thought this corporate behavior unusual or wrong.

One lone voice eventually raised during this period of "doldrums" belonged to a lawyer from Waterville named Jerome G. Daviau. In a muckraking book called *Maine's Life Blood*, published locally, he applied a lawyer's analysis to Maine's problems, particularly to how they affected its waterways, its "life blood," and in sharp, unlawyerlike language, cried out in condemnation of the status quo. As stated in his preface:

> States, like families, have skeletons in their closets. Not
> only have I rattled a few, but I have tried to illuminate
> every dark recess and corner of the closets.

Whether Daviau gets into every dark recess and corner is debatable. His targets are fairly obvious—one-party rule, water pollution, destruction of fisheries, deliberate lack of economic development in order to keep wages low, wildlife decimation, and a compliant media and state government. Butchery of the forests, such a burning issue in our times, is passed off with the backhanded comments: "We had lumber once. All we have left is pulpwood." And, "We do not have enough timberland left to support another papermill."

The paper companies are right up with the power companies as villains of the piece. In referring to "an active conspiracy by some industries to deprive the people of Maine of their rights to public water and to sabotage all efforts towards industrial expansion," Daviau names names. The bad guys are Hollingsworth and Whitney, Great Northern, the Kennebec Log Driving Company, and the Penobscot Paper Company, among the pulp and paper set, and Central Maine Power and Bangor Hydro-Electric, among the energy producers. "Their common interest in the public waters bands them together in a solid phalanx against the people," Daviau asserts.

Later, he tells a cautionary tale to illustrate how this interlocking works. It is the story of Axel Smedberg, the proprietor of a small hotel and cabins near the shores of Lake Moxie, once a great fishing spot. In the spring and summer, Smedberg ran his hotel and cabins for anglers and in the winter, he trapped. He had a nice living until the Moxie Dam Company began fooling with the water levels. Smedberg was reluctant to complain because he leased his land from Great Northern, which was a stockholder in the Moxie Dam Company. When at last he and others in the locality spoke to the dam manager about the fish kill, they were told the drawdown would continue and they could do nothing about it. Then, learning that Moxie Dam, under its charter from the state, had no right to lower the water level, Smedberg took the matter to court. The court, however, refused to act nor would the Somerset County attorney. Next, Great Northern canceled Smedberg's lease and made him remove his cabins. The commissioner of the State Department of Inland Fisheries and Game remained resolutely silent.

All of which, in Daviau's telling of it, added up to the stranglehold certain interests had on the State of Maine in that period. The one-party domination by the Republicans was likened to the one-party domination in the South by the Democrats. And one-party domination, Daviau reminded his readers, "results not only in political stagnation but also in social and economic stagnation."

To illustrate an aspect of these effects, Daviau quoted a businessman in rural Aroostook writing to Governor Burton Cross about the "appalling" exodus of labor from the county.

The Republican chief executive, in Daviau's words, "dutifully administered the usual soporific of misinformation that has made Maine's curtain of ignorance what it is." Cross flat-out denied Maine was losing population and if statistics showed a drop, it merely reflected Maine men leaving to join the armed forces. Daviau came back with U.S. Department of Commerce figures, subtracting those in the service, that showed a net loss of 76,372 from 1940–50.

Pollution in Maine rivers—some characterized as the worst in the U.S.—was attacked by saying that 97 percent was caused by industry and a mere 3 percent by municipal waste. Daviau was adamant industry should clean up its mess first and scoffed at the notion the paper companies would leave the state if forced to clean up. The state's program to deal with the problem—a water classification system—he labeled a "deception," a device to allow companies to continue to dump their wastes. "Implicit in river classification is the relegation of some waters to open sewers.... It's the Class D classification the industries are interested in.... These are the waters the industrial bloc has preempted through years of deception, corruption, and fraud."

Equally infuriating to Daviau was industry's preemption of economic development on the state level. There was no government agency to lure new industries. Thus, responsibility had been given to a twelve-member Maine Development Commission, headed by Harold F. Schnurle, a vice-president of Central Maine Power and the company's chief lobbyist. Their total concentration of effort, Daviau complained, was on the tourist business, a deliberate attempt to keep wages low, labor seasonal, and big, better-paying companies out. "Maine must aim at a few large, heavy industries, the very kind the industrial bloc has discouraged for years," Daviau declared.

Daviau's generally forgotten but illustrative attack on the status quo was published in 1958, after the first crack in the monolithic surface of Maine public life had appeared in the gubernatorial election of 1954. Edmund S. Muskie, a Democrat (and Catholic, no less) had been elected, to everyone's astonishment and, no doubt, Jerome Daviau's delight at the success of his fellow Waterville attorney. But *Maine's Life Blood* is almost as harsh on Muskie as on the Industrial-Republican Complex. Daviau tells of working with Muskie on a Maine Rivers Authority bill and then being let down when the governor withdrew his support. Even Muskie's key first term accomplishment — the establishment of a State Department of Economic Development — lost favor with Daviau when the Associated Industries of Maine was allowed to work with them. Daviau again felt betrayed after Muskie failed to make good on his brave talk about cleaning up the rivers. Daviau did not attempt to hide his bitterness.

> The Governor timidly took the well worn path to the right, though he occasionally looked longingly to the left, perhaps aware that greatness did not lie in the direction he was traveling.... The die was cast. The rivers would remain polluted and the clam flats unproductive, and further inroads in our coastal fisheries would be tolerated....

Knowing Ed Muskie, he must have been furious upon reading these words and defensive in his forceful way. For his surprise political success was mostly won by him personally, not by a sea change in the attitudes of Maine people. They were still hard-rock Republicans, even if "Muskie Republicans," and the hegemony of the GOP was still stiflingly strong—even after Ed Muskie's four years in office.

This newly elected Democratic chief executive, the first since Louis Brann twenty years earlier, had a legislature to deal with of a house split 117 Republicans to 34 Democrats and a senate of 27 Republicans to 6 Democrats. It could override a veto in the blink of an eye. In addition, he had the Executive Council, made up of 7 Republicans, usually all party activists, whose consent was needed for any important appointments. Department heads, too, stayed, so Muskie had to deal with personnel who owed their jobs to the GOP Almost the only people he could call his own were his immediate staff.

In other words, despite his amazing victory over Burton Cross, he had to tread lightly. It was the spark of a revolution, not the overturn of a set of conditions developing since before the Civil War. His gains were painfully slow.

Daviau's Maine Rivers Authority bill appeared so politically impracticable that it had to be introduced—by Representative Albert Bernier of Waterville—under the rubric "by request," which meant the sponsor, himself, didn't support it. The industrial lobbyists had a field day attacking the measure.

The breath of fresh air filling sails in the "doldrums" of these decades was admittedly weak and seemingly not long-lasting. But while backing off in his first term from a slam-bang attack on water pollution or even from mild remedies like finishing the classifications or adding more public members to the Water Improvement Commission, Muskie, by his second term, was speaking out more forcefully. "Surely, it is beyond argument," he declared, "that an abundant supply of clean water is essential to our industrial growth, to meet our domestic needs, to encourage the natural reproduction of fish in our streams, and to our coastal economy."

Eventually, he was off to Washington, D.C., and the distinguished career that earned him, among other things, the title of "Mr. Clean."

He was followed in the governor's office by another Democrat, a Waterville chiropractor named Dr. Clinton Clausen. One Muskie achievement had been to change the gubernatorial term in Maine to four years from two. Clausen thus became the first to take office under the extended term but died less than six months later and his place was taken by the Republican Senate President John H. Reed. For the next seven years, the Republican hegemony continued in much the same fashion as before, while Maine, itself, imperceptibly, was changing politically, if not economically.

In 1966 Reed sought a second four-year term to add to his seven years. The rallying cry of his opponents, "Seven, not eleven," was actually coined by a primary foe. In the general election, the Democratic nominee, Secretary of State Kenneth M. Curtis, used the refrain, as well, but relied more on the positive aspects of his campaign, including a plan—the Maine Action Plan—which was a series of proposals to move the state forward on all fronts, particularly in economic development, which meant the "big industries" Daviau had considered so important.

Ken Curtis called this "off-trend development."

The wind was up. New life was stirring Down East. Repercussions were felt throughout the Maine Woods, too—the scene of many of the titanic clashes about to occur.

NOTES

1 David Nevin, *Muskie of Maine.* New York: Random House, 1972.

2 Duane Lockard, *New England State Politics.* Princeton, NJ: Priceton University Press, 1959.

3 Nevin, page 148.

4 Ibid., pages 148–49.

TWENTY

Megaprojects and Megacontroversies

I T REALLY ALL BEGAN with Quoddy. Had this ambitious project for harnessing the tides in Passamaquoddy Bay been created when proposed in the 1920s by dam engineer Dexter P. Cooper, the idea of "non-trend development" for Maine might well have become more acceptable. There is evidence that Franklin Delano Roosevelt, Cooper's friend and neighbor on Campobello Island, spoke favorably about its prospects at Eastport as early as 1920, when he was campaigning for vice-president. Some years later, a referendum to exempt the project from Maine's Fernald Law, which prevented the export of power, was passed overwhelmingly—53,000 to 7,000 statewide and 9,855 to 119 in Washington County—giving Quoddy a definite green light. In 1926 Cooper received a preliminary permit from the Federal Power Commission, and in 1928 acquired a New Brunswick charter for the Canadian company he'd formed.

Yet this tidal dam was never built. Not even after FDR's election could Dexter Cooper's dream achieve more than the erecting of a housing site—Quoddy Village—for those who were to do the work. By the late 1930s, it had lost FDR's support and the U.S. Senate then killed any further funding.

After John F. Kennedy's election in 1960, the idea was revived. Except, in a report issued by Secretary of the Interior Stewart Udall, Quoddy was no longer a stand-alone project. It was to be linked to a dam on the upper St. John River so that "peaking power" could be added to the steady flow from the tidal operation. Only in this way, the report maintained, could there be a favorable cost-benefit ratio—i.e., more money generated than spent.

Upstream on the St. John no dams had yet been built. But soon a flurry of proposals began. The Army Corps of Engineers had its plan for a dam at Rankin Rapids, southwest of the town of St. Francis, and a private group, calling itself the Citizens Committee for the Maine Power Authority, had a rival proposal at Cross Rock in the same vicinity. Later, the most viable of the options—twin dams at Dickey and Lincoln School farther west—entered the lists.

The trouble with the first two projects was they flooded the Allagash River—the quintessential "wild river" in Maine—an icon of sorts, even in an age when conservation and wilderness values were anything but in the ascendance. Since 1957 the National Park Service had been studying the area for possible inclusion in its system.

Meanwhile, another factor was entering this equation—the start of an organized, grass-roots, widespread conservation group in Maine. Percival Baxter had been acting pretty much on his own, and by 1949 was even running into resistance from local sportsmen, while Jerome Daviau's was a single voice, too, and, in the words of one who knew him, "he had a pen and a manner dipped in vitriol," which didn't help his cause.

Yet soon another forceful environmental pioneer arrived on the scene in the '50s—Ezra James Briggs of Caribou, ex-ski trooper, hunter, fisherman, and investment consultant. He was as outspoken as Daviau but with a charm and humor that could cajole a roomful of hostile trappers into uproarious laughter, ending with a round of applause (which I once saw him do in Augusta on a bill to get rid of the coyote bounty). Characteristically, in describing his early days in the legislature, Jim stated: "Some people today might call me a voice crying in the wilderness. Back then, they just called me nuts."

On May 14, 1959, a small knot of like-minded men met in Jim Briggs's senate office in Augusta. They represented eight different organizations and included figures like Charles Bradford, then superintendent of state parks; Alonzo Garcelon, descendant of a Maine governor, a dentist active with the Maine Rifle and Pistol Association; Wendell Hadlock of the newly formed Nature Conservancy; and Robert Patterson, a trustee of the Maine Audubon Society.

At this meeting, the Natural Resources Council of Maine was

born, an umbrella organization dedicated to protecting the state's environment. Bob Patterson, a landscape architect from Mount Desert, was the initial president. Another early member of the board was a lawyer from Skowhegan, Clinton "Bill" Townsend, who represented the Somerset County Water District. Bill has said that the NRCM's initial program rested on three pillars: 1) preserve the Allagash; 2) oppose the spraying of DDT; 3) oppose dams.

In business with a three-year grant from David Rockefeller, which allowed them to hire an executive director, the Council tackled the Allagash issue first. A Washington-based environmental research firm, the Conservation Foundation, was hired to do a thorough study of the Allagash, to consider the environmental and economic implications of a possible wilderness preserve. The national park idea was still a possibility, but sparked opposition. Indeed, in November 1960, Supreme Court Justice William O. Douglas wrote Percival Baxter, told him he'd just canoed the Allagash, and expressed his dismay that a national park there would mean roads and hotels. Could not the Allagash be put under the Baxter State Park Authority? The answer was apparently no, but the idea of a *state* entity was in the air.

The report commissioned by NRCM sparked enough interest for the 100th Legislature to assign its single body allowed to do studies, the Legislative Research Committee, to probe the matter and come back with recommendations. Their key suggestion was to create an Allagash River Authority to formulate plans for the "preservation of the natural beauty and wilderness character" of the Allagash area. The next legislature created that Authority, composed of state officials and a University of Maine forestry professor. Governor John H. Reed, who had been sympathetic enough to let his name be used as honorary chair of the Natural Resources Council, added an Advisory Council that included Bob Patterson and Bill Townsend.

A funny thing happened on the way to the next legislature, the 102nd. In the presidential election of 1964, Lyndon Johnson beat Barry Goldwater in a landslide and did it in Republican Maine, too. Because the state still had straight-ticket voting, the legislature unexpectedly became Democratic. The momentum for an Allagash bill had already been building. The new turn of events made it seem possible.

Still, a problem for the Democrats, especially northern ones, was the strong support for Dickey-Lincoln in their constituencies and they needed to keep that idea alive, as well as to save the Allagash. Senator Elmer Violette from the St. John Valley town of Van Buren exemplified the dilemma in a speech seeking support for an order he introduced to study the issue further rather than act precipitously on the matter. Violette, a lawyer and later a state supreme court justice, was then chair of the Judiciary Committee and he told his senate colleagues straight out that he was for a combination of development of the Quoddy-Dickey-Lincoln Project "in conjunction with the preservation of the Allagash Riverway." He added he was the first candidate in Maine to urge state control of the Allagash and was personally opposed to the Cross Rock Dam.

Using the argument that a number of proposals for the upper St. John and Allagash were before the 102nd and a move afoot in Congress for Quoddy-Dickey-Lincoln, along with a bill for money to states to preserve wild rivers, Violette proposed that a study committee of four senators and five representatives hold hearings and thoroughly determine the best course of action. He said it was necessary to know the President's position on Quoddy-Dickey-Lincoln, to clarify Interior Secretary Udall's willingness to recommend a State Waterway and ended with a warning that "if Cross Rock looks as if it were going to pass, Uncle Sam will come in and take over the entire area."

Opponents of any delay used a similar argument. If they didn't act right away, the feds would grab the Allagash.

Violette's order was not accepted in the house and almost died in nonconcurrence between the two bodies. An element of opposition to the Allagash Wilderness Waterway, itself, entered the debate. An editorial was read in which the *Bangor Daily News*, then an ultra-conservative paper, called it "a very costly museum benefiting a few, only 1,000 hardy canoe campers, at the expense of many."

In January of 1966, at a special session, the Allagash issue returned, both as an act to create the Waterway and a bond of $1.5 million to pay for it. The *Bangor Daily News* still railed about its 1,000 canoeing buffs but opposition was minimal. Only 12 votes against the Waterway in the house and 102 in favor; the bond issue did almost as well and the senate passed it unanimously. When the same body finally enacted the Waterway bill, Elmer Violette was brought to the podium and made president pro-tem in order to deliver a speech about this "historic piece of legislation." In the fall of 1967 the people of Maine approved the bond.

Despite fears to the contrary, the Cross Rock deal was dead. In retrospect, what was being proposed could hardly pass a straight-face test today. Bill Townsend remembers going to a hearing and seeing "four rows of proponents, all New York types, people hoping to make money from it," including John Mitchell, President Nixon's later disgraced attorney general. The prospectus, describing Grand Allagash Lake—the 225,000-acre impoundment created by the flooding from the main dam—tried to emphasize the recreational benefits, particularly fishing. In the small print, however, it was admitted that keeping out yellow perch would be a problem, and thirteen more small dams would be needed. Then, too, fluctuating water levels for salmon spawning would cause trouble; that would require another twelve water control dams. If that was not enough difficulty, five outstanding trout streams would be inundated for half their lengths and would need dredging to open them to brookies. The winter drawdown for power generation would result in "desiccation and death for all lake trout [togue] eggs" in the areas left unwatered, plus leave flooded tree stands on the bottom of Grand Allagash Lake that would have to be marked with buoys to warn unwary fishermen. The roads and hotels dreaded by Justice Douglas were an asset to boast about: "a well-laid-out development of two- to three-bedroom homes," for tourist rental, a large motel, marina, boat basin, 300 trailer locations, vehicular bridge, dining center, etc., etc.

In contrast, Dickey-Lincoln could be advertised as "an environmentalist dam." Once it was determined in D.C. that Quoddy's cost-benefit ratio was hopeless under any circumstances, Dickey-Lincoln, it was also deemed, could still stand alone as a viable project.

By then, Maine had a new governor—Ken Curtis. The young

secretary of state, prior to entering state service, had been the federal ARA (Area Redevelopment Agency) director in northern Maine. He was a passionate proponent of large-scale projects to move the economy of this underdeveloped and relatively impoverished region of Maine. During his tenure, proposals started coming thick and fast.

Some, he inherited, like Dickey-Lincoln. Particularly controversial, too, was an attempt already started to diversify the agriculture of Aroostook County—add sugar beets as a crop alongside the famous potatoes. Because the sugar beet processing plant needed (or said it did) to pollute a class A stream (the Prestile), a vicious battle had been waged in the 102nd Legislature. Conservationists mobilized and, while that battle was lost, opponents felt vindicated when the effort failed, mainly because Fred Vahlsing, its promoter, stopped paying the farmers and they stopped growing beets.

Such evanescent solutions to Maine's economic backwardness were usually first touted by promoters like Vahlsing—moneyed people from "Away." It was, in a sense, an answer to Jerome Daviau's populist charge that a conspiracy of existing industries had combined to keep other industries and good-paying jobs out of the state.

Often, in the megacontroversies that swirled about these proposals, it was an intra-industry battle that played out Down East, as in the case of the oil ports.

These coastal projects, which started showing up in October 1968, have a tangential relation to the Maine Woods, in that, if built, some would have had a significant impact on the economy of northern Maine. The whole thing began with a Vahlsing-like promoter named Jack Evans, a Welshman who had worked for Royal Dutch Shell and was married to a native of Millinocket. His brainstorm was to have Maine apply for a foreign trade zone in Portland, with a subzone at Machiasport, where the world's largest oil refinery would be built to handle oil imported by the Occidental Oil Company from Libya and Venezuela. It was a legal way to get around the oil import quotas imposed through Congress by domestic oil producers, which had the result of making New Englanders pay a much higher price for fuel. One indignant industry opponent likened Evans's scheme to the "freeloading of hippies."

Another blockbuster project was offered by John King of the King Resources Company, who signed a lease with Maine to explore 3 million acres of seabed in the Gulf of Maine for oil and establish a refinery at an old navy oil depot on Long Island in Casco Bay. The federal government immediately challenged the state's legal ability to grant offshore rights.

The contorted maneuvers on these fronts, particularly who was going to do what out to sea and in Washington County with its deep water close to shore to receive huge tankers, have been well documented in a 1975 book by Peter Bradford, an assistant to Governor Curtis in the negotiations.[1] Much of the confusion involved the entry of other players, including the establishment, pro-import-restriction Atlantic Richfield Company, proposing an operation at Eastport, and statements like that of their ally Robert Monks,[2] when ARCO's entry was announced: "This is the biggest day in Maine's history. This is bound to cause industrialization the like of which Maine has never experienced," followed by the formation of anti-industrialization groups with names like Keep Oil Out and Citizens Who Care. In the waning days of the boom, the Pittston Company, better known for its coal, and the Gibbs Oil Company both tried to get into the act. Yet ultimately oil *was* kept out of Maine, except where its transport had existed before, such as in Portland, the East Coast's second-largest oil port, which handles all oil destined for Montreal.

As if these shocks to the nerves of coastal communities, with their many summer residents, weren't enough, another proposal weighed in for an aluminum smelter and nuclear power plant to be built at Trenton, the entrance to Mount Desert Island and Acadia National Park. A local option vote of the 500 townspeople defeated that plan by a two to one margin.

These types of crises eventually led to passage of two bills in the Maine legislature heralded as "landmark legislation." Fearing the state was vulnerable to large-scale projects, the Site Selection Law was passed, creating a Board of Environmental Protection and a process for approving or disapproving projects over a certain size. The second law, the Oil Conveyance Act, set up a method to deal with oil spills, using a tax imposed on every barrel of oil brought into Maine. Mostly this meant the pipeline to Montreal; the company controlling it, naturally, sued, but lost. Ironically, Ken Curtis, the prodevelopment governor, was hailed for such environmental triumphs.

In the 1970s, environmentalism was on the rise, in Maine, as in the rest of the nation. Actually, in 1969 the 104th Legislature took a tentative step to deal with the lack of any zoning or oversight in the state's Unorganized Territories, a land area of some 10 million acres. Initially, in forming the Land Use Regulation Commission, protection was given on a very limited basis to areas most threatened by development, but without any staff to enforce it.

On March 17, 1971, "An Act to Revise the Maine Land Use Regulation Law" came out of committee with a split report, nine to four, Ought-to-Pass—on beefing up LURC and adding authority over all 10 million acres.

The opposition seemed summed up by Representative James Dudley of Enfield (the most conservative legislator I ever served with, albeit a Democrat). Jim Dudley said:

> But let me tell you, with 10 million acres involved and the small bureaucracy in this State House capitol running it, it would be run very poorly. In my opinion, who can run it the best is the people that have owned it down through the years and have paid their good tax dollars and they involve hundreds of people. I think hundreds of people can do a better job of managing their own property...rather than a few people in Augusta.

Opposing this property rights sentiment from the north was an environmentalist legislator from the south, Representative Marian Fuller Brown of York, a Republican National Committeewoman. She spoke of threats to the area, like "proposals for multimillion-dollar, four-season recreation complexes, second home subdivisions, and leasing programs and vast expansion of mining for minerals." Another well-known Republican, Representative Don Collins of Caribou, told of the polluting of Madawaska Lake near his summer cottage in T16 R4 and of a logging company that built "an access road onto our private road and started hauling pulp right next to our cottage." It remained for his fellow Aroostook County lawmaker, Democratic Representative John L. Martin of Eagle Lake to supply a political note.

> You remember during the 104th session we passed for the first time a commission that we thought was going to do the job. I couldn't quite figure out why the lobbyists for the paper companies were so happy with us. They were happy because we had passed a bill that satisfied them...for all practical purposes...only 2 percent of the so-called wildlands of this state would actually be regulated by this commission.

On a bipartisan basis, an effective LURC was created and has been living a stormy existence ever since.

Bigelow Mountain—or the idea of turning part of it into one of those multimillion-dollar resorts Representative Marian Fuller Brown so deplored—was a long-running controversy. As early as 1966, the *Portland Press Herald* had announced that the International Design and Development Corp. of Boston was going "to start" construction of a major project along the mountain's slopes overlooking Flagstaff Lake. Four years later, the same announcement was made again. But in 1972, the effort really got underway, trying to head off a beginning attempt by conservation groups to protect the area, which had started with a proposal by the Appalachian Mountain Club to set aside 37,000 acres at Bigelow. The climbers and hikers were quickly joined by the Natural Resources Council and the Maine Department of Parks and Recreation, advocating a state park.

By November of 1972, the press was reporting the Bigelow situation had been complicated by the emergence of the public lots controversy in the legislature and the creation of an expanded LURC. As the year wound to a close, the Flagstaff Corp. announced its plans for the 8,000 acres it owned at the base of the mountain, which included a ski run. The owner of the corporation was a young man named John Marden, a New Zealander with a common Maine surname. His quasi-British accent in Augusta meetings soon displaced any idea that he was old Maine stock. However, I doubt chauvinism was why he fared so poorly in those halls of government. Ski resorts were not in high favor. Evergreen Valley, a massive project in Oxford County, backed by the credit of the state, had defaulted; Squaw Valley at Greenville, started by Scott Paper, lost so much money the company gave it to the state; and Mount Agamenticus, the Big A, in Representative Brown's own town of York, was about to go belly up. Also, the environmental movement, despite prognostications by political pundits that there would be an anti-environmental counterrevolution in this session, still packed a punch.

For much of 1973 there was no decision as LURC held hearings on the ski resort proposal. In November LURC gave it preliminary approval; ten days later, by a four to one vote, the agency reversed itself. The Flagstaff Corp. then went to court. Another four years were needed to settle the matter. A citizen's group, led by environmental activist Lance Tapley, gathered enough signatures for a referendum. It won narrowly in June 1976, despite the public opposition of Governor James Longley. In August 1978, Flagstaff Corp. sold its Bigelow holdings. Swaps of public lots and gifts of land by the J. M. Huber Co. and Great Northern helped build up the 35,000-acre Bigelow Preserve that now exists.

Public lots—what are they? Or what were they in 1972 after a Portland newspaper reporter, Bob Cummings, revealed that 400,000 acres of state land had somehow over the past century inadvertently ended up in private hands. As a newly elected member of the Maine legislature, sorting out this controversy was my baptism of fire on an issue of major importance to the state and the North Woods, since I was put on a special select committee to deal with the problem.

Public lots, themselves, were areas marked off in every township by the Massachusetts General Court when they had Maine surveyed after the Revolution. Originally, four of these "reserved" lots existed in each 23,000 acres comprising a township—one to support the minister, one his church, one to support the schoolteacher, and one his or her school. It was an assumption that all townships thus laid out would be eventually converted to towns, with their own governments, which could then fund these services. But, as we know, much of Maine was never settled. In 1850 the Maine legislature authorized the sale of the right to cut timber and grass on these reserved lots—primarily as a defense against timber thieves. Ever since, they had been pretty much forgotten, with the owners treating the property as their own and buying and selling such rights, although the state had never relinquished its title.

This was the bombshell Bob Cummings's articles had exploded. What should the state do? The legislature's answer was to form our special committee, led by Senator Harrison Richardson, a feisty Republican from Cumberland County.

The committee had a number of "heavy hitters"—the other Republican senator was Kenneth MacLeod, a former senate president, and the Democratic senator was Robert Clifford, later a Maine supreme court justice. House members included the GOP Majority Leader Larry Simpson; Linwood Palmer, later a GOP candidate for governor; Jim Briggs; and future speaker, John Martin. Besides trying to figure out an answer to the public lots conundrum, we also stuck our noses (led by Harry Richardson) into other areas of interest in the woods. "Forest Practices" was a big concern, and we held hearings in seventeen locations around Maine, receiving input and investigating bad practices. An especially egregious situation was the Beaudry Lumber Company's operations at Heald Pond in Bald Mountain Township, where considerable erosion had occurred. A letter in his inimitable style from Jim Briggs to Harry Richardson referred to our efforts to dig into this affair:

"I am struck by the belligerence of some witnesses to come before our committee," Jim began. He referred, in particular, to a "Mr. Fiske" who "had a chip on his shoulder" because the committee was seeking "information on an illegal, undesirable forest practice committed by themselves about which they would just as soon forget." Then, he lambasted the present forest commissioner:

> For Fred Holt to state he has no complaints about bad cutting practices is astonishing. I have such complaints all the time, most often from citizens I regard as responsible. Why does the Maine Forestry Department always seem to have this type of individual at the top?
>
> P.S. Tomorrow I am riding the Bangor and Aroostook

(Maine's Fastest Hound Dog) diesel to Van Buren so the railroad crew can show me the terrible cutting practices along the way. They initiated this. I didn't. Maybe they should take Fred Holt!

Another of the committee's concerns was the state's practice of leasing camp lots on its own territory. These leases, which often had elements of favoritism about them, were put on hold by our committee—no new ones until 1980. This drew some colorful correspondence from one Wendell H. Austin of Wytopitlock, who asked to be made an exception so he could build a small camp on a lake:

> In the meantime, I intend to dig a spring for water, bury my garbage, have an outdoor deep-deep toilet and prevent forest fires and live within all Maine laws, if you will give me a lease. We owe $4,500 on a $3,000 house, have an old '66 car and canoe and $87 a week workman's comp.... We don't have much money and we don't have much fun.... YOU CAN HELP.

Austin, who said he had been disabled in a sawmill accident, promised to go to "U.S. Senators and Congressmen" if we didn't assist him.

When it looked as if an accord might be reached between Great Northern and the state on a swap of public lots, International Paper and others raised the issue that reserved lots could only be used for school purposes, not for recreation, which was the state's goal in this instance.

An exhaustive study was done by an assistant attorney general, Lee Schepps, covering a number of legal points. His review of past statutes and law cases showed conclusively the state could do whatever it wanted with this property of theirs. They could even sell the lots or assemble them into "large contiguous quantities of land" far in excess of 1,000 acres. Furthermore, Schepps stated:

> Substantially all grass and timber rights on the public lots terminate upon the organization of the township from which the public lot was reserved into a plantation.

Because the owners of the cutting rights in the 1970s were maintaining that their ancestors had received them in perpetuity, the above provision led to the committee's most startling and controversial proposal. This was the legislation that came to be known as the "Grand Plantations Bill."

It was Harry Richardson's brainchild. Harry had never been a "play-it-safe" politician. When Republican house majority leader, he took an active hand in reshaping Governor Ken Curtis's call for a state income tax and forcibly pushed the hated tax through the legislature. Here, again, he was offending strong forces in the Republican Party, whose gubernatorial primary he was about to enter, by proposing to strip some of them in one fell swoop of land they had considered their own for generations.

Simply put, the "Grand Plantations Bill" would have divided all the Unorganized Territories into eight oversized plantation governments—a plantation being a hybrid—partly a town, but run by county commissioners.

The heavily debated measure came from our committee with a split report, five to five, and was presented to a special session in February 1974. The Republican-controlled senate beat it almost three to one, despite (or perhaps because of) Harry Richardson's statement it wouldn't affect his primary campaign (which he lost). In the also Republican house, we weren't as badly trounced, 85 to 50. My own remarks at the time strike me now as disingenuous, saying it was "merely an organizational device for dividing our Unorganized Territories...into a self-governing entity...." No mention that this was really a legislative ruse to reacquire our long-lost public lots on the cheap.

Ultimately, the notion of exchanging state land with nice timber stands for scenic public lots took hold. Equivalent value was the key. The first agreement apparently was one reached by Governor Ken Curtis and Robert Hellendale, president of Great Northern, on December 5, 1974, and was incorporated in a resolve sponsored on a bipartisan basis by John Martin and Linwood Palmer. Those two gentlemen and myself later sponsored "An Act to Improve the Management of the Public Lands," establishing a Bureau of Public Lands in the Department of Conservation and empowering it to continue the land swaps until the equivalent of all the public lots was recovered. In time this was done, and the state has gained some magnificent properties as "Maine Public Reserved Land," like the

De Bouillie Mountains, Gero Island, Duck Lake, Squapan, etc.

Until almost the 1990s, the saga (or threat, in some people's minds) of the Dickey-Lincoln dam hung over the Maine conservation-development scene. In public memory, it was torpedoed because it would have destroyed an endangered plant, the once-thought-extinct snapdragon called Furbish's lousewort. Or at least the media, with its love of simplistic sensation, inserted this memorable angle and wrote it large. The real story, of course, was far more complex.

After a Congressional House Committee in 1983 deauthorized the Lincoln School dam, thus ending any hope of its being financed, the entire project was declared officially dead. But a Maine paper in 1984, perhaps with the wishful hope of more headlines to come, pointed out that the U.S. Senate—no doubt because of Senator George Mitchell's prodding—refused to concur. Technically, then, that dam on the northern St. John still had a spark of theoretical life.

But to go back: Dickey-Lincoln's first open opponent in the hitherto-supportive Maine congressional delegation was the Republican First District congressman, David Emery of Rockland. Elected to the Maine house while in his early twenties, Dave Emery was a maverick and so conservative we used to say of him jokingly, "he's twenty-five, going on seventy-five." In 1974 he stunned Maine by defeating the popular, previously unbeatable incumbent, Democrat Peter Kyros. Emery had already shown his independent streak during the 1960s income tax debate by presenting his own tax plan and, once on the federal scene, he seemed on a similar quixotic quest in his determined opposition to Dickey-Lincoln. All the other major state politicos—U.S. Senators Edmund Muskie, Margaret Chase Smith, Bill Hathaway (who defeated Mrs. Smith), George Mitchell (who replaced Muskie), Congressman Bill Cohen, and Governor James Longley—were still resolutely for the dam. Emery tried to cook up an alternative. Using three undergraduate engineering students from Worcester Polytech, he presented a report detailing six potential power sites in Maine that would provide three-quarters of the energy of Dickey-Lincoln at a much cheaper cost. This end-run fared no better than his tax plan.

Implicit in his opposition to Dickey-Lincoln was the under-played hand of Maine's commercial power companies and their allies throughout New England and the nation. No public power had been permitted in New England. They wished to keep it that way. And, fortuitously for them, they soon had conservationists to hide behind.

Some conservationists had paid lip service to Dickey-Lincoln as a "conservationist's dam"—i.e., that it wouldn't flood the Allagash (or only a small part of it). Once Cross Rock and Rankin Rapids were eliminated, the environmentalists were no longer tolerant of Dickey-Lincoln.

New Yorker writer John McPhee, in a piece entitled, "The Keel of Lake Dickey," recorded direly that the dam would be bigger than Aswan, the twelfth largest on earth, flooding fifty-seven miles back up the St. John, leaving 90,000 acres of stumps on its lake bottom and a shoreline of 300,000 acres of mud—and for what? *725 megawattts of electricity for two and a half hours a day.* "That's all.... It's a soupçon...."

That same year, 1974, eleven years after the project had first been bruited, U.S. Senator William Hathaway, a liberal Democrat, was already criticizing its green opponents. In October 1976 Maine's prime outfitter of sportsmen, the L. L. Bean Company, joined the chorus of opponents. A month later, the Furbish's louse-wort discovery surfaced. The next year, the Second District congressman, William S. Cohen, changed his position; four years earlier, Republican Cohen had urged President Richard Nixon to "reconsider" his refusal to include Dickey-Lincoln in his budget. Exactly one year after Cohen's apostasy, Governor James Longley announced his change of heart.

A day before he did, Longley wrote to President Jimmy Carter, justifying his new position. In the sprawling, prolix style for which he was famous, Maine's first Independent governor started by referring to a decision Carter had made as governor of Georgia in regard to the Sprewell Bluff dam. Then, concerning Dickey-Lincoln, he came right out and called it "grossly unfair to the present and future generations of Maine people and a waste of federal and State of Maine taxpayer dollars." He urged the president to join him in opposition and also chimed in on the environmental impact— 88,000 acres flooded, 206,000 acres of forest land "isolated from

Maine wood markets to the extent that access and egress would be through Canada for the most part," but as a conservative business-man, he was perhaps more in his element attacking the project's preference for selling power to public bodies and energy co-ops.

Despite the defection of major officeholders such as Cohen and Longley, Dickey-Lincoln still wouldn't die. In May 1981 Dickey appeared finally dead, but Lincoln School was still alive. The stake in the heart came with the House Public Works' de-authorization vote in 1983. The vampire's ghost, however, still haunted the upper St. John until time ran out—seven years after the Senate refused to join the House.

Meanwhile, a crisis of monumental proportions loomed for Maine in general and the Maine North Woods in particular. This was the famous Indian Land Claims controversy, which had its origin because a white man named William Plaisted, the owner of some tourist cabins in Washington County, tried to cut a road to them through property members of the Passamaquoddy nation consid-ered rightly their own. This time, the usually passive natives reacted, blocked the road-building, were arrested, and hired a counter-culture-type defense lawyer. When the lawyer, himself, was arrested for marijuana possession, he was replaced by Tom Tureen, a young law student from St. Louis. Tureen's research led him to the "Indian Non-Intercourse Act," passed by Congress in 1790.

This law had been put into effect because the newly estab-lished U.S. government was concerned that states might be contra-dicting federal policies vis-à-vis tribes in the U.S. They felt relations with the Indians, like those with foreign nations, belonged under federal jurisdiction and so the Indian Non-Intercourse Act made it plain no treaty between a state and an Indian tribe after 1790 was valid unless ratified by Congress. Readers may remember the Rev-erend Daniel Little and his vain attempts to persuade the Penob-scots to ratify a treaty in 1788, so that it was after 1790 before they signed an accord with Massachusetts. The same was true of the Pas-samaquoddies. Furthermore, Tureen discovered, those two post-1790 treaties were never even submitted to Congress.

So thousands upon thousands of acres of land had been taken from Maine Indians after 1790 through treaties legally null and void.

It appeared that the titles to two-thirds of Maine's land area were clouded.

To most Maine people, this seemed like the most preposterous idea ever voiced. Yet on June 2, 1972, Tureen went into federal court and received an order from a highly respected, Maine-raised judge, Edward T. Gignoux, requiring the U.S. Justice Department to represent the Indians.

It took three years for a higher court to uphold Judge Gignoux's ruling that the Non-Intercourse Act applied to Maine's tribes. By then, Jim Longley was governor and he vociferously refused to concede that the claim had merit, an adamant position also endorsed by Attorney General Joseph Brennan. Their stonewalling was subsequently undermined when Ropes and Grey, the prestigious Boston bond counsel, refused to give unqualified backing to municipal bonds in the disputed area. A sale of $427 million of these bonds was halted.

Tom Tureen let it be known that the two $150 million damage suits he'd brought represented only the Indians' loss of rent on their property. The real cost would be $25 billion.

Naturally, this was a bit of posturing and the Indians showed a willingness to settle for less — stating, too, they would not go after homeowners nor small-property holders.

The Maine congressional delegation tried to pass legislation extinguishing the Indians' claims. All attempts failed. President Jimmy Carter then attempted to broker a compromise. An agreement was reached, but ran into bitter opposition from Governor Longley, GOP Congressmen Cohen and Emery, and Democrat Attorney General Brennan. However, when Republicans gained control of the legislature and a new attorney general, Richard Cohen, entered office, he advised the state to settle. U.S. Senators Ed Muskie and Bill Hathaway agreed, and a federal appropriation of $81.5 million went to the two Indian tribes. So harsh were the feelings, however, that Congressman Bill Cohen was able to use the issue to help unseat Senator Bill Hathaway.

The agreement, a landmark settlement in U.S.-Native American relations, still has its defenders and detractors and has placed the two principal tribes — the Penobscots and Passamaquoddies,

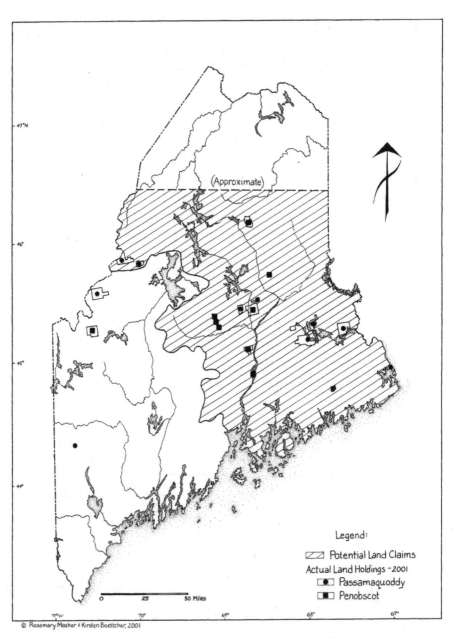

(Approximate)

Legend:

▨ Potential Land Claims

Actual Land Holdings -2001

⬤ Passamaquoddy

■ Penobscot

0   25   50 Miles

Land Subject to the Original Penobscot–Passamaquoddy Land Claim

plus additions of Micmac and Maliseet groups—in a new relationship with the state of Maine. The essence of this new situation created by the placing of the tribes on a less subservient basis has been aptly encapsulated in the title of a 1997 report commissioned by the Maine Indian Tribal-State Commission to assess the results of the Settlement seventeen years later. It was called: *At Loggerheads*.

The Commission was created by the Settlement Act as a forum for ironing out differences in what its report, itself, deemed the "Uneasy Relationship" between the two entities. The composition of this body tries to set a balance, with eight members—four natives, four from the state—and a ninth member, a chairperson, chosen unanimously by the others. It has operated since 1983, and a reading of its publications would furnish more than enough material for a book or two on the aftermath of the settlement and the difficulties that ensue from the tension of two different sovereignties trying to operate under a single governmental roof.

Broadly speaking, under the Settlement Act, the tribes were given money in exchange for the extinguishment of their claims—some millions for a trust fund, others for buying land—and set free from the state as Maine's responsibility (the state office for Indian Affairs was abolished) while given responsibilities of their own as a quasi-municipality, but with some rights not afforded to other Mainers or their communities. The $81.5 million was divided equally between the Penobscots and Passamaquoddies and a goodly chunk of it set aside for the 150,000 acres each was allowed to buy from willing sellers, the first of which was the Dead River Company. Later on, two smaller Abenaki groups—the Houlton band of Maliseets and the Aroostook band of Micmacs—were allowed to partake of some of the federal largesse. Their tribes—most of whose members live in Canada—had also owned land in Maine and, like the Penobscots and Passamaquoddies, they traded their claims for cash and a different relationship.

In January 1981, the *Bangor Daily News*, the conservative northern Maine newspaper that had fought the Indian claims all along, declared prophetically: "We should probably anticipate a chain of continued litigation over what the Indian settlement actually means." This wasn't just sour grapes, since a beginning conflict had already emerged. The question had arisen: was the state of Maine obligated to continue funding housing, sewage, and water projects already under construction on the three reservations—Penobscot Indian Island, Passamaquoddy Pleasant Point, and Indian Township. Although Governor Joseph Brennan included funding for one year in his budget, his Commissioner of Finance and Administration Rodney Scribner insisted Maine's financial obligations had ended with the Indian Land Claims Settlement. Incidentally, Scribner had previously served as the state's commissioner of Indian Affairs and was generally considered sympathetic to the natives. Other problems soon surfaced. While Indian lands were opened to non-Indian hunters and trappers, they were told they needed special permits in addition to those they had to buy from the state. When the *Bangor Daily News*, responding to the outcries of local sportsmen, editorialized that, in revenge, Maine Indians should lose their privilege of free hunting and fishing licenses, the young Penobscot governor, Tim Love, shot back that the Settlement Act retained those rights for the tribes since they had never relinquished them, even in the "illegal treaties of 1796, 1818, and 1820."

Possibly the biggest hassle was the long-running one of allowing gambling on Indian territory—most specifically the high-stakes bingo or beano games that attracted players from all over the state. This question went all the way to the U.S. Supreme Court, which upheld the state supreme court's shutting down of Indian gaming by denying to review it for "want of a substantial federal question." Four years later, after a different U.S. Supreme Court ruling, the legislature at the prompting of Attorney General James Tierney, enacted legislation to permit the games to return.

Tom Tureen, the Indians' lawyer who conceived their case and brought it to a seemingly successful conclusion, was well aware of the problems of a political compromise solution. In an afterword to Paul Brodeur's book, *Restitution*, which details this and another case in Massachusetts, he wrote that although his victory for the Maine Indians was the greatest for any of the American Indians in the history of the U.S., it was:

> ...nonetheless difficult for many of the Indians to accept.... Some of the more militant tribal members

considered any resolution that did not return all the land in question and provide for absolute sovereign independence of the tribes to be a sell-out....[3]

Nature's own assault on the Maine Woods in those years, as fierce in its own way as the Native American assault on ownership, was the extended spruce budworm outbreak, a periodic plague of insects, last experienced in the 1920s, that returned to decimate thousands upon thousands of forest acres.

As a Maine legislator in the 1980s, I co-chaired the Audit and Program Review Committee—a body that on a rotating basis studied each operation of state government—and the spraying operation to combat these larval pests was one we examined. I had my first personal view of the moths these larvae turned into on a trip to Mt. Kineo. We were standing under the floodlights at the wharf at Rockwood that night, waiting for a friend to pick up our family in his boat. From the lake's surface to the lights 20 feet above us rose a solid wall of winged bugs. Touch a tree and hosts of these gray-brown creatures would flutter out. Later, flying in a state helicopter, we could see the damage in acres upon acres of wispy, almost naked trees.

The spraying program had become controversial. Originally, the paper companies had such political clout they were able to push through a state appropriation to pay for the spraying and do it on an emergency basis without a word of questioning. By the 1980s, this was no longer the case and they were footing some of the bill. Our committee became involved when a whistleblower reported violations in International Paper's compliance with the spraying rules. We traveled to the Presque Isle airport, the headquarters for a fleet of crop-duster planes, held hearings, interrogated all, and listened to the anguished outcries of certain IP executives who deeply resented having anyone look over their shoulders. The whistleblower, to them, was simply a disgruntled employee trying to mess up perfect operations.

IP, like other powerful groups whose will had been law in the woods, were reacting to a change in attitude toward them permeating state government. Concern about the environment had brought in regulation and was making life more difficult. LURC was a major bane, since prior to its existence there were no rules in the Unorganized Territories and they felt, from their point of view, that some of these new rules were both heavy-handed and unnecessary.

Ronald Lovaglio, manager of forest management for IP, came before our committee in 1983 with his company's major complaints against LURC, and they well illustrate the attitude then prevalent in the forest industry. Since 1994, incidentally, Ron has been commissioner of the Maine Department of Conservation. He had three beefs: that LURC was requiring protection of unmapped streams; that their turnaround time for granting permits was too long; and that LURC had no industry representative on it. His words on the last point even have a bit of poignancy, somewhat akin, Lear-like, to a dethroned monarch, arguing for a concession to his past status:

It is unthinkable that the industry that contributes more labor and proprietor's income, more to the gross state product, more to the value of production in manufacturing, and more to the state's export base, can't get a clear, firm voice on the Land Use Regulation Commission.

It is unthinkable that the industry that is responsible for seven million acres, the very acres that everyone is working so diligently to protect, is treated an outsider looking in.

A group can't begin to live up to its social responsibility when the very society that wants it to be responsible continues to treat it as an outcast.

The composition of LURC seventeen years later remains as contentious as ever. Recently, the idea surfaced that the commission should be elected and only by voters who live in the Unorganized Territories. The legislature had previously required that four of the seven appointed members be from the Unorganized Territories. Critics pointed out that the land being regulated was under state jurisdiction and therefore should have state representation.

Another large-scale economic development versus environment project in the Maine North Woods, coming fairly late upon the scene in 1984, was the Big A dam. In a sense, it was a "last hurrah" for giant private industrial undertakings like the one that bulled through Flagstaff Lake.

The Big A was the nickname for the unpronounceable Ambejackmockamus Falls, which came in two sizes, Big and Little, four miles below Ripogenus Dam on the West Branch of the Penobscot. The Great Northern Paper Company, reorganized in 1970 with the Nekoosa-Edwards Mills of Wisconsin to become Great Northern Nekoosa, proposed a 36-megawatt dam in this area, mostly to support its own plants. There was some indication the company had grabbed this property when it learned an outside group was planning to file with the Federal Energy Regulatory Commission (FERC) to build a hydroelectric generating station there. This was a period when the Maine Public Utilities Commission was encouraging hydro power additions to the state's energy mix by giving their builders a generous rate they could charge. Great Northern loudly advertised it would be displacing 430,000 barrels of oil a year and, although it didn't say so, the suspicion was strong that part of its motive was to sell its surplus power to the state's utilities. The total price tag of the project was $96 million.

Opposition was immediate. Leading the charge was another industry—a new one in the North Woods—whitewater rafting companies that made a living by taking tourists through those rapids scheduled to be flooded. Also in the forefront of the opponents were salmon fishermen, upset that some of the best waters in the world for their favorite species would be drowned. Other environmentalists joined in on general anti-dam principles. The company argued that the dam was necessary to its continued existence and saving the jobs of its employees at the Millinocket and East Millinocket mills. The unions became ardent proponents. A battle royal on the lines of Dickey-Lincoln thus ensued, except business and labor were now allied in a head-on clash with the greens.

The legislature was quite pro-Big A. Union support for the dam helped bring over many Democrats, including House Speaker John Martin and Senate President Charles Pray, to combine with pro-business Republicans willing to help a paper company. The critical issue in Augusta was the reversal of a condition that LURC, the overseeing agency, had put on its four to three approval vote—namely, that the company had to guarantee no job losses as the result of a project declared essential to saving jobs. A bill to remove this clause passed the house, but bogged down in the senate.

On March 13, 1986, Great Northern Nekoosa, seeing it would not win in the senate and knowing it would have to cut several hundred jobs to make its plan work, abandoned the Big A. No matter that some of the whitewater rafters had changed their positions. The environmentalists once more had beaten back a megaproject.

One incident during this heated contest involved an anti-Big A Republican state senator from Bangor who by then was quite well known. His name, alone, made him stand out—Howard Trotzky—and he was an anomaly Down East, a New York City-raised transplant with an accent to match, full of chutzpah, who had made his mark crusading to end the log drives on Maine rivers. In 1976 the legislature had enacted that ban, and it must be said the paper companies didn't fight strenuously, since they had found it cheaper and less wasteful to transport their logs by truck. The explosion of road building in the North Woods dates from this period. During the Big A fight, Trotzky, who had worked as a whitewater rafting guide, caused Great Northern Nekoosa a brief flare-up of embarrassment by producing a self-serving advertisement of theirs from the past which claimed they were building one of their roads—the Golden Road—in order to save Big Ambejackmockamus Falls, which now they planned to destroy.

One more megaproject must be mentioned. Its demise is of recent origin—February 29, 1996—when Governor Angus King announced the state would no longer support the creation of a cargo container port at Sears Island. For more than a decade, state government had tried to build it and the feds, particularly through the Environmental Protection Agency, had thrown up roadblocks. The Sierra Club, taking the lead, then instituted lawsuits, tying up construction from 1985–88 and again in 1989–92.

Quieter in their opposition were the two major ports on the Maine coast, Portland and Eastport. They did not want a third major port as a competitor. Yet the Maine Department of Transportation, which was spearheading the effort, harped on the large amounts of freight slated to pass through the new terminal annually, citing the president of the Bangor and Aroostook Railroad, who talked of 92,600 containers and 300,000 tons of noncontainerized items. Wood chips exported to Europe were to be a prime component, a prospect that delighted forest owners.

Yet, in the end, after almost $20 million had been spent on planning, environmental studies, and initial construction, Governor King decided the $70 million cost, to which Sears Island had ballooned, would not pay for itself. Reluctantly, and with blasts at "misguided environmentalists and irresponsible federal regulators" he claimed had elevated the price tag, he withdrew.

Amid much sound and fury, it could be said little if anything had been done to change Maine's economic direction through glitzy build-ups of its infrastructure.

"Pickerel" seemingly had won out over "payroll" in that classically stated Maine either-or choice couched in lingo depicting the environment versus the economy.

How Maine escapes this conundrum and continues to feed its people, to grow, even to flourish, has turned away from the grandiose. Or, rather, the nature of that grandiosity has changed — huge land sales, gigantic park proposals, easements on close to a million acres — the "howling wilderness" still left in the north, half the acreage of the state or better, has a great big question mark hanging over it. Rooted in the past, never really settled, an "Amazon" in the minds of many Americans, it is yet like that blank spot on the map that so intrigued me years ago in Manhattan, not exactly terra incognita, since people do know it, but a chunk of mother earth that for one reason or another hasn't been smothered in habitation. What will become of this remnant of the wildlands now that the dams and the oil refineries and aluminum smelters and superports have seemingly been ruled out?

NOTES

1 Peter Amory Bradford, *Fragile Structures*. New York: Harper's Magazine Press, 1975.
2 His father-in-law owned Sprague Oil, which had a monopoly on oil distribution in Maine, and he was working with ARCO.
3 Paul Brodeur, *Restitution*. Boston: Northeastern University Press, 1985.

TWENTY-ONE

And the Future Is —

THE LATE PAUL MCCANN, longtime spokesman for the Great Northern Paper Company, was a short, intense, fiercely loyal, and thoroughly likable person. Before his death, Paul, who considered himself a journalist at heart, wrote a short history of the company's fortunes during the 1970s and 1980s. His title, alone, illuminates Paul's view of what was happening at Great Northern, even before its hostile takeover by Georgia-Pacific, subsequent sale to Bowater, and recent re-sale to Canadian interests. Paul McCann called the booklet, *Timber! The Fall of Maine's Paper Giant.*[1]

"My company, right or wrong" might have been his motto—and the company to which he felt devoted was clearly the original organization created by Garrett Schenck and "Baron" Fred Gilbert. Paul's chronicle is an insider's look at the deterioration of GNP's dominance in the Maine Woods and, if "the past is prologue," his brief paean to GNP's lost glory makes a good vantage from which to foretell future trends.

We start with an attitude expressed when the spruce budworm crisis hit in the 1970s. Paul quotes state entomologist Robley Nash saying he had never in his career "witnessed the grave and extensive holocaust posed to Maine forests by the budworm for 1975," and that a $3.6 million spraying effort with Zectran, Fenithrothion, and Sevin, the costs shared by federal and state governments and private landowners, was the answer.

Historically, industrial foresters and state personnel had a close working relationship, but "all that changed," Paul said, "when forestry was submerged in a 'super' Department of Conservation."

Worse, Governor James Longley felt that state money spent on spraying was an unwarranted subsidy to the paper industry and, as a GNP employee remarked: "Power was shifting to southern Maine where there was little understanding of forest management, only a dread of spraying." Paul was equally opinionated on why the feds resisted:

> In Washington, dollar-hungry bureaucrats begrudged the annual drain of millions of dollars for spruce bud-worm control from budgets which otherwise would have been spent on managing federal lands mostly in the west. Environmentalists also became policy makers in the Carter administration.[2]

With enough paper company clout left in the Maine legislature, "objections to spraying were overruled in Augusta," a situation Paul attributed to "public understanding and tolerance, if the spraying was done with care." It was an alleged lack of care by IP that had brought our committee to Presque Isle to witness the crop-duster planes coming and going, like swarms of insects, themselves. By the end of the program—perhaps also due to "public under-standing"—Zectran and Sevin had been dropped in favor of Bt (*Bacillus thuringiensis*), a bacteria that feeds on budworm larvae and whose use is more benign than a chemical approach.

As baneful for Great Northern as the ascendancy of environmental thinking was also an internal change. This was the 1970 merger of Great Northern with Nekoosa-Edwards. GNP was now GNN. Paul McCann doesn't openly criticize the action, but obliquely does so by detailing its effect two decades later:

> For Great Northern Paper, the 1980s end with a company that had been a money-maker for its first fifty years, and was now a loser month after month. Once the largest single employer among operating companies within GNN, it was now fourth. Once the operating company with the most production capacity in GNN, it was now fourth.[3]

The company had literally gone south. GNN's priority for expansion began to be in places like Cedar Springs, Georgia; Ash-down, Arkansas; and Leaf River, Mississippi. When GNN acquired

Owens-Illinois's Forest Products Company, Virginia was added. Maine was becoming a minor player. Even when a $155 million modernization at East Millinocket was announced, the cheering was short-lived. Less than a year later came the chilling news that 1,200 to 1,400 GNP jobs would be eliminated over time. Three of eleven paper machines were shut down in Millinocket and one of five in East Millinocket. Talk of revitalizing Millinocket in a joint venture with a German partner, M. D. Papier, came to nothing; by 1989 GNN had started seeking permits for a new Millinocket plant when another business-oriented blow was dealt to Maine's one-time King of the Woods. The Georgia-Pacific Company launched its $3.8 billion hostile bid for Great Northern Nekoosa.

T. Marshall Hahn, G-P's chairman, was determined to make his company the largest forest products company in the world. GNN, based in Stamford, Connecticut, but a Maine corporation, tried to cloak itself as a hometown boy and rally the state's public opinion and media against the sale. The results were meager and the forced marriage went through.

It wasn't long before Georgia-Pacific sold off its Maine assets, and Great Northern, with its two big mills and 2 million acres went to the Bowater Corporation of South Carolina, which originally had been a British company. This international stage relevant to the Maine Woods was made vivid to me on a trade mission trip I took to Taiwan in October 1998 with my old boss, ex-Governor Ken Curtis. As a member of Bowater's Board of Directors, Ken was, among other things, trying to find possible Taiwanese investors for the Millinocket paper mill. This was well before Bowater's later surprise decision to sell all of its Maine holdings. We were met in Taipei by Bowater's man in the Far East and appointments were made for Ken, but there were no takers.

I knew personally, too, of anxiety in Millinocket, having been there that September for the "End of the Trail Days" celebration the city had arranged. Talking to local folks I met, the uncertainty about their future was palpable; one millworker talked about how they were down to four paper machines. Since the Bowater sale, the apprehension can only have grown. A friend of mine, Millinocket-born and raised, told of going to Millinocket after his mother's death and trying to have her home appraised by a local bank. "We'll loan a certain amount on any house," he was told. "But we won't do any appraisals. We just don't know where values are going."

If the major industrial firms have reached the point in Maine where—to use Paul McCann's metaphoric title—they can come crashing down to a cry of "Timber!," what *does* the future hold? At best, these are uncertain times. Since I began this book, Champion Paper, which showed us their painstaking efforts to try to be responsible consumers of the resource and still stay in business, has been sold. At first, it was rumored they were going to a Finnish company; then the buyer turned out to be International Paper. Since then, IP has closed Champion's stud mill at Costigan.

A different peek into the clouded crystal ball comes from another longtime player on this forested field—one of those family held operations involving land bought long ago in great swaths and held ever since. The Baskahegan Company, a mere eighty years old, is not as venerable as some others in the same genre. But according to the principal family member and company president, Roger Milliken, Jr., in his 1983 book, *Forest for the Trees: A History of the Baskahegan Company,*[4] its roots go back much farther in that northernmost section of Washington County close to the Aroostook line. Still fairly isolated today, the area was opened up somewhat when John A. Poor's transitory European and North American Railway passed Danforth in 1871 on its way to Vanceboro and helped it become the major town in the region. An equally transitory industry of peeling hemlock bark for tanneries helped, too, in stimulating a local economy.

After the Civil War, the Shaw brothers of Massachusetts bought thousands of acres in Washington County and set up a number of tanneries, the one at Grand Lake Stream allegedly the largest in the world. Here was a whole other mode of operation in the Maine Woods, trees taken for their bark, not their wood, and insect-swarming piles of it left along roadsides and lake shores. In 1883 Shaw Brothers failed and so did the tanning industry in this part of Maine, leaving thousands of acres up for grabs.

The man who picked up many of the pieces was Henry H. Putnam of Danforth. Civil War veteran, stagecoach driver, liquor-seller, shopkeeper, Putnam spent most of his spare cash buying land. He also built mills, took over the dam on Baskahegan Lake, generated power, and was, in this remote corner of Maine, a one-man, miniature version of a Great Northern or an International Paper. To those whose toes he stepped on, the "King of Danforth" was a "penny-pinching bastard who would chisel and chisel and chisel." In 1920, left without an heir, Putnam sold land, mills, and dam for $890,000 to the newly formed Baskahegan Company. The chief money man behind this venture was Gerrish H. Milliken, a wealthy textile company president from New York, whose father had come from Portland.

The man on the scene, who essentially developed the company, was John E. Kelley of Winn, an experienced lumberman who had worked on Fred Gilbert's 1901 West Branch drive and then had become a "John Ross" of the East Branch. He stayed with the Baskahegan Company from its inception until 1955 when he fell ill and died shortly afterward.

At his home near Cumberland Center, Roger Milliken, Jr., related the story of "Blackhawk" Putnam and the other antecedents of the company he now heads. The premise of my visit was my interest in how he saw a family company like his, with large acreage in the Maine North Woods, coping with trends that seemed to be developing in an ever-more-volatile line of business. So understanding Baskahegan's past was a necessary prelude.

For thirty years, from 1937 to 1967, Roger said, the company did very little cutting of its lands. They had about 100,000 acres. Worried about timber stealing, they eventually contracted with their neighbor, the Dead River Company, to supply a pine mill in Princeton, but in 1981 this connection was severed and they began to do their own harvesting. They hired Phillip Conkling, a forester out of the Yale School of Forestry (today executive director of the Island Institute in Rockland), and after he left in 1983, they managed their own operations with Roger at the helm. Their goal was "to grow value for their products." Quality hardwood like bird's-eye maple, which brought $200 a cord, could be measured against spruce at $70 a cord. The objectives of companies like Baskahegan were much different from pulp and paper companies who were "slaves to their mills and keeping them running."

It was interesting to learn Roger Milliken, Jr., not only considers himself an environmentalist, he is currently president of the Nature Conservancy of Maine. He described how the attitudes of the major landowners have changed dramatically since the 1980s when they fought obdurately against LURC restrictions. "Today, we wouldn't do anything differently," he said. He referred to the early resistance to better road standards and how shortsighted it had been to object to water bars that kept their roads from being flooded or streams from filling with silt. He said, with some amazement, that operators previously would bulldoze right down to impermeable soil in order to build a road base.

Companies like his had "a different ethic of care." They could look long-term in their objective of growing value, work with "big, healthy, native species" and have a "sense of legacy." Some 4 to 6 million acres were owned by such family groups, including small woodlot owners. The pulp and paper companies now owned less, but one of the biggest landowners of all—the Irving Company—he put in a separate classification: "clearly industrial in its methods," albeit a family company with a long-term focus.

Imperceptibly, our conversation drifted to the present forces arraigned within the Maine Woods: the paper companies, with their 3 million acres, like Inexcon, Mead, International Paper, SAPPI, from South Africa, with their mills (having sold all their land), the Canadian company Fraser Paper, with their mill in Madawaska, Fort James (formerly James River); the big commercial landowners, like Plum Creek, who bought the SAPPI lands, Wagner, who bought Stowell and Great Northern lands. Then, Roger cited a Wall Street dictum: Land is unproductive, so get rid of it.

A term new to me entered the discussion: a TIMO, a Timber Investment Management Organization. Plum Creek is an example; so is John Hancock. Roger said he was worried about them as players "because they had promised returns to their investors that were greater than the biological possibility of the land." The only means to this end were to sell the land for high-priced camp lots or to "way overcut."

The latter subject brought up another new term—"liquidators." With mills desperate for wood, these operators would supply them on a large scale. They are "rational economic men," Roger said. "They cut everything. Then, they cut the land up into lots and sell to out-of-staters." In a sense, they have to—to keep their equipment and men working—to pay off their overhead.

The "highest supplier" of the mills in this fashion, according to Roger, was Herb Haynes of Winn. Here was a man who would buy 25,000 acres at a time and clear it of timber. Some TIMOs were selling to him and other similar contractors. "Those were the guys who funded Mary Adams," Roger said, and as we slipped into a conversation about the past two referenda, I remembered Mary's speaking to me of Herb Haynes with great reverence. I also learned that Roger had been one of the architects of the "Compact"—backed by big companies, Governor Angus King, and establishment environmental groups—the "third way" that had failed. One of its major points had been a requirement to leave two or three more cords per acre than present law required. TIMOs also competed with liquidators and environmentalists for land. He cited the upper St. John purchase—a merry-go-round with a liquidation logger offering $41.5 million, a TIMO (Wagner) $40 million, and the Nature Conservancy $35 million. In the end, the others pulled out and the Nature Conservancy won. It was a close thing.

"The next five years will be a shakeout," Roger said. Some of the deals made were not economically defensible, he insisted. The conventional wisdom was that these lands would produce a 2 to 4 percent return beyond inflation—not a good bargain for investors. The most value was selling into the lumber market, which was what Baskahegan was doing. But a problem was finding an outlet for the thinnings necessary to grow a bumper crop of quality trees. Bio-mass was one answer, but bio-mass was a shaky business and if those bio-mass plants went out, so would sawmills for lumber.

We did not talk specifically about the most recent forestry referendum in Maine. I did, however, notice the "NO on 3" bumpersticker on his car in the driveway, opposing the latest effort to impose cutting restrictions, which on November 7, 2000, was defeated overwhelmingly, 70 percent to 30 percent. One of its arguments had been based on a state report that more wood was being

The Interrupted Forest

cut annually in Maine than was being replaced. This was the implicit negative in Roger Milliken's appraisal of the future in the woods, with the liquidators and TIMOs and pressures on paper companies as contributing factors, and was a challenge not about to go away. What I felt from him might be a hint of a solution was what could happen in the upper St. John. The Nature Conservancy, like Baskahegan, like the Pingree heirs, would manage their lands for value, would cut them, but keeping them as close to wild as possible yet with their heads above water financially, their lands open to careful recreation, maintaining a tradition. The astounding success of the Nature Conservancy in raising the money it needed for the upper St. John was perhaps a case in point.

Similar success attended the New England Forestry Foundation of Groton, Massachusetts, in raising almost $30 million to purchase a conservation easement on the lands in Maine owned by the heirs of David Pingree, billed as "the largest forestland easement in the United States." Whereas the upper St. John purchase was 185,000 acres, the Pingree lands total 755,000 acres and spread from the west in the Rangeley Lakes region to the Aroostook and upper Machias River watersheds, with parts of the Allagash and upper St. John. The pitch was:

> The easement removes forever the ability to develop
> these lands, and assures that future generations of own-
> ers will practice sustainable forestry, much as the Pin-
> gree family has since 1840....

To a certain degree, it could be argued the Pingree heirs were simply being given a tidy sum of cash to continue what they've always done—log their forests. Yet, theoretically, at least, without the easement, a new generation, hard up for money, might put all or part of the Pingree acreage on the block and have TIMOs or liquidators descend.

Thus, a multipronged effort has been underway—through outright and easement purchases to bring the acreage equivalent of more than several Baxter Parks into public or quasi-public hands. Other large chunks include state of Maine acquisitions from Plum Creek on the eastern shore of Moosehead Lake, the west outlet of the Kennebec River, and portions of Mount Abraham and of the north shore of Flagstaff Lake. An ambitious 656,000-acre proposal targeting the West Branch of the Penobscot involves Wagner Company-managed land that the state, in partnership with the Forest Society of Maine, will concurrently buy and/or protect with easements. An interesting easement on 22,000 acres owned by the Robbins family lumber interests on Nicatous Lake will allow them to continue logging the specialty trees—white pine—they bring to their mill in Searsmont, but also allow for the saving of large old pines used by bald eagles for nesting.

The attraction of easements to landowners has been explained by Sally Stockwell, conservation director of the Maine Audubon Society. It is an answer of sorts to the threat TIMOs pose—that these new forest owners may need to cut more and more wood to pay off debt or satisfy investors. Woodlands, she says, are seen as "stable, long-term investments in portfolios that also include high-growth, riskier stocks. They're counting on a 7 or 8 percent return, but if they can add to that by selling conservation easements, they will."

Not everyone is happy with the idea of conservation easements. Steve Swift, at the time chair of the Forest Ecology Network, the organization formed by Jonathan Carter, sounded this note in a letter to the *Portland Press Herald*:

> ...please let me vent my frustration with some environmentalists. Please abandon the idea that development easements are the answer. They are just ways for landowners to make more money while clear-cutting, over-cutting, and herbiciding.

In another part of his letter, Swift pleaded for an alternative—his organization's project to establish a 3 million-acre national park in the Maine North Woods, and then he commented on a new wrinkle in this game of Maine Forest Monopoly—the purchase by billionaire John Malone, the cable company mogul, of an entire lake. Malone's 15,000-acre ownership gave him control of Spencer Lake in northwest Somerset County, a favorite fishing spot, and had drawn the wrath of "folks from one end to the other...muttering how there ought to be a law against rich jerks turning Maine wilderness into their private fiefdoms," as Steve Swift wryly put it.

Since to Swift this "the land is ours, even if we don't own it"

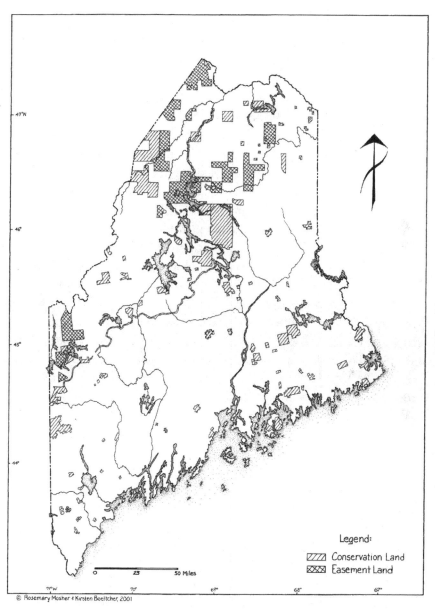

Major Conservation Purchases and Easements, 2001

357

sentiment seemed the ultimate in hypocrisy, tongue in cheek, he defended John Malone:

> My pet peeve is not with the man fortunate enough to own one of Maine's treasures. I'm peeved with the property rights crowd who are upset with this sale. After all, that's what property rights are about.
>
> The new owner doesn't care to share the deer, fish, and hiking trails. Yet the property rights crowd has opposed every effort to create public lands such as the Maine Woods National Park.

Malone, himself, has said he has no intention of not adhering to the tradition that wildlands, including his, will be open for recreation. But folks may have to sign in, so there can be some control and for their own safety. He also will ask for respect for the land. "Carry your trash out. Don't tear up the roads during mud season."

A new term has since been coined to label Malone and his fellow high-roller consumers of Maine real estate. They are now "kingdom buyers" in the local media. Close on the heels of Malone have been Richard Brown, a technology company chief from Texas, whose 20,000-acre purchase includes more than three miles of waterfront on Moosehead Lake, and Chris Nash, a shopping mall developer from Massachusetts who bought 1,153 acres on Chesuncook Lake. In the case of the latter property, it was land the state's Bureau of Parks and Recreation had tried to buy, but its owner, Herb Haynes, the notorious so-called timber liquidator, apparently preferred to sell to a private party. Prices per acre in Maine for kingdom lots appear to be far less than in the West, particularly Montana and Idaho, where companies such as Plum Creek have been selling similar giant-sized pieces for years. That has Maine environmentalists concerned about the effect on their efforts to preserve the character of the North Woods, since land prices are inexorably rising as a result of these sales and other 1,000-plus-acre tracts are on the market. Nor do Malone's and Brown's (and others') assurances that their land will now be protected from development and kept open to the public allay all fears.

The attitude of many proponents of saving these areas can be summed up in the opinion of Steve Swift that, "the only true protection that will leave a lasting legacy for future generations" is public ownership in the form of a national park.

What of the national park? What are its prospects in the years to come? If, as proponents claim, the polls show a 63 percent approval for it in Maine, why does there seem to be such determined political opposition?

Part of it, in my opinion, is style. Although some of the park's strongest proponents, like Jym St. Pierre, are Maine natives, the impression remains that the effort is spearheaded by people from "Away"—and the pejorative opinion in Maine of such strangers when they rub you the wrong way is that "they're trying to tell us what to do." In a conversation about the St. John purchase with a Nature Conservancy spokesperson, I was told how careful they were in their public relations—taking great pains to connect with all stakeholders in the region: assuring leaseholders they would still have their leases, hunters and fishermen they would still have access, and recreation businesses that there would still be camping and canoeing, etc. The Nature Conservancy, too, would be considered from "Away," but they were treading very lightly and listening. The national park, in the grandeur of its vision and the single-mindedness of its champions, has a different feel. It is portrayed, even subliminally when not explicitly, as the answer to what happens when the present major industry—pulp and paper—dies. Trips to Minnesota, to see the Boundary Park and its economic revival— well intentioned as they are—simply reinforce the impression the present way of life is doomed. Thus, the rash of bumperstickers: NO RESTORE FOR ME, or RESTORE BOSTON LEAVE OUR MAINE WAY OF LIFE ALONE. Instead of instilling hope, the national park idea subtly says, "The game is over. You must try something else. And this is it."

Then, there are the three referenda that have rattled cages. Jonathan Carter is right in saying these three votes have raised the consciousness of forestry issues in Maine to a level that never otherwise would have been reached. But they have angered people, too. The November 2000 election also spread those ill feelings to small woodlot owners throughout the state, since previous votes had been confined to restrictions in the Unorganized Territories. A fourth referendum—this time to ban herbicide spraying—is in the offing.

Admittedly, the great success a year earlier, in November 1999, of a $50 million bond issue for land acquisition might argue for the national park. Despite strident opposition from property rights groups, the measure passed 68 to 32 percent. Even in the rural north, it was heavily supported.

Yet, when at Jonathan Carter's request, I tried to sound out our Second District congressman's feelings about a federal feasibility study of a Maine Woods national park in his bailiwick, I was advised that Representative John Baldacci was strongly opposed to the idea. Knowing John as an elected official with a keen ear to his constituents' wishes, I saw that fact as indicative of attitudes in the north country. I was also told that Congress as a whole was not particularly enamored of the National Park Service at this time.

It strikes me as ironic that Maine seems to have been more accepting of the national park idea earlier in the past century than it is today. Percival Baxter's harping on the recreational intrusions of a national park in the 1930s may have accelerated the sense we could be losing some of the precise wilderness values we sought to maintain because of such a park's attraction to visitors and the Service's mandate to cater to them. Acadia National Park, while beautiful and of significant economic value to Maine, has created an extensive atmosphere of visual pollution along its entranceway. The reaction to a national park—and fear of one—was a goad to the state's creation of an Allagash Wilderness Waterway—and our own Maine Department of Conservation's opening up additional recreational access points to it has been a target for considerable criticism.

Plus 3 million acres, in one fell swoop, raises lots of questions to current users of the forest. Hunting and fishing? Camp lot leases? Fire control? Snowmobiles? Is this a means, once and for all, of putting the pulp and paper companies out of business? What about *any* lumbering? Even Baxter Park, forever wild, has its experimental forestry.

One thing is certain. The national park concept will continue to be pushed.

And so will the notion of wilderness.

There is a good deal of writing these days about wilderness. Some of it is incomprehensible. In one of my less charitable moods, I once wondered aloud: "Where has all the bad writing gone, now that Marxism and Freudianism have fallen from intellectual favor?" and concluded it has descended into "wilderness-babble," as epitomized in this passage from a book of essays on the subject, entitled *Wild Ideas:*

> Is there, then, yet another mode of absence or invisibility entirely endemic to the presence of the surrounding earth? I have already noticed here within the perceivable present, the hidden nature of what lies behind the tree trunks and stones that surround me, which corresponds to the unseen character of those lands entirely beyond the horizon of the perceivable present, from whence numerous entities enter the visible terrain and into which various phenomena withdraw, recede and finally vanish from view....[5]

Perhaps my countersnobbism derives from the fear that this awakened interest in wilderness as a concept—and a political goal—will be made too precious and brittle by an overdose of academic attention. It is, nevertheless, interesting to find in another essay in this same book a perspicacious view of the history of our perception of the concept: that is, its journey to the present-day from what the author calls "classical wilderness" and "romantic wilderness."

> The classical view places wilderness as something to be feared, an area of waste and desolation inhabited by wild animals, savages, and perhaps even supernatural evil....
>
> The romantic view sees wilderness as an untouched space that human contact corrupts and degrades. In this conception, the wilderness is a place to be revered, a place of deep spiritual significance, and a symbol of earthly paradise.[6]

The first perception, our heritage from the Puritans, remains with us still. Maine's own Stephen King has written a novel, *The Girl Who Loved Tom Gordon*, in which America's and the world's favorite plumber of our hidden nightmares finds one in the plight of a young girl lost in the contemporary woods on the Maine-New Hampshire border. The monster lurking in these mosquito- and no-see-um-filled, swampy, trackless, "desolate wastes" is real enough. It turns out to be a rogue black bear. Here are no sylvan forests, boon to the spirits of those who come for a day's hike; it's a scary wildland where there's nothing to eat but berries, and a puny human is prey to the elements. And this is a book written now—with the Boston Red Sox games on a portable radio as a form of salvation—not a tract from the era of John Winthrop and Cotton Mather, condemnatory of the "howling wilderness" beyond the "Hedge" of civilized Massachusetts Bay.

But, then again, Thoreau once wrote that "a howling wilderness doesn't howl." And Andrew Light, the author of the definitions of classical and romantic wilderness cited above also adds this kicker to the current love affair with the romantic version, that, "The history of human encroachment into the wild represents a steady fall from grace rather than a victory over dark places."

In a country whose government passed a "Wilderness Act," would a good-old Maine country boy like Stephen King advocate bulldozing that wilderness in which his pre-teen heroine passed her ordeal? I think not. Or, such notions would assail mostly deaf ears, for today we tend to regard wilderness, as Andrew Light says, "as a fairly innocuous place in terms of its dangers to man...a sense of the wild as something to be set aside and respected so it can serve as a conduit for beneficial natural experience."[7]

It is not surprising, therefore, that contributors to the Natural Resources Council of Maine's special publication, *Reflections on the Future of Maine's Environment,* should pine in print for a refuge, a park, whatever, of one, two, three million acres, to be an inherent fixture in the Maine of tomorrow. It is not necessarily specified to be a national park, with the local aversion to federal influence possibly in the back of their minds. But a real wilderness, roadless, forever wild, is clearly in the psyche of many Mainers and on a scale that dwarfs what Percival Baxter accomplished. His example is before them—that he bucked an attitude dismissive of *his* wilderness idea (the *Portland Press Herald* called it the "silliest" proposition ever to come before the Maine legislature)—and touched a nerve that carried his gesture eventually to a triumph bordering on saintliness.

In fact, wilderness designated as such has been established in Maine within that section of the White Mountains National Forest tucked into the western part of the state. It was not done without controversy and delay, although accomplished in an era when the idea of setting off roadless areas of a national forest seemed less of a raging firestorm than it is today, after President Clinton's executive order doing it wholesale throughout the country.

The Maine Wilderness Act of 1990, sponsored in Congress by Maine's then U.S. Senators George Mitchell and Bill Cohen, added 12,000 acres in Maine to the almost 100,000 acres in New Hampshire put into the National Wilderness Preservation System. The idea had been hanging fire since 1973, and much of the stumbling revolved around the Caribou-Speckled Mountain region, as to whether it should be included or not. In the end, under the bipartisan Mitchell-Cohen effort and with the support of the Bush administration, the bill was signed into law on September 28, 1990, containing Caribou-Speckled Mountain. Perhaps as a sop to the woods products industry in and around Bethel, language was included that, unless specifically authorized by Congress, the U.S. Department of Agriculture (which runs the national forests) "shall not conduct any further statewide roadless area reviews of national forest systems in Maine" and that no protective perimeters or buffer zones would be allowed around the wilderness area.

If "wilderness" in even larger chunks is ever restored to the Maine North Woods, my own instinct is that it will have to arrive in a different package from the traditional federal acquisition, including a national park. New forms of protection will have to be invented, nor can they be superimposed. After all, Baxter, himself, tried a conventional governmental way, was shot down repeatedly, and then devised his own highly individualistic but successful route to his objective.

"Wilderness," one is surprised to learn in the readings, was never included as a word in any Native American language. On second thought, this may not be so strange. They had words for the natural features that were part of their lives; twenty words for river in one California tribe. But since the overall environment did not seem separate or distinct or alien for them, there was no reference point against which to set anything. Concurrently, the tribes have a keen sense of the past. They have never forgotten this land was once theirs, at least in the sense of what each tribe or clan claimed for its own hunting ground. Each year now, the Penobscots stage a 100-mile run to their sacred mountain, Katahdin. They do not really recognize Percival Baxter's act of buying the area and donating it to the state. They have sought a special location inside the park they can call their own, for the purposes of this run and its accompanying celebration.

Now that their landholdings have been increased significantly thanks to the settlement (116,000 acres for the Penobscots and 144,000 for the Passamaquoddies), the chances for conflict, if anything, have multiplied. It is interesting to note that the Passamaquoddies have ended up buying the Plaisted tourist cabins where the whole confrontation began, but the dimensions of the struggle for jurisdiction over tribal lands may yet again go all the way to the highest authorities in D.C.

A hint of the potential problem was apparent to me one summer day in Costigan, a town bordering the Penobscot River, north of Bangor. At a rest stop, placards welcomed the traveler to "the Penobscot River, home of the Penobscot Nation," with a map showing the section from Lincoln to Milford and a reminder that all of the islands belonged to the Penobscot Reservation. Permits for picking fiddleheads or for duck hunting were to be sought from the Penobscot Nation's Department of Natural Resources. That department also had a Water Resources Program, testing some seventy-five sites in the Penobscot basin and a statement was included that, "Clean water is important to the Penobscot Nation." That the present conditions were not what they might be was implicit in a warning posted nearby by the Maine Toxics Action Coalition, telling people, especially pregnant women, to be careful about eating river fish.

Not long afterward, headlines in Maine newspapers told of a clash between the tribes and the state over water quality, with the Penobscots and Passamaquoddies wanting the U.S. Environmental Protection Agency to control water regulation near their lands, not the State Department of Environmental Protection. As part of a lawsuit filed by three paper companies who had the opposite desire, the tribes were ordered to turn over documents relating to their water regulations and the tribal authorities refused. Threatened with jail, they appealed to the Maine Supreme Court. For them, it was a much bigger battle—once more a question of sovereignty.

Not winning their case with the Maine Supreme Court, which said they had to turn over documents that were not internal tribal matters, the "nations," as they prefer to call themselves, talked of taking their case to the U.S. Supreme Court. In an unrelated matter, appearing at the same time, the federal Department of Justice filed notice it might seek up to $60 million from the bankrupt Lincoln Pulp and Paper Company for polluting the Penobscot River with dioxin, some of which sum, if collected, would go to compensate the Penobscot tribe. That the famous Land Claims Settlement has not quieted such disputes with the descendants of the Native Americans adds yet another dimension to the future of the Maine North Woods, as does the tendency of the younger generations of the Penobscots, Passamaquoddies, Maliseets, and Micmacs to revert to native language learning and spiritual beliefs.

There is also a new global ethic at work in these parts. Strong fears have surfaced about our planet and the overall impact of an ever-increasing, ever-consuming species (our own) upon its no longer inexhaustible resources. Global warming, while not totally accepted as proven, has brought trees into another light—as "carbon sinks"—instruments for reducing the oversupply of carbon dioxide in the atmosphere. That green leaves consume oodles of this gas in order to photosynthesize and give us oxygen argues for keeping and planting ever more of them. One frustrated logger, in rebuttal, has counter-argued replacements will grow, anyway, even if you clear-cut and, besides, worldwide, the forests represent only a minuscule percentage factor. He does admit there is a problem, however, by trusting instead in the immense contribution of phytoplankton, the nearly invisible plants in ocean water, to accomplish the absorption of carbon dioxide.

A far more experienced observer of the woods than myself has attempted a long-range prediction for the "Northern Forest," not just the Maine Woods but the entire temperate forest in the northeastern section of the United States, from New England to Pennsylvania. Lloyd C. Irland is a professional forester, a graduate of the Yale School of Forestry and Environmental Studies, a veteran of Maine state government and a highly respected consultant in the field. At the close of his latest book, *The Northeast's Changing Forests,*[8] he includes some recommendations:

The acreage of the Wild Forest should be increased, perhaps by 50 percent.

Vigorous steps are needed to save what remains of the Suburban Forest.

The Recreational Forest needs to be better managed and its expansion restrained.

The concerns of landscape management must be addressed and the region must make its own maximum contributions to reducing ozone, sulfur, and greenhouse gas emissions.

Access to private forests for fishing, birding, hunting, and simply enjoying the woods must be ensured.

In a sense, Irland herewith encompasses everything that is going on today, while simultaneously he argues for new leaders and new policies, and then states an obvious conclusion: that "one reality will abide: the northeast will remain, as it was in 1620, a region of forests."

That's probably not a fair place to end. Something more heroic is needed for a subject so heroic. Will the clash of titans in the North Woods terminate, not with a bang but a whimper, as natural tendencies, like water, follow paths of least resistance? It may be hard for an author to come to such a conclusion—and for an ex-politician turned author, no less. But despite all the hoopla and the media attention, the changes in the Maine North Woods will, I'm sure, have that same slow accumulation of compiled mini-events by which nature most often comports itself, inexorable in the final analysis but hard to quantify and even discern as they are happening.

Yes, but in Maine, as never before, we will be watching closely.

NOTES

1 Paul K. McCann, *Timber! The Fall of Maine's Paper Giant*. Printed by the *Ellsworth American*, Ellsworth, ME: 1994.

2 Ibid., page 22.

3 Ibid., page 7.

4 Roger Milliken, Jr., *Forest for the Trees: A History of the Baskahegan Company*. Self-published. Cumberland, ME: 1983.

5 David Rothenberg, ed., *Wild Ideas*. Minneapolis and London: University of Minnesota Press, 1995. Page 112.

6 Ibid., pages 195–96.

7 Ibid., page 196.

8 Lloyd C. Irland, *The Northeast's Changing Forest*. Harvard Forest, Petersham, MA: Harvard University Press, 1999.

AFTERWORD

HENRY DAVID THOREAU, jolted from his perhaps complacent view of nature as seen in its tamer Massachusetts setting by his trips to the Maine wilds, wrote of "uninterrupted forests." The impact of his observations that resulted not only remains with us today but appears to have spawned an intellectual and emotional movement that grows stronger every day as the forest (worldwide) is more and more *interrupted*. Maine, in effect, as it grapples with the future of its woods, is but a microcosm. Yet what a vast microcosm it has turned out to be, what a vast story.

Here, in this relatively small corner of North America, is a saga, mirroring much of world history, which in many respects primarily concerns the relationship of our species with its environment or, more precisely, the *Nature* it occupies. Homo Sapiens' use of land dominates the tale, once the processes of geology and biology have given us the "garden" in which to live. Thus, tribes develop and clans within tribes, and a rhythm to life arises, as we have seen signaled in the Wabanaki ways that preceded the arrival of more sophisticated Europeans who clashed with them over what? Mostly over land.

Noblemen came from England and France, seeking to add to their estates and pay for them with the work (and rent) of tenants, while commoners found a "commons" beyond belief in its magnitude—land seemingly for the taking—or at least that was the innate sense inculcated in the average Anglo-Saxon immigrant, whose roots have engendered that unspoken attitude that "the land is ours even if we don't own it" so prevalent still in many parts of Maine.

The Interrupted Forest

The self-made speculator and businessman developed quite naturally out of the overriding Western belief that the "howling wilderness" needed to be cut down and converted to use in a manner the Native Americans could never have imagined. Nor was this solely a phenomenon in Maine's "uninterrupted forest." The pre-Revolution history of America finds even the father of our country, George Washington, deep into land ventures in the West and South, and after independence the trend accelerated, as we have seen, with his cronies Henry Knox and William Bingham and their huge purchases of property in Maine.

A strongly contributing factor of the American Revolution was Great Britain's Proclamation of 1763, cutting off American access to the lands beyond the Appalachians. Land hunger drove the country's thrust westward, as surely as a river flows to the sea. The story of the public lands, the Homestead Acts, and the politics surround that them is as deeply imbedded in the fabric of our nation-building as was the flood of settlers into Maine, most of them second- and third-generation Puritans whose forebears' removal to the New World may have been as much or more connected to a lust for land as to any desire for religious independence.

So then, how does one relate to Nature? Thoreau supplies one answer. Hugh Chisholm and Garrett Schenck supply another. A whole new set of battles replace the older clashes of Dissenter versus Church of England, white versus red, Brits against the French. The interruptions in the forest grow so great that fear of depletion brings new controversy. Game laws. LURC. Trying to ban clear-cutting. The aftermath of a Land Claims Settlement.

It is an accident of history, with an assist from geography, that almost half of Maine was never populated. It was not for want of trying. John Alfred Poor was an interesting industrial visionary. His railroads, both those he constructed and another he merely planned, were to turn Maine into a rival of Massachusetts or even New York in the global economy. He thought big—transcontinentally and internationally—with Portland and Bangor as the hubs—but in the end, his dreams were as evanescent as the megaprojects proposed a century later to spur the "non-trend" development of the upper half of the state: Quoddy and Dickey-Lincoln and the Big A and big oil.

So nothing significant was built and *they did not come*, except to "cut and run," and a resource remained for us to fight about.

Some still bedevil us—like the 700,000 acres the legislature voted to give away to John A. Poor's European and North American Railway. Years later Percy Baxter was wont to decry this as a prime example of "boondoggle" and "corruption" in nineteenth-century land dealings. Where did those acres end up? One Maine historian points a finger at the Bangor banker George K. Jewett, who was president of the line at the time of its dissolution—a mystery still inviting its historical sleuth.

Traveling around Maine, one sporadically if not constantly encounters evidence of the collective memory of this forest past. That rest stop at Costigan, aside from its notices by the Penobscot Nation, contains a memorial stone, erected in 1994, to the "PENOBSCOT RIVER DRIVERS, Men of Courage Who Moved Logs Down this River from Forest to Mill." Nearby is the Maine Forest and Logging Museum at Leonard's Mills in Bradley, with its memorial to yet another set of obscure lumbermen, in this case the Blackman brothers, most memorable for their first names of Elmanan, Alanson, and Hyrganus; their contributions to logging were not inconsiderable but mostly occur after they went west to Puget Sound. Farther north on the memory trail is the much better known Lumberman's Museum in Patten, a complex of nine buildings showing exactly how the fabled, red-shirted woodsmen lived and worked. Even on the tourist attraction-cluttered road from Ellsworth to Mount Desert, there is a "lumberjack" show to attract visitors.

Headlines continue almost nonstop. In the *Maine Times*, in their January 11–17, 2001, issue, the whole front page was ablaze with an exclusive exposé of Herb Haynes, MAINE'S NEW PAUL BUNYAN, the story of the chief *liquidator* woods operator who "cuts $100 million worth of wood a year." The next week they followed up with a real scoop—the first interview allegedly ever allowed by the reclusive man from Winn who contributed more than $30,000 to defeat the forestry referenda in 1997 and 2000 that would have restricted his operations. In the flesh, he turned out to be more human than his reputation as the "bad boy" of liquidation harvesting—a seventy-year-old home-grown veteran of the generation in the forest industry who had witnessed the "transformation...from the horses/ax era, to the skidder/chain saw period, and then to mechanized harvester marvels of the last fifteen years," as reporter Phyllis Austin wrote in her interview. She also described Haynes as "gracious and humorous." Whatever else he may be, Herb Haynes is a major if not well-publicized player on today's Maine North Woods scene, lumbering thousands of acres yearly and spending millions of dollars each year to buy land to strip.

The multimillion-dollar expenditures in competition with Herb Haynes of environmental groups like the Nature Conservancy and New England Forestry Foundation have been touched upon, but the woods all over Maine are full of other like-minded but smaller groups who come to light only now and then, or accidentally, as happened at a party when I learned about Pierce Pond and the Maine Wilderness Watershed Trust. Pierce Pond is near the Forks and Bingham in western Maine, a sort of private enclave to which families have been going for generations. Twelve years ago, seeking to protect the Pierce Pond watershed, they formed the MWWT and now are dealing with the impact of Plum Creek's purchase of land in that watershed and the logging and, particularly worrisome, road-building in the area, which has accompanied it. On land that they, themselves, have bought, they are moving ahead with forest regeneration.

Land trusts throughout the state are active as never before, saving natural landmarks, battling developers, or trying to get to threatened acreage first. Sawyer Mountain, Agamenticus—just in my own York County. It is news that Maine has established its *ecological reserves*, 70,000 acres to help preserve distinct ecosystem types, thanks to a bill the legislature recently passed overwhelmingly. The lawmakers are no longer giving away acreage to railroads.

Enough. Material abounds. Maine history, past and in the making, is by all accounts, on a roll. Molly Spotted Elk and Fly Rod Crosby have come out of the mists, as the biographies of these exceptional Maine women have been published. Dr. Sylvester Gardiner, the great Kennebec proprietor, has been similarly resurrected.

The "White Indians" have come alive in the prose of Alan Taylor. We learn more about the real Native Americans in works they produce themselves, like the *Wabanakis of Maine and the Maritimes* resource book. There is a "Wabanaki Awareness Day" in the state capitol building.

Attention is being paid, even as our statehouse in Augusta is renovated, not only to preserve what's there, but to interpret a person's contribution that heretofore had been no more than an unidentified portrait of a pompous-looking nineteenth-century man with mutton chop whiskers. Maine no longer feels it can ignore any facet of its heritage, nor rely on puff pieces that masquerade the real truth. Today's headlines make so much more sense when historical memory can put them in context and add to the public debate. That is especially applicable to the future ruckuses that are sure to bloom over the land question in Maine, whether on a small scale in the settled parts of the state or in massive confrontations in that vast, tree-covered expanse north, west, and east, that still can be called *wild*.

BIBLIOGRAPHY

Adams, Charles Francis. *Three Episodes of Massachusetts History, Volume I*. Boston: Houghton Mifflin, 1892.

Adams, Henry. *The United States in 1800*. Ithaca, NY: Cornell University Press, 1955 (reprint).

Adams, James Truslow. *Revolutionary New England*. Boston: Atlantic Monthly Press, 1923. An interesting, ultraconservative, even pro-Tory point of view.

Ahlin, John Howard. *Maine Rubicon: Downeast Settlers During the American Revolution*. Camden, ME: Picton Press, 1966.

Albert, L'abbé Thomas. *Histoire du Madawaska*. Quebec: Imprimerie Franciscaine Missionnaire (Franciscan Missionary Printery), 1920.

Alberts, Robert C. *The Golden Voyage: The Life and Times of William Bingham, 1752–1804*. Boston: Houghton Mifflin, 1969. An excellent biography.

Albion, Robert Greenhalgh. *Forests and Sea Power: The Timber Problem of the Royal Navy, 1652–1862*. Cambridge, MA: Harvard University Press, 1926. A seminal work on forest politics in England and colonial New England.

Allis, Frederick, Jr. *Guide to the Microfilm Edition of the Benjamin Lincoln Papers*. Boston: Massachusetts Historical Society, 1967.

_____. *William Bingham's Maine Lands, 1790–1820*. Boston: The Colonial Society of Massachusetts, 1954. More than 1,000 pages, this is the ultimate work on Bingham's purchase, the largest in Maine history, by one of my history teachers at Phillips Academy, Andover.

American Friends Service Committee's American Indian Program. *The Wabanakis of Maine and the Maritimes*. Bath, ME: 1989. An extremely useful book, presenting the Native American viewpoint.

Anastas, Peter. *Glooskap's Children: Encounters with the Penobscot Indians of Maine*. Boston: Beacon Press, 1973.

Andrews, Charles M. *Narrative of the Insurrections*. New York: Charles Scribner's Sons, 1915.

Angier, Jerry and Herb Cleves. *Bangor and Aroostook: The Maine Railroad*. Littleton, MA: Flying Yankee enterprises, 1986.

Atkinson, Minnie. *Hinckley Township or Grand Lake Stream Plantation: A Sketch*. Newburyport, MA: Newburyport Herald Press, 1920. An obscure but entertaining bit of local history.

Audette, Susan with David E. Baker. *The Old Town Canoe Company: Our First Hundred Years*. Gardiner, ME: Tilbury House, Publishers, 1998.

Avery, Myron. *Collections*. Many volumes of letters, etc., now at The Maine Room, Maine State Library, Augusta. His correspondence on the 1937 national park idea and clash with Percival Baxter is particularly revealing.

Bailyn, Bernard. *The Peopling of British North America: An Introduction*. Madison, WI: University of Wisconsin Press, 1985.

Bailyn, Bernard and Philip D. Morgan, eds. *Strangers Within the Realm: Cultural Margins of the First British Empire*. Chapel Hill, NC, and London: University of North Carolina Press, 1989.

Baker, Emerson. "The World of Thomas Gorges," *American Beginnings*. Lincoln, NE: University of Nebraska Press, 1994.

Baker, Emerson with John G. Reid. *The New England Knight: Sir William Phips, 1651–1695*. Toronto, Buffalo, NY, and London: University of Toronto Press, 1998.

Bangor and Aroostook Railroad. *In the Maine Woods*. 1904 and 1924 editions of a tourism publication of the Bangor and Aroostook, promoting the Maine North Woods.

Bangor, City of. *The Centennial Celebration*. Bangor, ME: Benjamin A. Brown, printer, 1870.

Bangor Daily Whig and Courier. April, May, and June, 1842.

Bangor Historical Society. *Proceedings, 1914–15*. Bangor, ME: 1916. Addresses by Congressman Frank E. Guernsey and Professor Lucius H. Merrill of the University of Maine on making the Katahdin area into a national park.

Barry, William David and Geraldine Tidd Scott. "Charting a Wilderness," *Down East* Magazine. Camden, ME: June 1995.

Batinsk, Michael C. *Jonathan Belcher, Colonial Governor*. Lexington, KY: University of Kentucky Press, 1996.

Baxter, James Phinney. *Sir Ferdinando Gorges and the Province of Maine*. Boston: The Prince Society, 1890.

Beck, Horace. *The Folklore of Maine*. Philadelphia: J. P. Lippincott Co., 1957.

Beem, Edgar Allen. "The Lost Village of Flagstaff," *Down East* Magazine. Camden, ME: 1994.

Bemis, Samuel Flagg, ed. *The American Secretaries of State and Their Diplomacy*. New York: Cooper Square Publishers, 1963.

———. *The Diplomacy of the American Revolution*. Bloomington, IN: Indiana University Press, 1957.

Bennett, Dean. *Allagash: Maine's Wild and Scenic River*. Camden, ME: Down East Books, 1994.

Bennett, Randall H. *Bethel, Maine: An Illustrated History*. Bethel, ME: Bethel Historical Society, 1991.

Berkhofer, Robert F. *The White Man's Indian*. New York: Vintage Books, 1979.

Billias, George Athan. *The Massachusetts Land Bankers of 1740*. Orono, ME: University of Maine Press, 1959.

Botkin, B. H., ed. *A Treasury of New England Folklore*. New York: Bonanza Books, 1947.

Bower, Frank Colburn. *It Began with the Wasps*. Newcomen Society, 1949. A history of papermaking.

Bradford, Peter Amory. *Fragile Structures*. New York: Harper's Magazine Press, 1975.

Bradley, James W. *Origins and Ancestors: Investigating New England's Paleo Indians*. Andover, MA: Robert S. Peabody Museum of Archaeology, Phillips Academy, 1998.

Brain, Jeffrey. *The Popham Colony*. Salem, MA: Peabody Essex Museum, 2000.

Bramwell, Anna. *Ecology in the 20th Century: A History*. New Haven and London: Yale University Press, 1989.

Braun, Esther and David. *The First Peoples of the Northeast*. Lincoln, MA: Mocassin Press, 1994.

Brebner, John Bartlett. *The Neutral Yankees of Nova Scotia*. New York: Columbia University Press, 1937.

Brooks, David. "The Eastern Maritime Boundary Between the United States and Canada," pubished in *EOS*, vol. 65, no. 50, a publication of the American Geophysical Union, 1954. Brooks, an oceanographer at Texas A & M, is a native of Eastport, Maine.

Brooks, John K. *Our Scene: Gems of Downeast Maine*. Gardiner, ME: State Publishing Co., 1989.

Brown, Joseph Epes. *The Spiritual Legacy of the American Indian*. New York: Crossroads Publishing Co., 1991.

Bunting, W. H. *A Day's Work: A Sampler of Historic Maine Photographs, 1860–1920, Part I*. Gardiner, ME: Tilbury House, Publishers and Maine Preservation, 1997.

Burrage, Henry S. *The Beginnings of Colonial Maine, 1602–1658*. Augusta, ME: printed for the State of Maine, 1914.

_____. *Gorges and the Grant of the Province of Maine*. Augusta, ME: printed for the State of Maine, 1923.

Butterfield, L. H., ed. *The Adams Papers: Diary and Autobiography, Series I*. Cambridge, MA: Harvard University Press, 1961.

Calef, John. *The Siege of Penobscot*. New York: New York Times and Arno Press, 1971 (reprint).

Callahan, North. *Henry Knox: General Washington's General*. South Brunswick and New York: A. S. Barnes and Co., 1958.

Calloway, Colin, ed. *Dawnland Encounters*. Hanover, NH, and London: University Press of New England, 1991.

Carroll, Peter H. *Puritanism and the Wilderness: The Intellectual Significance of the New*

England Frontier, 1629–1700. New York and London: Columbia University Press, 1969.

Chamberlain, John. *The Enterprising Americans: A Business History of the United States*. New York, Evanston, IL, and London: Harper and Row, 1961.

Chandler, E. J. *Ancient Sagadahoc: A Narrative History*. Thomaston, ME: self-published, 1997.

Chaney, Michael. "White Pine on the Saco River: An Oral History of River Driving in Southern Maine," *Northeast Folklore*, vol. XXIX, 1990.

Chase, Edward E. *Maine's Railroads*. Portland, ME: A. J. Huston, printer, 1926.

Chase, Henry. "Sketch of Governor Abner Coburn," *Representative Men of Maine*. Portland, ME: The Lakeside Press, 1893.

Chute, Robert. *Thirteen Moons*. Brunswick, ME: Blackberry Press, 1978.

Clark, Charles E. *The Eastern Frontier: The Settlement of Northern New England, 1610–1763*. New York: Alfred A. Knopf, Inc., 1970. Doesn't cover much in very northern Maine.

Coe, Eben S. *Services in Memory of Eben S. Coe*. Derry, NH: Charles Bartlett, printer, 1901.

Cook, Don. *The Long Fuse: How England Lost the American Colonies, 1760–1785*. New York: The Atlantic Monthly Press, 1995.

Coolidge, Olivia E. *Colonial Entrepreneur: Dr. Sylvester Gardiner and the Settlement of Maine's Kennebec Valley*. Gardiner, ME: Tilbury House, Publishers and the Gardiner Library Association, 1999.

Coolidge, Philip T. *History of the Maine Woods*. Bangor, ME: Furbish-Roberts Printing Co., 1963. This is one of the major studies of lumbering in Maine.

Cooper, James Fenimore. *The Wept of Wish-Ton-Wish*. New York and London: The Cooperative Publication Society, n.d.

Cormack, Lesley B. *Charting the Empire: Geography at the English Universities, 1580–1620*. Chicago: University of Chicago Press, 1997. A masterful work.

Corrigan, Paul. *At the Grave of the Unknown River Driver: Poems of the Upcountry*. Unity, ME: North Country Press, 1992.

Cowan, Sara J. "Revolutionary War Bounty Lands in Maine." Master's thesis. New York: Columbia University, 1954.

Cronon, William. *Changes in the Land*. New York: Hall and Wang, 1978. A trailblazing ecological study.

Cyr, Soeur Marguerite S. M. *Notre Album Culturel*. St. John Valley Bilingual Education Program, 1976.

Daly, Herman E. *Beyond Growth*. Boston: Beacon Press, 1996.

Danforth, Susan. *The Land of Norumbega: Maine in the Age of Exploration and Settlement*. Portland, ME: Maine Humanities Council, 1988. Catalog of exhibition.

Daviau, Jerome G. *Maine's Lifeblood*. Portland, ME: House of Falmouth, Inc., 1958. A classic polemic.

Davies, Godfrey. *The Early Stuarts*. Oxford, England: Clarendon Press, 1937.

The Interrupted Forest

Davis, Albert H. *History of Ellsworth, Maine.* Lewiston, ME: Lewiston Journal Workshop, 1927.

Davis, Harold A. "An International Community on the St. Croix, 1604–1930," *University of Maine Studies,* second series, no. 64, 1950.

Day, Holman. *King Spruce.* New York: A. L. Burt and Co., 1908. His best-known novel.

Delbanco, Andrew. *The Death of Satan: How Americans Have Lost the Sense of Evil.* New York: Farrar, Straus and Giroux, 1995.

Dietz, Lew. *The Allagash.* New York: Holt, Rinehart and Winston, 1968. A classic work by a great friend of mine.

_____. *Touch of Wildness: A Maine Woods Journal.* Camden, ME: Down East Books, 1957; New York: Holt, Rinehart and Winston, 1970.

Dobbs, David and Richard Ober. *The Northern Forest.* White River Junction, VT: Chelsea Green Publishing Co., 1995.

Dolan, Edward F. *The American Wilderness and Its Future: Conservation versus Use.* New York: Franklin Watts, 1992.

Dow, Charles. "Violette's Allagash: A Political History of the Preservation of the Legendary Waterway." Independent writing requirement project. Portland, ME: University of Maine Law School, n.d.

Drake, Francis S. *Life and Correspondence of Henry Knox.* Boston: Samuel O. Drake, 1873.

Drayton, Michael. *Poems.* London: W. Stansby for John Smethwicke, 1619. From a 1969 reprint.

Drinnon, Richard. *Facing West: Indian Hating and Empire Building.* New York: Schocken Books, 1980.

Dunn, Richard S. *Puritans and Yankees; The Winthrop Dynasty of New England, 1630–1717.* Princeton, NJ: Princeton University Press, 1962. A very useful study.

Eckstorm, Fannie Hardy. "History of the Chadwick Survey," *Sprague's Journal of Maine History,* vol. 14, no. 2.

_____. *Old John Neptune and Other Indian Shamans.* Orono, ME: University of Maine Press, a Marsh Island Reprint, 1980.

_____. *The Penobscot Man.* Boston: Houghton Mifflin, 1904.

_____. "Tales of the Maine Woods: Two *Forest and Stream* Essays," reprinted in *Northeast Folklore,* vol. XXXIV, 1999. Written under her maiden name, Fannie Pearson Hardy. This includes her famous essay on Maine Game Laws. What would we Maine historians do without Fannie?

Eckstorm, Fannie Hardy and Mary Winslow Smyth. *Minstrelsy of Maine.* Ann Arbor, MI: Gryphon Books, 1971. Reprint of 1927 Houghton Mifflin edition.

Ellis, David M., ed. *The Frontier in American Development.* Ithaca, NY, and London: Cornell University Press, 1969.

Ellis, George E. *Memoir of Jared Sparks.* Cambridge, MA: Massachusetts Historical

Society, press of John Wilson and Co., 1868.

Feller, Daniel. *The Public Lands in Jacksonian Politics.* Madison, WI: University of Wisconsin Press, 1984.

Fisher, David Hackett. *Albion's Seed.* Oxford and New York: Oxford University Press, 1989. An extraordinary work on the types of English who first settled North America.

Fitzpatrick, Rory. *God's Frontiersman.* London: Weidenfeld and Nicolson, 1989.

Foster, Benjamin Browne. *Down East Diary.* Orono, ME: University of Maine Press, 1975 (reprint).

Gaffney, Thomas. "Maine's Mr. Smith: A Study of the Career of Francis O. J. Smith, Politician and Entrepreneur." Ph.D. thesis. Orono, ME: University of Maine, 1979.

Garber, Frederick. *Thoreau's Redemptive Imagination.* New York: New York University Press, 1977.

Gerritt, Greg. *A Campaign for the Forest: The Campaign to Ban Clearcutting in Maine in 1996.* Raymond, ME: Leopold Press, Inc., 1996. A polemical book, but full of information.

Gilman, William H., ed. *Selected Writings of Ralph Waldo Emerson.* New York: Penguin Books, 1965.

Gilpatrick, Gil. *Allagash: The Story of Maine's Legendary Wilderness Waterway.* Skowhegan, ME: self-published, 1995.

Godfrey, John Edwards. "The Ancient Penobscot," *Maine Historical Society Collections.* Series 1, vol. 7. Extremely good on land negotiations with the Penobscots.

_____. *The Journals of John Edwards Godfrey, Maine, 1863–1869.* Rockland, ME: Courier Gazette, 1979 reprint.

_____. *The Revolution of American Conservatism.* New York, Evanston, IL, and London: Harper and Row, 1965.

Graham, Ada and Frank Graham, Jr. *Kate Furbish and the Flora of Maine.* Gardiner, ME: Tilbury House, Publishers, 1995.

Greenleaf, Moses. *A Survey of the State of Maine in Reference to Its Geographical Features, Statistics, and Political Economy.* Augusta, ME: Maine State Museum, 1970. Reprint of the 1829 edition, the classic pioneering work of Maine's foremost and earliest surveyor and promoter.

Griffiths, Thomas Morgan. *Major General Henry Knox and the Last Heirs to Montpelier.* Monmouth, ME: Monmouth Press, 1965.

Hakluyt, Richard. *Voyages to the New World.* Edited by David Freeman Hawke. Indianapolis and New York: Bobbs-Merrill Co., Inc., 1972. A compilation of Hakluyt's historic collection of exploration tales.

Hale, Richard Walden. *The Story of Bar Harbor.* New York: Ives Washburn, Inc., 1949.

Hall, Clayton, Jane Thomas, and Elizabeth Harmon. *Chimney Pond Tales: Yarns Told by Leroy Dudley.* Cumberland, ME: Pamola Press, 1991.

Hall, Michael Garibaldi. *Edward Randolph and the American Colonies, 1676–1703*. Chapel Hill, NC: University of North Carolina Press, 1960. An excellent biography of this rascally enemy of the Puritans.

Hallock, Charles. "Life Among the Loggers," *Harper's New Monthly Magazine*, March 1860.

Hamlin, Ardeanna. *Pink Chimneys: A Novel of Nineteenth-Century Maine*. Gardiner, ME: Tilbury House, Publishers, 1987.

Hamlin, Helen. *Nine Mile Bridge: Three Years in the Maine Woods*. New York: W. W. Norton, 1945. Reprinted in 1973 by Down East Books.

———. *Pine, Potatoes, and People: The Story of Aroostook*. New York: W. W. Norton and Co., 1948.

Hanneman, Paul. *Little Known Historical Facts about Bangor and the North Country*. Bangor, ME: Bangor Historical Society, 1952.

Harding, Walter, George Brenner, and Paul Doyle, eds. *Henry David Thoreau: Studies and Commentaries*. Cranbury, NJ: Farleigh Dickinson University Press, 1972.

Hatch, Louis. *Maine: A History*. New York: American Historical Society, 1919.

Hawthorne, Nathaniel. *The Whole History of Grandfather's Chair and Biographical Stories*. Boston: Houghton-Mifflin, 1900. This has been reprinted.

Hempstead, Alfred Geer. *The Penobscot Boom and the Development of the West Branch of the Penobscot for Log Driving, 1825–1931*. Orono, ME: University of Maine Press, 1931. Reprinted in 1975.

Henretta, James A. *Salutary Neglect: Colonial Administration under the Duke of Newcastle*. Princeton, NJ: Princeton University Press, 1972.

Hill, Christopher. *The Century of Revolution, 1603–1714*. New York and London: W. W. Norton, 1961.

———. *Liberty and the Law*. London: Penguin Books, 1996. Hill is one of England's foremost modern social historians.

———. *Society and Puritanism in Pre-Revolutionary England*. London: Penguin Books, 1964.

Holbrook, Stewart. *Tall Timber*. New York, The MacMillan Co., 1960.

———. "The Flowering of a Lumber Town," *White Pine and Blue Water: A Maine Reader*. Edited by Henry Beston. Camden, ME: Down East Books, 1950.

Hosmer, James Kendall, ed. *Winthrop's Journal*. New York: Charles Scribner's Sons, 1908.

Houghton, Vinal A. *The Story of an Old New England Town: A History of Lee, Maine*. Wilton, ME: Nelson Printers, 1926.

Houpt, William Parry. "Maine Logging and Its Reflections in the Work of Holman Day." Ph.D. thesis. University of Pennsylvania, 1964.

Howarth, William. *Thoreau in the Mountains*. New York: Farrar, Straus and Giroux, 1982.

Huber, J. Parker. *The Wildest Country: A Guide to Thoreau's Maine*. Boston: Appalachian Mountain Club, 1981.

Huntington, Samuel P. *The Clash of Civilizations: Remaking of World Order.* New York: Simon and Schuster, 1996. A provocative thesis regarding current world events.

Hutchinson, Bruce. *The Struggle for the Border.* New York, London, Toronto: Longmans, Green and Co., 1955.

Hutchinson, Thomas. *The History of the Colony of and Province of Massachusetts Bay.* Cambridge, MA: Harvard University Press, 1936. Reprint.

Irland, Lloyd C. *The Northeast's Changing Forest.* Harvard Forest, Petersham, MA: Harvard University Press, 1999.

_____. "Rufus Putnam's Ghost: Maine's Public Lands, 1783–1820." Speech given at the Maine Humanities Council conference on statehood, December 2–3, 1983.

Irwin, Margaret. *The Great Lucifer: A Portrait of Sir Walter Raleigh.* London: Allison and Busby, Ltd., 1998. Reprint.

Ives, Edward. *George Magoon and the Downeast Game War.* Urbana, IL: Univeristy of Illinois Press, 1988.

_____. *Joe Scott, the Woodsman-Songwriter.* Urbana, IL: University of Illinois Press, 1978.

Jennings, Francis. *The Invasion of America: Indians, Colonialism, and the Cant of Conquest.* Chapel Hill, NC: Institute of Early American History and Culture, University of North Carolina, 1975.

Jewett, Fred Eugene. *A Financial History of Maine.* New York: Columbia University Press, 1937.

Johnson, Charles E. *Coo-Aush-Akee Country.* Norway, ME: Oxford Hills Press, 1976.

Johnson, Muriel Sampson. *Early Families of Gouldsboro, Maine.* Camden, ME: Picton Press, 1990.

Jones, Howard. *To the Webster-Ashburton Treaty.* Chapel Hill, NC: University of North Carolina Press, 1977.

Jones, Page Helen. *Evolution of a Valley: The Androscoggin Story.* Caanan, NH: Phoenix Publishing, 1975.

Josselyn, John. *An Account of Two Voyages in New England.* London: G. Widdows, 1674.

_____. *New England Rarities Discovered.* London: G. Widdows, 1672; Boston, MA: Massachusetts Historical Society, 1972 reprint.

Judd, Richard W. *Aroostook: A Century of Logging in Northern Maine.* Orono, ME: University of Maine Press, 1989.

_____. *Common Lands, Common People: The Origins of Conservation in Northern Maine.* Cambridge, MA: Harvard University Press, 1997. Dick Judd's books are always excellent.

Kammen, Michael. *The Origins of the American Constitution: A Documentary History.* London: Penguin Books, 1986.

Karliner, Joshua. *The Corporate Planet: Ecology and Politics in the Age of Globalization.*

San Francisco: Sierra Club Books, 1997.

Kavenagh, W. Keith. *Foundations of Colonial America*. New York: Chelsea House Publishers, 1973.

Kellman, Peter. "People's Republic of Jay: The Story of the Paperworkers' Union and the Future of Labor." Unpublished manuscript, n.d.

Kendall, David. *Glaciers and Granite*. Unity, ME: North Country Press, 1987.

Kershaw, Gordon E. *The Kennebeck Proprietors*. Somersworth, NH: New Hampshire Publishing Co., 1975. A seminal work on one of the "great proprietors" and land acquisition in colonial Maine.

Kevitt, Chester B. *General Solomon Lovell and the Penobscot Expedition, 1779*. Weymouth, MA: Town of Weymouth, 1976.

Kilby, William Henry. *Eastport and Passamaquoddy*. Eastport, ME: Edward E. Shead and Co., 1888; Eastport/Moose Island, ME: Border Historical Society, 1982 reprint.

King, Stephen. *The Girl Who Loved Tom Gordon*. New York: Scribner, 1999.

Kirkland, Edward C. *Men, Cities, and Transportation: A Study in New England History, 1820–1900*. Cambridge, MA: Harvard University Press, 1948.

Lansky, Mitch. *Beyond the Beauty Strip: Saving What's Left of Our Forests*. Gardiner, ME: Tilbury House, Publishers, 1991. An all-important polemical book in opening the debate on forest practices in Maine.

Leach, Douglas Edward. *The Northern Colonial Frontier, 1607–1763*. New York: Holt, Rinehart and Winston, 1966.

Leamon, James S. *Revolution Downeast: The War for American Independence in Maine*. Amherst, MA: University of Massachusetts Press, in cooperation with the Maine Historical Society, 1993. A first-rate piece of work.

Leger, Sister Mary Celeste. *The Catholic Indian Missions in Maine, 1611–1820*. Washington, DC: Catholic University Press, 1929.

Leland, Charles G. *The Algonquin Legends of New England*. Boston: Houghton-Mifflin, 1884. Still a classic.

Lenentine, Charlotte. *Madawaska: A Chapter in Maine-New Brunswick Relations*. Madawaska, ME: Madawaska Historical Society, 1975. Thesis for the University of Rochester.

Lepore, Jill. *The Name of War: King Philip's War and the Origins of American Identity*. New York: Vintage Books, 1999.

Libby, Lorraine. *Old Times on the Sawacatok*. Limington, ME: privately printed.

Lockard, Duane. *New England State Politics*. Princeton, NJ: Princeton University Press, 1959.

Looney, John Francis. "The King's Representative: Benning Wentworth, Colonial Governor. Dissertation, Lehigh University, 1961.

Lowell, James Russell. *A Moosehead Journal*. Boston: Ticknor and Fields, 1864. An overwritten travelogue by the famous poet and littérateur.

Lynch, John F. *The Advocate: An Autobiography and Series of Reminiscences*. Portland, ME: George D. Loring, 1916.

MacDonald, M. A. *Rebels and Royalists: The Lives and Material Culture of New Brunswick's Early English-Speaking Settlers, 1758–1783.* Frederickton, NB: New Ireland Press, 1990.

MacLeish, William H. *The Day Before America: Changing the Nature of a Continent.* Boston: Houghton-Mifflin, 1994.

Main, Jackson Turner. *The Anti-Federalists: Critics of the Constitution, 1781–1788.* New York and London: W. W. Norton and Co., 1974. Reprint.

Maine Bureau of Industrial and Labor Statistics. *Commissioner's Report, 1903.* Excellent on the development of Millinocket and Rumford Falls paper companies.

Maine Forest Commissioner. "History of the Wild Lands of Maine," *Seventh Report.* Waterville, ME: Waterville Sentinel Publishing Co., 1908.

Maine Historical Society Collections. Series 2, vol. XXI, Portland, ME: Fred L. Tower Co.

_____. "Tercentenary of De Monts Settlement at St. Croix Island," 1905.

_____. Volume 4, part II.

Maine Land Agent. *A Circular from the Land Office Descriptive of the Public Lands of Maine.* Bangor, ME: Bartlett and Burr, printers, 1858.

_____. *Report,* 1872.

Maine Legislature. "Documents Relating to Trespassers on the Public Lands." 19th Legislature, 1839. Confidential message to Governor John Fairfield.

Maine State Chamber of Commerce and Agricultural League. *History of the Wild Lands of Maine.* Portland, ME: published by the organization in 1986.

Maine, State of. "Report on Public Reserved Lots." Chapter 76, *Resolves of 1961.* Prepared by State Forestry Department, 1963.

Maine Writers Research Club. *Maine Indians in History and Legends.* Portland, ME: Severn, Wylie, Jewett Co., 1952.

Manning, Samuel F. *New England Masts and the King's Broad Arrow.* Kennebunk, ME: Thomas Murphy, Publisher, 1979. New edition distributed by Tilbury House, Publishers, 2000.

Marchand, Peter J. *North Woods: An Inside Look at the Nature of Forests in the Northeast.* Boston: Appalachian Mountain Club, 1987.

Marr, Harriet Webster. *The Old New England Academies.* New York: Coronet Press Books, 1959.

Massachusetts House of Representatives. Volume I. Boston: Massachusetts Historical Society, 1919.

McCann, Paul K. *Timber! The Fall of Maine's Paper Giant.* Ellsworth, ME: printed by the Ellsworth American, 1994.

McGrath, Anna Fields, ed. *The County, Land of Promise: A Pictorial History of Aroostook County, Maine.* Norfolk, VA: The Donning Co., 1989.

McIntyre, Ruth A. *Debts Hopeful and Desperate: Financing the Plymouth Colony.* Plymouth, MA: Plimoth Plantation, Inc., 1963.

McKenney, C. Ross and David Kendall. *Language of the Forest.* Unity, ME: North

Country Press, 1996.

McKibben, Bill. *The End of Nature.* New York: Doubleday, 1990. Reprint.

McLane, Charles B. *Islands of the Mid-Maine Coast: Mt. Desert to Machias Bay. Volume II.* Falmouth, ME: The Kennebec River Press, 1989. Now distributed by Tilbury House, Publishers.

McLeod, John E. *The Northern: The Way I Remember.* Millinocket, ME: The Great Northern Paper Co., n.d. Condensed version.

Mendenhall, T. C. *Twenty Unsettled Miles in the Northeast Boundary.* Worcester, MA: Press of Charles Hamilton, 1897.

Merk, Frederick, *Fruits of Propaganda in the Tyler Administration.* Cambridge, MA: Harvard University Press, 1971.

Merrill, Midge. *A Remarkable Man from Bradley, Maine.* Old Town, ME: Penobscot Press, 1993.

Miller, Perry. *Errand Into the Wilderness.* New York: Harper and Row, 1964. Reprint.

Milliken, Roger, Jr. *Forest for the Trees: A History of the Baskahegan Co.* Cumberland, ME: self-published, 1983.

Mitchell, Roger E. *I'm a Man That Works: The Biography of Don Mitchell of Merrill, Maine.* Orono, ME: University of Maine Printing Office, 1979.

Moody, Robert Earle. "Maine Frontier." Ph.D. thesis. New Haven, CT, Yale University, 1933.

Morris, Richard B. *The Peacemakers: The Great Powers and American Independence.* New York: Harper and Row, 1965. Very helpful information on the 1783 Treaty of Peace.

Morrison, Kenneth M. *The Embattled Northeast: The Illusive Ideal of Alliance in Abenaki-Euramerican Relations.* Berkeley, CA: University of California Press, 1984.

Morrison, Samuel Eliot. *The Story of the "Old Colony" of New Plymouth.* New York: Alfred A. Knopf, 1956.

Morton, A. C. *Report of A. C. Morton, Civil Engineer: Survey of the European and North American Railway.* Portland, ME: Harman and Williams, Printers, 1851.

Moulton, Augustus Freedom. *Memorials of Maine.* New York: American Historical Society, 1916.

Mundy, James H. *Hard Times, Hard Men.* Scarborough, ME: Harp Publications, 1990. Early history of Bangor Irish.

Munson, Gorham Bert. *Penobscot: Down East Paradise.* Philadelphia: Lippincott, 1959.

Murchie, Guy. *St. Croix: The Sentinel River.* New York: Duell, Sloan and Pearce, 1947.

Nevin, David. *Muskie of Maine.* New York: Random House, 1972.

Northeast Folklore Center. *Northeast Folklore.* Winter 1958. Published at Orono, Maine.

Northland, William Dummer. *The Bay Colony.* Boston: Estes and Lauriat, 1896.

Oelschlaeger, Max. *The Idea of Wilderness*. New Haven, CT, and London: Yale University Press, 1991.

Osborn, William C. *The Paper Plantation*. New York: Viking Press, 1974. A study by Ralph Nader's group on the pulp and paper industry.

Paine, Albert Ware. "The Territorial History of Bangor and Vicinity." *Maine Historical Society Collections*, vol. 9, article 9, 1882.

Paine, Lincoln P. *Down East: A Maritime History of Maine*. Gardiner, ME: Tilbury House, Publishers and OpSail Maine 2000.

Palfrey, John Gorham. *History of New England*. Boston: Little, Brown and Co., 1890.

Parker, Everett L. *Beyond Moosehead*. Greenville, ME: Moosehead Communications, Inc., 1996.

Pattangall, William. "The Maine Hall of Fame," *The Maine Democrat*, published in Waterville, 1909, 1910.

Peffer, E. Louise. *The Closing of the Public Domain*. Palo Alto, CA: Stanford University Press, 1951.

Perreault. Gene N. *Memories Grow on Trees: L'Arbre des Memoires*. Durham, NH: Department of Media Services, University of New Hampshire, 1986. On the French in the lumbering industry in Maine.

Pike, Robert E. *Spiked Boots*. Dublin, NH: Yankee Books, 1959.

_____. *Tall Trees, Tough Men*. New York: W. W. Norton and Co., 1984.

Piscataquis County Historical Society. *Collections: The Northeast Boundary Controversy and the Aroostook War*. Dover-Foxcroft, ME: Dover Observatory Press, 1910.

Platt, David, ed. *The Penobscot: The Forest, River, and Bay*. Rockland, ME: Island Institute, 1996.

Plumb, J. H. *England in the Eighteenth Century*. London: Penguin Books, 1950.

Poor, John A. "Communication to the Legislature of Massachusetts for State Aid, Memorial of the European and North American Railway," 1866.

Poor, Laura Elizabeth, ed. *The First International Railway and the Colonization of New England*. New York and London: G. P. Putnam's Sons, 1892.

Porter, H. C. *Puritanism in Tudor England*. Columbia, SC: University of South Carolina Press, 1971.

Probert, Randall. *A Forgotten Legacy: The Matagamon Region*. Self-published, 1998.

Putnam, Cora M. *The Story of Houlton*. Portland, ME: House of Falmouth, Inc., 1958.

Raddall, Thomas H. *The Path of Destiny*. Garden City, NY: Doubleday and Co., 1957.

Rawlyk, George. *Essay on the Atlantic Provinces*. Toronto: McClelland and Stewart Ltd., 1967.

_____. *Nova Scotia's Massachusetts*. Montreal and London: McGill-Queens University Press, 1978.

Reid, John G. *Maine, Charles II, and Massachusetts: Governmental Relationships in Early Northern New England.* Portland, ME: Maine Historical Society, 1977.

Ring, Elizabeth. *Maine in the Making of the Nation, 1783–1870.* Camden, ME: Picton Press, 1996.

Robotti, Frances Diane. *Chronicles of Old Salem.* Salem, MA: 1948.

Rolde, Neil. *Maine: A Narrative History.* Gardiner, ME: Tilbury House, Publishers, 1990.

Rose-Troup, Frances. *The Massachusetts Bay Company and Its Predecessors.* New York: The Grafton Press, 1930.

Rothenberg, David, ed. *Wild Ideas.* Minneapolis, MN: University of Minnesota Press, 1995.

Rothwell, Robert L., ed. *Henry David Thoreau: An American Landscape. Selected Writings.* New York: Paragon House, 1991.

Rowse, A. L. *The Expansion of Elizabethan England.* New York: St. Martin's Press, 1955.

Saltonstall, Richard, Jr. *Maine Pilgrimage: The Search for an American Way of Life.* Boston, MA: Little, Brown and Co., 1974. A fine book by a fine writer who died too young.

Sanger, David. *Discovering Maine's Archaeological Heritage.* Augusta, ME: Maine Historic Preservation Commission, 1979.

Sawtelle, William Otis. *Historic Trails and Waterways of Maine.* Augusta, ME: Maine Development Commission, 1932.

———. *William Bingham of Philadelphia and His Maine Lands.* An address to the Genealogical Society of Pennsylvania. Lancaster, PA: Wickersham Press, 1926.

Scee, Trudy Irene. *In the Deeds We Trust: Baxter State Park, 1970–1994.* Standish, ME: Tower Publishing, 1999.

Scontras, Charles A. "Non-Adversarial Labor Relationships in 19th-Century Maine: The S. D. Warren Co.," *Maine History,* vol. 37, nos. 1–2, Summer-Fall 1997.

———. *Organized Labor in Maine: 20th-Century Origins.* Orono, ME: University of Maine Press, 1985.

Scott, Geraldine Tidd. *Tier of Common Blood: A History of Maine's Northeast Boundary Dispute with Great Britain, 1783–1842.* Bowie, MD: Heritage Books, Inc., 1992.

Sellars, Richard West. *Preserving Nature in the National Parks: A History.* New Haven and London: Yale University Press, 1997.

Sewall, George T. *To Katahdin: The 1876 Adventures of Four Young Men and a Boat.* Gardiner, ME: Tilbury House, Publishers and Friends of the Maine State Museum, 2000. A reprint.

Shakespeare, William. *The Tempest.* Edited by David Bevington. New York: Bantam Books, 1980.

Shands, William E. and Robert G. Healy. *The Lands Nobody Wanted.* Washington,

DC: The Conservation Foundation, 1979.

Shepherd, Jack. *The Forest Killers*. New York: Weybright and Talley, 1975.

Sloane, Robert K. *The Courthouses of Maine*. Woolwich, ME: Maine Lawyers Review, 1998.

Smith, David C. *A History of Lumbering in Maine, 1861–1960*. Orono, ME: University of Maine Press, 1972. The workhorse.

_____. *History of Papermaking in the United States, 1691–1969*. New York: Lockwood Publishing Co., 1970.

_____. "Wood Pulp Paper Comes to the Northeast, 1865–1900," *Forest History*. April 1966.

Smith, Edward Ware. *The One-Eyed Poacher and the Maine Woods*. Camden, ME: Down East Books Quality Reprint, 1955.

Smith, Page. *John Adams, Volume 1*. Garden City, NY: Doubleday and Co., 1962.

Smith, Seba. *Way Down East*. Philadelphia: John E. Potter and Co., 1854.

Smith, Wynifred Staples. *Pines and Pioneers*. Weld, ME: Keim Publications, 1965.

Speck, Frank. *Penobscot Man*. Orono, ME: University of Maine Press, 1997 reprint. A classic work on the Penobscot Indians.

Spencer, Wilbur D. *Pioneers on Maine Rivers*. Portland, ME: Lakeside Printing, 1930; Bowie, MT: Heritage Books, 1990.

Sprague, Richard S., ed. "A Handful of Spice. Essays," *University of Maine Studies*, No. 88, 1968. Useful for accounts of Ralph Waldo Emerson's early visits to Bangor.

Springer, John S. *Forest Life and Forest Trees*. Somersworth, NH: New Hampshire Publishing Company reprint, 1971. This was the first real book on logging.

Staples, Arthur G. *The Inner Man*. Lewiston, ME: Lewiston Evening Journal Publications, 1923.

Stephenson, George M. *The Political History of the Public Lands, 1840–1862*. Boston: Richard G. Badger Co., 1917.

Stevens, David H. *Report of State Owned Rights in Timber and Grass on Reserved Lands in Unorganized Territory*. Augusta, ME: State Tax Assessor's Office, 1946.

Street, George E. *Mount Desert: A History*. Boston: Houghton-Mifflin, 1926.

Sylvester, Herbert Milton. *Indian Wars of New England*. Boston: W. B. Clarke Co., 1910.

Tawney, R. H. *Business and Politics under James I*. Cambridge, England: University Press, 1958.

Taylor, Alan. *Liberty Men and Great Proprietors*. Chapel Hill, NC, and London: University of North Carolina Press, 1990. Pioneering work on land squatters in Maine.

_____. *William Cooper's Town: Power and Persuasion on the Frontier of the Early American Republic*. New York: Vintage Books, 1996. Pulitzer prize-winning book on a speculator extraordinaire who was also James Fenimore Cooper's father.

Taylor, Aline S. *The French Baron of Pentagoët: Baron St. Castin and the Struggle for Empire in Early New England*. Camden, ME: Picton Press, 1998.

Taylor, John. *Works, Volume I.* 1630.

Thoreau, Henry David. *The Maine Woods.* New York: Bramhall House reprint, 1950. The bible of wilderness and also a realistic portrait of the Maine Woods of its time.

———. *A Year in Thoreau's Journal, 1851.* London, Penguin Books reprint, 1993.

Tokar, Brian. *Earth for Sale: Reclaiming Ecology in the Age of Corporate Greenwash.* Boston: South End Press, 1997.

Trask, William Blake, ed. *Letters of Colonel Thomas Westbrook and Others Relative to Indian Affairs in Maine, 1722–26.* Boston: George E. Littlefield, 1901.

True, Dr. Nathaniel Tuckerman. *The History of Bethel, Maine.* Bowie, MD: Heritage Books, Inc., 1994.

Turner, Philip B. *First John.* Bar Harbor, ME: Acadia Publishing Co., 1991. Historic fiction about Aroostook in the 1860s and 1870s, based on historic figures.

———. *Rooster: The Story of Aroostook County.* Bar Harbor, ME: Acadia Publishing Co., 1988. Non-fiction, but written in a fictional style.

Vickery, James B., ed. *Illustrated History of the City of Bangor.* Bangor, ME: Bangor Bicentennial Committee, 1976.

Vickery, Jim Dale. *Wilderness Visionaries.* Minocqua, WI: North Woods Press, Inc., 1994.

Walker, Ernest George. *Embden, Town of Yore.* Skowhegan, ME: Independent-Reporter, copublisher and printer, 1954.

Wall, Robert Emmet Jr. *Massachusetts Bay: The Crucial Decade, 1640–50.* New Haven, CT: Yale University Press, 1972.

Ward, Reverend Julius H. "Moosehead Lake," *Harper's New Monthly Magazine,* August 1875. Good example of early tourism promotion.

Warren, J. A. *A History of the S. D. Warren Co., 1854–1954.* Westbrook, ME: self-published, 1954.

Webber, G. Pierce. "The Webber Timberlands: An Horatio Alger Story," *The Northeast Logger,* December 1962.

Webster, George Oliver. *Pentagoët.* Rockport, Me: House of Falmouth, 1955.

Wendell, Barrett. *Cotton Mather, the Puritan Priest.* New York: Harcourt, Brace and World., Inc., 1963. Reprint of 1891 edition.

Wertenbaker, Thomas Jefferson. *The Puritan Oligarchy: The Founding of American Civilization.* New York and London: Charles Scribner's Sons, 1947.

Wessels, Tom. *Reading the Forested Landscape: A Natural History of New England.* Woodstock, NY: The Countryman Press, 1997.

Westcott, Richard R. "A History of Maine Politics, 1840–1856." Dissertation. Orono, Maine: University of Maine.

White, John W. "Early Transportation in Northernmost New England." Master's thesis. Orono, ME: University of Maine, 1952.

Whitgift, John. *Works.* Cambridge, England: University Press, 1851–1853.

Whitney, S. H. *The Kennebec Valley.* Augusta, ME: Sprague, Burleigh, and Flynt, 1887.

Wight, D. B. *The Wild River Wilderness: A Saga of Northern New England.* Littleton, NH: Courier Printing Co., 1971. Very good on the lost town of Hastings, ME, and the Maine portion of the White Mountains National Forest.

Wildenson, Paul Wendell. "Protagonist of Prudence: A Biography of John Wentworth." Dissertation. Durham, NH: University of New Hampshire, 1977.

Wilkins, Austin H. *Ten Million Acres of Timber.* Woolwich, ME: TBW Books, 1978. History of the Maine Forest Service by a former forest commissioner.

Williams, Ben Ames. *Come Spring.* Union, ME: republished by the Union Historical Society, 2000. Epic novel of the settling of this mid-coast town.

_____. *The Strange Woman.* Boston: Houghton-Mifflin, 1941. Long novel based on the history of Bangor.

Williams, Charles E. *The Life of Abner Coburn: A Review of the Public and Private Career of the Late Ex-Governor of Maine.* Bangor, ME: Press of Thomas W. Burr, 1885.

Williams, William Carlos. *In the American Grain.* New York: New Directions Publishing Co., 1956.

Williamson, Joseph. "General Samuel Waldo," *Maine Historical Society Collections.* Vol. 9, 1887.

_____. "Journal of the Voyage of Governor Thomas Pownall from Boston," *Maine Historical Society Collections.* Series 1, vol. 5.

——. "The Proposed Province of New Ireland," *Maine Historical Society Collections.* Vol. 7.

Wilson, Charles Morrow. *Aroostook, Our Last Frontier.* Brattleboro, VT: Stephen Daye Press, 1937.

Winthrop, Theodore. *Life in the Open.* Boston: Ticknor and Fields, 1863. An overlooked classic by a promising writer, killed at an early age in the Civil War.

Wood, Carolyn A. *Reflections from Eddington.* Eddington, ME: Eddington Bicentennial Committee, 1976.

Wood, Richard G. *A History of Lumbering in Maine, 1820–1861.* Orono, ME: University of Maine Press, 1961. Original edition, 1935. Another workhorse.

Wright, Esther Clark. *The Loyalists of New Brunswick.* Yarmouth, NS: Sentinel Printing Ltd., 1955.

Wyman, Mary Alice. *Two American Pioneers: Seba Smith and Elizabeth Oakes Smith.* New York: Columbia University Press, 1927.

York, Vincent. *The Sandy River and Its Valley.* Farmington, ME: Knowlton and McLeary Co., 1976.

Young, Muriel. *My Life as a Maine IAC.* Orono, ME: Puckerbrush Press, 1984. Enigmatic title, enigmatic book, filled with odd bits of information.

Zolz, Abigail Ewing and Marilyn Zoidis. *Woodsmen and Whigs.* Virginia Beach, VA: The Donning Co., 1991.

INDEX